Weary Sons of Conrad

THEORY AND PEDAGOGY

Kristi E. Siegel
General Editor

Vol. 3

PETER LANG
New York • Washington, D.C./Baltimore • Bern
Frankfurt am Main • Berlin • Brussels • Vienna • Oxford

Brenda Cooper

Weary Sons of Conrad

White Fiction Against the
Grain of Africa's Dark Heart

PETER LANG
New York • Washington, D.C./Baltimore • Bern
Frankfurt am Main • Berlin • Brussels • Vienna • Oxford

Library of Congress Cataloging-in-Publication Data

Cooper, Brenda.
 Weary sons of Conrad: white fiction against the grain
 of Africa's dark heart / Brenda Cooper.
 p. cm. — (Travel writing across the disciplines; vol. 3)
 Includes bibliographical references (p.) and index.
 1. English fiction—20th century—History and criticism. 2. Africa—
In literature. 3. American fiction—White authors—History and criticism.
 4. American fiction—Male authors—History and criticism. 5. English fiction—
White authors—History and criticism. 6. American fiction—20th century—History
and criticism. 7. English fiction—Male authors—History and criticism. 8. Conrad,
 Joseph, 1857-1924—Influence. 9. Race in literature. I. Title. II. Series.
 PR129.A35 C66   823'.9109326—dc21   2002016256
 ISBN 0-8204-5682-9
 ISSN 1525-9722

Die Deutsche Bibliothek-CIP-Einheitsaufnahme

Cooper, Brenda:
 Weary sons of Conrad: white fiction against the grain
 of Africa's dark heart / Brenda Cooper.
 –New York; Washington, D.C./Baltimore; Bern;
 Frankfurt am Main; Berlin; Brussels; Vienna; Oxford: Lang.
 (Travel writing across the disciplines; Vol. 3)
 ISBN 0-8204-5682-9

Cover photo: *Arms Interwined* by Hans Neleman
(Courtesy of The Image Bank)

Cover design by Lisa Dillon

The paper in this book meets the guidelines for permanence and durability
of the Committee on Production Guidelines for Book Longevity
of the Council of Library Resources.

© 2002 Peter Lang Publishing, Inc., New York

All rights reserved.
Reprint or reproduction, even partially, in all forms such as microfilm,
xerography, microfiche, microcard, and offset strictly prohibited.

Printed in the United States of America

DEDICATION

To Martin

ACKNOWLEDGMENTS

Thanks to Meg Samuelson, my research assistant stalwart. My colleagues in the Centre for African Studies at the University of Cape Town provide me a very special working environment. Adam and Sara Cooper enable and facilitate all my endeavours. Martin Hall reads, edits and makes everything possible.

TABLE OF CONTENTS

Part One: Introduction

CHAPTER ONE:
Sons of the Circus: Orientalist and Africanist Writing   1

Part Two: Sons as Explorers

CHAPTER TWO:
"The Niger remained a mystery": Fetishes, Bodies and Books in
T. Coraghessan Boyle's *Water Music*   35

CHAPTER THREE:
The Anti-Quest and the Migrating Tale: Lawrence Norfolk's
The Pope's Rhinoceros (and *Lemprière's Dictionary*)   69

Part Three: Sons and Apes

CHAPTER FOUR:
The Battered Boys of Rice Burroughs: Tarzan and Jane Goodall   103

CHAPTER FIVE:
Chimp Wars, Guerilla Wars and Gender Wars: William Boyd's
Brazzaville Beach, Will Self's *Great Apes* and Peter Hoeg's
The Woman and the Ape   131

Part Four: Sons as Gay

CHAPTER SIX:
Secret Sharing: The Closet and Empire   161

CHAPTER SEVEN:
Out of the Closet? Alan Hollinghurst's *The Swimming-Pool Library*
and Patrick Roscoe's *The Lost Oasis*   191

Part Five: Sons of the Soil

CHAPTER EIGHT:
Crossing the Great Desert Void   229

CHAPTER NINE:
Hybrid Landscapes: Adam Thorpe's *Pieces of Light*   257

Part Six: Conclusion

CHAPTER TEN:
Sons of the Century   293

BIBLIOGRAPHY   325

INDEX   337

Part One: Introduction

CHAPTER ONE

Sons of the Circus: Orientalist and Africanist Writing

> "What do I expect of a weary god, of my weary self?"
> —Patrick Roscoe, *The Lost Oasis*

Into the Heart of Whiteness

This book is an investigation of contemporary imaging of Africa on the part of white, male and non-African writers. One big question motivates it. Is it possible for European and North American men to depict Africa in a wise and non-exploitative manner? Are these writers able to avoid the pitfalls, conventions, distortions and stereotypes, the exploitation, objectification and oppression all of which have historically characterised European representations of Africa?

The writers that I have chosen are politically aware and also sophisticated literary craftsmen. In other words, I am dealing with serious fiction on the part of writers who oppose racism, are aware of the nature and consequences of the history of imperialism and are struggling with patriarchy and gender stereotypes. All of this is what makes them weary in every sense of the word. They are wary of the machinations of language. They are aware of the powerful literary conventions and devices, metaphors and symbols attached to the relentless image of Africa as a heart of darkness. They are tired of being white men in the mould of their patriarchal forefathers.

This does not mean that their representations are immune from the pitfalls, tensions and contradictions that arise when adult knowledge encounters deeply embedded cultural archetypes and prejudices, literary conventions and traditions that have been imbibed from childhood. This book explores both the highs and lows of recent white, male representations of Africa.

My earlier research focussed on black African novels (Cooper, 1992, 1998). What emerged was the fact that a number of African writers and others from the once colonised world have undertaken the journey from Lagos, Trinidad or Accra to London or New York for longer or shorter stays. As Kobena Mercer emphasises in his *Welcome to the Jungle*, "*we are here because you were there*" (1994, 7). And Arjun Appadurai goes so far as to suggest that to journey intellectually into the sphere of postcoloniality, is to journey "into the heart of whiteness" (796). This is the fictional journey undertaken in the pages that follow. The point is that the network of influence now works in many directions simultaneously. If Chinua Achebe and Ngugi wa Thiong'o were affected by Conrad, then writers whose fictions will be occupying our attention, like William Boyd, Coraghessan Boyle, Patrick Roscoe, Lawrence Norfolk, Alan Hollinghurst and Adam Thorpe, are profoundly influenced by writers like Chinua Achebe, Ben Okri, Wole Soyinka and Salman Rushdie.

V.Y. Mudimbe, referring to black African writers of the first generation, writers like Achebe or Soyinka, asks under the subheading, "The Death of False Fathers", in his book, *The Idea of Africa*:

> What if the father to which you have subjected yourself is an impostor: a false father who wrongly usurped the position of authority? What happens then to the son? What about the status of memory: if I'm confronting a false father who has imposed a false word on me, what sort of memory am I rejecting? This has long been the case in colonized Black Africa: Having been drilled from textbooks that speak of "our ancestors, the Gauls," what happens when you wake up and discover that your ancestors were not the Gauls? Do you remain silent—or shout yourself hoarse? What are the implications here for a practice and politics of patrimony and tradition? (1994, 192)

One of my questions, in the pages that follow, is what happens when white men also wake up and discover that their fathers are false?

Weary Sons of Conrad is a title adapted from a book by the renowned French feminist, novelist and philosopher, Catherine Clement. Her book is entitled *Weary Sons of Freud* (1987) and she asks critical questions about the practices of the psychoanalysts in the generations following Freud—about their healing powers, or lack of them, about their politics, about their work ethics and their self-identities. I am asking what happens when late twentieth century white male writers realize that the milieu in which they have been nurtured is hostile to their politics, dreams and goals? How powerful are the survivals of imperial quests and heroic yearnings in the dreams and nightmares of these writers? And what are the influences of black writers and intellectuals on them? In addition, what happens, further along the line, when both white and black writers, in different yet related ways, discover that they continue to be bound by invisible, and therefore powerful, unconscious ties to these perhaps only partially false, white fathers? This Sara Suleri suggests accounts for the "complications of tone" in Salman Rushdie's *Shame*, but I suggest more widely applicable. She describes that novel's

> great embarrassment of what it must mean to be fathered by *Kim*. For Kipling's powerful transcultural fetish plays a secret role in the energies of Rushdie's abundant idiom, suggesting an ironic relation that deserves more careful reading. (178)

If part of the shame that Suleri identified is that both the white boy, Kim, and the black writer, Rushdie, share Kipling as their father, then their somewhat shared, somewhat false fathers place recent black and white writers in an ambivalent relationship of fraternity and we are looking at a paradigm shift, one that is crucial to this book:

> In place of the remorseless postcolonial paradigm of Prospero and Caliban, a new equation suggests itself: the complicity of comedy and shame that the postcolonial narrative must experience, when it acknowledges that it indeed descends from the jaunty adolescence of *Kim*. (Suleri, 178)

That 'remorseless' paradigm is, of course, none other than the key to the nature of colonialist discourse with its profound binary opposition between the Centre and the Periphery. What this paradigm is increasingly chafing against, is globalisation where the traffic between worlds is beginning to amount to a jam with borders under seige in all directions and where the keyword has become 'hybridity'. This must have consequences for the ways in which people see and represent themselves and others. This is particularly the case when those others are encountered, not by intrepid explorers in the bush, but in your own block, down the road, in your school, university, at work and in the cinema. What transformations have the writers and intellectuals of that so called Third World, made on the culture, self perception and subjectivity of so-called First World writers?

In other words, what are the changes since the Imperial age, which Said describes in his *Culture and Imperialism* as "a coherent, fully mobilized system of ideas" and which he dates as being as early as "near the end of the eighteenth century (1993, 58)"? This was the era of "the authority of the European observer – traveller, merchant, scholar, historian, novelist". It was a time of the absolute "hierarchy of spaces" between centre and various peripheries (Said, 1993, 58). This hierarchy may survive in many important ways, but it is certainly no longer absolute or entirely familiar. As Mary Louise Pratt questions, in response to *Culture and Imperialism*:

> How much explanatory power does the term *imperialism* have today? Or rather, what are the limits of its explanatory power as we approach the year 2000? (1994, 9)

In other words, the drift of Said's book implies a seamless continuum between those spatial metaphors, which developed about two hundred years ago and our current situation in late modernity. The reality is that geography and its tropes and myths have undergone a degree of radical shake-up. New beneficiaries cut across old national boundaries, while some of the old divisions and injustices are reinforced by new webs and exchanges. One thing is certain, the old polarity of the white, western male explorer/writer on his promontory height, observing natives in the bush below, is radically outdated, albeit that its survivals continue to scar the landscape. In part two of this book we shall see how the motif of the explorer into Africa is fictionalised and problematised.

And this a sophisticated and sensitive commentator like Said also knows. In an extraordinarily moving, autobiographical piece of writing, entitled "Between Worlds", after being diagnosed with cancer, and reviewing the nature of his own life trajectory, Said suggests his affinity with Conrad, an affinity which cuts across their profound differences:

> The first thing to acknowledge is the loss of home and language in the new setting, a loss that Conrad has the severity to portray as irredeemable, relentlessly anguished, raw, untreatable, always acute – which is why I have found myself over the years reading and writing about Conrad like a *cantus firmus*, a steady groundbass to much that I have experienced. (1998, 3)

If "Conrad had been there before me" (Said, 1998, 3) then so had Tarzan. Unlike Conrad's Kurtz, who is destroyed by his untrammelled urges and primitive passions, which have been released in Africa, Tarzan thrives in the jungle. There he lords it over the apes, the Africans and women, civilized or savage. Tarzan it is who clears the bush and constructs a path between England and the interior of Africa and back again, a journey he repeats, back and forth, through all the subsequent books, comics and films in which he stars. In this role he is tour guide and travel agent, interpreter and translator across the continents. And in so being he is on that razor edge between facilitating and betraying, often looking in both directions simultaneously. Sometimes speaking with a forked tongue, he denies his white father, whilst possibly speaking in a version of his language. At other times he speaks a new language and this different tongue has been forged out of the strange languages that his newfound black colleagues, fellow writers, journalists and teachers speak within the interior of the metropolis. See part three of this book for a discussion of apes and Tarzan tropes and their consequences.

The binary of coloniser versus colonised was never total and the cracks and fissures have opened wider in more recent years. The metropolis has been transformed culturally, politically and economically by immigrants from areas of the world it once colonised and equally those areas are themselves exposed to satellite dishes, webs, internet sites and Big Macs, which both transform them and which they domesticate. As Iain Chambers puts it;

> When occidental sounds, images, icons and languages travel elsewhere what remains peculiar to the West? What, in global transit, translation and transvaluation can be purified of its subsequent passage to reveal a pristine, original and essential core? Perhaps nothing. So the West, however violently and neurotically it seeks to preserve its powers and position, its centrality, is paradoxically destined to be deluded by its apparent global presence. In travelling elsewhere its languages return in other forms, following other rhythms, bearing other desires. *They cannot go home again. They are home.* (57, my emphasis)

Simon Gikandi's *Maps of Englishness* beckons beyond the metaphors of colonial conquest and into the heart of England, where once colonised writers and intellectuals, like himself, have made and continue to make, a profound impact on the "Maps of Englishness", his title. He tells us in the preface that "the critical cartography of this book...has been across a cultural landscape that stretches from East Africa to Scotland and Michigan" (xx). For him, positioned within this vast global landscape, "it has never been clear where the identity between colonizer and colonized ends and the difference between them begins" (2).

Gikandi is self consciously insistent in pointing us "in two related directions" (9). That is to say "that the colonized space was instrumental in the invention of Europe just as the idea of Europe was the condition for the possibility of the production of modern colonial and postcolonial society" (6). In other words, his book is predicated on the recognition of "the mutual imbrications of both the colonizer and the colonized in the making of modern social and cultural formations" (20).

Does this mean that the forces of globalisation have annihilated racial difference? Has it become irrelevant whether it is a Rushdie or an Irving who is describing India? Appadurai suggests that the opposite may be true— "I am now well advanced on the road to becoming a person of color" (802). Living and working in the U.S has heightened his sense of difference, but also sharpened his perception of the global ties that bind white and black in a postcolonial world. Or as Richard Dyer puts it in his study, simply entitled *White*, albeit the prevailing view is that "we are living now in a world of multiple identities, of hybridity, of decentredness and fragmentation", the reality is that "we have not yet reached a situation in which white people and white cultural agendas are no longer in the ascendant" (3).

In other words, Said's insistence on the continuing force, power and durability of his conception of Orientalism has some validity:

> Epistemologies, discourses, and methods like Orientalism are scarcely worth the name if they are reductively characterized as objects like shoes, patched when worn out, discarded and replaced with new objects when old and unfixable. The archival dignity, institutional authority, and patriarchal longevity of Orientalism should be taken seriously because in the aggregate these traits function as a worldview with considerable political force not easily brushed away as so much epistemology. (1989, 210–11)

Michael Gorra wonderfully illustrates both colonialist discourse and its qualification in the conclusion of the final chapter of his book, *After Empire*. He refers to an extraordinary moment in Rushdie's *The Satanic Verses*: "After his transformation into a human goat, Rushdie's Saladin Chamcha finds himself in a hospital full of other foreign beasts, including a manticore from Bombay" (1997, 74). I would like to give a rather fuller quote from the novel. The poor manticore, creature of fabulation, from Bombay, grinds its teeth in frustration and points to other Third World 'animals':

> There are businessmen from Nigeria who have grown sturdy tails. There is a group of holidaymakers from Senegal who were doing no more than changing planes when they were turned into slippery snakes. ...
> Every night I feel a different piece of me beginning to change. I've started, for example, to break wind continually. ...
> 'But how do they do it?' Chamcha wanted to know.
> *'They describe us'* the other whispered solemnly. *'That's all. They have the power of description, and we succumb to the pictures they construct'*. (Rushdie, 1988, 168, my emphasis)

Rushdie has pinpointed here the self fulfilling prophesies of Orientalist and Africanist colonial discourses, with their power to wreak havoc on the people they describe and oppress. Interestingly, however, Gorra is making a somewhat different point in his concluding chapter, entitled "A Redefinition of Englishness" where his comment in response to the desperate manticore is:

> But the map isn't pink anymore, and in describing *themselves*, in changing the face in England's mirror, such figures as Saladin may one day help loosen the coils of that island nation's seemingly endless past. (1997, 175, my emphasis)

Coraghessan Boyle, in his *Water Music*, which will occupy us in the next chapter, fortuitously defines the manticore, one of the mythical creatures with which Al-Idrisi populated the imagined banks of the elusive Niger River, "with its lion's torso and scorpion's tail and its nasty predilection for human flesh" (1981, 4). My question here is, as the bite of the former colonised transforms the shape of the Centre, how is Englishness, and whiteness more broadly, being redefined and what are the implications of this redefinition for the ways in which white writers represent the people and places of the ex-colonies?

A Son of the Circus: Orientalism

The East is a useful starting point for the examination of images of Africa. This is so not least of all because of the enormous influence of Edward Said's *Orientalism*, which is essential to an understanding of the deep-rooted conventions determining how the West represents the land and people of its colonies. Said illustrated how the West constructed knowledge of the Orient, linked to its own ruling interests. He defined "Orientalism as a Western style for dominating, restructuring, and having authority over the Orient" (1985, 3).

With this in mind, I want to skip over more than six hundred pages of John Irving's novel, *A Son of the Circus*, to his extraordinary ending. I am then going to draw from it some of the major themes, theories and methods that will be shaping *Weary Sons of Conrad*.

A Son of the Circus develops the character of a doctor—Farrokh Daruwalla—who was born in Bombay, studied medicine in Vienna, where he met his wife, and lives most of the time in Toronto, where he holds Canadian citizenship. Daruwalla can only be described as a darling, compassionate man, a true egalitarian, albeit one who is often bewildered and emotionally taxed. His holy grail is to find a cure for dwarfism; he tends crippled, poor children in his capacity as an orthopaedic surgeon; he volunteers as an AIDS worker in the Toronto hospice; he melds all of these good works into the metal of his endearing vices. These include a tendency to overindulge his palate and his eccentric pastime as a screenwriter of reactionary, Bollywood style movies, brimming with violence and florid romance. We are so very fond of him by the end of the novel.

Dr. Daruwalla is back in Toronto after all the excitement of murder and mayhem that had ensued in Bombay, and which I cannot go into here. One snowy, wintry night, he is standing on a street corner, waiting for his wife to arrive and drive them to a reading by a visiting Indian author. At this reading his wife and her friends expect him to have something special to say to this fellow Indian, an expectation that Farrokh Daruwalla feels is unrealistic. Across the road from where he is waiting, a mother and her small son are also standing in the snow and Farrokh sends them a big beaming smile. What he has momentarily forgotten, however, is "the racial wariness he might provoke in the woman, who now regarded his unfamiliar face in the streetlight…as she might have regarded the sudden appearance of a large, unleashed dog" (628). Daruwalla is not simply offended by her fear, but he is "shamed" by it. The boy's mother struggles with her "rising terror" and imagines that beneath his fine topcoat "there surely lurked a naked man who was dying to expose himself to her and her child" (629).

The boy, meanwhile, is full of the joys, not yet puffed up with the hatred and distrust of his parents, his tongue in the air to catch the sensation of snow melting upon it. He is filled with enthusiastic curiosity about "the exotic foreigner". Daruwalla, ever the rather bumbling well-intentioned, kindly man, impulsively sticks his tongue out too, no doubt as an attempt to defuse the situation. "But now" writes Irving with his inimitable humour, "the young mother could see that the foreigner was radically deranged; his mouth lolled open, with his tongue sticking out, and his eyes blinked as the snowflakes fell on his lashes" (629). "As for his eyelids" Irving continues, and these eyelids will be significant, as we shall see,

> Farrokh felt they were heavy; to the casual observer, his eyelids were puffy—his age, his tiredness, the years of beer and wine. But to this young mother, in her growing panic, they must have struck her as the eyelids of the demonic East; slightly beyond illumination in the streetlight, Dr. Daruwalla's eyes appeared to be hooded – like a serpent's. (630)

Irving's Dr. Daruwalla, carries the shades of the "Salman" Rushdie to whom *A Son of the Circus* is dedicated. Rushdie is known for his hooded eyelids, which are a striking feature of his appearance, or were. The Sunday Times of March 21st 1999 ran a feature headlined "Eye surgery lifts Salman Rushdie's brooding looks" and indicated that he has long suffered from a medical condition of the eyes. However, his surgery "casts him in a new light. Eyelids that rose barely above his irises have long lent the author a hoodlum's gaze" (Woods, 1). A hoodlum, or a shifty Oriental? (Interestingly, Rushdie does Irving a reciprocal gesture of acknowledgement in his *The Moor's Last Sigh* where he refers to one of Irving's characters from *A Son of the Circus*—his Inspector Dhar) (1995, 264).

Back to the boy, who cannot be restrained, and who rushes up to Farrokh. His terrified mother, who sees only a shifty eyed hoodlum, expects the worst – "how well she knew what would happen next":

> The black topcoat would open as she approached the stranger, and she would be confronted with the male genitalia of the *truly* inscrutable East. (630)

Redolent of Oliver Twist's cathartic, outrageous request for further nourishment, (Irving acknowledges his debt to Dickens, McCaffery, 6) the boy asks the bombshell, deceptively simple, question, to which I have been leading up—"'Excuse me', the little gentleman said. 'Where are you from?'" (630). This innocent enquiry sets up an agonised train in Daruwalla's mind, provoking as it does the good doctor's agony in searching for an identity, a search which characterises postcolonial traumas quite broadly:

> Well, that's the question, isn't it? Thought Dr. Daruwalla. It was always the question. For his whole adult life, it was the question he usually answered with the literal truth, which in his heart felt like a lie.
> "I'm from India," the doctor would say, but he didn't feel it; it didn't ring true. "I'm from Toronto," he sometimes said, but with more mischief than authority. Or else he would be clever. "I'm from Toronto, via Bombay," he would say. If he really wanted to be cute, he would answer, "I'm from Toronto, via Vienna and Bombay." He could go on, elaborating the lie – namely, that he was from *anywhere*.
> He could always enhance the European qualities of his education, if he chose; he could create a spicy masala mixture for his childhood in Bombay, giving his accent that Hindi flavor; he could also kill the conversation with his merciless, deadpan Torontonian reserve. ("As you may know, there are many Indians in Toronto," he could say, when he felt like it.) Dr Daruwalla could *seem* as comfortable with the places he'd lived as he was, truly, *un*comfortable.
> But suddenly the boy's innocence demanded of the doctor a different kind of truth; in the child's face, Dr. Daruwalla could discern only frank curiosity – only the most genuine desire to know. ...
> "Where are you from?" the child had asked him.
> Dr Daruwalla wished he knew; never had he so much wanted to tell the truth, and (more important) to feel that his response was as pure and natural as the currently falling snow. Bending close to the boy, so that the child could not mistake a word of his answer, and giving the boy's trusting hand a reflexive squeeze, the doctor spoke clearly in the sharp winter air. (631)

The reader, by this time, has herself been raised to a high pitch of interest in the answer Daruwalla will construct. It does not disappoint:

> "I'm from the circus," Farrokh said, without thinking—it was utterly spontaneous—but by the instant delight that was apparent in the child's broad smile and in his bright, admiring eyes, Dr. Daruwalla could tell that he'd answered the question correctly. What he saw in the boy's happy face was something he'd never felt before in his cold, adopted country. Such uncritical acceptance was the most satisfying pleasure that Dr. Daruwalla (or any immigrant of color) would ever know. (631)

After the boy and his mother have gone, the preoccupied Farrokh does not hear the racial abuse "Go home" flung at him from a passing car. He is too busy fantasising about his newfound home in the circus.

The circus, which is nowhere and goes everywhere, which is topsy turvey, extraordinary, the liminal abode of the gypsy, the migrant and the misfit. This carnivalesque fantasy brings Daruwalla comfort and a paradoxical sense of roots.

The woman was an ordinary, average protective Canadian mother "of medium height and figure" (629). Her assumptions about the East, and about Daruwalla as its representative, have filtered down to her from the vast resource of images, distortions and stereotypes, which she involuntarily acts upon. The mother is not original in her certainty that Indians are as inscrutable as they are demonic, sexually insatiable and perverse. Daruwalla's fine coat, indicative of his professional standing and privileges, is invisible to her, covered up as it is by the archetypal raincoat of the dirty old Oriental man.

Irving demonstrates here that it is possible for a white American male writer not only to have understood Orientalism, as outlined by Said, but also to have contested it. This is so, given the incredulity that he provokes in us when we are compelled to see Dr Daruwalla through the crazed lenses of the Canadian mother's Orientalist terror.

Even, however, as I myself propose that the late twentieth century is demanding additional insights, I accept the continuing relevance of Said's paradigm, to which Suleri referred earlier, of Prospero and Caliban, the Coloniser and the Colonised, which is so "remorseless". In other words, in order to capture the changes and the survivals and scars, I will describe the paradigm of Orientalism by way of a paradox; my first weary son contests its absoluteness, even as he illustrates its durability. In pondering this durability where the "heart of darkness" relocates inside the savage jungle of whiteness, we will throughout this book also have to consider the role of metaphor in ensuring the survival of the discourse.

An Enchanting Darkness: African Orientalism and European Hunger for Metaphor

Edward Said parallels his discussion of depictions of the East with representations of Africa and emphasises that "Conrad's Africans...come from a huge library of *Africanism*, so to speak" and that Conrad's "impressions of Africa were inevitably influenced by lore and writing about Africa" (1993, 67). These impressions then feed back into the history and geography of imperialism as "the work is extraordinarily caught up in, is indeed an organic part of, the "scramble for Africa" that was contemporary with Conrad's composition" (1993, 67–8).

Christopher Miller defines "Africanist" discourse as less about Africa than "born and nurtured in Europe of European ideas and concerns" (5). His study is "not of Africa but of the conditions within certain French and other European utterances that give rise to that peculiar empty profile called 'Africa'" (6).

However, while there are important similarities between the two discourses of Orientalism and Africanism, there are also profound differences. Miller's Africanism is "empty", because Africanism is lower in the cultural hierarchy than the Orient. Africa is, in fact, "the Other's other, the Orient's orient" (Miller, 16).

This sense of nullity, of absence and emptiness, as a core feature of Africanism is confirmed by Gikandi, also in relation to its contrast with Orientalism:

> Indeed, what makes Africa, as a colonial space, different from Asia is its innate capacity to reduce society to the same level as violent nature. ... It is not by accident, then, that whereas India's capacity for alienation is represented by such modernist writers as Kipling and Forster in terms of its cultural institutions (the Museum, Temple and Mosque), the most prominent insignia of Africanness in modernism is the forest. The African forest would hence appear to negate the ideals of culture and civilization. (169)

Or, as he sums it up "the forest, like the river in *Heart of Darkness*, is a powerful presence whose primary narrative function, however, is to call attention to equally powerful absences, namely, culture and civilization" (172). Dennis Hickey and Kenneth Wylie in *An Enchanting Darkness* summarise "the idea of Africa" as:

> a mysterious place of jungle, mountain, and plain, mostly unfamiliar or unknown even decades after everything has been "explored" time and again; the idea of Africa as a zoological Eden of infinite variety replete with primordial flora, fauna, and, above all, primitive people (a human museum of the picturesque and the exotic); and the image of Africa as a distant staging point for episodes of adventure and discovery. (186–7)

In part five of this book, I examine fictional depictions, which centre on the African landscape in more detail. For now, the key point is that Orientalism, and its African variations, provides a metaphorical lens through which some Europeans viewed the world and other people, as a mechanism for viewing themselves. This lens is constituted by gender as much as by race. Said described Orientalism as a "male conception of the world" (1985, 207) and Anne McClintock suggests that "Columbus's breast fantasy, like Haggard's map of Sheba's Breasts, draws on a long tradition of male travel as an erotics of ravishment" (22).

Why has Africa played such a central role, however, in the manufacture of this metaphorical lens? Or as Simon Gikandi puts it: "How and why does Africa come to occupy such an important role in the discourse of modernism?" Or as he says in another way, "why is the continent one of the important places in which European anxieties are staged or projected in the era of late colonialism, which is also the nascent moment of modernism?" (162). Part of his answer is that

> this space that threatens European subjectivity is, as many canonical readings of *Heart of Darkness* have argued for years, one of the few places in which this subject can *recode its world* or even hallow a space in which it can *contemplate itself.* (166, my emphases)

In contemplation of self, Europeans are hungry for metaphors, which contribute to the ever-elusive search for life's meaning. This search, however, is surely an appropriate and spiritual endeavour? This is not so when Europeans, in their quest for meaning, manipulate Africa and Africans in order to represent metaphorically the most feared, untrammelled, unsocialised and 'uncivilized', buried aspects of their Selves. As Ngugi wa Thiong'o put it, Conrad

> was telling his fellow Europeans: you go to Africa to civilize, to enlighten a heathen people; scratch that thin veneer of civilization and you will find the savagery of Africa in you too. (19)

Or, as Chinua Achebe has it, Africa is the place "where the wandering European may discover that the dark impulses and unspeakable appetites he has suppressed and forgotten through ages of civilization may spring into life again in answer to Africa's free and triumphant savagery" (5–6).

This metaphorical function of Africa in the European imaginary is captured by what V. Y. Mudimbe in his *The Invention of Africa*, terms "double representation" (1988, 8–9). "Double representation" is the European cultural tradition of simultaneous identification with, and distancing from, black people. Mudimbe illustrates this phenomenon by way of Hans Burgkmair's 1508 painting of an African family group in which "the painter has represented blackened whites" and done so in a way that "was not rare during the sixteenth and the seventeenth centuries" (1988, 8). What Mudimbe means by this double representation is that "sameness [is] signified by the *white* norm" and eventually that very sameness opens up inferior differences—"distinctions and separations" (1988, 8 & 9). In other words, "normative sameness" doubles up as "cultural distance, thanks to an accumulation of accidental differences, namely, nakedness, blackness, curly hair, bracelets, and strings of pearls" (1988, 9).

Mudimbe goes as far as to suggest that it is upon this double representation, this search for, and affirmation of, Self through the Other, that "the 'invention' of Africanism as a scientific discipline" is based (1988, 9). That is to say:

> The African has become not only the Other who is everyone else except me, but rather the key which, in its abnormal differences, specifies the identity of the Same. (1988, 12)

In fact, the power of metaphor in general lies in the tension between similarity and distance. As David Lodge explains, if metaphor is "based on a certain kind of similarity", then it simultaneously requires that the difference between "tenor and vehicle" is "not suppressed" (75). When the 'vehicle', however, is an African person, and when the difference between the 'tenor', which is European, and the African as 'vehicle' is based on racist assumptions, then double representation comes into full force and works against the interests and dignity of Africans.

This brings us back to the vexed question of whether all of this implies that people may not learn more about themselves through the comparison with others. Is it invariably problematic for people to travel to other places and cultures to come to greater self-knowledge? Why can't this urge to explore—our curiosity—be quite a universal and laudable mark of our humanity? This could be the case, except for the fact that there is the history of colonialism, exploitation and power imbalance between places that were colonised and the forces and individuals that colonised them. This imbalance is invoked and reinforced metaphorically, unless the history and the politics are understood and confronted directly. As Denis Porter points out, there is a profound contrast between European travel accounts of journeys within or outside of Europe because in the case of the latter, there is "a hegemonic geometry of center and periphery that conditions all perceptions of self and the Other" (19).

The bonds between power and knowledge become chains and ropes that entwine with the grey matter and embed in the psyche. This is why the conscious and intellectual project of re-writing history in fiction is only the tip of the proverbial mountain of ice for white writers, who wish to overturn the racist and patriarchal paradigms invested in representations of Africa. While Africanist discourse can only be understood as *originating* within a socio-economic plane of conquest and raw materials, of wealth, privilege and their conservation, its *perpetuation* can only be comprehended through its relationship with the deepest recesses of the mind.

The Stranglehold: Africanist Discourse and the Psyche

What we are about to touch on is no less than the relationship between the social and the sexual, the political and the psychological, the individual and the collective. Kaja Silverman's *Male Subjectivity at the Margins* addresses these relationships. She begins with a dedication to "the exploration of some 'deviant' masculinities" (1), of which some "say 'no' to power" (2). Her book's "Afterword" concludes:

> Finally, I have struggled to expose the murderous logic of traditional male subjectivity, and to articulate some alternative ways of inhabiting a...masculine body. The marginal male subjectivities that I have most fully valorized are those which absent themselves from the line of paternal succession. (389)

Silverman's key theoretical concept is "the dominant fiction". It is not a term that I find attractive, with its overtones of false consciousness and dominant ideology, both of which have a chequered past. Therefore, at the risk of doing irreparable damage to Silverman's argument, I am going to adapt some of her words and strip some (although not all) of her Freudian, Lacanian and Althusserian terminology. This is worth the effort in order to extract the pearls buried within her compelling celebration of those masculinities that have positioned themselves at the margins, away from the centres of traditional patriarchy.

Silverman's insistence throughout, which is the kernel of our agreement, is upon the indivisibility between questions of the nature of "the larger social order" (1) and of the individual psyche (16). In order to illustrate this syncretism between the social and the psychological, she remembers the unfashionable Marxist concept of ideology and insists that "in order for ideology to command belief, then, it must extend itself into the deepest reaches of the subject's identity and unconscious desire" (16). Ideology "permeates subjectivity" in a relationship of "absolute imbrication" (23). Her book explores "the subjective bases of social consensus, and the ideological bases of conventional psychic reality" (23).

Ideology is understood as ideas and feelings linked to social interests. These interests are vast and include the network of class, race and gender that underlies struggles over privilege and power. To this must be added the concept of discourse, especially variants of the Orientalism that we have been outlining. Discourse provides the media, the mechanisms, the conventions for expressing those interests in the traditions and conventions of language—the language of speech, of writing in all its genres—fiction, biography, history, political tracts, newspapers, and so on. These conventions develop histories and traditions of their own, which sometimes reinforce and sometimes skew the ideological interests which discourses are called upon to express.

Ideology and discourse may only be understood in relation to their role in shaping the individual's psyche if we add a third term, that of the Law. And this concept, of the Law, comes close to Silverman's 'dominant fiction' and can, I think, be used in place of it. The intellectual breakthrough, that I would agree with Silverman appears to have been prematurely discarded in theoretical writing, is Althusser's "Freud and Lacan" paper (1971).

Simply, what Althusser attempted to demonstrate in that paper was how the invariables of biology, interact with social and psychological forces, to give rise to socialised, individuated subjects. Lacan's so-called Imaginary Order is the early state of merged, narcissistic identification with the Mother. The process Althussser charts and elaborates upon, is Lacan's description of development into human subjectivity through the zone of the Symbolic Order of the Father, of the Law, enabling individuation, separation and maturity.

However, this maturity, in which language is acquired, civilized behaviour learnt, and taboos (such as that of incest) are obeyed, also involved repression of the powerful drives and instincts, desires and untrammelled urges of the earlier stage.

For the purposes of explanation, I am first going to take a demonic, cemented up version of what happens within the Capitalist, patriarchal subject formation of powerful, ruling white men, prior to problematising it. In order to become good citizens, speaking a language intelligible to others and obedient to the rules of the social order, we obey the Law. The Law is the mechanism for socialisation and it holds sway deep within the psyche of the individual growing into maturity. The Law, in other words, is a mechanism whereby individuals are forged in the fire of prohibition to emerge as socialised subjects. The Law can only be understood as the rules governing social consensus, if those rules are themselves understood to be deeply internalised and inherited mechanisms of human psychological development.

This is why Silverman likewise emphasises, that while there is "the capacity of discursive practice to challenge and transform" there are also "powerful constraints":

> Indeed, one of the major premises of this book is that there can be other kinds of subjectivity than those promoted by the dominant fiction. However, I am proposing that there is no subject whose identity and desires have not been shaped *to some degree* by it. (48)

This is why Silverman insists so vehemently that "ideology can so fully invade unconscious desire that it may come to define the psychic reality even of a subject who at a conscious level remains morally or ironically detached from it" (23). This helps solve the puzzle of writers who consciously reject their fathers, patriarchy, imperialism and racism and may yet involuntarily reaffirm and collude with some of these.

While it is imperative to contest Africanist discourse, it is impossible to ignore its sway. Although there is the danger of the symbiosis, where Africanist discourse continues to set the terms and where a dance of death is choreographed between father and son, it is unavoidably the case that this discourse continues to occupy the territory—the themes, language and style of the writer. The degree of success or failure of the novels in question relies to some extent on the nature of the writers' attempts to rip apart its tendrils. The tentacles of Africanist discourse wind around hearts and minds, starting at birth, as the Law, which enables the constitution of the subjectivity of what will become our adult writers, is set in motion. We will see the sweat and blood stains inscribed upon their fictions, as these writers tear away at that Law of their Fathers, often labouring under its surviving statutes. More about the sweat and blood in a moment.

The Law—in the Imperial and Postcolonial contexts we are examining—is a summation of the complex rules of the dominant power holders—the State, Patriarchy, Capitalism and Empire building. The Law is thus a mixed blessing. Mature individualisation and the acquisition of mutually intelligible, socially taught language, are achieved at the price of repressing untrammelled urges, instincts, and desires into a vast unconscious zone.

Coming now to our particular crunch, if that unconscious zone of Subjectivity is metaphorically understood as a place, then that place is all too often none other than Africa. This point cannot be emphasised enough. The dark, pre-socialised pre-civilized instincts of Western man, deeply repressed within his unconscious, has been represented in mainstream Western metaphor as African people, their wild sexuality, their savage customs, and by reference to their landscape, with its abundant jungles, wild bush and terrifying emptiness.

I think that this is what Roland Barthes captures in his essay, "African Grammar". He takes words in the European language, like "DISHONOR" or "DESTINY" or "MISSION" and illustrates how each of them operates "like a blank place in which we arrange the entire collection of inadmissible meanings and which we make sacred in the manner of a taboo" (104). The sacred meanings are deeply symbolic and linked to the imperial mission of France. He gives examples of their usage, such as "France has a mission in Africa" (105) or "the people whose destiny is linked to ours" (104). The African Grammar, then, is the shorthand language, built into the unconscious of French (or English) users and linked to assumptions about race and power.

This is, of course, not the whole story. Firstly, not all European men are equal and uniformly constituted as imperialists and patriarchs. Secondly, and linked to the first, the whole process is an excitingly unstable one, enabling people to transform themselves through acquiring alternative knowledge, a different politics and new gender awareness. This is Lemaire's point when she first of all affirms and summarises Lacan with her "as I understand it, the process of symbolization is what ensures the passage from nature to culture via the psychic" (63). She goes on to qualify the relentlessness of this process by emphasising that the unconscious is formed by "as many elements which derive strictly from private experiences as there are elements attributable to the social instance" (63). Indeed, the child's

> cognitive syntheses of experience will be made within a culture which has already thought for him, but which, because of the variety of its members, does nevertheless leave him a certain margin for personal creativity. He will then continually remake these syntheses in the course of his own historicity, and in a world which is continually changing. These syntheses show the human tendency to question things, one example of which is *the psychoanalytic cure, another being theoretical research*. (64, my emphasis)

What is clear is that The Law cannot be understood as a monolith. There are many gateways, constituting subjects as Patriarchs or Revolutionaries, Gay or Straight, Capitalist or Hippie. The Law is an unstable zone of competing rules, clubs, churches, families, histories, survivals, sub-groups and counter cultures. Patriarchal capitalism may be dominant in the West, but individuals, writers and others, are variously constituted into their positions, which are both determined by forces beyond their control and are unique and idiosyncratic, individual and mobile. This is McClintock's point when she raises severe reservations with Lacanian theory in general and the Law in particular:

> For Lacan, the name of the father is equivalent to the entire symbolic realm, to culture itself. But then the dominant male culture becomes, at a stroke, synonymous with *all* culture. To be the phallus in Lacan's text is to find one's meaning only through the logic of the paternal law; it is to be entirely contained within the terms of phallocentricism. (197)

More about the phallus in a moment. For now, McClintock appropriately contests "the artificial unity of a single, universal patriarchy" and invokes "those differences that might call into question the very concept of the Western Law of the Father" (198). In other words

> Lacan erases the theoretical possibility of multiple, contradictory and historically changing symbols of desire. Most crucially, there is no room under Lacan's sovereign Name of the Father for a historical investigation of why *there is not one patriarchy, but many*. (197, my emphasis)

This is to say, the monolithic Law of Patriarchy

cannot account either descriptively or analytically for historical contradictions and imbalances in power *between* men. Nor can it account for the history of masculine powers that are not invested in metaphors of paternity; nor for ... black, colonized and otherwise disenfranchised men. (197)

In part four of this book, I examine gay writing in relation to representations of Africa or India. However, what is also true is that it is not only disenfranchised or gay men, who attempt to disinvest from those patriarchal metaphors and to construct alternative identities. There are straight white men, writers like John Irving and others who form the subject of this book, who understand the shackles of patriarchy and the power of figurative troping and who are attempting to break these open. 'Understand' is a keyword. David Spurr emphasises that in the conception of discourse is an understanding "that power and knowledge are joined, but this juncture is imperfect; discourse can be not only an instrument or an effect of power, but also a point of *resistance*" (184). In the concluding chapter of Spurr's book, he asks how writing might "find its way out of this entrapment?" (187). He suggests that

> The first step toward an alternative to colonial discourse, for Western readers at least, has to be *a critical understanding of its structures*. (185)

That critical understanding, which may be gained by research, by life experience, or whatever, has then to be translated into a literary method, language and style, which will, again either consciously undercut the metaphors of colonialist discourse, or be unconsciously sabotaged by them, or any number of contradictory, tense, or ambiguous possibilities in between. For all the theoretical and political transformation that writers may make, and alternative subjectivities through which they are constituted, the rebellion against the tropes of Africanism will not succeed, if all the figurative conventions of the discourse are not attacked head on.

And with this link between the metaphoric, the unconscious and Africa, between language, subjectivity and conventions of representation, we have to re-visit to Lacan's Imaginary and Symbolic dimensions. This we have to do in order to strengthen our understanding of how the discourse embeds by way of the cultural symbols and metaphors at hand – tropes which dictate the nature of the representations Africa or the Orient in certain prescribed ways.

Anika Lemaire refers to Lacan's Symbolic in a way that is a cross between his specialised usage and the more conventional meaning of the symbolic. She suggests that "the Imaginary is everything in the human mind and its reflexive life which is in a state of flux before the fixation is effected by the symbol" (61). Furthermore, "the process of symbolization is what ensures the passage from nature to culture via the psychic" (63). Or as

Anthony Wilden describes it, there is "a passage from the ... 'empty words' of an Imaginary discourse to the 'full words' of a Symbolic discourse" (21). If these words, which are "full" and replete with cultural meaning and imperial power, then what potential lies in those "empty words" to impact on the presiding codes?

The answer lies in the proposition that if there are two psychological dimensions—the Symbolic and the Imaginary—then there are two poles of language, which correspond to them to some suggestive, albeit murky, degree. These are metaphor and metonymy respectively. Roman Jakobson and Morris Halle, popularised this distinction as early as 1956 and it has since been quite widely used and variously applied. And with such distinctions and how they operate in language and in the bodies and souls of writers (not to be too melodramatic about it), we begin to see the outlines of an alternative route than the force propelling us through the relentless tunnel vision of the patriarchs and imperialists. With this to spur us onwards, what precisely is the relationship between metaphor and metonymy?

Breaking the Stranglehold of Discourse: Language and Subjectivity

The figurative language of metaphor strives for revelation via comparison, for understanding that comes with the deep connections and meaningful associations between people, places and objects. Master Texts are metaphoric discourses writ large out of which flow innumerable mini figures of speech. These, through constant usage, become universalised as ways of seeing the world, and all its people, through Western eyes.

If metaphor is meaningful connection, metonymy is its opposite. It is fluke, coincidence and contiguity, Lacan's accidental or contingent, as in strangers sitting next to one another on proverbial trains. The nature of metonymic relationships is characterised by happenstance, by a lack of design or quest. Metonymy is the opposite of the metaphoric language of the Law in the Symbolic, where codes of social subjectivity are stored and fixed. Linda Fleck, by way of detailed quotation from Lacan, gives his description of "a radical shift from metonymy to metaphor", where the metaphoric pole is "'the signifying quest' where the subject is called upon 'to become that which I [the speaking subject] am, to come into being'" (269, single quotes from Lacan). She enlarges, by reference to Lacan's *Ecrits*:

> In his seminar on Freud's technical writings, Lacan, as was his wont, turned to literature, to a poem by Angelus Silesius, to deliver the essential message of metaphor. (269)

To give this message, Fleck quotes from Lacan, who is attempting to distinguish between "contingency and essence". Lacan, remember, favours the Symbolic meaningfulness over what he would characterise as the immature condition of the random Imaginary:

> *Man, become essential: for when the world passes*
> *The contingent falls away and the essential remains.*

This is the road to 'normality' and Fleck emphasises Lacan's celebration of this journey from metonymy to metaphor:

> This is indeed what the end of analysis is about. ... *It is then that the contingent falls away*—the accidental, the trauma, the snags of history. *And it is being that comes to be constituted then.* (269, her emphasis)

To sum up, what Fleck is emphasising is that, according to Lacan, it is with the metamorphosis from the accidental of metonymy to the meaningfulness of metaphor, that subjectivity becomes constituted in the fullness of significant language. I have been suggesting the opposite—that full subjectivity, within the Western, patriarchal social context, is not necessarily so desirable. Or, as Durham and Fernandez put it, metaphor is part of "the 'inner storehouse' of a culture and its sets of cultural assumptions or models" [read discourse]; Metonymy, on the other hand, is characterised by its "volatility" and is therefore more "highly individualised" and "freely assembled and dissembled according to particular experience and circumstance" (195). In other words, it is metonymy, rather than the more granite and collective signfications of metaphor, that lends itself to intervention and transformation:

> It is in the realm of metonymic associatons, indeed, that conventions may be challenged, and hence metonymy is a trope most suitable for either asserting or challenging established hierarchies and conventions—for asserting and/or challenging worldviews indeed! (Durham and Fernandez, 198)

And "the structure of the world, sustained by an authoritative and legitimating metaphor" may be challenged through the use of the metonymic" (Durham and Fernandez, 209).

If the tentacles of Africanist discourse are inexorably entangled and knotted around Western metaphors, then a possible route for writers, desperate to avoid their strangling grip, is to attempt to cleanse their language of metaphor in some kind of recourse to the metonymic dimension. I would myself be most reluctant to prescribe which conventions writers may use. If writers are to avoid the quicksands of the tropes of Colonial power, however, then quite conscious and possibly desperate measures need to be taken, in opposition to the modernist metaphoric pull of gravity.

What is certain is that, given the power of discourse and the moral imperatives embedded in the very structures of narrative, it at that level of those devices, techniques, tropes, subtexts, hidden messages and figurative language that transformation also has to take place. An alternative representation

> would have to do more than simply stand in an ideological opposition to the prevailing discourses of power. ...This writing would act as a kind of guerrilla resistance to the discourse of colonialism: evading the power of that discourse by harassing its encamped position, by exposing its logic to view, and by maintaining a perpetual openness to the unexpected, to the chance disclosure of some truth that would otherwise remain closed off by the boundaries of discourse. (Spurr, 195)

Whatever devices are conjured up, moreover, this would simply be prior to the growth of the inevitable new symbolisms and meaningful connections of language and history, as metonyms ignite themselves against the blandness of happenstance. For, as David Lodge explains, no matter what "fresh materials" are thrown up, "there is nowhere else for discourse to go except between these two poles" (220) and that "although the metonymic text retards and resists the act of interpretation which will convert it into total metaphor, it cannot postpone that act indefinitely" (110). Nor should it. The big question, of course, is whether these new meanings, when and where they arise, are different from the blueprint of the dominant white, male Bigfoot. What should be noted is while the necessity for confronting and torpedoing the tropes is certain, the mechanisms for so doing, be they Realist or Postmodern conventions, or whatever undreamt of means, are not at all predetermined. We will see later that some of the devices of postmodernism have both been harnessed to the project of exposing that blueprint and also unwittingly to reinforcing it.

Another cautionary note is in order. All of these concepts—metonymy, the Symbolic, Orientalism and so on—are themselves constructs. They are props and tools to assist us in understanding forces, and also people, who are complex, contradictory and elusive in their uniqueness and unpredictability. We would do well not to take our tools too literally or use them to construct coffins into which we force the weird and wonderful fictions that emerge like Jacks out of their boxes in the chapters that follow. Jakobson and Lacan understand metaphor and metonymy differently, in ways that I don't really want to get into (Lacan, 1977, xiv). Maria Ruegg goes so far as to suggest that the distinction between metaphor and metonymy results in "a misleading oversimplification of what language does" (145). She emphasises "the impossibility of separating the two imaginary axes of "similarity" and "contiguity" given "the inevitable mimetic *play* between a multiplicity of codes, texts, context: play which implicates *all* discourse in a complex, ambiguous, undecidable web" (146).

Indeed, but for all her wonderful skepticism and stripped of its layers of dross, Ruegg *does* find Lacanian concepts usable, albeit "all the scientific clap-trap Lacan employs" (147). What Lacanian terminology gives us is the ability to link language, rhetoric, the psyche and the body in productive ways, despite the necessity of dismantling some of Lacan's own patriarchal assumptions. Paradoxically, even as we are now approaching Lacan's road to the metaphoric Emperor, the Phallus, the King that we can and must strip and de-throne, we are enabled to do so by the language and concepts with which we are provided in the Lacanian paradigm.

Ruegg puts it bluntly—"the master symbol" of the Lacanian code "is the phallus" (153). If the metaphor of the phallus is the dragon guarding the gateway into the Symbolic, how may the sensitive boy grow into an unpatriarchal man, short of castrating himself or, perplexingly, short of embarking, as dragon slayer, on new quests that reinscribe him as Adventurer Imperialist? One route that has been suggested is to de-trope the phallus, return it to the body part as penis and then to re-imagine the male body in new metaphoric language. If the darkness is race, then the heart is the body and possibly one route out of the bog of metaphor is that both have to be re-materialised in the literal language of metonymy.

The problems inherent in the 'sane' path towards subjectivity, with all the metaphors and baggage that comes along with it, has led to the search for alternatives to Symbolic subjectivity, not least of all that of 'madness'.
Two theorists, who have played with alternatives to the Freudian/Lacanian model of subject constitution are Gilles Deleuze and Felix Guattari. They propose a "fundamental difference between psychoanalysis" and what they call "schizoanalysis" in their *Anti-Oedipus: Capitalism and Schizophrenia* (1984, 351). They go so far as to suggest that "a revolution ... can proceed only by way of a critique of Oedipus" (1984, 75).

There is, of course, the enormous danger of idealising schizophrenia. Anyone who has ever encountered this dread disease would be outraged at the slightest hint that the schizophrenic somehow leads a better life than the subject fully constituted by way of the Symbolic zone. As Goodchild explains, they [Deleuze and Guattari] do not intend "to turn the schizo into a postmodern hero" (82). And as they themselves put it, they are not suggesting "that the revolutionary is schizophrenic" (1984, 379). What they do propose is a radically different body and language as the only route away from the Oedipal Law. In their language, they contrast the "schizobody" as opposed to the oedipalised body. The "schizobody" is what they call "the Body without Organs". The schizophrenic lives right on the boundary. The rest of us "never reach the Body without Organs, you can't reach it, you are forever attaining it, it is a limit" (1987, 150). Instead of the multiple prohibitions and Laws of the Oedipal unconscious, the "schizoanalytic unconscious", embedded in its Body without Organs, is an unbounded, smooth space, one capable of infinite desire and limitless metamorphoses. In this scenario "nothing is primal" (1984, 77). This alternative space, however, when occupied in part by writers and others, provides the capacity for a different form of social engagement, one, moreover, that may interrogate the problematic bonds between Oedipal subjectivity and patriarchy, imperialism and exploitation. Philip Goodchild, in his study of Deleuze and Guattari, explains how schizophrenia arises "where Oedipus does not take root at all" (90). Desire is liberated, rather than repressed and this "allows the development *of a fantasy* not normalized or inscribed by the dominant structures of society" (Goodchild, 90, my emphasis).

What will emerge in the chapters that follow is how often the fantasies of our writers return to schizophrenic, deranged minds and the creation of science-fictionalised, non Oedipalised new species. Is it not the fantasy of breaking away from the stranglehold of 'normality' with the baggage that this seems to bring along with it? And do they, in their search for imagined, unheard of beings, bodies and language babbles, in places far from home, avoid the traps and the snares of old Africanist metaphors and the symbols, which enabled imperial plunder?

Circuses, Devils and Literary Devices: Weary Sons on a Tightrope

Does postmodernism, by definition, break the symbolic heart in which metaphoric meaning is pumped through the body of the culture? Postmodernism takes Henry James's deep code, that modernist trope of the figure in the carpet as interpretive key, and reduces it to a stain, the insignificance perhaps of wine accidentally spilled. It is not the blood of Christ or anyone else for that matter:

> 'Where is the figure in the carpet?'asks a character in Donald Barthelme's *Snow White* (1967), alluding to the title of a story by Henry James that has become proverbial among modern critics as an image of the goal of interpretation; but he adds disconcertingly: 'Or is it just ... carpet?' A lot of postmodernist writing implies that experience is 'just carpet' and that whatever patterns we discern in it are wholly illusory, comforting fictions. (Lodge, 226)

Postmodernism, at that moment in which it de-rails master texts, enters an exquisite unity of purpose with postcolonialism, which latches onto the particular meta-narrative that it hates most—that of the civilizing mission of the imperialist/robber. There are, however, as many versions of postmodernism as there are narratives, and at that magical moment of joint cause, postmodernism reaches its far boundary and parts company with a postcolonialism which would attempt to pose an alternative, re-written story of the true past, which the coloniser obliterated. When postmodernism, moreover, is simply lack, a deconstruction of deconstructions, the fun and games of smashing, exposing, stripping and ridiculing, when the lifted mask reveals only a great emptiness, then the culture's storehouse is defended by default. This, I would like to suggest occurs in David Caute's novel, *Fatima's Scarf*, where Salman Rushdie is reincarnated once again, but this time as African Devil.

Caute's protagonist, Gamal Rahman, is unambiguously and overtly a fictional reincarnation of the author of *The Satanic Verses* and Caute's novel reconstructs the events surrounding the publication of Rushdie's, thinly veiled as *The Devil: an Interview*:

> The press can talk of nothing else: first the public, ceremonial burning of a book outside a British City Hall—and now a death sentence on a British citizen (albeit naturalized) handed down by a foreign Head of State! Bruddersford is crawling with photographers and television crews cruising the modest, sensible streets of Tanner and Bellingham in search of turbaned fanatics, veiled girls—the dark and dangerous Orient. (24)

And with this twisted tongue reference to turbans, veils and dark dangers, we are in no doubt that Caute fully understands and critiques the prejudices of Orientalism. How is it possible, in that case, that he reproduces them so profoundly in his fiction, as we shall see he does? Caute is a respected commentator on the history of the Left, especially of the French Left, and has written extensively, both fiction and non-fiction, on the organic relationship between history, politics and personal relationships. Born in 'Rhodesia', he also has a complex feel for Africa and produced the *Fontana Modern Masters* book on Fanon. In addition, his astute knowledge of British party politics, of local government and of British culture, prejudices and principles, should have enabled him to place the Rushdie affair into quite complex perspective. What is very interesting is that when he writes within realist and more strongly metonymic conventions of description, this he is indeed able to accomplish.

For example, in this political and historical mode of analysis, Caute demonstrates how the reactions to Rahman's book are more about the plight, poverty and power brokering within a quite heterogeneous British Muslim community. Izza Shah, Chairman of the Islamic Council, tells his daughter, Fatima, about the history of Muslims in Bruddersford, which is both about the racist host community and the gap between the generations, a gap, which is growing:

'We could not find accommodations. Nobody was prepared to let us into their homes. We were living all cramped up, twenty to thirty people in a three-bedroom house.'
'Twenty to thirty!'
'The Council houses we couldn't get either. ...
And then we lost our jobs. Cutbacks. ...Our jobs were the first to go. They threw us out of the mills. Our younger men led some bitter strikes. ...
Then we had Paki-bashing. And we were fighting back always. ...
Our children were growing up "modern", despising our customs. They became angry, we could not reach them. *Only now, with this Rahman book, are we reaching them*'. (61 & 2, my emphasis)

All of this has tremendous reverberations in the real life situation, as analysed by Muslim commentators at the time. (See Appignanesi and Maitland,72 &129). When the mode of the novel moves, however, into ridicule, as when Izza Shah makes his "brief statement to the waiting reporters", in what is described as "his uniquely opaque English", why do I feel so uneasy?

'We Muslims was insulted. And we is continuing this campaign until we gets apology. We have support of Muslim states, all unanimous. Insulting Islam is depriving me of existence. It's wiping my face from Earth.' (71)

When Caute moves from the intricacies of British political jostling and brokering, to depicting British Muslims as characters, their homes, their speech, their dreams and obsessions, in the postmodern mode of irony, farce and satire, he falls into the Orientalising that we discussed at the outset. We laugh at Izzah's mistakes and have little insight to his fluency in his own language and his Islamic scholarly achievements that have brought him to seniority within the community. His grammar and imperfect English expressing high feeling infantilises and feminises him, within the mould of overwrought, emotional Oriental gentleman.

These problems are magnified in the characterisation of Rahman/Rushdie himself. In this first, Bruddersford section, prior to any close encounter with him, we learn that "Gamal Rahman dropped from the sky, horns glowing, his sulphuric breath choking the city" (80). The echoes of the opening scene of *The Satanic Verses* are as obvious as the reference to Rahman's "rolling, lusting eyes" (75), repeated later by reference to how his lids hood his "bulging eyes" (299). Gamal, growing up in Cairo, is a strange, overweight and over-sexed boy with repulsive habits—"fat Egyptian boy with high forehead and large, revolving eyes" (235)—"fat-floppy Gamal's sweat, which no deodorant can conquer" (349). Caute goes even further. Like the twinned characters of Gibreel and Chamcha of Rushdie's novel, Rahman, no angel in the first place, has his demonic flip side, which is even more of a horrible parody of sinister Eastern lunatic bombing terrorist—Iqbal Iqbal, who smiles "his awful smile", displays his fake Koran, which houses a bomb and confesses to Haqq – "'I am Gamal Rahman. Or I might be. You never know. Shaytan lurks in all of us.'" (216).

He does indeed shoot and kill the mayor of Bruddersford (on whom he has laid and executed his own lunatic fatwa) and on arrest "claims to be Gamal Rahman" (528). The Chinese box postmodern device of the novel is to reveal that all the snide comments about the Muslim characters have been written by the fictional writer in the novel, Gamal Rahman himself. That is to say, Rahman is constructed by Caute as the writer/creator of all the characters—those inhabiting Bruddersford, Cairo and even his own self-portrait. This provides Rahman with an ironic self-portrait and also a smokescreen for the real life writer, David Caute, who is the true, concealed narrator, within the narrator.

John Irving's *A Son of the Circus* is also postmodernist in crucial ways. It too abounds with the pastiche of postmodern splintered selves and also of Dickensian realism, which seals the splinteredness of postmodern riot. We have mixed blood children, confusion of identity (as between twins separated at birth and raised on different continents) confusion of gender (including a sex changed key character and Hijras, or eunuch transvestites) all of which make a mockery of fixed identities and celebrate the cutting across polarities, such as between white and black, male and female, East and West.

Furthermore, Irving appears to be grappling with some of the issues of breaking out of conventional forms of subjectivity, which we discussed above. Debra Shostak notes "Irving's preoccupation in his novels with fathers—absent fathers, unknown fathers, surrogate fathers, dangerous fathers" (134) and *The Son of the Circus* is, of course, no exception. If Daruwalla's Father is the circus, then he is constructed in a Subjectivity whose Law is quite other than the Western Phallic one. Shostak points out that Irving's interest in the figure of the father "lies in his symbolic power as origin of and authority over narrative and artistic identity" (135). Ultimately, she continues, Irving's aim is

> to beget or engender himself without the help of fathers, to make himself subject to himself and subject in narrative. Paternal authority is thus conceived in metaphoric relation to the power to narrate. (135)

It is, then, only through inventing the language of his own fiction that the self is conceptualised as freed from the Father's word. And the power to narrate, Irving emphasises in an interview, is linked to making his narratives "as absolutely linear as possible" (McCaffery, 11); he seeks to make his narrative "as unconvoluted" as he can (McCaffery, 17). He has said: "'I follow the form of the nineteenth-century novel. ... I'm old-fashioned, a storyteller'" (Shostak, 132) and Shostak suggests that his mode of writing is "comic realism... and the master is Charles Dickens" (132).

While Irving has certainly transformed Dickens's *oeuvre* with his overlay of postmodern pastiche on the linear framework, the resultant palimpsest retains the metonymic bent of realism and is a mode of writing that Irving has designed in order to distance his fiction from the Modernist language of the metaphorical Fathers.

Caute's split and macabre Rushdie clone, on the other hand, ends up as a Muslim caricature, within the mode of Orientalism's metaphorical discourse. Caute's politics are at their best, in fact, only when his irony is used against the British characters. For example, the character, Ali Cheema, a scholar and cultural hybrid, turns the tables on his arrogant and ignorant BBC interviewer, in classical postmodern fashion:

> 'Shall I explain what the Liberal Inquisition is? The Liberal Inquisition brings *you* to interrogate *me* in my home. The cameras ensure that the audience identifies with *your* Caucasion journey to the oriental "belljar"—these alien, marginal, dark-skinned Believers who speak funny English. Why doesn't your producer send me and my canvas travel bag from Bruddersford to the South, questing and probing among all these exotic media people and famous liberal writers? Why am I not allowed to drink tea in your pinewood-fitted kitchen and then comment direct-to-camera? Why not turn the lens around? (493)

While this offers a warning about too readily linking devices (such as postmodernism's tools) and their political consequences, this example raises the spectre of another all too familiar issue. Am I saying that white writers may only offer up *a self-critique* using all the available literary devices at hand with which to do so? Yes and no. Writing within the history of imperialism and by means of its conventions, means occupying a battleground littered with unexploded minefields. Furthermore, given the enormous suffering caused by Western Imperialism and its arsenal of racism enshrined in its discourses, makes certain demands on white writers. And this brings me to the concluding part of this introductory chapter.

Tarzan, Tact and some Conclusions

The problem began at an emotional, gut level, where I experienced great unease and embarrassment with Caute's characters, and especially with Gamal Rahman, the putative author. This contrasted with my sense of being moved by Irving's Farrokh Daruwalla.

Daruwalla's little drama of immense significance is enacted within the glittering Canadian heart of whiteness, in the driving snow, under the lamplight. Irving is on home ground and secure in the critique of the vicious racism of the shouted insult from the car. This is Irving's depiction of the Canada he knows and has himself adopted as one of his homes, rather than of India, albeit that the bulk of the novel takes place there. As Irving states in his foreword:

> This novel isn't about India. I don't know India. I was there only once, for less than a month. When I was there, I was struck by the country's foreignness; it remains obdurately foreign to me. But long before I went to India, I began to imagine a man who has been born there and has moved away; I imagined a character who keeps coming back again and again. He is compelled to keep returning yet, with each return trip, his sense of India's foreignness only deepens. India remains unyieldingly foreign, even to him. (vii)

And later, in conversation with Laurel Graeber, Irving explains that *A Son of the Circus* was born in the heart of snowy whiteness of Canada, confirming my sense of the significance of the setting of the ending:

> Although John Irving's new novel, "A Son of the Circus," takes place largely in India, it was born on a snowy street corner in Toronto, one of two locations the author calls home.
> "I saw a man, well dressed and dignified, who was what newspapers call an 'immigrant of color,'" Mr. Irving said in a telephone interview from southern Vermont, where he also lives. "I recall thinking that the richness of his past life could never be accessible to me."
> But Mr. Irving, who is 52, made it accessible through the creation of Dr. Farrokh Daruwalla, his kind hearted hero. (1 & 22)

It is at this crossroads of cultural intersection that Irving's own identity surfaces, as a writer, uneasy with many of his culture's dominant values, one who has travelled and, significantly, like Daruwalla, has studied in Vienna, with whom he identifies across the racial divide.

I began this study firmly of the belief that the race or gender of the writer was irrelevant and that the only criterion for the success or failure of the fictional politics and aesthetics of representing Africa rests with the novel itself. I was determined not to engage in the well tread debates over whether men can represent women, whites depict blacks, and *vice verse* in both instances. I still hope not to linger on this well beaten track too long.

I also began with the assumption that debates about who has a voice and who should be silent were spurious. Everyone has a voice and the only question at issue is what they say and in whose interests they speak. The white, western man's Master Text, revealed as none other than the self interested discourse of Orientalism or Africanism, should not give way to the black, postcolonial intellectual man's discourse, in which new power and knowledge deals are clinched. If Edward Said, Arjun Appadurai and Simon

Gikandi are our new Fathers, whose Law constitutes our psyches, where is the gain?

In practice it is not so simple.

Firstly, and this point must be made with all the nuance I can muster, Caute cannot assume immunity from assumptions that he, like most whites, are racist in their attitudes to Egyptians, to Muslims, to black British citizens in general.

R. Radhakrishnan, in asking some cogent questions of Edward Said's *Orientalism*, helps me to frame my misgivings:

> The purpose of *Orientalism*, it seems to me, was not to suggest that there is a perfect insider's point of view that can tell *the* correct story of the Orient. The intention was to show the complicity of a certain kind of knowledge with imperialist, colonialist interests. Orientalist knowledges are dominant – not hegemonic: exploitative, colonizing, and invasive. How then do we distinguish between good and bad, just and unjust representations? What is the relationship between who is making the representation and what is being said? Does it matter who is speaking? (15)

When Salman Rushdie parodies and caricatures Muslim fundamentalism from within his own background, he is grappling with his own past and history. Even in this situation, he has given grave offence. I was intrigued by the undertow of reservation in the support for Rushdie on the part of Edward Said himself:

> Above all, however, there rises the question that people from the Islamic world ask: Why must a Moslem, who could be defending and sympathetically interpreting us, now represent us so roughly, so expertly and so disrespectfully to an audience also primed to excoriate our traditions, reality, history, religion, language, and origin? Why, in other words, must a member of our culture join the legions of Orientalists in Orientalizing Islam so radically and unfairly? (in Appignanesi & Maitland, 176)

Said is donning his own mask as he asks his question in the name of "people from the Islamic world" but in his own particular language of critique of Orientalism. He goes on to concede, however, that Rushdie, writing from within Muslim culture, has produced in *The Satanic Verses* "*a self-representation*" (in Appignanesi & Maitland, 177).

I myself would reject the suggestion that only Muslims may critique Muslim fundamentalism. What I am accepting is that a white man wishing to make the critique, given the history of Western exploitation and prejudice, has massive constraints upon him regarding how to do so. He has to find ways of indicating that the lunacy of rabid fundamentalism is counterbalanced by other Islamic practices and without leaving the impression of a mad and horrible religion in general. This is especially so, given that he is white. And this is so in practice, no matter how unacceptable it appears to be in theory.

Does Caute not do this with a sympathetic character in the novel like Nazreen? To some extent he does. She is the community teacher, who is very sane and rational, wishes to read the contentious book and judge its nature for herself and attempts to mediate between the Muslim community and the school principal. Nazreen, most interestingly, is one of the few characters not drawn in the style of satire. Take this moment in the novel when she is driving to the airport to fetch her father and she is frightened by the English landscape:

> Tremulously driving up to the 'knobbly backbone of England'—she does not know Mr J.B. Priestley's work—Nasreen shudders as the high moorlands come into view. Inside the car, with the heater on and the radio playing, she feels safe enough, but the road is narrow, the culverts deep. Sadar Baj Hussein has never taken his family weekend-picnicking on Bodkin Top or High Grave or Black Moor or Five Gates End, where, Priestley reflected, 'in summer you can wander...all day, listening to the larks, and never meet a soul'. Bruddersford's Muslims are not keen on never meeting a soul, and still less keen on the soul you might meet in that void. The djinns of the Pennines are not friendly to dark skins. (137)

This depiction is of a black woman on the part of a white man, but it takes her fears seriously, within the language of sympathy and realism, rather than satire and ridicule. It acknowledges cultural difference within a race and gender depiction that is complex; it acknowledges the racist discourse of British culture. It provides an alternative to the horrible image of the shrill, possessed Fatima, of the novel's title, and her band of black burka-ed harpies that form a chorus in the novel's wings. Caute, however, undermines his own achievement with regard to Nazreen and goes and condemns Islam as a whole, behind his postmodern pose. He has Gamal state sadly in the 'Epilogue', addressed as always to his absent father, "'I'm sorry Nazreen had no luck but she was born into the wrong religion for luck'" (555). This is an extraordinary indictment of the entire religion, and one which Caute is presumptuous to make.

I confess that the issues are not as clear cut as I once thought before working my way through the treasure trove of original, struggling, experimental novels described in the chapters that follow. Michael Gorra in a rather wonderful paper entitled "Tact and Tarzan" says that he thinks "that the Tarzan books are where I first learned to recognize a literary convention" (1991, 87) and he proceeds to question, as we have been doing in relation to the conventions of Africanist discourse, "when does metaphor become harmful? Is a writer ever entitled to see a place that's not his own in metaphoric terms?" (1991, 88). He offers us a blunt, empirical object, which is "tact", and which may not be able to sustain the heavy weight of all of this theory we have covered, but yet felt enormously right and comforting as a contribution to the measure of our writers' ability to come to Africa and to find an appropriate voice in which to write about it. He suggests that

> negotiating the issues of Otherness calls for what I think of as tact. For tact requires that you know the limits of your knowledge, that you know how your point of view is situated in the contingencies of history, that you know too how that Other sees the issues with which you attempt to deal and know when to use that point of view to qualify your own. But it is also important to say what tact does not mean: it does not mean discounting my own views simply because they are Western or white, and it does not mean trying to match somebody else's simply because they are not. It is instead a way of avoiding orthodoxy, and thereby makes possible that necessary conversation across the dividing lines of Otherness. No method, and no theory, can compensate for its absence.
> And yet it seems a matter of impossible delicacy. (1991, 91)

Perhaps Irving's version of this delicacy is his comment that "grace and affection...mean a great deal to me in evaluating other writers", qualities he ascribes to Dickens, among others, whose "ultimate structure is graceful and whose ultimate feeling for people is fondness" (McCaffery, 18). Caute's disdain for people, when those people include persons from cultures and backgrounds other than his own, contributes unwittingly to his culture's tradition of Orientalist discourse. And I would agree that after all of our defining of difficult terms and concepts, there is a moment of almost indescribable good manners blended with humility that is called for when writers pack their literary bags and journey to Africa.

In summary, the connections that I have been building are between postmodernism, the mortified male body, discourse and the representation of Africa. Lacanian theory positioned the Phallus, symbol of male power, as the keeper of the Law, within the Symbolic as the site of the construction of human subjectivity, the acquisition of language and with it, the unconscious. Emanating from the authority of this Name of the Father, are the multiple Master Narratives of mainstream Western culture. The master narrative is a mega-metaphor, a store house of the culture's common knowledge and out of it comes the countless mini-metaphors and plots, stories and films that comprise the 'common sense' of Western knowledge of other places and people. Postmodernism may or may not reveal Master Texts as mere representations rather than reality, as stories, among them that of the white imperialist male, who brings the light of civilization to the dark and savage people of Asia or Africa. The conventions of Realism too may contest the powerful metaphors of Western culture and in so doing, demote the perfect built body of Superman and Tarzan, icons of white, Western male power.

Perhaps in the process the Phallus will be made visible and become the vulnerable flesh that it is. Perhaps not. What is the case is that the traditions and conventions of representation on the part of the West must be identified and attacked if writers are to transform them. In so doing they must re-make themselves not only as writers, but as men.

Finally, what is clear in all of these forces and determinations of the social, economic, psychic and cultural is that ultimately, as Fred Pfeil puts it "the very concept and normative definition of white straight masculinity" is "unsettled" (1998, 182). The chapters that follow will question the extent to which the writers under discussion find their way through the labyrinth of unequal power and privilege, of the psyche and the tropes that leave their fossilized imprint upon it. Have they armed themselves with new understandings and crafty devices as they pick their way, wearily, warily and tactfully, into the African fictional zone?

As the chapters unfold, new and different words, concepts and methods emerge. I have not attempted to unify the book by applying the same methodology in each part. This would be to do damage to the unique styles and projects of the heterogeneous novels under discussion. It would be to place the writers in a formulaic box of my making, rather than to listen as carefully as I can to their voices. Ultimately, I wish to communicate with all the tact that I can muster, the humour and ruefulness of some latter-day Tarzans who admit their fear of heights, the pain of penitent sons of Conrad, who understand the manipulations of narrative and who do not confuse the profits of ivory with the invention of local 'brutes'.

Part Two:
Sons as Explorers

CHAPTER TWO

"The Niger remained a mystery": Fetishes, Bodies and Books in T. Coraghessan Boyle's *Water Music*

Selves and Things: Introduction

Two eras criss-cross this part of the book. Firstly, we will enter into the late eighteenth century at its millennium, on the cusp of the period of the famous nineteenth century explorers and of the formal colonial occupation of African territory. This we will do with T. Coraghessan Boyle, who re-writes and fictionalises the story of the two expeditions undertaken by Mungo Park in his search for the contours of the Niger River in his first novel, *Water Music*. In the next chapter, we will go even further back in time with Lawrence Norfolk, to the Renaissance and its voyages of discovery as we search for a rhinoceros for a corrupt Pope in his *The Pope's Rhinoceros*.

Boyle begins with a powerful critique of European greed, competitiveness and entitlement with regard to Africa:

> Pliny the elder painted the Niger gold and christened it black, and Alexander's scouts inflamed him with tales of the river of rivers where lords and ladies sat in gardens of lotus and drank from cups of hammered gold. And now, at the end of the Age of Enlightenment and the beginning of the Age of Imbursement, France wanted the Niger, Britain wanted it, Holland, Portugal and Denmark. (1981, 4)

The extent to which *Water Music* is written against the grain, or swept along with the current, of the conventions of Africanism will emerge as we travel with Boyle's Mungo Park and Ned Rise towards the River Niger. One thing is certain, we can only understand Boyle's novel in the context of another era, that of the heady period of the American sixties of his young adulthood, when he and others like him, were dodging the draft, dropping out and flying high on drugs and booze. They were searching for an identity at a time when the generation gap became a chasm and the Third World offered up alternative fathers to these white sons, fathers like Che Guevara, Mao

Zedong and Frans Fanon (Jameson, 1988, 188). These fathers opened up new vistas, providing a likely explanation for the fact that when Boyle turned to writing a novel for the first time, as opposed to short stories, he journeyed to Africa, searching for roots, origins of Rivers, of Fathers and Mothers, of the self. This is, of course, a dangerous past-time, reeking of the old stereotype of Africanism where white boys travel to—from their perspective—the ends of the earth to discover their essences.

Again, does Boyle write or contest such a novel? This question should be posed in the context of the distance between the young Boyle, who was nineteen during the heyday of the Vietnam War, and the contemporary novelist, of our own times. About two decades on from Vietnam, Boyle constructs a fiction about Africa from the vantage point of an omniscient narrator, who comments upon, judges and invents multiple characters and possibilities. This he does with the assistance of a generation of postcolonial writers on his doorstep, writers that influence and sway his vision, like Gabriel Garcia Marquez. This Third World, magical realist presence entwines with that of the great nineteenth century social realist, Charles Dickens, both of whom are acknowledged influences on Boyle (Friend, 50, Adams, 59).

If multiple eras echo and entwine in the historical framework of Boyle's *Water Music* then the novel also plays to many *selves* that Boyle explores. The bulk of this chapter deals with what I will suggest are five different Boyles, who occupy the enlarged quartet of *Water Music*. These are the characters of Mungo Park himself, of Ned Rise, an underclass ex-prisoner on his expedition, and of an unfortunate victim named, significantly, Boyles. The fourth, intriguingly, is Mungo's black African guide, Johnson. The final Boyle inscribed in the *Water Music* is an omniscient narrator, who in true nineteenth century mode of Realism, knows all and whose seeing-eye carries moral weightiness. Although in an important sense, all of these characters are both Boyle and not Boyle, the crucial link between them, one which cut across race, is the fact of Boyle's background as a North American of poor Irish descent, as will become clear:

> His father, a school-bus driver, and his mother, a secretary, were alcoholics. ... When he was 17, Boyle foresightedly changed his name from Thomas John Boyle— his father's name—to the memorable battle cry T. Coraghessan Boyle, the trumpeting "Coraghessan" (pronounced cor-RAG-a-sen) taken from his mother's family. (Friend, 68)

At the same time, the novel is peppered with significant, magical objects, fetishes that light a path along the river, guiding us as to the direction and meaning of all the searching. These are a clarinet and a pistol, the highly suggestive African carving that Mungo finds and takes from the courtyard of the potentate of the village where he first encounters the Niger, the chicken carcass around Johnson's neck and, of course, last and perhaps most significantly, and as always, the Book itself.

To sum up, the threads that Boyle weaves together, as history transforms into the discourse of his fiction, are his many selves striving for subjectivity and magical things, or fetishes, which, as "compromise objects" (McClintock, 202) attempt to resolve complex tensions in both who he is, how he writes and what has gone before. The nature of these symbolic objects will be explored in the light of the many faces of Coraghessan Boyle.

Will the Real Boyle Please Rise?

My sub-title has been adapted from Chris Denina, whose profile of Boyle asks for the real Boyle to "stand up". I think that Boyle would like Ned Rise of *Water Music* to respond to the call. The pun is Boyle's as the novel traces the fortunes of the upwardly mobile Ned. But first, Boyle himself. Denina entitles his piece thus, given that:

> Friends know him as Tom Boyle, his students know him as T.C. Boyle and readers around the world know him as T. Coraghessan Boyle.
> With a different name for each part of his life, one might be confused as to exactly who he is. (7)

Or as Boyle himself puts it – "'the audience thinks, 'He's *bad*'":

> "They want me to be running wild, to die young. But you could also present me as the family man with a Ph.D. who's been with his wife for 20 years, loves his three kids, is a tenured professor at U.S.C., lives in the suburbs and plants trees in his backyard". (Friend, 66)

But the audience wants Boyle to be bad, because this is the image that Boyle cultivates. He and his buddies get drunk, wake up in strange places, "burn dolls' heads in fireplaces" (Friend, 66). In younger days, "they drank hard, wore torn leather jackets, peeled out in the family station wagon and busted up churches" (Friend, 66).

An important short story of Boyle's, "Greasy Lake", begins with just such a bunch of 'bad' boy buddies as Boyle hung out with in the sixties. The story opens thus:

> We were all dangerous characters then. We wore torn-up leather jackets, slouched around with toothpicks in our mouths, sniffed glue and ether and what somebody claimed was cocaine. When we wheeled our parents' whining station wagons out into the street we left a patch of rubber half a block long. We drank gin and grape juice, Tango, Thunderbird, and Bali Hai. We were nineteen. We were bad. (1986, 1)

This murky lake, I will suggest, is not only the Vietnamese "nightmarish swamp, the crucible of a forming consciousness, as it was for the United States" (Walker, 251) but the dangerous, crocodile infested, mosquito-lined, disease-bearing waters of the River Niger. This association between the two waters is made in a telling comment of Walker's that "the three friends go searching for the heart of darkness at Greasy Lake" (248–9). Conrad's trope of Africa is involuntarily conjured up by dark, murky places, where violent and criminal events are enacted, and adolescents develop a little self-knowledge.

The relationship between the historical period of the sixties, Boyle's search for a workable identity in the context of his particular family background and his fictional journey to Africa at the turn of the last century, is a complex one. Fredric Jameson's essay, entitled "Periodizing the 60s", suggests that the Third World is where it all began:

> It does not seem particularly controversial to mark the beginnings of what will come to be called the 60s in the Third World with the great movement of decolonization in British and French Africa. (1988, 180)

Jameson suggests that "the overall dynamic of Third World history during this period" exerted "some privileged relationship of influence on the unfolding of a First World 60s" (1988, 180). The 60s was a period in which the Law of the white, Western Fathers is interrogated and splintered with the phrase "generation gap" achieving popular, colloquial usage. What seemed to be marked was:

> the decisive end of the well-known passing of the torch to a younger generation of leadership, as well as the dramatic defeat of some new spirit of public or civic idealism. (Jameson, 1988, 183)

The sixties was the decade in which the indivisibility of the personal and the political became the creed of the young, where the search for an individual identity was forged within resistance to the politics and lifestyle of the Elders, to the Law of the false Fathers. This included their wars, their state and their ideology of racism, sexism and lack of respect for the planet. Into this gap moved new Fathers and role models and profound new questions about the relationship between Self and Other. Into this space Jameson plots the powerful influence of Sartre, and through him, of Fanon.

Invented Fathers across the line of culture and colour—Fanon, Mao, Castro—provided new Laws through which these white, receptive, immature subjects attempted to constitute themselves. They took up the banner of anti-racism and sexism and linked their anti-war demonstrations to a green revolution where noxious gases as weapons of war symbolised their biological fathers' lack of care in securing the heritage of the earth. In this regard, Jameson, with reference to the theories of Ernst Mandel, describes how the 60s in which colonialism gives way to neo-colonialism also saw the demise of the untouched, natural world, symbolised by the remote areas of the map, as viewed from the West:

> Late capitalism can therefore be described as the moment when the last vestiges of Nature which survived on into classical capitalism are at length eliminated: namely the Third World and the unconscious. The 60s will then have been the momentous transformational period when this systemic restructuring takes place on a global scale. (1988, 207)

We encounter again that powerful link between the Western unconscious and its imaginary Third World space of emptiness of culture, of Nature in its purest form, which for the young hippies of the sixties, also signified escape from their 'false fathers'. The search for untrammelled Nature, linked to unbridled sexuality, is a significant recurrent preoccupation in Boyle's genre. And often it is water that encompasses the tension between that natural state as bliss and as demonic, threatening and disease infected. There is the greasy lake; there is also the pond with the wild, "pullulating" toads in the story "Hopes Rise" (1994). In *Water Music*, it is the ambivalent pull of the River Niger that summonses Mungo Park, whose exploring passion enthrals Coraghessan Boyle, even as it repels him.

Soft White Underbelly: Mungo Park

"Soft White Underbelly" is the first sub-heading of the novel, which begins in 1795 with Mungo in dire straits, captured by the Moors, about to have his eyes gouged out. It appears as if Boyle is distancing himself from the persona of the explorer, as the omniscient narrator, who knows exactly what is going on, parodies Mungo's ignorant and naïve delusions of grandeur:

> But now they seem to be fitting something over his head...a helmet? Do they expect him to go to battle for them? Or have they finally come to their senses and decided to measure him for a crown?
> The explorer grins stupidly beneath his brazen cap (1981, 9)

Boyle's irony punctures the myth of the intrepid explorer with his heroic stature and all-seeing eyes, and begins with a Mungo Park, who is silly and arrogant, albeit good-natured. Far from gazing from his privileged promontory, Mungo Park is blindfolded by the Moors and stared at by them with shock and distaste. The Moors gaze at his white skin and peculiar eye colour with horrified incredulity. It is he who is the Other.

Johnson, Mungo's African guide, is the one who is in touch with reality and aware of the peril of the situation. Boyle uses Johnson's voice to caricature Mungo Park, and others like him, in their postures as intrepid adventurers:

> "Mr. Park," Johnson whispers. "What you got that thing on your head for? Don't you realize what they doin' to you?"
> "Johnson, jolly old Johnson. How good to hear your voice."
> "They puttin' out your eyes, Mr. Park". (1981, 9)

Boyle repeatedly debunks and satirises the image of Park as heroic adventurer and uses Johnson as his agent in a way that extends his role way beyond that recorded in Park's own memoir where Johnson, his guide, plays quite a minor role. In true colonial style, Park may ride on a horse while Johnson walks, but the horse is disgusting, given to "senile farting—great gaseous exhalations that swept the sun from the sky and made all the world a sink" (1981, 14). Also note the irony that Johnson is better educated than Park, that he speaks in an ironic mode which is too sophisticated for Mungo—he quips that the clapped out horse is "Rocinante"—"however, the allusion was lost on the explorer (1981, 14)".

After he had been taken prisoner by the Moors, moreover, Mungo himself ponders the difference between the romantic dream of exploring and the harsh reality:

> The explorer never dreamed it would be like this—so confused, so demeaning. And so hot. He had pictured himself astride a handsome mount, his coat pressed and linen snowy, leading a group of local wogs and half-wits and kings to the verdant banks of the river of legend. Yet here he is...a prisoner for all intents and purposes, his horse wheezing and farting, his underwear binding at the crotch. Is there no sense of proportion in the world? (1981, 64)

Park's arrogance and ignorance of local conditions and culture repeatedly get him into life threatening trouble, from which Johnson has to bale him out. Park's foolish unawareness makes Johnson bitter about wandering "all over the continent, risking life and limb to bail out some half-witted, glory-hungry son of a crofter" (1981, 102).

This brings us to the climatic anti-climax of Park reaching the River Niger and ascertaining the direction of its flow—to the East. The crucial point is that surrounding this River is densely populated land, great masses of people who live their daily lives sustained by its waters. In what sense, then, can the River Niger have been "discovered"? Boyle makes this point wonderfully, turning the tables on the explorer's Gaze, as local inhabitants on high look down at this white lunatic in wonder:

> People—packed in like bees in a hive—as far as the eye can see. There must be three or four thousand of them, hanging from windows, treetops, roofs, perched on shoulders, the backs of camels, straining on tiptoe. The banks of the river are black with them, scores in water up to their ankles, knees, necks, scores more bobbing in pirogues and coracles. All gathered to stand hushed and appalled while this impossible, inexplicable presence, this man in the moon fallen to earth, this white demon from hell chants, screeches, laughs, gibbers and sings, churning up the water, cursing the crops, bringing the sky down, and who knows what else? (1981, 103)

Mungo is utterly unaware of the effects of his actions, his strangeness and the threat that this poses to local sensibilities. Enveloped in his own mission, narcissistically, "Mungo Park is kicking up a froth and singing 'God Save the King' at the top of his lungs" (1981, 103). Indeed, while Mungo is prancing about and destroying any basis of trust with local people, it is again Johnson who is urgently aware of the necessity of first paying their respects to the local ruler, the potentate of Bambarra. This is an astute fictionalisation of Mary Louise Pratt's famous observation:

> As a rule the "discovery" of sites like Lake Tanganyika involved making one's way to the region and asking the local inhabitants if they knew of any big lakes, etc. in the area, then hiring them to take you there, whereupon with their guidance and support, you proceeded to discover what they already knew. (1992, 202)

On his second expedition, moreover, Park has not developed more humility or wisdom and by refusing the advice of Johnson (now called Isaaco for reasons that will emerge) he leads his men and himself to their slow and painful deaths—all except one, Ned Rise. Mungo Park's pig-headedness, moreover, embodies the predictable racism just beneath the surface of his boyish charm. When Johnson becomes convinced that the expedition is doomed to failure and that they should turn back, Park refuses this advice. Johnson is adamant that he will not continue and offers Park his precious silver-plated pistol for good luck. In a shocking moment, Boyle whisks away the safety net of his irony and irreverence and has Park scream "'Get out, nigger!'" (1981, 386). The racial insult, the word, 'nigger' is the bullet shot at the possibility of genuine friendship across the line of race. All of this is, of course, highly anachronistic, given that the shock is induced by twentieth century sensibilities. But with that verbal missile Boyle obliterates Mungo's relationship with Johnson and banishes the black man from the novel:

> Johnson's face showed nothing. He pushed himself up, brushed off his toga, and stepped out of Mungo Park's life. Forever. (1981, 386)

This is wonderful. The clear, crisp, single word 'forever' is uncompromising in its recognition of racism as an absolute divide between the men.

Having said all of this, however, I would like to suggest that *Water Music*'s apparent caricature and distance from the character of Mungo Park embodies a simultaneous identity between Boyd and his doomed explorer. Park embodies Boyle's own underbelly of guilt as American, white and privileged, guilt to which Boyle has confessed:

> I was mollycoddled and brooded over by a plethoric society, a society of abundance unparalleled at any time anywhere in history, and that society made me into a rebel with many causes and no real fear of retribution, save for the occasional judicious (and sometimes judicial) spanking. (In response to Krishna Baldev Vaid, 1996, 548)

"Rara Avis", a short story in the *Greasy Lake* collection, captures Boyle's sense of collusion and white male culpability. It describes a wonderful bird that lands on the roof of the furniture store of some small town:

> There it was: stark and anomalous, a relic of a time before shopping centers, tract houses, gas stations, and landfill, a thing of swamps and tidal flats, of ooze, fetid water, and rich black festering muck. In the context of the minutely ordered universe of suburbia, it was startling, as unexpected as a downed meteor or the carcass of a woolly mammoth. I shouted out, whooped with surprise and sudden joy. (1986, 198)

Again there is Nature, watery, uncivilized and black. And the boy, first person narrator, is utterly captivated by its power in the face of encroaching shopping malls. Crowds gather in wonderment and then a sudden wind exposes the bird's weakness, its vulnerability—a wound beneath the feathers—"secret, raw, red, and wet" (1986, 202). The last words of the story are chilling in their abrupt unexpectedness:

> I threw the first stone. (1986, 202)

Boyle may fool about, joke, hide behind his irony and his irreverence, but when he strikes a serious note, it is a blow. This is the same verbal stone, "nigger", flung at his guide by Mungo Park in *Water Music*. It is a self-conscious device—as Boyle puts it – "'I really like the power of stopping the laughter and turning it to horror'" (in Friend, 50). He enlarges:

> 'It's very powerful when the safety net drops away from the comic universe where nothing can go wrong, and there's this overpowering, terrible violence.' (in Friend, 50)

Why did the boy do it? Six weeks earlier he had been initiated into masculine subjectivity as he had stood with his father and watched an abandoned house burn:

> I stood beside my father, leaned against him, the acrid, unforgiving stink of the smoke almost drowned in the elemental odor of his seat, the odor of armpit and crotch and secret hair, the sematic animal scent of him that had always repelled me—until that moment. (1986, 199)

Always fathers and ambivalence. A violent male bonding moment, conjuring the power of its corrosive aggressive sexuality, which is evoked six weeks later by two strangers, also watching the bird—"they were lean and seedy, unshaven, slouching behind the brims of their hats" (1986, 202). What Boyle is poetically and humbly acknowledging is the way in which white male Subjectivity passes through the gates of the Law of the problematic Fathers, giving rise to a measure of fraught collusion with their violence and cruelty.

What is born, of course, is a terrible and ultimately divided Self, a Subjectivity bathed in the culture of violence, war and discrimination, which is simultaneously reluctant and eventually desperate to be different. And again there is the underbelly, the sting in the tale, where Africa becomes metaphor for those compelling, watery, sexual spaces of fecund slime and exotic creatures—bird and black person shockingly linked—all victims of white violence. But there are further, more positive points of identity between Boyle and his adventuring, white protagonist.

The Compelling Music of Distant Waters

Like the boyish and confused protagonists of some of Boyle's short stories, it does appear that Mungo Park was, in reality, in the historical record, quite a sweet and gentle man. It is in relation to the type of character of Mungo Park that Pratt develops a more generalised trope of exploration, which she terms "anti-conquest". By this she refers to "the strategies of representation whereby European bourgeois subjects seek to secure their innocence in the same moment as they assert European hegemony" (1992, 7). And she indicates specifically in relation to Park that:

> In comparison with a great many other travellers, especially some of the Victorians who followed him, Park affirms plausible worlds of African agency and experience. His relational approach to culture raises genuine possibilities of critical self-questioning. At the same time, though they are relativized, or even parodied, European ideologies are never questioned directly. Park's book owes much of its power to this combination of humanism, egalitarianism, and critical relativism anchored securely in a sense of European authenticity, power, and legitimacy. (1992, 84)

This trope, nearly two centuries later, seems to resonate powerfully with the criticism Boyle makes of himself and of and his contemporaries. Peace Corps volunteers, writers and teachers, well-meaning seekers after goodness and innocence, they nonetheless threw those stones, and in whom something monstrous, white, male and oppressive, was reproduced. And if this means anything, it means that Boyle is simultaneously aware of the contradictions between innocence and imperial power and also culpable of being an anti-conquest man himself, as we shall see.

Furthermore, the roots of the ambivalence that both Pratt and Boyle display lie with the attractive, rebellious side of the adventurer. He may survey the scene like a king and represent, and even consolidate imperial interests; he may have little interest or respect for the people and landscapes to which he journeys, but he has the courage to risk overstepping the bounds of accepted behaviour. He dares all, breaks the rules and the boundaries of his own self-knowledge. This Boyle admires and it is this that gives an edge to the critique of these arrogant, ignorant men, who despise settled Patriarchy even as they dominate and oppress their Penelopes who wait back home.

Johnson does not understand "this explorin' business" given that Park has "been starved and abused, sick with the ague and the fever" robbed of all his worldly goods and reduced to eating roasted paw pads of the jackal. Park's genuinely inspiring answer is that he learns something new every day, that:

> I want to know the unknowable, see the unseen, scale mountains and look behind the stars. I want to fill in the maps, lecture the geographers, hold up a torch for the academicians. The Niger...think of it, Johnson. No white man has ever laid eyes upon it. I'll have seen what none of them have—not the Laird of Dumfries, nor Charles Fox, nor the King himself". (1981, 90)

There is poetry in Mungo Park's exceptional urge for adventure and exploration. The adventurer may be the imperialist's lookout, but he is also the unruly wild man, who rebelliously contests the Law of the Fathers. Hayden White, in an early paper, "The Forms of Wildness: Archaeology of an Idea", describes how:

> the Archetypal wild men of the Old Testament are the great rebels against the Lord, the God-challengers, the antiprophets, giants, nomads—men like Cain, Ham, and Ishmael, the very kinds of "heroes" who, in Greek mythology and legend, might have enjoyed a place of honor beside Prometheus, Odysseus, and Oedipus. ...They are depicted as wild men inhabiting a wild land, above all as hunters, sewers of confusion, damned, and generative of races that live in irredeemable ignorance or outright violation of the laws that God has laid down for the governance of the cosmos. (14)

They are bad. They are men with whom Boyle would identify; they are Salman Rushdie's characters in his latest novel, *The Ground Beneath her Feet*, in which Rushdie himself writes a version of the Odysseus myth:

> Among the great struggles of man—good/evil, reason/unreason, etc.—there is also this mighty conflict between the fantasy of Home and the fantasy of Away, the dream of roots and the mirage of the journey. ....Off you'd go, off your turf, beyond family and clan and nation and race, flying untouchably over the minefields of taboo, until you stood at last at the last gateway, the most forbidden of all doors. Where your blood sings in your ears, *Don't even think about it.* And you think about it, you cross that final frontier, and perhaps, perhaps—we'll see how the tale works out—you have finally gone too far, and are destroyed. (1999, 55)

Is this not precisely what Mungo Park dared? When he heard the voice in his ears warning him to turn back, he decided instead to go too far and was destroyed. And is there not a big part of Co-RAG-hessan Boyle who admires that recklessness. It is no coincidence that it is Rushdie himself who says approvingly of *Water Music* on its front cover that it is "crammed with disgusting, filthy ideas".

Paul Zweig calls these adventuring men "escape artists" and suggests that:

> The adventurer pokes holes in the walled city, and we breathe more freely for having seen that it is possible to do so. (60)

Boyle, part of the sixties generation, identified with the rebel, the reckless, brave man, who broke god's Laws, who, remember, on wild nights out, wrecked churches and despised settled domesticity. Boyle empathises with poor old Mungo, who once home and married, after his first and before his second expedition, is domesticated, bored and claustrophobic:

> He tries to imagine himself in twenty years, his hair gone white, fifteen children clamoring for meat and milk and sugar buns, new suits and dresses, schoolbooks, dowries, university fees.
> "Three's enough, " he tells Ailie, but she just looks at him out of the corner of her eye, sly and suggestive, fertile as Niger mud. "I want bairns to remember you by when you go off and leave me," she says, no trace of humor in her voice, each child a new link in the chain that binds him to her". (1981, 272)

University fees? Surely more of a concern of Coraghesson Boyle's than of Mungo Park? Ailie may have only produced three children thus far, the same number, note, as Boyle has, but she is capable of producing fifteen, all for the purpose of slyly enslaving her man. And so we are quite pleased when Mungo gives her the slip and we share his sense of justification when he writes to her from his next expedition:

> 'The Yarrow is tame, life is tame. There are wonders out there, wonders waiting for the right man to risk all to reveal them. I am that man, Ailie, I am that man.' (1981, 294)

We too can almost hear the music of the lure to explore and to break the bonds of convention when, with Ailie we re-read the letter and see scribbled inside the leaf of the envelope the following words:

> I can hear it in my dreams, hear it in the morning when I wake and the birds are in the trees—a rustling, a tinkling—a sound of music. You know what it is? The Niger. Rushing, falling, heaving toward its hidden mouth, toward the sea. That's what I hear Ailie, day and night. Music. (1981, 294)

The reader is with Mungo and with Boyle and we understand more than Ailie does when all she can hear is the wail of infants—"The baby cried out. She dropped the envelope in the fireplace" (1981, 294). However, the portrait of Mungo remains quite contradictory. He is also such a ridiculous figure when he plays out this urge in Africa. The novel, moreover, also has a great deal of sympathy for Ailie, who is quite literally left holding the babies, who never reaches her potential and ends up sad, drained and very lonely.

In many ways Boyle's novel conforms to the adventurer genre, as described in Paul Zweig's book of that title. In a chapter entitled "The Flight from Women", Zweig defines the adventurer as being "in flight from women" (61)—"the woman he defeats expresses the bewitching domesticity of the house" (69). Zweig sums up adventure as an imperfect form of "initiation into the emperion of the masculine" (71). It "represents a poignant male fantasy: moved by his desire to vanquish the many faces of woman, he reinvents the shape of manhood itself so as to free it from its multiple attachments to the feminine" (79). This dimension of the Mungo Park story surely comes close to the marrow of Boyle's own issues.

What these macho adventurers have is a love/hate relationship with their wives, who are simultaneously the snare and the lure—home and unexplored territory. Ailie is, remember, "fertile as Niger mud" and this ambivalence of male desire is also a part of the adventuring paradigm:

> As for Kurtz in *Heart of Darkness*, and Gawain in the medieval epic, the adversary in the bedroom and the adversary in the forest are one. (Zweig, 72).

And so Ailie

moves like a creature born to water. Moves with an easy fluid athletic grace, moves with a beauty that catches in his throat. He loses her momentarily in a shimmering crescent of reflected sun, only to watch her re-emerge in an aureole of light, transfigured in that flashing instant to something beyond flesh and blood, something mythic and eternal. How could he ever leave her? (1981, 273)

The music of the water is the fatal siren calling out to intrepid white men to adventure, ironically leaving behind a wife in pursuit of a mermaid, woman as both the object of desire and impediment to achieving it. Nonetheless, the empathy with Mungo's (albeit naïve, arrogant, stupid, suicidal) urge to freedom and adventure, away from the deathly dull, ordinary, good citizenship of Peebles and good works as family, country bumpkin doctor is palpable.

The mixed message of woman as perplexingly both ensnaring wife and object of the adventurer's quest is embodied in the strange, magical wooden carving that Mungo brings back from his first expedition, a fetish discovered by Ailie.

"The tree is festooned with human skulls": African Orientalism

[She] turns it over in her hands. Smooth, black. So black it seems to drink in light and swallow it. At first she can make no sense of the thing, but then as she traces the thickly carved lines it comes to her: a woman. Ponderous, disproportionate, her head the size of an acorn, sagging dugs, abdomen and nates distended to cruelly absurd proportions. She looks closer. The woman's feet are like trees, each toe a bole. And what's this? Tortuous, secretive, black on black, a snake winds its way up her leg.

Ailie stares down at the figurine for a long while, lost in the pure rich glossy blackness of it, and then she begins to shiver. A night breeze lifts the curtains. Naked, she sets it down on the table and moves for the wardrobe and her nightgown. Outside the crickets stir. (1981, 244–5)

The mixed emotions are reflected in Ailie's response to this strange object. Ailie identifies with her as a woman with a body, which echoes Ailie's own desire for a pregnant, fertile shape. However, she is also mysterious Africa, Ailie's rival for Mungo. How did Mungo acquire it? We suspect that he stole it, in the mode of European plunder of African treasures.

At the cathartic moment of encountering the Niger, Johnson, we recall, had insisted that Mungo pay his respects to the potentate of Bambarra, an important ruler called Mansong. In the main courtyard of the palace, Mungo encounters "an enormous snaking fig tree" with all the overtones of the original tree of knowledge. As he looks more closely at this tree, "the stumbling explorer"

is chilled to discover that the tree is festooned with human skulls, and a number of carved figures depicting unnatural acts: autofellatio, pederasty, the eating of excrement. *The most arresting statue, its features greedily distorted, shows a pregnant woman with the multiple dugs of a dog either swallowing or regurgitating a serpent, which is in turn either swallowing or regurgitating the head of an infant.* (1981, 110, my emphasis)

"'Mansong is disembowelin' thirty-seven slaves in your honor'" (1981, 114). The 'civilized' Park is utterly horrified—"he grits his teeth and tries to think of Scotland, of barbered hills, open white faces, safety and sanity" (1981, 114).

There is worse to come. He has to drink blood with the Potentate to seal their agreement (1981, 115) which also includes fifty thousand cowrie shells, but nowhere mentions a gift of the carving, which we must assume, Mungo stole from the Tree of Knowledge, Adam turned Eve in Edenic Africa. Why did he do this? It is obviously to him a horrible, demonic unnatural figure in a pantheon of decadent, depraved acts of child sex, auto penis sucking and greed, along with, note, hags and pregnancy. The multiple dugs of the woman signify the many sources of ambivalent power she carries over men as mother, wife, sexual partner, keeper of the keys to domestic bliss and tamed imprisonment. She is a source of greed, unbridled sexuality, rampant fecundity and cannibalising ferocity and also of fatal attraction for the adventurer.

This takes us back to Mungo's love-hatred towards Ailie, his horror of domestic imprisonment and what he sees as her rampant fertility. This gross fecundity cuts across race. In Africa, Mungo encounters a character called Fatima. She is the wife of Ali, vicious leader of the Moors and implacable enemy of Park. She, however, becomes enamoured of our explorer and he views her as an enormous, pulsating sexual goddess—"she is gargantuan, elephantine, her great bundled turban and glowing *jubbah* like a pair of circus tents (1981, 46)". Her body is likened, again in familiar fashion, to the land that the intrepid adventurer is exploring. Fatima's seduction of Park occurs in a section entitled '*New Continents, Ancient Rivers*' (1981, 51). Exploration is likened to mounting this vast sensuous and disgusting woman. Boyd's irony is limitless and the description includes a bizarre and suggestive recipe for stuffed baked camel (1981, 54). In case we did not get the point, Boyle describes how

> he scrambles atop her, feeling for toeholds—so much terrain to explore—mountains, valleys and rifts, new continents, ancient rivers. (1981, 58)

As always, Boyle is ambivalent and hiding behind his irony, a concealment which enables both a critique of Orientalism and a collusion with it. The irony, in addition, blurs both a rejection of patriarchy and a patriarchal distaste for domesticity and the powerful female body. Boyle certainly demonstrates how both Fatima and Ailie, albeit in different ways, are oppressed by their husbands. Fatima was delivered by her father to her husband, packaged plump in ways that men of that culture find sexually satisfying. She is first force-fed and then becomes a gargantuan eating machine of indescribably enormous proportions:

> "And when you come of age you will continue to eat – day and night. That is your duty. To your father, and to your husband. He will have a rod!" her father shouted. "A rod like this one. And he will thrash you as I am thrashing you now and as I will thrash you tomorrow and the next day and the day after that!" Suddenly the venerables were on their feet, as if this were some sort of signal. Fatima looked up, her cheeks swollen with mush, and gasped: a hideous unnatural change had come over them. Where before they'd been flaccid, now they were hard. Wizened old turkey cocks, their members engorged, they closed in on her. "Thrash you!" her father shrieked and they began pumping at themselves, milking their rods with a whack and thwap, their faces strained and distant, beatific even. (1981, 24)

These orgies of eating, drinking and masturbating may caricature male decadence, but they also enter a grotesque union with Africanist discourse in cahoots with Orientalism and even patriarchy itself. Women, white or black, are briefly united in the novel by their fecundity, which the novel, for all its critiques, finds grotesque:

> At night [Ailie] lights candles before the carved black statue that squats in the center of her dressing table like an icon, and once he caught her rubbing its swollen belly before climbing into bed. Touch her and she's pregnant again. (1981, 272)

To sum up, if we have seen Boyle's simultaneous critique of, and attraction towards, Mungo Park and all he stands for, then the device he chooses for handling this tension is irony, a mode that can enable the writer to speak with a forked tongue. This it can do with a range of political consequences. The problem that arises is that it becomes a blunt instrument when directed against all and sundry, within a context of reluctance to single out Mungo Park, for especially punitive treatment. In this way, Boyle appears to mute the critique of Park via the mechanism of even-handedness, where everyone receives the butt of his gallows humour, his irreverence and refusal to bow to any form of political correctness. This mode is dangerous within the minefield of Africanist Discourse.

In other words, if Park and the explorer *persona*, are being debunked, aspects of Orientalism and Africanist discourse seem simultaneously to be being reinforced. For example, while Mungo is depicted as naïve and arrogant when he is captured by the Moors, they are also portrayed negatively, if anything more so than Mungo Park—"The Moors looked as if they'd just cooked and eaten their mothers" (1981, 14) and their savage cruelty is embodied in their weapons "that hacked rather than thrust: a single blow could remove a limb, separate a shoulder, cleave a head" (1981, 14). Ali, their leader, is a Mafioso-style thug, who either gets paid for his "protection" by the "Kafir towns within his compass" or "if not, he hacks half the villagers to pieces and takes twice as much" (1981, 66).

It seems as if in a desperate attempt to avoid political correctness, which the irreverent, outrageous Cor-RAG-essan does, he has to couch his critique in a caul of stereotype about Africa and about Moors. There is, thus, a kind of double irony, of critique of the explorer, his arrogance and his ignorance in a shell of destructive irony about the land and people he moves among:

> The rest is just about what you'd expect. Dusty streets, consumptive cattle, woman with haunted eyes and children with distended bellies and hunger-bleached hair. These are the hard times, the long lingering days before the rains. Udders dry, grain reserves shot. (1981, 65)

On the second expedition we are quickly re-introduced to the familiar picture of the European's Africa of stench, pestilence and exotic and horrible, fatal disease:

> Spotted fever, yaws, typhus and trypanosomiasis throve here. Hook-worm, cholera and plague. There was bilharzia and guinea worm in the drinking water, hydrophobia in the sharp incisors of bats and wolves, filariasis in the saliva of mosquitoes and horseflies. Step outside, take a bath, drink the water or put a scrap of food in your mouth and you've got them all—bacilli, spirilla and cocci, viruses, fungi, nematodes, trematodes and amoebae—all eating away at your marrow and organs, blurring your vision, sapping your fiber, eradicating your memory as neatly as an eraser moving over the scribbled wisdom of a blackboard. (1981, 297)

The African people in this desolate, taxing environment simply add to the explorer's torments and are thieves and predators:

> And so the villagers turn out like flies, like jackals, like hyenas. To steal something from these pale, puking, shit-stinking white men becomes a matter of honor with them. ...They are ubiquitous, merciless. (1981, 352)

The villagers compared to insects and animals in the muck of the disease-infested land, softens and contextualises Boyle's simultaneous critique of the Vietnam war style brutality of two of Mungo's men, Martyn and M'Keal, who "enthusiastically cut down a pair of elderly egg women as they teeter up the road" (1981, 353). We will encounter Boyle's double-edged irony again. For now, Johnson may have walked out of the story, but we have not quite finished with him. Just when African Orientalist discourse appears victorious, we must look again at Boyle's extraordinary portrayal of Mungo Park's guide, who is another of Boyle's personas.

"Johnson's price was the complete works of Shakespeare"

We have already seen the ways in which Johnson's perspective, his gaze, on Mungo Park, brings the explorer down to size. In being the one who distances from the heroic explorer by viewing, criticising, and having superior knowledge to Park, he increasingly becomes the omniscient narrator's moral touchstone.

This he can be because Boyle constructs Johnson autobiographically, as he enacts Boyle's own struggles to forge an invented persona. In this novel where appearances are always deceptive, it appears as if Johnson's history is totally different from Boyle's, emerging as it does out of a different time, place and culture. We will see, however, that this is both true and untrue. Like Boyle, his name changes—"his mother did not name him Johnson. She called him Katunga—Katunga Oyo" (1981, 10). He is of the Mandingo tribe. At thirteen he is kidnapped by Foulah herdsmen, who sold him to a slave merchant, thence to an American slaver, bound for South Carolina, where he works on the plantation of a Sir Reginald Durfeys, and is promoted to house servant. Thereafter, he goes to London as valet of Sir Reginald where he, again like Boyle, remakes himself through the study of the great canon of classics of literature:

> He began to educate himself in the library at Piltdown, the Durfeys' country estate. He learnt Greek and Latin. He read the Ancients. He read the Moderns. He read Smollett, Ben Jonson, Moliere, Swift. He spoke of Pope as if he'd known him personally, denigrated the puerility of Richardson, and was so taken with Fielding that he actually attempted a Mandingo translation of *Amelia*. (1981, 11)

The reference to Piltdown is telling as the site of a notorious forgery where fossil fragments were found of what became known as the Piltdown man. This Piltdown man raised questions about the origins of the human species, which were thought to be in Africa, and which now seemed to have relocated to England. Subsequently, it emerged that the Piltdown man was a big hoax of fake parts, deliberately designed to confuse (Britannica, 9, 1993, 445). Katunga Oyo, whose true origins were in Africa, deliberately re-designs himself by way of English culture. Tribesman parading as English gentleman is itself a hoax of a kind. Sir Reginald is Henry Higgens and Johnson is Eliza Doolittle, upwardly mobile through reinvention. The gender and race crossover, from overtones of the white woman, Eliza Doolittle, to black man, and from Katunga Oyo to Johnson, is all part of the pattern of translating the self.

Boyle too changed his life by way of studying the English classics, changed his name and his station in life. His stories recount youthful rebellion in anger and violence whose overtones are audible in the incident where Johnson kills a man in a duel because the "red-faced gentleman with muttonchop whiskers called him a 'dammed Hottentot nigger' and invited him to fight for his life" (1981, 11). Johnson is sentenced to be hanged, but Sir Reginald's influence commutes the sentence to transportation in shackles back to Africa.

In Africa, Johnson escapes back to his village, described by Boyle in terms of the "Merrie Africa" trope, just in case we were taking Johnson too seriously:

> It rained. Crops grew, goats fattened. He lived in a hut, went barefoot, wrapped a strip of broadcloth round his chest and loins and called it a toga. He gave himself over to sensuality.
> Within five years Johnson was providing for three wives and eleven children—fourteen mouths—plus an assortment of dogs, simians, rope squirrels and skinks. Still, he wasn't exactly working himself to the bone—no, he cashed in instead on his reputation as a man of letters. (1981, 12)

In this *"Paradise Regained"* (1981, 13) he happily remains until a letter arrives from Sir Reginald, who is a founding member of the Africa Association, introducing Mungo Park and asking Johnson to act as guide and interpreter, in return for which he can name his price:

> Johnson's price was the complete works of Shakespeare, in quarto volumes, just as they had appeared on the shelves of Sir Reginald's library. (1981, 13)

We will return to the Shakespeare after this summary of Johnson's life trajectory. What we have already seen is the crucial role played by Johnson, who is more leader than guide to the foolhardy Mungo. On the first expedition, his role is suddenly and dramatically curtailed when Johnson is, supposedly, devoured by a crocodile (1981, 149). (In Mungo Park's original journal, well into the second expedition, the guide, Isaaco, who is a different person from the Johnson of the first expedition, is lacerated by a crocodile and goes to a nearby village to recuperate (1954, 326).

On his ill-fated second expedition, Park realizes he desperately needs a guide—locals are hostile and thieving and the expedition endangered. He goes back to Johnson's old village to see if he can recruit someone from there. To his amazement and delight, he finds Johnson, who had not died at all in the crocodile incident. He is older, wiser and transformed into a new person, Isaaco. (Isaaco was the name of the guide on the real Mungo Park's second expedition). Isaaco has changed more than his name and is a more angry and assertive man than he was in the past. It takes all of Mungo's powers of persuasion to bring him on board the expedition. What has not changed, is Johnson's love of English literature and his perception of its worth. Again he is offered to name his price. He is coy, hard to get, but finally:

> Johnson's face seems to soften. He takes a long reflective sip of tea, then tips the cap back on his head and puckers up his lips as though stifling a grin. "It'll cost you dear," he says finally. "I want Milton, Dryden and Pope. Leather-bound, gilt titles". (1981, 342)

And then, later, as an afterthought:

> Johnson takes the explorer's wrists and pulls him forward. "Listen," he says, his voice low, confidential, "the Pope I want signed". (1981, 343)

This is funny and wonderful, but of course, deadly serious. Johnson is portrayed as dignified and smart, a man who knows the value of things. He is not beguiled by the mirrors, beads and worthless trinkets, which whites bring as false exchange to bedazzle the natives. Johnson is a marvellous creation, and it is in the light of the influence of postcolonial scholars and magical realists, like Salman Rushdie, Gabriel Garcia Marquez and Homi Bhabha that we may more fully understand him.

Bhabha emphasises the power of the English book and begins his classic essay, "Signs Taken for Wonders: Questions of ambivalence and authority under a tree outside Delhi, May 1817", set in 1817, not much later than the setting of *Water Music*:

> It is with the emblem of the English book—'signs taken for wonders'—as an insignia of colonial authority and a signifier of colonial desire and discipline, that I want to begin this chapter. (1994a, 102)

These books, "these texts of the civilizing mission", Bhabha suggests, signify that authority in terms of "the name of the father and the author" (1994a, 105). The Law, by way of whose prejudiced, exploitative and imperialistic rules, becomes the gateway to colonised, oppressed subjectivity. Its Tablets are carried down from the heights of the imperial centres by stern fathers, colonial administrators, governors, missionaries and, not least of all, teachers bearing Shakespeare, Pope and the bible.

And as always, this is only part of the story. The guts of Bhabha's theoretical contribution has been to conceptualise the covert, wily, subversive devices by which these colonised subjects indeed pass through those sacred gateways of the white fathers, but via a devious route that leads to unexpected places. Thus they make themselves into unstable and potentially unruly subjects. This Bhabha has demonstrated variously through concepts of mimicry and ambivalence and via third spaces, such as cracks and interstices. Johnson renames himself Isaaco from the European bible, but as an act of empowerment. The English lifestyle Johnson/Isaaco, appears to imitate slavishly, as in the following description of his hut, is deceptive:

> But what makes this one different, what makes it extraordinary and special, unlike any other hut in the whole of Africa, what makes it Johnson's hut, is the bookshelf, bathed in overhead light until it looks ghostly and illusory: the bookshelf, neatly constructed of bamboo and hemp and lined with the complete works of Shakespeare, quarto volumes, bound in leather. (1981, 338-9)

He may imitate the mores of Sir Reginald's library, bizarrely in his hut in deepest Africa, but his authority over Mungo Park is ultimately indisputable and he can name his price, a price which will utterly transform the power balance between them. No illusion, the books provide not only symbolic value, but real wealth that enables Isaaco to have become a man of substance. This is so because he has always been able to pay for services like "a week's food and lodging" with "some couplets from Herrick and Donne" (1981, 141). For, as Bhabha says, "the colonial presence is always ambivalent":

> If these scenes, as I have narrated them, suggest the triumph of the writ of colonialist power, then it must be conceded that the wily letter of the law inscribes a much more ambivalent text of authority. For it is in-between the edict of Englishness and the assault of the dark unruly spaces of the earth, through an act of repetition, that the colonial text emerges uncertainly. (1994a, 107)

Johnson anticipates the twentieth century migrant cosmopolitans, who are the products of many cultures and influences. We saw that Johnson has lived in North America and England, has partaken of the wealth of English books in the library of his employer. At the same time, he retains a deep belief in the customs and religion of the African community where he was born and raised to adulthood. He, like his maker, who identifies with him, uses an ironic tongue to bridge the alternative worldviews and identities that he juggles. This unstable package of Christian knowledge, indigenous belief structures, scientific understanding, Western literary appreciation, the supernatural, magical and pre-industrial frameworks, fragilely tied together by parody, satire and smokescreen, is identifiable as a magical realist mode (see Cooper, 1998).

And this brings us to the point that if Charles Dickens is the white father of the London of this novel, then Gabriel Garcia Marquez is the black father

"The Niger remained a mystery" 55

of Johnson and magical realism is the mode by which we can most easily come to grips with his mixed parts. Tad Friend refers to Marquez as one of Boyle's "polestars" (50). The utterly carnivalesque Segu, an African town, capital of Bambarra, is culled straight out of a Marquez mode. It is presented through the eyes of an old "witchdoctor", Eboe, a character who is critical in filling in other aspects of the kaleidoscope that is Johnson's background:

> According to old Eboe, who twice visited the city in his youth, it's a wide-open place, awash in palm wine, mead and *sooloo* beer, the streets ringing with wanton laughter, snatches of song, the shriek of cockfights, the alleys packed full of whores with brass rings round their necks and skin like the bottom of a well. There are jugglers and dwarfs and acrobats, men who bite the heads from chickens, marvels untold. Water flows uphill in Segu. People speak backward. (1981, 93)

Along with his European, if informal, education there is Johnson's ambiguous belief in the supernatural. The ambiguity is signalled, as always, by the ironic mode. The tongue-in-cheek "I'm a Animist" (1981, 46), which, like all forked tongues, contains a qualified truth. Johnson, always the translator, explains to Mungo that the old Eboe has "'his *mojo* workin...'you know: magic, black arts, hoodoo and voodoo. Nobody messes with a witch doctor'" (1981, 91). "Hoodoo and voodoo" appear to distance Johnson from the belief, as well as his description of Eboe as "runnin' around with that chicken tucked under his chin" (1981, 92), but for all its flippancy, this is a serious warning to Mungo that:

> this is Africa, man. The eye of the needle, mother of mystery, heart of darkness. And this old naked black man here with his feet all crusted up and his penis danglin' in the mud—he don't fool round". (1981, 92)

Johnson's faith in the forces over which Eboe has sway is signified by the powerful fetish of the guinea hen that hangs around his neck. At one point, Mungo and Johnson think that the old man has died and Johnson attempts to removes the fetish. Eboe, who had simply been sleeping, awakes:

> 'You want?' The old man's Mandingo is thick as a sleeping potion.
> 'No!' pleads Johnson. 'No!'
> Then suddenly, with a motion so quick and smooth it defies the eye, Eboe loops the grisly thing through the air. A flutter of feathers, and it catches Johnson's neck like a noose. FOOMP! The bird strikes his chest, and dangles. Maggots wriggle in the folds of his belly. Flies orbit his head. His face makes the Pieta look like a portrait of joy.
> The explorer is mystified, mouth agape, witness to some primitive rite. 'Johnson,' he says, astonished. 'Cut it loose. Toss it in the bushes.'
> Old Eboe is grinning ear to ear.
> Johnson hangs his head. 'I can't,' he whispers. (1981, 96)

Note the enormous significance here of the fact that Johnson believes in the power of the fetish and loses all his irony—he is desperate not to have the thing and once it is around his neck he is unable to get rid of it. Of further interest, is the precise meaning of the fetish, in relation to the Law. Johnson, whose edge of irony immediately returns, explains that members of Eboe's village, when threatened by attack from outside, appealed to him "to appease Chakalla, god of violated taboos, by assumin' all the sins of the townspeople" (1981, 108) in order to appease this god and have his assistance in turning back the invading army. With the fetish around his neck, Johnson is now the carrier, the custodian of acceptable social behaviour:

> "So now I've got to answer to Chakalla for every little broken taboo in the history of that godforsaken backwater hamlet. Every time a pregnant woman eats an egg or a boy copulates with a pangolin. Every time a young girl walks backward under a crescent moon, rubs her face with hoona sap or plucks her pubic hair with her right hand. (1981, 109)

For all the irony of the language and the reluctance of Johnson to bear this burden, it is significant that he becomes the keeper of the Law of Chakalla. He takes on the role of alternative keeper of different taboos from those sacred, European and Christian prohibitions, which are the passwords into the Symbolic arena of full Western subjectivity. Johnson makes the comparison overtly in response to Mungo's incredulity:

> The explorer looks as if he's just swallowed a fork. "But you're joking. You don't mean to say you believe all that mumbo jumbo?"
> "No more unreasonable than believin' in virgin births or ladders to heaven."
> "You mean—you question the Bible?" Mungo is shocked to his roots. Lord, they're savages, he's thinking. Dress them up, educate them, do what you will. Their minds are in the jungle". (1981, 108)

The important point, and one that Bhabha has emphasised, is that these colonised subjects find ways of turning the tables and empowering themselves by way of their many inheritances. The hybrid bag of tools at Johnson's disposal is potent and useable:

> And so, model of prudence and preparedness that he is, Johnson has taken measures to insure against an untimely deluge: that is, he has concocted a potent antipluvial fetish consisting of the chucked scales of a small dune-dwelling lizard, a square inch of camel tripe, a pinch of sulfur and six lines of Milton's 'L'Allegro'. (1981, 344)

There is, furthermore, authorial weight which corroborates the old man's powers. The warning to Mungo is necessitated by the explorer's wish to have

Eboe tell his fortune, as Mungo puts it in the language of gypsies of his own culture. What ensues is one of the nodule points of the novel:

> He rises shakily and takes hold of the explorer's hand, scrutinizing it as if it were a text or a painting. His leathery old fingers play over the knuckles and joints, a wild bolt lights the sky, thunder steps down like a giant walking the earth. ...Finally he looks down into the huge white palm and his eyes go wide. He is stung, stricken. (1981, 92)

These powers of prediction are proven by the suggestion that Eboe foresaw in Mungo's palm the explorer's violent and terrible end in the next expedition. In the final, searing dispute between Mungo and his guide, when Isaaco is desperately imploring Mungo to turn back he says "'don't go because you won't come back. Remember Eboe?'" (386). Mungo, of course, refuses to remember and indeed, he does not come back. But we, the readers, remember Eboe's prophesy when a demoralised and defeated Mungo Park crashes to his death in the very river that so enchanted and hypnotised him.

Johnson is a slippery and interesting character. He happily integrates local custom and belief with his English high culture and includes a wonderful dose of humour and irony as the meld between them. He is indeed the high priest of Chakalla, redolent of local alternatives to the false universality of the European psyche. Despite all the difficulties we have been encountering as regards stereotypes of Africa unwittingly reinforced in *Water Music*, Johnson is a funny, profound developed and intriguing character, written against the grain of the dark heart.

Finally, if the identification between Boyle and his invention, Johnson, is to be fully understood, we have to turn to another character, the one who is probably the key to the composite, splintered Coraghessan persona—the underclass Londoner, Ned Rise, with whom the novel concludes, and in whom it ultimately places its trust.

"[Ned Rise] had a mission ... to take charge of the expedition"

We first encounter Ned pickled in gin—a picaresque scoundrel—and apparently, a parody of Mungo Park, the heroic explorer, as he looks around the filthy cellar that he inexplicably finds himself in—"then he scans the room through half-closed lids, feeling *a bit like an explorer* setting foot on a new continent" (1981, 6, my emphasis). The comparison seems bizarre, but will become less so. Given what we know, moreover, about Boyle's own alcoholic carousings, we can assume that this overhung awakening is autobiographical.

The reverberations between Ned and Mungo, for all of the enormous social gulf between them, is emphasised. At one point, Ned appears to have drowned in the Thames, reminding us that Mungo was nearly drowned in the sand storm (1981, 69). Mungo, moreover, himself awakes overhung and disoriented in a cellar, just like Rise (1981, 74–5). A section called 'LAZARUS', in fact, could apply either to Ned returned from the dead after a bungled hanging, the result of his having been unjustly accused of murder, or to Mungo returned from Africa, from where he was assumed to have died on the first expedition (1981, 202). The novel appears to be warning us to be sceptical of appearances—Mungo is not as much of a hero as we thought and Ned will become more of one later. This is itself a commentary on the overblown importance given to big names and fancy pants explorers. Who has ever heard of Ned Rise, fictional invention of Boyle, but no doubt with real life counterparts, the scum of the London pavement? (Who has heard of Isaaco, the guide on the famous expedition, who was not a fiction?)

I am suggesting that the links between Ned and Mungo relate powerfully to their both being alternative personas for Coraghessan Boyle. We can speculate as to the origins of this split persona. As an American of Irish background, whose parents were of the lower social order and who abused alcohol, Boyle must have felt a class difference from his more waspish fellows. This is so notwithstanding his simultaneous sense of being first generation American and privileged. If Mungo Park represents Boyle's own soft white American underbelly, then Ned Rise signifies his drunken Irish roots (albeit that Park hails from Scotland, a marginalized part of Britain, not altogether dissimilar from Ireland).

Ned's background is truly ghoulish—his alcoholic single mother/whore died before he was six. A crone harridan witch tries to kidnap him, only for him to be saved by the sadistic and vicious "bad father", Edward Pin, who cuts off the first joint of the finger and thumb of one hand with a meat cleaver so that he can be a better beggar. Unsurprisingly, Pin dies a gruesome, drunken death and Ned lives on the streets for some years, begging, stealing and eating rubbish—a barbaric life without love or comfort.

Ned's life suddenly takes an upward turn in the mode of what we now can recognise as the recurrent Eliza Doolittle myth. He bumps into a wealthy, eccentric man, Prentiss Barrenboyne, who plays a clarinet in the park and who "owned a block of houses in Mayfair" (1981, 39). Ned is genuinely captivated by the clarinet and ends up being taken into Barrenboyne's house:

> Officially he was established in the house as a servant, but Barrenboyne, won over by the lad's ingenuous and consuming enthusiasm for the clarinet, came to treat him more like a member of the family. He bought him clothes, gave him milk and chops and drippings, taught him to read and how to balance a teacup on his knee. There were trips to the concert hall, the theater, the shipyard and the zoo. A tutor was

engaged. Ned acquired the rudiments of orthography, geometry, piscatology, a phrase or two of French, and a profound loathing for the Classics. (1981, 40)

Here comes the plot puzzle. Ned's idyll is suddenly terminated when Barrenboyne is killed in a duel. The duel is with "a blackamoor" against whom he had flung a racial insult. In one of those plot coincidences so beloved of nineteenth century novelists, the "negro" will turn out to be none other than Johnson. Barrenboyne is both the kindly, benevolent man, who lifted a boy out of the gutter, as well as the rude racist, who had "called him [Johnson] a 'dammed Hottentot nigger' and invited him to fight for his life" (1981, 11). This perplexingly splintered portrayal of Barrenboyne requires some unpacking.

The only way to interpret this apparently contradictory character portrayal, and these all too fortuitous coincidences, is to understand Boyle's Irish background within the North American context. Boyle loves to name his characters allegorically and we must interpret the symbolism of these names with his own humorous light touch. "Prentiss Barrenboyne" has overtones of the Protestant defeat of the Roman Catholic, within the historical context of the war between them in Northern Ireland in the seventeenth century. "On 7th December 1688 thirteen young A*pprentice* Boys closed the gates of Londonderry against the advancing Catholic army of King James II" and they defended the city until they were relieved and in the Battle of *Boyne* in 1690, the Protestants were victorious, on behalf of English colonialism in Ireland, a victory that was 'barren' for the Catholics. The Protestants celebrate what is for them the great courage of the so-called "Prentiss boys" with a parade twice a year (http:www.ulsterweb.freeservers. com/apprentice_boys.html)

What Boyd appears to be doing, is transcribing onto the racial dimension the violent history of his Irish past. Prentiss Barrenboyne, may be a kindly old gent, but he is a rich racist property owner and on the wrong side. Associated with Protestant imperialism in Ireland, he is damned for expressing racist attitudes to black people. The transposition onto race, and onto Africa, of Irishness finds its rationale in the fact that the Irish, who first immigrated to North America, were regarded as the lowest of the low—in fact as the same as the Negroes. Noel Ignatiev, in a book tellingly entitled *How the Irish Became White* suggests that in America the Irish "commonly found themselves thrown together with free Negroes...and developed a common culture of the lowly" (2).

Johnson, the black man, is a persona for the Irish Boyd and furthermore reverses history and wins the battle against the Boyne in the duel, a victory, which has the unforeseen consequence of sending him across the seas to his origins in Africa.

As homeless scum on London streets, Ned's destiny and oppression reverberates with Johnson's. He too is picked up by mainstream English paternalism, but can only finally Rise, by shaking off all connotations of Irishness/Blackness. This is the essence of Boyle's own identity dilemmas. He has become a middle class academic, and in so doing, has become a first generation white man, exploring, in Ignatiev's words "what did it mean to the Irish to become white in America?" (2). The stage for playing out this question, however, and this is crucial, is Africa, where Ned Rise, working class London convict (read Irish dregs) arrives in Africa (read North America) where he discovers upward mobility by becoming a white king among the natives. It is this quest, this life trajectory, which takes over the novel. We thought we were following Mungo Park and his adventures in Africa. Slowly and subtly the novel's sub-text erupts to the surface and takes over the quest. This confusion between the voyage of discovery we thought we were on and the true, more hidden object of exploration is a theme that will recur in the next chapter and most spectacularly in chapter seven. The use of Africa as foil for these subterranean issues of identity, however, has consequences, which are not always sufficiently foreseen by these writers with good intentions. Bearing this in mind, let us trace the Rise of Ned.

Ned will rise and fall many times through his picaresque life in ways that would take too long to recount. Suffice it to say that he falls foul of the law more than once and ends up, in yet another reversal, by being sent from England to the slave shipping Fort at Goree in Africa as a convict, along with his mate, Billy Boyes:

> And so, in the early fall of that year, Ned and Billy are transferred from the black stinking hold of the *Cerberus* to the black stinking hold of the H.M.S. *Feckless*, and deposited, soaked in their own vomit, at Goree—Fort Goree, on the island of the same name off the coast of West Africa. Fort Goree, gateway to the Niger and bastion of rot. (1981, 289)

Billy, also of the squalid London streets, is a ghost of Ned, his partner in petty crime, in grand booze-ups, penury, piss and penal lock up. He is insignificant except for two powerful signals that Boyle sends us to make us take notice of him. The first, in a novel of identity exploration and the significance of names, is the fact that Billy's surname is 'Boyles', signalling another identification between a character and his author. The second is Boyles's spectacular death in Africa. We will explore the link between these two at the appropriate time in Ned's life, given that Boyles is Ned's fictional shadow and his foil. Ned's life determines the nature of that of his mate.

Ned and Billy manage to get themselves chosen to join Park's second expedition for purely un-heroic self-interested reasons—they have been promised that if they survive, they can return home, free men. What becomes readily apparent, and links Ned and Johnson in this context, is that Ned is sharper and far more in touch with reality than is Mungo:

> What he does know is that the expedition is a shambles. Already. Seven days out of Pisania and confusion is the order of the day: soldiers bitching, negroes pilfering, asses collapsing under the weight of panniers loaded with lead shot. Right from the beginning Ned has had his doubts. (1981, 326)

Unfortunately, what we see again here, is the double bind from which Boyle cannot seem to extricate himself. He is able to make the perceptive critique of the adventurer hero only in the negative language of the discourse of Africanism, of "pilfering negroes" and this is nowhere more apparent than the events leading up to the horrific, savage murder of Billy Boyles. The trigger begins to tighten when the expedition's asses run rampant, trampling crops and inciting the locals to battle. But look at the highly problematic description of the attack and finally the capture of Boyles:

> Swarming like insects, the farmers converge on the first of the asses, inundating the hapless animal in a flurry of flailing hoes and bloody spears. Killer bees, locusts, army ants, they break open the crates and fight over the trade goods, rip the ass's limbs from the sockets, strip off the skin and butcher it on the spot, already rising up in group frenzy to seek out the rest of the malefactors, equine and human alike. (1981, 330)

The comparison between the local inhabitants and insects, bees, ants and locusts is, of course, highly questionable. It is true that what is concealed beneath the florid prose of blood, violence and savage mob frenzy is that these strange whites and their asses are trampling preciously cultivated crops from which the people derive a life and death subsistence living. But the impression of gratuitous violence indulged in by savages for its own sake is reinforced in what is to come. Poor Billy Boyles was last seen in this massacre "swallowed up in the black mass like a feather in an inkwell" (330). In one of Boyle's bullet phrases, we suddenly hear about Billy's fate in that "it was Ned Rise who cut Billy down":

> Ned could see the long purpling scar running from Billy's ribcage to his waist and disappearing into the folds of his trousers. They'd cut him open is what they'd done. Cut him open and stuffed him like a partridge. With sand. (1981, 333)

And here comes the point of Billy Boyles and the cathartic turning point of the novel. We see the meaning of Ned's name as he literally rises up the wall to rescue Boyles's dead, mutilated body, and as he does so, he figuratively rises out of the muck of his previous life:

> In the silence and the heat, under the sky that fell back to the verges of deep black space and hid all that terror and emptiness beneath a specious screen of blue, Ned was undergoing a transformation. With each inch he rose, each crease and depression his fingers and toes sought out, he felt it charging him, this new sense of himself and the bleak bitter universe, as if the wall were some oracle, some Grail, some radiator of cosmic reality. (1981, 333–334)

This 'Grail', the re-making of Ned Rise, and not Mungo Park's false sense of discovery of the source of the Niger, becomes the novel's true quest. Out of Billy's death and the threat posed by the local population, Ned comes to the realization that his only salvation lies in taking over the leadership of the expedition from Mungo Park:

> Ned reached out and hacked at the rope in a fury. I don't deserve this, I don't—he repeated over and over, as if he were praying. He wanted to die, he wanted to live. Then it came to him, hard and sudden, in a flash of recognition—he had a mission on earth. He could almost hear the trumpets of the archangels, the crackle of ancient scrolls. Ned Rise, elected in a burst of radiance. He had a mission and this was it: to eliminate Smirke, [his old adversary from London] seduce Park and take charge of the expedition. Or they were all doomed. Like Billy. (1981, 334)

It is inspired. You rise or you fall. You are a victim of your difficult circumstances or you overcome them and are reincarnated. Mungo Park, his river, his ego, his quest, the outcome of which was known from the beginning anyway, recedes. Here is a new hero, a brand new and potentially radical goal. The focus shifts to the underdog, be he a penniless product of the London streets, or a drunken Irish Catholic. Brutalised, criminalised, bashed and beaten and mutilated, Ned Rise is going to empower himself, take control of his life and turn it around. The identification between author and character is undeniable, for all the differences in their times and places.

Remember Haydon White identified the archetypal wild men of the Old Testament as, among other things, *black,* descendants of Ham with the twin attributes of "grossness and rebelliousness" (15). That is to say, Ned begins as a 'black' man, the scum, the lowest of the low, an Irishman. Boyle, with the deftness and the magical licence of his craft, is conjurer, pulling white monkeys out of black hats and enacting his own history as Irish, as newborn intellectual, as cross-dresser and man of many, hybrid parts. Ned Rise, like the Irish of Boyle's parentage, becomes a white man in Africa. Boyle may feel guilt about his choice, but what are the alternatives?

And so, at this moment, Boyle acknowledges the privileges of race as he has Ned realize that it is only in Africa and as a white man, that someone of his class background stands any chance of a dignified life, given the deep class oppression that exists in England in general and in the brutal, poverty stricken streets of London in particular. So "maybe he won't return to

London" (1981, 420). He has developed great self-knowledge and has the measure of Park and his idiocy. He realizes that back in London "the high and mighty Mungo Park" would not have given him "a second glance" (1981, 420). And

> Homeless, fatherless, with neither prospects nor hope, Ned has begun to see this bleak, stinking, oppressive continent in a new light, as a place of beginnings as well as endings. (1981, 420)

The echoes with America are subtle, understated and crucial. There too was a new continent, filled with bleakness and oppression, but also a place of opportunity, but only for some. Likewise, only as a white man in Africa could Ned rise out of the pit of London squalor. The problem, and it appears insurmountable, is that when a writer uses Africa as metaphor for identity discovery, within even Boyle's complex understanding of history and oppression, he buys into Africanist discourse. This is so because of the history of unequal power between Africa and, say, America. They cannot be transposed without violent consequences. After Conrad, white men cannot come to find their dark, or even their light sides in Africa.

In order to substantiate this critique we must wind back the reel of the novel's action to the last days of the expedition and to the fall of Mungo Park and the victorious survival of Ned Rise.

Fetishes, Figments, Bodies and Books: Conclusions

We enter the mythical, timeless Africa of European imagining, almost a precise replica of Conrad's surrealistic boat as it sails down the river. As Mungo Park and his men become more and more insane, deranged and out of touch with reality, we become slowly aware that the perspective that is taking over is that of the omniscient narrator:

> It is like descending into the body, this penetration of the river, like passing through veins and arteries and great dripping organs, like exploring the chambers of the heart or reaching out for the impalpable soul. Earth, forest, sky, water: the river thrums with the beat of life. Mungo feels it—as steady and pervasive as the ticking of a supernal clock—feels it through the searing windless days and the utter nights that fall back to the rim of the void. Ned Rise feels it, and even M'Keal. A presence. A mystery. ... *It is almost as if they've fallen under a spell, the explorer and his men*. ... (1981, 391, my emphasis)

As the survivors sail along in the grip of this spell, relentlessly towards their destruction, it can only be Coraghessan Boyle in his own voice, who is unbound by the spell and can view the whole scene clearly. Why the mystery and the evil enchantment, if not emanating out of the very earth and water of

Africa, whose landscape continues to be aestheticised and mythologised—"as if their blood were flowing in sympathetic confluence with the river" (1981, 391).

The specific place and time stop and enter a kind of universal space of threat and hell. This is signalled by the fact that inexplicably Park's German-made infallible watch stops (1981, 396):

> Now, sweeping along on the dark flood, that time seems as remote as the Age of Dinosaurs. He slaps the watch in his palm, holds it up to his ear. Raucous, derisive, the invisible forest howls at him with a thousand voices. Mungo looks up at the sky, at the shifting stars and the planets in their loops, and drops the silent timepiece into the flat black soup of the river. (1981, 397)

If time is frozen, it is the time not of the present, but the ancient past, the Age of the Dinosaurs, the wild, howling forest, whose thousand voices include those of the wild natives who are out there to get them—"stirred-up naked savages yabbering threats and insults" (1981, 400). Thus we follow the doomed boat with Boyle's guiding eye into that *static time* when "it is noon, forever" and they are headed into the desert, "into the glare, into the very maw of mystery" (1981, 402). And yet, lest we forget Boyle's astute politics and ironic even-handedness to the fault discussed already, look at how degenerate these white explorers are:

> Their hair, thick with grease and dust, trails down their shoulders, their beards reach their waists. The proud red uniforms have long since degenerated to tatters—to loincloths—and the once-glistening boots have fallen to pieces. Unwashed, undisciplined, underfed, thin of rib and cloudy of eye, their skin blotched and sun-scorched, their bare feet blistered, they could be the last remnant of some ancient tribe emigrating to a new homeland, they could be cave dwellers, scavengers, eaters of offal and raw flesh. (1981, 402)

But again, like Kurtz gone native—savages in loincloths—these sad soldiers have found their nemesis in Africa. Relentlessly on they sail, until they reach the fateful rapids and the black hordes, all of whom knew that the river would turn and the whites would be cannon fodder for their bows and arrows, until "they're over the side" (1981, 427). There is no one left to view the naked, black savages on the shore, other than our omniscient narrator:

> Above, on the rocks, ten thousand voices whoop in triumph and exaltation. Barefooted, naked, their faces disfigured with ritual scars and gashes of paint, black faces, black bodies, the tribesmen embrace, kiss their sworn enemies, dance in one another's arms. (1981, 427)

This narrator, with all the authority of his omniscience, is able to tell us that "the Niger remained a mystery" (1981, 435), above and beyond Ned, after the demise of Boyles and Mungo and the exit of Johnson. In a 'Coda' to the novel, however, we discover that Ned, and Ned alone, does indeed survive—"a man totally unknown to the public, a pariah of sorts, a man who had been born to poverty and experienced the miracle of resurrection" (1981, 432). Ned, after his baptism in the waters of the Niger, is being re-born and his body is cleansed as his identity is being reconstituted:

> He [Ned] stared at the polished surface of the rock before him, a trickle of water washing his legs and groin. (1981, 433)

Boyle desperately wants it all. If he is enacting the Irish birth into North American privilege, then by transposing this re-birth into Africa, he fantasises a different way of becoming whole, within a narrative of hippie peace and love. In other words, Ned is not only returning to some organicist African essence, but also entering an alternative social order:

> Then there was another sound, breathy and melodic, no mere birdsong, no illusion created by rubbing branches or mimetic streams—it was the sound of music, *the sound of civilization and humanity.* Had he died after all? (1981, 433, my emphasis)

Edenic Africa, paradise after all, Ned finds himself looking at gentle brown people, totally idealised and simultaneously diminished as children—

> little people, no bigger than children, standing out in the open now and gazing at him out of their placid umber eyes. They were naked, these people, their limbs bundles of fiber, their abdomens swollen like the rounded pouting bellies of infants. And they weren't black—not exactly—they were more the color of acorns or hazelnuts. (1981, 434)

The new God the Father, a little miniature man, repeatedly compared to a child, does not carry the big penis of the repressive Western male—"his pubic hair was a snarl of white wire from which the rutted gray penis hung like a badge" (1981, 434). Does he come to attack Ned, who sees something glinted in his hand—"a knife? a gun?":

> But then suddenly he knew what that refulgent, light-gathering object was, knew why they were offering it to him, knew what he would do and how he would survive. All at once he could see into the future. He was no outcast, no criminal, no orphan—he was a messiah.
> The old man handed him the clarinet. It was still damp from its soaking but the pads were clear, the keys undamaged. The drum thumped, the flutes skirled. He put it to his lips – they were smiling now, ranged round him like precocious children—he put it to his lips, and played (1981, 434–5)

Gun versus clarinet. Make music not war—the clarinet, not the vicious duelling gun, the bloodshed of bad wars, in North Ireland or in Vietnam. The clarinet, it turns out, is a fetish, a magical object that can lift Ned up, make him rise and find safety and peace away from both the doomed boat of exploration and the filthy pavements of rat infested, gin soaked London. What could be more sixties than the white male refusal of the gun, the bad war, male aggression, linked to the camera and the gaze? What could be more obvious in its place than a musical instrument, being one of the major mechanisms by which young people at the time expressed their rebellion, their aspirations and their slogans?

The youth have passed a vote of no confidence on their elders, on the White Western man, and in so doing, their the ultimate discovery is not of the origins of the River Niger, but of nothing less than humanity itself. The original father, a little brown elder, becomes the wellspring of all original fathering—"he could have been the first man on earth, father of us all" (1981, 434). What could be more problematic than the manipulation of African landscapes and inhabitants to play out this privileged, white, hippie regeneration? This depiction can only be accounted for in the light of the desperation of Boyle to find a new Father, a different Law whose transformed precepts would inaugurate new human subjectivity and a brand new male body.

The new Father is innocent as a child with a miniature body. He is not the macho man with the sweaty crotch, with the big penis, the gun, who initiates boys in the rituals of gay bashing, race hatred and the murder of innocent women and children in illegitimate wars. He is also not a black African, but rather a miniaturised, lighter and more marginalized man. Embodied in the magical object of the clarinet is the body of the pygmy as idealised alternative to White Western male sexuality in general, as symbolised by the phallus, in particular. And in so transforming his male subjectivity, Ned is fulfilling the wish of his maker, of Coraghessan Boyle, with whom he is very closely identified, he and he alone, by the novel's extraordinary climax.

That is probably the best one can say about this climactic depiction. The worst hardly bears outlining, of people as children, the past of the European; inhabitants of Africa as gullible and waiting for the messiah, the saviour, in the form of Ned Rise, Tarzan, or any of the other megalomaniacal, malcontented white men, who manipulate faraway people and lands. The critical point, and this goes right to the heart of Africanism, is the real loss of any kind of autonomous existence of local people and their spirituality, their customs and culture. The protest against the Vietnam War was necessary and admirable, but what becomes highly problematic is when it is waged by means of the objectification and appropriation of people, like the pygmies, who are manipulated in the crisis in Western masculinity. These people are nowhere represented realistically in terms of their own struggles, desires and issues. Their bodies are expropriated, infantilised and inscribed in the terms of the white man's desires.

The gun, the clarinet, chicken carcass and the demonic carving all link male bodies, beliefs, sexuality and subjectivity. However, perhaps the most powerful fetish of all is the written word, the English book, as Johnson found to his great advantage. Boyle's own discovery is, of course, the novel we have been reading, *Water Music* itself. If *Water Music*, Boyle's first novel, assisted him in remaking himself as a new man, a writer, an intellectual, a rebel against the values of a powerful North American society, a bridge between old and new selves, a platform, a politics, a big belly laugh, if the novel is all of this, then it is usefully seen as a "compromise object" as described by Anne McClintock in her definition of the fetish, which is:

> the displacement onto an object (or person) of contradictions that the individual cannot resolve at a personal level. These contradictions may originate as social contradictions but are lived with profound intensity in the imagination and the flesh. The fetish thus stands at the cross-roads of psychoanalysis and social history, inhabiting the threshold of both personal and historical memory. The fetish marks a crisis in social meaning as the embodiment of an impossible irresolution. The contradiction is displaced onto and embodied in the fetish object. ... By displacing power onto the fetish, then manipulating the fetish, the individual gains symbolic control over what might otherwise be terrifying ambiguities. (184)

The book, as magical, compromise object, becomes the Father and remakes Boyle in its image, but at a price.

Ailie receives no more letters from either husband or son. The last lines of the novel read:

> She sat by the window a long while, the envelope heavy in her hand, a pale alien light blanching the shrubs, the rooftops, the trees, until even the distant hills were drained of color and life. On the shelf behind her, oiled and black, sat the ebony figurine: gravid, obscene, another artefact.
> There were no more letters. (1981, 437)

The obscene, oily and black fetish has executed its mysterious magic and husband and son have succumbed to its evil hypnotic power. And yet, it would be an injustice to this vast and intriguing novel to end with the image of the malevolent carving redolent with European myths of the African primitive. The novel's other side, its ability to rise above these myths, even as it perpetuates them, resides in Johnson, the man, who with straight back and dignity intact says "no" to Mungo Park, walks out on the doomed

European expedition and returns to his marvellous hut, which we see through Mungo's amazed, European eyes:

> He [Mungo] replaces the volume and then notices Johnson's writing desk—no more than a leaf really—squeezed up against a square shutter cut into the thatch. Slips of papyrus paper, an earthenware jar of quills and a pot of indigo ink: tools of the trade. *Never underestimate the power of the written word, Mr. Park,* he would say if he were here now. ... (1981, 339)

This brings us to another writer, Lawrence Norfolk, whose novels powerfully refuse to underestimate both the written word and the spoken tale. Stories entwine the explorers who hear, read and tell them, sometimes with dire consequences.

CHAPTER THREE

The Anti-Quest and the Migrating Tale: Lawrence Norfolk's *The Pope's Rhinoceros* (and *Lemprière's Dictionary*)

The Enlightenment and the Renaissance, through the Splintering Prism of the late Twentieth Century

Lawrence Norfolk's first novel, *Lemprière's Dictionary*, is set in the eighteenth century. Profoundly and self consciously anachronistic, it takes its Enlightenment protagonist, Lemprière, whose vision is tellingly myopic, through a journey of twentieth century preoccupations with splintered identities, fractured bodies and the breaking of boundaries in the realm of cyberspace. Specifically, Lemprière travels from the small island of Jersey of his birth, to London to settle his murdered father's affairs and to uncover the mysteries surrounding his father's death. In the process, he exposes the vicious greed and rapacious imperialism of the East India Company.

It is no coincidence that both *Lemprière's Dictionary* and *Water Music* take us back into that period. Donna Heiland suggests that recent fictional interest in the eighteenth century is so great as to constitute "a genuine literary subgenre" (109). If the unified subject is the opposite of our splintered subjectivities, he remains present for us, perhaps as object of fascination, or even of nostalgic longing in our times. In addition, there is the collusion between imperialism and this Cartesian subject:

> The construction of the Cartesian subject as a distinctively human mind attached to an animal/mechanical body had everything to do with rationalizing an imperialism that would put the European *mind* in control of the colonial *body*, and put *us* in control of *them*. (Heiland, 109)

A similar comparison between the eighteenth and twentieth centuries, and the archetypal men they embody, is made by Stephen Bann in his paper intriguingly entitled "From Captain Cook to Neil Armstrong: colonial exploration and the structure of landscape" (1990). Bann's Mungo Park persona is Captain Cook, the man whose use of "the Latinate categories of the Linnaean system" enabled him to name "the legendary 500 and more varieties of eucalyptus native to the Australian sub-continent" (215). With the "gradual atrophy", however, of blank spaces on the map, which have enabled adventuring men to set off into the horizon on voyages of discovery, the twentieth century has given rise "to an increasingly strong preoccupation with the vertical dimension" (Bann, 225).

What this means is that the newer urge to explore upward on the vertical plane, "the moon landing", effects "a qualitative change in the systems of measurement through which we adjust our relationship to the natural world" (Bann, 225). Or as Bryld and Lykke put it, "our 'high' and 'deep' frontiers...satisfy the desire for vast and sublime wilderness areas" (21), a desire which becomes acute in the context of the disappearance of that wilderness:

> The 'insurmountable' mountains, 'impenetrable' forests and deserts of early modernity have long since been 'conquered', as have the 'dark' continents and 'virgin lands' of the classic colonialist period. (Bryld & Lykke, 20)

Norfolk's eighteenth century novel can only be understood through the hindsighted prism of the late twentieth century disillusionment with old quests, its pulverising of boundaries, with real and virtual reality, with damaged bodies and split minds and cyborgs generating new species. All of this is captured by Norfolk's *Lemprière's Dictionary*, in which the sinister East India Company Cabbala meets "deep beneath the sleeping city" (1991, 48) in a giant fossilized dinosaur carcass—"once it was a mountain of flesh, red throbbing meat, and muscle. Now it is dead stone with its veins sucked dry as dust and all its arteries blown out clean by time" (1991, 113). We are warned that, like the dinosaur's demise, the certainties and quests of this era will give way and become extinct.

In fact, both of Norfolk's novels travel back in time in order to say important things about our present. The second novel also travels widely in geographical space. Its sites are Rome, the bleak German island of Usedom and most importantly for our purposes, the old West African kingdom of Benin, and so, for the moment, let us travel right back to the sixteenth century, to *The Pope's Rhinoceros*, which is the focus of this chapter.

A Rapacious Pope and the Rhinoceros of Benin

> And yet [the Pope] craves marvels and prodigies before allies and armies. I tell you, a dragon, a gryphon, and a centaur would secure Africk, the Indies and the New World, all three. (*The Pope's Rhinoceros*, 1997, 199)

The Anti-Quest and the Migrating Tale

Renaissance Rome in the early sixteenth century is a dirty, putrefying, rat infested stink hole in which greedy European nations compete for the favours of a corrupt and decadent Pope. The year is 1513 and the Spanish and Portuguese vie for a Papal Bull guaranteeing possession of their overseas conquests:

> Invisible lines divided unseen seas, snaked about coasts and islands whose positions seemed to shift with the whims of the popes: Cape Verde, the Canaries, Cape Bojador, Antilla. ...Now, in the open seas three hundred and seventy leagues west of the Cape Verde isles, a frontier begins. A line is drawn. Portugal stands back to back with Spain. (Norfolk, 1997, 194)

We are quite clear that whatever exploring and questing after dreams and visions happens in this book, it does so benchmarked by the rampantly material—by gold and greed and promises of the untold wealth in faraway places.

The new Pope, Leo X, is being lavishly installed with pomp, ceremony and fanfare that drowns his unsavoury past and fills the vacuum of spirituality with spectacle. False father, he over-indulges, farts, hunts and covers up his role in past wars and massacres. But this charlatan has power.

Much of this is historically accurate, down to the Pope's painful anal fistula that Norfolk includes in his novel, as well as the real names of Pope, Spanish and Portuguese ambassadors, the Pope's secretary and the famous line of demarcation, as documented in Silvio A. Bedini's *The Pope's Elephant*. Bedini also describes the custom whereby European sovereigns, on the election of a new Pope, send ambassadors to Rome, providing "opportunities for unlimited ostentation," reflecting "the importance of the sovereign and his achievements," to say nothing of the plea for favours with regard to overseas possessions (18–19). Bedini explains that Leo valued above all other gifts, "the most unusual exotic birds and beasts from Africa and Asia" (27). Exotic flora and fauna from faraway places, are trophies for European lusts and greed. Norfolk takes up the tale. Faria, the Portuguese ambassador, in a joint Papal audience with the Spanish Ambassador, Vich, asks the Pope in some exasperation, "'what is it that you want?'" To which the Pope replies:

> "Plinius tells a wonderful tale in his Natural History," he says with sudden enthusiasm. 'Every beast has its adversary, the Lion and the Tiger, the Tortoise and Eagle. ...There are others, though I forget them now. Even Hanno has his enemy, the one he must live to destroy". (1997, 183)

The fabled adversary of the elephant is, of course, the rhinoceros. The coded message implies that whichever nation brings Hanno his adversary, enabling a glorious war of the exotic animals, will win the Pope's Bull bestowing sovereignty over other lands and people. And so events are set in motion for an expedition to Africa to find a rhinoceros for a Pope and thereby to enable Europe to grow rich on the spoils of the East. This is framed within Norfolk's ironic critique of the arrogant imperialist assumptions, whims and avarice on the part of these Europeans, both secular and, supposedly, spiritual.

The protagonist of this novel is called Salvestro. He is the man who forms part of the expedition to Africa to find this exotic animal. We will follow his destiny with amazement and compassion.

Salvestro is crying for his mother: Murder, Rape and the Quest for Buried Cities

The plot is dense and labyrinthine, making the attempt to summarise it somewhat futile. Norfolk loves big novels, or as he puts it, "long, messy, flawed, excessive books" (1994, 6). Peter Keough manages quite deftly to summarise Salvestro's background:

> Born on the far northern German island of Usedom, Salvestro the boy barely escapes with his life when a lynch mob of islanders drowns his mother as a witch. After swimming to the mainland, he roams the woods a feral child until pressed into the service of the christian Free Society, a squalid band of mercenaries. ...When the disasters of battle set Salvestro and his comrade Bernardo to flight, they return to Usedom...and the pair is enlisted as guides for Father Jorg and his company of fractious monks on pilgrimage to Rome to beseech the pope for money to rebuild their crumbling abbey. There, inevitably and implausibly, Salvestro and Bernardo entangle themselves in the most daunting and capricious quest of all—the search for the pope's rhinoceros. (1)

The novel plays with time, and does not follow this order, but in order to understand the analysis that follows, it may be helpful to emphasise this linear breakdown. In other words, Salvestro grows up in Usedom, from which he flees the crowd, which is eager to drown him too, after his mother is murdered. He returns there as a young man, in order to find his mother's lost city, about which we will hear more, and this is where the novel opens. He is not successful, but he falls into the company of a group of monks. He establishes a relationship with their leader, Father Jorg, a good man, who enlists his assistance in leading them to Rome for an audience with the Pope. We will also encounter the saintly Father Jorg again. In Rome he stumbles into the expedition to Africa to find the rhinoceros. He returns with it (or an effigy of it at least) to Rome, from which he finally comes full circle back to Usedom, where the novel ends.

The Anti-Quest and the Migrating Tale 73

And so, sandwiched between the Roman jostlings and politicking and vying for power, are the two other sites, Salvestro's birthplace at the very beginning of the novel and the Africa to which he adventures near its end, before returning to Rome and then finally back to Usedom. Both of these other places are at the point of Christianity's aggressive drive to establish its sovereignty—the far Northern German island of Usedom in the Baltic Sea and the kingdom of Benin in West Africa. The novel concludes in Usedom, narratively enclosing, surrounding and barricading the European centre. These sites comment politically and morally on events in Europe at the very moment of the birth of the Renaissance's celebration of secular human subjectivity. It is interesting to note, however, that Africa is hardly mentioned by the Eurocentric reviewers of the novel (Keates, Keough, Moore and Parini). What I will be illustrating is how utterly crucial Africa is to the entire outcome of the narrative.

The definitive experience of Salvestro's life is witnessing that brutal murder of his mother, who was accused of witchcraft by the bigoted Christian islanders. The origins of this accusation and murder lie in the different culture of her extinct community, which lives only in the stories Salvestro's mother tells him. She speaks about the god she worships, Svantovit, a deity, which had followers, in reality:

> Arkona, West Slavic citadel-temple of the god Svantovit, dating from the 9th–10th century AD and destroyed in 1168/69 by Christian Danes when they stormed the island of Rugen in the southwestern Baltic. (Britannica, 1, 1993, 559)

We will discover extraordinary overtones between this pre-Christian Baltic island and pre-colonial Benin, towards the end of the novel. As for Salvestro's mother's stories, they are taken as the proof of the family's heathen beliefs. In fact, fundamental to this novel's design is the material role played by stories, here and elsewhere, in the destinies of the characters and in the history of cultures.

What makes matters worse, is that Salvestro, inadvertently, and with childish innocence, contributed to his mother's vile end by telling her secret tales of her god to his friend, Ewald, for whose father Salvestro's mother works, gutting fish. His mother, note, is dark, foreign to the bulk of the Christian islanders. She has the blackest hair on the island and speaks words that Salvestro himself does not understand (1997, 18). They are shunned by the islanders because they are different, heathen and savage. They are the last of a dying breed and their culture is disappearing in the face of the Christian onslaught. In this, I must emphasise, there are clear parallels with Africa on the cusp of the colonial era.

In this way, Norfolk sets up our white explorer/protagonist as both victim and perpetrator. He played a part in the terrible loss his mother—"he should not have told Ewald his mother's secret" (1997, 21). But he also joins the European quest to plunder Africa of her treasures; he is the last of a dying breed and also a man, who suffers at the hands of dominant patriarchy. This double role Norfolk demonstrates by way of a most horrible fictional depiction of rape. In one of the wars that Salvestro inexplicably finds himself caught up in, a bunch of soldiers brutally gang rape a woman. The only way that Salvestro can think of to attempt to save her from their violence, brutality and murder, is to take over from them and pretend to wish to rape her too. It is clear that he does this out of the memory of the terrible victimisation of his mother and his inability to help her then. It is a ghastly nightmare:

> She smelt of urine and sour sweat. He had expected that, but as he laid his length over hers, he felt the coldness of her flesh, its clamminess. He entered her quickly, and turned his head away from hers, as the curly-haired boy had done, feeling himself shrink from her. She was formless. He felt nothing as he pumped and jerked about inside her. With his eyes screwed tight he imagined their positions reversed, or himself somehow looking down on the act being committed. ...And the darkness which was the water in the cask, or only his eyes shut tight. Or the dormitory, her, now. ...Or a long time ago, and there. And her. (1997, 257)

Salvestro's loss of the language of subjectivity is as significant as the fact that he is depicted as both rapist and victim as he imagines their "positions reversed". The link between the woman and his mother is made here and again a bit later in Rome when he re-lives the rape in which "his disowned carcass couples with hers" (1997, 261). Note that it is his mother's body that he imagines jerking in death, uncertain whether he saw it, or conjured it out of his own body, which also jerked about during the rape, merging the three of them—mother, unknown raped woman and Salvestro himself, victims all:

> Her bent body jerks about like a puppet's—did he see that? The water folded her shrieks in its custodial silence. The dulled drumbeat of his blood drowned her out as the weight of the Achter-wasser pushed in on him. Is that what she heard too? As they picked her up, one on each side, as they pushed her head forward? As they drowned her there, that night, in a barrel of rainwater? ...No one hears and no one cares. Little liquid hiccups and half-stifled sobs erupt unvigorously and sink swiftly in the night's tarry silence. It's too late. It always is. Salvestro is crying for his mother. (1997, 262)

As we saw, Salvestro was inadvertently partly responsible for his mother's death by betraying the secrets of her beliefs and then again he is caught up in the gang of rapists and the woman dies after he has entered her. By this means, Norfolk both deplores male violence on women, but also, most movingly, captures the ways in which some gentle and unwilling men are drawn into patriarchy, become at least partly complicit with it and are themselves wounded and scarred in the process. I think this is what lends passion and dignity to this great novel. Norfolk, in other words, confronts gender in terms of an understanding of how men can be oppressed at the hands of their fellow, brutal, macho, mates, but acknowledges the tinge of power, collusion and guilt that accompanies white male suffering.

At the opening of the novel, the adult Salvestro has returned to the site of his birth and his loss, Usedom, and with his friend, Bernardo, is attempting, futilely, to plumb the deeps and discover the buried, sacred city of Vineta. Salvestro "remembered his earlier self leaning forward across the fire to catch his mother's words as she told him of their ancestors' city and its riches" (1997, 12). She tells also of a war that lasted a hundred years as the Christian invaders built their churches and attempted to destroy the ways of the people that came before them—"They muttered curses against their temples, and against their god Svantovit" (1997, 13). Before a final battle, that would have been decisive, there was a terrible storm and Vineta, which "was built on an arm of land that stuck out into the sea" was cast asunder into "the bottom of the sea":

> "And Vineta is still there,' he murmured, "with all its temples and their treasure. ...."
> ...And its people too, his mother had said. Our people. When the water was clear, she told him, you might see them walking in the watery streets. Svantovit was down there with them. (1997, 14)

Salvestro's quest, then, is to find the lost city of Vineta in order to vindicate his mother, to re-discover his watery past and his future identity. In addition, Norfolk is signalling that this book is a commentary on another novel, Thomas Pynchon's *V*, to which point we will return later on in the chapter.

What is clear here is that if Salvestro is an explorer—seeking Vineta or the rhinoceros in Benin—he is no ordinary adventurer. He may wear the costume of such a person, the trappings that have been bought for him by the Spanish to deck him out for the journey to Africa, but he is not the soldier or adventurer so dear to the dominant mode of fiction set in faraway lands:

> He did not question his isolation any more than he had his ostracism from the islanders, or the other soldiers at Prato. Private Salvestro. Explorer Salvestro. He was neither, never had been. He had to wrap himself in a swagger to be offered a seat. Play the fool in his gaudy motley. ...The chain looked stupid. None of his

costumes truly fitted. He did not belong, and any who belonged with him, they did not belong either. (1997, 404)

What he, in fact, seeks to recover is his past and his identity. Whether he is ultimately successful is another, murky matter which we will come to in due course. Norfolk devises an image of Salvestro's search for his true being in the form of "the Water-man". A kind of reflection of Salvestro in the water, this image symbolises very powerfully Salvestro's beginnings, horrors, but also the source of his potential recovery of self. Salvestro had not always carried this name (reminiscent of many of Boyles's characters in the previous chapter). Back in Usedom he had been Niklot, a name he had dropped when he ran away from the horrors of his birthplace, a name and a past life he has difficulty owning. In Benin, he has this fusion nightmare, that he is back in Usedom, desperately seeking the lost Vineta, but he has become black:

> Water-man looked up at him, aping the motions of his limbs. He looked ridiculous, his arms and legs flopping about, his body hanging in the water down there while his own teetered on the raw edge above. ...The Water-man was breaking up, coming apart, his mouth widening impossibly.
> To swallow him?
> *Niklot!*
> Not yet. The men around him are silent...unreachable as they search for missing walls and ramparts, listen for the hum of voices, clatter of footsteps, for the clangour of drowned Vineta. ...
> *Salvestro!* ...
> He glanced down at him again, then stared. Now how had he failed to notice that before? The Water-man was black.
> "Salvestro! Salvestro, wake up!"
> "Niklot," he mumbled, coming blearily awake, "I am called. Or was". (1997, 663)

Note how this dream foregrounds the parallels between the history of the Baltic and of Africa. Note also the image of his flopping body, reminiscent of the jerking pangs of his mother and the grotesque movements in the rape, now built into his struggle for self-image as the jerking-flopping causes his reflection to distort and fall apart. More importantly, this key passage alerts us to the events that will climax the novel when the "not yet" becomes now. What occupies us crucially right at this moment, however, is the link between Salvestro's past in Usedom, where the lost city of Vineta and its gods and customs symbolise Salvestro's pre-Christian roots, and this present in Benin.

The narrative provides a plot explanation for this image of blackness, given that an African boy is looking at the half sleeping Salvestro, who has sailed to Benin and who dreams him as the image of the Water-man, but Norfolk assures us this boy is not himself the Water-man:

> There was a face staring into his, a black face, not old, not young, and *not the Water-man's either*. A youth, he decided. (1997, 663, my emphasis)

The identity, which is quite unambiguous, is between Salvestro in the past as Niklot, as pre-Christian and hounded by the new Christian order and this boy, also part of a pre-colonial culture. This boy is learning bronze casting, an apprentice who listens to the stories of his cultural heritage, just as Niklot had listened to his mother's stories. Benin, too, is a society persecuted by slavery and awaiting colonial occupation and plunder, which will result in much of the bronze and the golden treasures illicitly finding their way back to the banks and museums of Europe.

Having traced Salvestro's journeys from Usedom to Rome to Benin, we need to go back to Rome and discover how, and why, and with what consequences, one of the fellow travellers to Benin is an African woman called Usse, a woman who is driven to action by stories. Usse's journey is from her home, Benin, to Rome as a slave. In Rome she overhears and imperfectly interprets European stories, stories she listens to with an ear attuned to the tales of her own culture. She finds a way to return to Benin armed with a deadly cocktail of stories.

A City of Two Tales: The Splintered Rhinoceros

Usse, or Eusebia, as we first are introduced to her, is originally from Benin. She was enslaved and shipped to Rome, where we find her. She manages to inveigle her way aboard the ship in search of the rhinoceros for the Pope, a ship carrying Salvestro, his big, somewhat simple friend, Bernardo, and the soldier, Diego.

Back in Africa, Eusebia, too, it turns out, has another life and a different name. She metamorphoses into the important princess called Usse, with her hair "braided in locks which shot out of her head in all directions" and her ichi-marks on her face highlighted by the dark blue of uli berries. All this, along with her new authoritativeness and power, results in Salvestro, Bernardo and Diego concealing "their shock at her transformation" (1997, 601).

Most intriguingly, it is Usse who turns the story of the four of them, herself, Salvestro, Bernardo and Diego, into a local folktale of the battle between rhinoceros and elephant, Ezodu and Enyi:

> Soldier, Giant, and Thief. It was like the beginning of a children's tale: "Tortoise and Leopard were out walking in the forest...or Hare and Dog met one day at the waterhole. ..." She felt drowsy even with the motions of the boat, the muddy-watery

smell in the air, the little grunts of the paddlers whose rhythm never changed. Soldier, Giant, and Thief went in a boat to a strange country with a fierce princess called Usse. They wanted to catch the ugliest beast in the world. ...

Ezodu and Enyi were walking in the forest. ...Eh, Usse? Remember that one, my fierce little princess? (1997, 603)

Whose is the italicised voice that intrudes into Ussse's story and why is Salvestro the thief in this story? What is he stealing? It appears that Salvestro is picking up the static of Usse's father's voice from the dead, possibly creating some interference. Her father's tone is strangely altered:

Father?
Ezodu and Enyi were once the best of friends. They used to meet at the waterhole, eh? Heh, heh, heh, heh. ...
And then he was gone. She sat up quickly. Gone as abruptly as he had come. Her father playing tricks on her? Strange. Not like him. (1997, 604)

Then Usse notices Salvestro:

He was sitting bolt upright, a puzzled expression on his face which she could see only because he turned his head to left and right; his baffled, startled, searching head. With its spying eyes and its thieving ears. Could he have heard too? *Was it possible that a White-man could hear such voices?* (1997, 604, my emphasis)

That indeed is the question, the one motivating this entire study. Norfolk is aware of the necessity of exchange and dialogue, in place of objectifying people from cultures different from his own. He is also keenly attuned to the postmodern urgency of dismantling master texts of the West. As Iain Chambers puts it:

As authority slips from my hands into the hands of others, they, too, become the authors, the subjects, not simply the effects or objects of my ethnography.
But sometimes we fail to hear and merely register a silence. For our loss of authority is not usually the result of our benevolence; ...it is invariably the outcome of struggle, contestation and a refusal on the part of another being to register our presence. (51)

Norfolk has a profound understanding of this contestation and refusal, as well as of different points of view, histories and interests. He does not, however, give us any idealised new dialogue between the black woman and the white man. Usse does not acknowledge Salvestro—she has been through too much at the hands of the slavers and Roman masters and mistresses. She deeply resents what she sees as Salvestro's intrusion into her communication with her father and brands him a thief of her vital messages, pirating her line to the ancestors. As for Salvestro, he receives no divine knowledge; he does not understand what he is hearing, can only hear partially and this is not least of all because he speaks a different language. He is merely tormented by the buzz in his head and the headaches it induces:

> Then, once again the voices had started up, more insistent than ever before. He had tossed and turned under their assault, trying to shake them out of his head, but they were trapped in there and there was no means of escape. (1997, 643–4)

Why Salvestro? Cutting across race and gender in quite a bold way, Norfolk draws clear associations between him and Usse. Like Salvestro, Usse too has more than one name:

> Diego stared at her. "She is called Eusebia," he said. "Or Usse."
> In response to this, Eusebia-or-Usse snorted dismissively.
> "Usse" she said. "Eusebia is only fit for scrubbing people's feet."
> "Usse," Salvestro echoed absently. "Eusebia" and "Usse." "Salvestro" and "Niklot," who was far away, and long ago. Dropped somewhere and lost. What was "Salvestro" fit for? (1997, 549)

With unmistakable overtones of Salvestro, who survives the attempted drowning of himself, along with his mother, Usse also

> undrowned herself and came back; the River's voice drummed in her ears, a voice she alone had dared to hear. She was painted and armoured, moving her own mass against the current. (1997, 602)

Salvestro's position as the last of the Baltic, 'pagan' and pre-Christian community, with all the overtones of ethnic cleansing, anachronistically invoked by the recent and terrible history of Bosnia, provides an extraordinary safeguard against essentialising. In other words, oppression, victimisation and witch-hunting are not the preserve of any pre-determined grouping, but are historically and politically contextual.

In constructing this interface between Rome and Benin, moreover, Norfolk is reconstructing fictionally a cultural and historical reality. As Stuart Hall puts it:

> Since the Sixteenth Century, these different temporalities and histories have been irrevocably and violently yoked together. This certainly does not mean that they ever were or are *the same*. Their grossly unequal trajectories, which formed the very ground of political antagonism and cultural resistance, have nevertheless been impossible to disentangle, conceptualise or narrate as discrete entities. (252)

What this means is that from that time "the very notion of an autonomous, self-produced and self-identical cultural identity" is torpedoed, in that such an identity "had in fact to be discursively constructed in and through 'the Other', through a system of similarities and differences"(252). And this brings us most precisely to the question of Salvestro, in Benin in the sixteenth century, as part of a European mission of discovery and plunder, who becomes plugged in, albeit imperfectly, to the voice of Usse's ancestor, the King.

Salvestro's listening is not altogether passive, notwithstanding that he is involuntarily on a receptive wavelength. Does not the Eze Nri in his new mocking voice refer to the particular story of the elephant and the rhinoceros, precisely because of what is on *Salvestro's*, as opposed to Usse's mind—the search for the rhinoceros? It is Salvestro's history, surely, that transforms Usse's father's tone.

The local story is filtered through two authoritative male voices, pillars of power in the community. The one is the voice Usse hears of her dead, but not yet buried father, the Eze Nri, the Ruler. The other voice of authority is that of a character to whom we now must turn. He is known only as "the old man", the master craftsman in bronze casting, the cultural custodian and reservoir of the communal memory.

The Stratigraphy of Stories Cast in Bronze

Usse's father, the Eze Nri, the king, is the ultimate word of the local Law and Usse, as his eldest child, on his death is responsible for the ritual of his cleansing and burial. It is the old craftsman, whose sacred role it is to execute a bronze of the king. He tells stories to his boy apprentice as he works. Stories and bronze casting, for which Benin was renowned, mutually enrich each other. It is thus impossible to disentangle the literal from the figurative dimensions, as stories and bronze, the material and the spiritual, body and soul, entwine and comment on each other and on the past. If the bronze is a permanent record of the past told in stories, then it also celebrates and enshrines the body:

> The Eze Nri carried his ancestors' memories in his head and their bodies in a piece of bronze so they would not be lost in that way either. Bodies were important too. (1997, 622)

At "the core" of the casting made by the old man is the "the clay stump" which, most suggestively, turns out to be a large, realistically moulded penis:

> It was a carefully modelled clay penis, at least eight inches long, standing upright on its base with a shaft, a head, and a fat vein winding up its side like a half-submerged python. (1997, 597)

The Anti-Quest and the Migrating Tale

It may well form the core of a sacred object, but it, and the craftsman's attitude to it and in relation to his wife, Iguedo, is wonderfully bawdy, irreverent and resounding with all the joyful bodily lewdness of the carnivalesque:

> Iguedo walked in, took one look at the thing, and began hooting with laughter.
> "What's this then, old man?" She gasped between guffaws. "Your eyes going the same way your balls did?" She picked up the penis and began waving it around. "You make this to keep me company, old man?"
> The old man was cackling away as she jabbed it at him.
> "Careful," he protested. It's not...It's not..." He couldn't get it out.
> "It's not hard yet? That what you want to say?" It set her off again. "Not hard yet. Oh dear, it hasn't been hard since Eri's time."
> They both collapsed, laughing too hard to stand now. (1997, 597)

Penis and phallus, physical body and Law of the ancestors, both, the clay object will provide the core of the bronze. It is, in other words, both the body of the Eze Nri, fetish signifier of the ultimate pantheon of Law-givers and ancestors, but also the penis, the old man's body part that he wishes to insert into the body of Iguedo, his wife. This he attempts to impart to the predictably disgusted adolescent boy, who does not yet understand the layers of wax, clay and bronze, of sacred, sensual and secular, that go into the complex process he is learning:

> "That wax, pick it up—go on—that's for the model. You'll get the trick of it. And this," he picked the clay *phallus* "will be inside it, just like this," he moved as though to open his wrap, "will be inside old Iguedo. Eh, Iguedo?"...
> The boy dropped the wax and seized his chance to stalk out. They were crude and stupid. But tomorrow, he thought, tomorrow he would learn bronze-casting. (1997, 600, my emphasis)

What he learns is that the crudeness, the "obscene stump of clay" is crucial to the casting:

> The old man took the stump and, holding its base with his fingertips, dipped its length very quickly into the melting-bowl, as though he were stabbing the molten wax, then keeping its 'head' pointing downwards, he brought it straight up, swung his arm sideways, and plunged it into the bucket. When he pulled it out again the clay was coated with a thin sheath of wax. The old man held the shaft still while drops of water slid down its sides, shook the last few back into the bucket with a single motion of his wrist, then dipped the stump back into the wax to begin the procedure again. The wax formed a sheen over the dark-red clay, then a milky coating as the wax thickened. (1997, 624–5)

The bronze casting is intricately and realistically described. This technology, painstakingly executed in layers and stages, is literally a part of Benin's cultural record and heritage. It is also a metaphor for the richness of the cultural past, including its receptacle of history—the stories, which are told and re-told. These stories provide the fabric of the society's history within an oral culture and also the individual's sense of identity. The bronze of the Eze Nri incorporates all the layers of previous Law-givers and the casting of the layers happens crucially in conjunction with the telling of founding stories, something the boy still has to learn:

> "Layers," said the old man. "Smooth even layers." The clay stump was the core and the clay in which they would later encase the wax was the mould. The wax itself was the image of the casting and the casting was of the Eze Nri who was not one man but many, each one encasing the last all the way back to Eri. ...
> When the layers had reached the thickness of a man's arm, the old man had dipped the wax into the water for the last time and bade the boy fetch the basket which held his modelling tools. ... (1997, 625–6)

The boy's apprenticeship in bronze casting is simultaneously his initiation into the world of the secret stories of the men. As the old man's hands moved "busily around the wax, turning it this way and that while he hacked and pared at great speed" he tells the story of the first Eze Nri, Eri:

> "Eri sat on an anthill," said the old man, "and all around him the land was soft as mud. Useless. Couldn't grow a thing in it. ... Are you listening, cloth-ears?"
> "Yes," he mumbled. "Eri sat on an anthill."
> Everybody knew this story. He was supposed to be learning bronze-casting, not listening to tales his mother had told him when he barely reached her knee. (1997, 626)

The old man tells the boy the full, the true and the only partly generally known story of the origins of the line of power and also of elephant and rhinoceros. The first Eze Nri, Eri, had not one, as was generally thought, but two, sons—Ifikuanim and a nameless brother. When Eri died the brothers "cut his land in two," East and West of the river. The brothers are true opposites of each other. Whereas Ifikuanim clears the bush and cultivates and tames the land, his brother loves to hunt the wild animals within the undisturbed forest:

> The old man told how on his side of the river Ifikuanim cleared the forest and planted yam and coco-palm, how he caught goats and tamed them, then cattle, even dogs. ...
> "but the other brother didn't like the hoe, didn't like the axe, didn't like felling, or clearing, or planting, or weeding. He didn't like the sun either. What he liked was hunting. He kept his land as forest and he kept himself within it." (1997, 640)

The Anti-Quest and the Migrating Tale

Light and dark, but not good and bad. The brothers supplement each other and the land. The forest has always been the place of tradition, of the spirits and wild things, a place with which you meddle at your peril. The forest brother "was a good hunter, even the leopard feared him" (1997, 641) but he could not hunt enough to feed his people and he encroached on the land of Ifikuanim, who conspired with Enyi, the elephant, who helped him catch his brother, who he horribly captured in clay and metamorphosed into an angry, repressed and vicious rhinoceros:

> "They caught him by the waterhole, just as Enyi promised, and they rolled him in the clay there till he was covered from head to foot. Then they rolled him some more, until the weight of the clay was so heavy that he could not stand. He fell on all fours like an animal. They stripped off his necklaces of leopard teeth. They took his hunting horn and stuck it on the end of his nose. Every time he tried to run back into the forest, Enyi and Ifikuanim herded him back to the waterhole and rolled him in the clay again. They held him down until the sun had dried it hard". (1997, 641)

In so doing, they violated the balance between change and tradition, between light and dark, forest and farm and left to future generations an inheritance of impurity. This is how Usse interprets the voice of her father repeatedly pointing to Enyi and Ezodu. This, moreover, is how European and African stories mingle as Usse travels the globe along the middle passage and divines the message from the Pope, with his obsession with elephant and rhinoceros, with the riches of Africa and the sweat and blood of its enslaved populations. In other words, Usse reads the designs of the Pope, who desires to enslave the rhinoceros, as the harbinger of the curse on the land bequeathed by Enyi and Ifikuanim, when they stripped the hunter of his forest, his traditions and his humanity and trapped him in clay:

> "None of them know anything, except this 'Pope.' Why else does he send these White-men? What does he tell them to bring him, eh? Tortoise? Baboon?" (1997, 613)

Usse has read the Pope's desires through that founding story of Enyi and Ezodu, within a growing crisis in the region with regard to trading with whites and the selling of slaves. The people are desperate for answers within the growing crisis. They had gathered together "for the palaver which had turned Onitsha from a village into a transitory city" (1997, 607). At this crucial moment, Usse returns miraculously, having escaped her enslavement—"a living ju-ju which confronted and dazzled them" (1997, 611). She comes with an extraordinary solution. They must kill all their wealth in livestock to purify the land in a blood ritual. Usse's uncle,

Namoke, buys into Usse's vision and refers the men to the powerful and secret founding story, something like the Western Oedipal Myth:

> He began by speaking of Eri and his first son. ...Then he spoke of the second son, which was *a story reserved by the men of Nzemabua, a secret they shared*. It would draw them tighter together. He told them of the fight in the mud by the waterhole...and moving back and forth over the protagonists and their actions, pointing out this or that detail or implication, *slowly recasting the story* and even signalling that he was doing this by the repetition of stock phrases until their meaning began to shift and grow slippery; he would discard them then and adopt others. (1997, 934–5, my emphases)

Albeit a story reserved for men, Usse seems to know of it, perhaps by way of her uneven, warped position, as privileged yet female in the home of the king; perhaps she heard this story too only partially, through walls and static. Whatever the case, the dreadful 'solution' she posed gathers momentum. What is clear from the turmoil already bubbling in the area is that "the rite had already begun, the call to gather the beasts was already ringing through the Obiri, already unstoppable" (1997, 636). And then all "eyes were fixed on Usse":

> *Gather the animals.*
> Her lips echoed the command, forming the words the men...would echo themselves until they amplified and magnified...Their legacy was an old mistake; an ancient stain. They were choiceless custodians, debtors to an old story. ...(1997, 636)

And so this is what the Portuguese sailors, trophy hunters too, also seeking Papal bulls and an African rhinoceros, see on their arrival in Benin:

> The men of the *Adjuda* looked about them in amazement. They were surrounded by a herd of goats.
> "And look there!" shouted Estevao. He was pointing upriver, beyond the *Lucia*.
> Another flotilla was advancing.
> "Good God!" said Dom Francisco. "Pigs!"
> And more goats, and small oxen, and whole flocks of squawking chickens. ... (1997, 529)

In a suicidal cleansing operation, a tribute to the hunter, the forest and cultural purity and in resistance to white desire for rhinoceroses and slaves, the people have sacrificed their livestock, their subsistence and livelihood— their pigs, goats, chickens and oxen.

"The Allegory Becomes Flesh"

What Norfolk appears to be asking, and it is a profound question, is what are the concrete consequences when stories, voices, quests and desires from one culture invade and bombard other places, landscapes and people? What are the rifts and fissures that crack the landscape when the power imbalances between different parts of the globe precipitate cultural earthquakes?

Norfolk seems to have ruptured the narrative stranglehold of the Eurocentric master text by way of this intriguing interplay between West African and European stories, which become entwined and mutually implicated. In this he appears to have met the challenge thrown out by Iain Chambers to Westerners, of breaking with the occidental pattern of locating "their displaced desires and neuroses" at the "margins, those other 'times' and places". Instead, *"the allegory becomes flesh"* when

> the tempo and the linear calculus of 'modernisation,' 'knowledge' and 'progress' is radically unsettled by *a diverse rendering of a myth that is unavoidably translated into localised realities* and forced to accommodate travesties, transgressions and the particular tenacities of asymmetrical ways of being and inhabiting the apparently universal shaping of the world. (Chambers, 55, my emphasis)

The translation of myths, stories, echoes and reverberations between and across continents, provides the links in the narrative chain of *The Pope's Rhinoceros*. The asymmetry of power between cultures and the travesties of plunder and slavery ensure that these links are both jagged and tenuous. The static, interference, distortion, misheard whispers through keyholes, headache inducing buzz in the head of strange tongues and foreign words, all contribute to a network that is both implicated, global and disjunctural, jarring and un-romanticised.

Crucially, Norfolk accepts that the myths, metaphors and archetypes of Western culture have to be cleansed of their tropes and figures, if the discourse and the oppression that it carries with it, is to be challenged and defeated. The adventurers and explorers, who are the carriers of these myths and legends, have to be stopped in their tracks. And paradoxically, it is at the service of this truth that postmodern intertexts and rhetorical gymnastics are invoked in the novel.

But breaking the chain of linked stories and their surviving associations tends to leave jagged and dangerous edges. The story of Usse has undeniable echoes with another African story, one that also became flesh and blood and was played out far from Benin, in Southern Africa, but over three centuries later in which a young and obsessed girl also influenced her community to destroy their livestock. As outlined by J.B Peires in his *The Dead Will Arise*, which is a detailed treatment of this event in South African history:

> Nongqawuse said that she had met with a 'new people' from over the sea, who were the ancestors of the living Xhosa. They told her that the dead were preparing to rise again, and wonderful new cattle too, but first the people must kill their cattle and destroy their corn which was contaminated and impure. (311)

As Peires begins his book:

> Few people who hear the story of Nongqawuse—the young girl whose fantastic promise of the resurrection lured an entire people to death by starvation—ever forget it. ...And while the Xhosa nation was lying prostrate and defenceless, Sir George Grey...trampled on this human wreckage...and seized more than half of Xhosaland for a colony of white settlement. (ix)

While there are clear differences, Norfolk's is also a tale of young woman, who incites the people, also through her uncle, to sacrifice their livestock in the perceived interests of preventing white colonial expansion. Norfolk (in conversation with me) denies the South African Cattle Killing as a powerful influence on his novel and refers rather to brutal internal self-destruction, violence and cannibalism later in Benin itself, which, like in Southern Africa, by way of divide and rule, enabled colonialism to make its inroads.

The overtones with the South African Cattle Killing are, however, too clear for the text not to partake in that story. The problem is that by linking two events that took place in very different parts of Africa, many hundreds of years apart, tends to buy into the stereotype of freezing Africa in time and space. This is reinforced, to some extent, in the echoes between Vineta and Nri, for all the potential richness of this comparison referred to earlier. Is the identification between the white man's past and the black boy's present another example of Africa as the youth of Western civilization? Johannes Fabian in his *Time and the Other* emphasises that if you do not situate other cultures in the same time frame as yourself, if you deny them what he calls "coevalness"—simultaneous time—then you cannot engage in a dialogue between equals (25). "Communication," he insists "is, ultimately, about creating shared Time" (31).

A further point made by Fabian, in fact, is that by freezing non-Western places in time is to produce time as a space—the Western past becomes a continent, a place—Africa. There is, in other words, an "implied affirmation of difference as *distance*" (16). Given this link between "visualization and spatialization" (Fabian, 121), "relations between the West and its Other...were conceived not only as difference, but as distance in space *and* time" (Fabian, 147). This has enormous implications for the ways in which the landscape is described, when it is conceptualised in temporal terms as the past of the protagonist. In this light, look at the consequences of the fact that

The Anti-Quest and the Migrating Tale

Benin, the distant place of his present, reminds Salvestro of Usedom, his past and origins:

> There was a time—a long time ago and a long way away—when he would have been at home here. The trees and bushes, thickets of cedar-scrub and thorn-breaks evoke another forest, damper and colder but still recognisable in this monstrous and exaggerated version. Can he sink back into that? Can this forest in some sense be that one? (1997, 620)

The landscape is "monstrous and exaggerated" and Norfolk, as omniscient narrator, objectifies and aestheticises it, at times, in the language of excess problematised by David Spurr in his *The Rhetoric of Empire* (18). There are many examples of which the following is just one. Note all the alliteration, rhyming, repetition and dense, luxuriant imaging:

> There are no shadows—the light is too vague—but only a murky chiaroscuro which furs the forest and blurs its denizens, breaking outlines and bleeding hues so that they muddy themselves in one another, producing a homogenising surfeit of hessians and khakis. Seen in the sub-light of the forest-floor, one patch of forest really is much like another. Viewed sideways, most of what's in it is too. Along the lateral axis of homologue and homage, the massive flanged buttresses of the cottonwood trees might as well be twenty foot termite nests, or the rotting stumps of dead cedars, or creeper-strangled satinwoods, while the creepers and lianas themselves resemble—rather obviously—snakes both large and small. (1997, 619)

In creating this fecund, yet homogenous landscape, where plants resemble animals in a surfeit of browns, where, to the white onlooker, no doubt, and not to local people, one patch of the forest is much like another, Benin in 1516 might as well be the Eastern Cape in 1856, and both of them are frozen in the chronology of Salvestro's past.

But, at the same time, Norfolk backs away from this scenario. Salvestro answers his question—"can this forest in some sense be that one?"—in the negative:

> No, it's either too far or not far enough. If he's going back anywhere it's not to the forest. Not that one, and not this one either. He owes himself elsewhere, and to different creditors (1997, 621)

This identification and also distancing is very interesting. I have emphasised that Norfolk wrote male collusion into his novel, even as he simultaneously rescued his hero from its clutches. He appears in this way to acknowledge also the inevitability of his seeing other places and cultures through his own Western gaze.

We have charted the de-stabilisation of the process through which inhabitants of Benin were socially and psychologically constituted as subjects through their rituals, their rulers, their stories, art and culture. It was a patriarchal society, phallic to the core, but no more patriarchal than Europe, no less civilized than Rome. The Laws of the Father are in crisis, both in Rome, where a vain and ruthless Pope holds sway and in Benin where a dead ruler speaks in tongues to a deranged daughter. If the Eze Nri is rendered ineffectual, his messages from the grave involuntarily intercepted and distorted by the white man, then the big white Father, the Pope, fares no better. And it is back to Rome that we must go to attend the spectacle of his exposure and dismantling and to discover the outcome of the quest for the rhinoceros grail. In so doing, we will touch again on Norfolk's first novel, *Lemprière's Dictionary*.

Exploding Myths: the Alphabet as Bomb

The vain and silly Pope is avidly awaiting the delivery of his animal spoils from Africa. He has had "an ornamental platform" specially designed for himself, in the middle of the water, down which the rhinoceros captured from Africa will triumphantly sail. Coward that he is, he will not risk being caught in the cross-fire of this battle or falling into the water, and so "he, Leo, will sit on the throne in effigy, for someone else will actually do the sitting" (1997, 685). The chosen effigy turns out to be none other than the saintly Father Jorg, who, remember, Salvestro helped to reach Rome from Usedom. The arrogant Pope, who is more interested in spoils than in poor monasteries in outlying areas, has not agreed to see him and he is now blind and reduced to rags and near starvation. Ironically, it is Father Jorg, who is now to sit on the throne and act the part of the Pope. Jorg, actually more holy than the Pope, is "costumed appropriately as a Pope," with "a papier-mache mitre" (1997, 722).

The irony is multi-layered as another effigy—that of the rhinoceros—is called for. This is as a result of the unfortunate drowning of the live creature, shipwrecked *en route* to Rome.

> The Beast is not just dead. It's stuffed, the leathery products of Groot's bakery proving ideal for fitting into those difficult niches and corners with which the Beast's awkward gutted interior abounded. (1997, 730–1)

The spirit of this stuffing of the Pope's rhinoceros is true, albeit that in the letter of what happened, it was stuffed with straw, not bread, and done so by the Portuguese and not the Spanish. Thus filled, "the mounted rhinoceros was placed on board another ship and sent off to Rome a second time, much as if the shipwreck had not occurred" (Bedini, 129).

The Anti-Quest and the Migrating Tale

What will become increasingly clear is that Salvestro's re-birth into subjectivity, into a Symbolic zone, is frustrated as much by the parody of the Law of the ludicrous, vain and criminal Pope, as by his effigy, Father Jorg, whose authority and church is in shreds. Salvestro spots Father Jorg at once and is not fooled by the pantomime. The key and crucial references to Salvestro's identity as mixed and changing, as racially kinetic, refers again to the fluid image of the Water-man:

> The Water-man was there on the very edge of his vision, waving to him and retreating. The figure turned white then black, slate-grey and bottle-green, dissolved into ripples and emerged again. What colour is he? wondered Salvestro. And what colour himself, when water will take on any colour offered it? The flat greys of near-tidelessness and near-saltlessness, a dull tinge of yellow. He is not long for that now, although there are no 'true colours' and it will not—cannot—happen here. Tonight he is invisible, the colour of *Ro*-ma, which will forget him the moment he is gone. (1997, 719)

Again, this Water-man, his inner soul, his *chi* as the West Africans would have it, is linked to, and interrogates race, as it kaleidoscopically changes shape and colour. Again, there is the anticipation of something about to happen to Salvestro but not yet. For now, he dives into the water, determined to reach and rescue Father Jorg. It is over to him to find redemption for the transgressions and tragedies of his past. Water, as always is crucial. It was the scene of his mother's drowning and his own un-drowning and first re-birth. As Salvestro reaches, saves and has to carry Father Jorg, freeing him from humiliation and farce, so the rhinoceros spectacularly self-destructs. Allegory becomes flesh and flesh explodes in the face of the reality of the death of false fathers:

> "Salvestro? Is that you?"
> "It is, Father Jorg. I'm in here. Underneath you."
> *Then the Beast explodes.*
> The force shoots fragments of Beast-skin and sodden bread high and wide into the air in a spray of grey tatters and pinkish-white clods which spatter the waiting crowds. (1997, 735, my emphasis)

Exploding clods of many stories across time and space. There is the story, originating with Plinius, of elephant and rhinoceros as natural enemies and Pope Leo X's obsession with such animals and such adversaries. There is the reality, told by Bedini, of "the papal elephant featured in carvings of ivory objects brought back to Europe from Africa by Portuguese traders in the sixteenth century":

> In the course of recent studies of carved African ivories, several representations of elephants were discovered that apparently had been based on European images of Hanno...produced by the Sapi peoples of the Portuguese colony Sierra Leone. (202)

"The praiseworthy traits of the elephants," Kim Hall suggests by reference to Renaissance texts in another mythical rendering, "were the attributes Europeans came to value in the perfect colonial subject" (50–1). There are reverberations here with Hanno, the affectionate and obedient elephant pet that Leo doted upon. This contrasts with the fractious rhinoceros, endowed not with the white and precious tusks, but with the lethal and ugly horn:

> a huge head swung over and blotted out the sky. A head the size of a water barrel. Eyes like a snake. A horn on the end of its nose. (Norfolk, 1997, 667)

It is with the rhinoceros, not the servile elephant, that Usse herself is associated—rebellious, disobedient escaped slave, wild like the hunter, untamed, like the forest. Her father finds her "too impatient...and too wild" (1997, 605) causing him to observe that "sometimes I think she is Ezodu herself..." (1997, 606). She is the white man's trophy, an exotic beast stolen and transported to foreign places. She becomes the combative, repulsive rhinoceros, wreaking havoc on her own people.

And with the explosion of the beast and the clods of narrative shrapnel that are released, we are thrown back to an earlier Norfolk tale and a climactic moment in it. In *Lemprière's Dictionary*, we find statuettes, which represent the array of mythical gods and goddesses. These are pulverised right near the end of the novel, revealing the illicit, buried East India Company gold they conceal. There were "Minerva, Juno, Venus, Diana, surrounded by her nymphs, Hercules strangling the vipers, Jove with his thunder-bolt, Neptune with an urn, satyrs, dryads, and hamadryads" (1991, 415). During the course of the narrative, all of these are hammered to bits:

> Limbs and heads were broken off. Torsos which fell to the ground were cracked open, and soon a cloud of off-white dust hung over the carnage. ...Faces and fingers splintered under the hammer blows until every figure lay smashed. The dust began to settle. Eben saw the first man bend and lift something heavy from the rubble. ...
> "Gold". (1991, 415)

This battleground against the concealing myths lies at the heart of that novel and the dictionary of its title and explains both the explosion of the rhinoceros and the quest for it of this one. And so, at this climactic sixteenth century Roman moment, we must pause and travel back to Norfolk's first novel and forward two centuries in order to do so. We must, in other words, look at Lemprière and his dictionary a bit more closely.

At the outset, Lemprière constitutes himself through the heroic myths and legends that he reads about as a scholar—"Strange beasts slavered before his sword, turned their spit red. He dried the tears of ox-eyed women and broke the chains which bound them to the black rock" (1991, 8).

During the course of the novel, Lemprière is purged of those legends in what I will refer to in chapter eight in relation to Alan Hollinghurst, as the process of de-fetishization. It is via the tools of language reduced to their pips as the arbitrary signs and squiggles that make up our letters, that this cleansing process takes place. And Norfolk makes the process visceral, like the blowing away of snot from the nostrils:

> "ABC." Lemprière sniffed. "D." He wiped his nose, then thought to do the same for his eyeglasses. "E." He sniffed again. Lemprière nursed a slight dislike of the letter "E." The look of it, but also its pronunciation which seemed to him misleading. "Eeee." How many times did "E" sound like "Eeee"? Its vagaries seemed to imply a new vowel, a "yur" or "er," an "eh." It was a promiscuous, fawning surd, continually merging with its neighboring consonants ("R" in particular), confirming Lemprière's view of it as a perfidious little hieroglyph: "E", ee, *eeyurgh*." He looked at the page in front of him and noticed that the left lens of his eyeglasses was now lightly smeared with snot. (1991, 205)

Note the "neigboring consonants"—the metonymy of the random sounds creating onomatopoetic meaning. The texture, feel and shape of the letters as objects, as real and physical as snot, removes Lemprière away from the imaginary world of myth and legend. His dictionary gives rise to the process whereby "buried legends cracked through the generations' interment" (1991, 244) and the "old heroes were being dispossessed" (1991, 277). Rome, Carthage, and "all the cities which had folded one inside the other" become paper chains as "his dictionary...filled itself at the expense of these streets" (1991, 294). As he nears completion of his dictionary, "another month and the strange gray city would be empty, all its citizens interred with only his entries for headstones" (1991, 295). Allegory becomes flesh once more.

The overtones with Pynchon's novel are unmistakable in both of Norfolk's fictions, given that Pynchon introduces the quest for **V** as linked to two places—Valletta and the mythical city of Vheissu. And in the emphasis on an alphabetal sign as the arbitrary link between all the different possible Vs in Pynchon's book that are mentioned—Venus, Veronica, Victoria, Vesuvius, Venezuela, and so on—we gain clues not only to Salvestro's echoed quest for Vineta, but to Lemprière's project in writing his dictionary. *The Pope's Rhinoceros* is intriguingly dedicated to "Vineeta" (the same name as the ship on which reunited lovers sail away in an unexpectedly happy ending of *Lemprière*).The Vheisus, Vineetas, Vinetas and Vallettas all jostle about in their proximity to one another in *Lemprière's Dictionary*. But consider this for the biggest coincidence of all. In conversation with Norfolk, in answer to a chance question I happened to put to him, I learnt that his wife's name is Vineeta. Like the coincidence of *B*enin and the *B*altic, new associations are made, as Norfolk departs in a crucial way from Pynchon and finds his *V*.

Look, for example, at Pynchon's vignette also obliterating these figurative monoliths in *V*, by way of reference to Henry James's famous, modernist, figure in the carpet. Two men are pacing a carpet. They

> turn the corner by the allegorical statue of Tragedy. Their feet crush unicorns and peacocks that repeat diamond-fashion the entire length of the carpet. ... Light from outside, late summer light now falls through a single window, turning the statue and the figured carpet to a monochrome orange. (93)

We have Pynchon's constant reminders about the folly of metaphor and the dangers of pursuing the tropes and symbols that ensnare us—the room that we try to turn into Church, into the confessional, is a delusion—"The room simply is. To occupy it, and find a metaphor there for memory, is our own fault" (304). Pynchon becomes quite passionate in the reiteration of this folly of poets, "cloaking" as they do, "that innate mindlessness" of our universe "with comfortable and pious metaphor" (326). We are warned, therefore, not to seek in the symbolic significance of "V" this poetic deception and, along with Pynchon's protagonist, we are increasingly suspicious that all that V adds up to is "the recurrence of an initial and a few dead objects" (445). In fact, says Pynchon, "V. is a country of coincidence" (450). Or, "V. might be no more a she than a sailing vessel or a nation" (226). Norfolk shares Pynchon's playfulness and scepticism up to a point. In *Lemprière's Dictionary*, it *is* most surely a sailing vessel, the *Vineeta*, in which the lovers happily sail away and to which *The Pope's Rhinoceros* is dedicated—"For Vineeta". This is so because, notwithstanding that Norfolk is building in a coded dedication to his wife, Lemprière is victorious over the discourse—eventually "he had them all"—that is to say, he has captured all the myths and legends and tamed them in his dictionary. As a result, and unlike Salvestro whose elusive Water-man reflects his lack:

> The well in the courtyard showed [Lemprière] a face a hundred times more beautiful than his own, *but it was himself, not Narcissus*, peering into the water. (1991, 317, my emphasis)

Love is the elusive V and it is surely found in the happy ending of *Lemprière's Dictionary*. And here, alphabets, coincidences and the re-

The Anti-Quest and the Migrating Tale

formation of new meanings find happy congruence. If Lemprière finds his identity in the watery reflection, what of Salvestro, the Renaissance man? Has his time come?

The Pope's Rhinoceros began with Salvestro's search for the lost city of Vineta, and thereby for his past, his mother and his salvation. What he eventually finds and brings to Rome is the stuffed Rhinoceros, bulging with multiple inflammable stories. In return for bringing back the beast, he is offered the gift of hearing the Pope's confession, a pantomime that turns all too real, given the Pope's crimes and transgressions. The perplexed Salvestro is thrown into confusion as he stands in judgement against the Father, that "plump and jolly" Pope, who directly and indirectly has been responsible for so much death and suffering. Salvestro has never had a stable point of moral reference and, like the drowning man, his life of persecution at the hands of cruel and narrow bigotry passes before his eyes:

> He thinks of a boy white, silent, diving for Vineta. Ashore, an identical creature creeps into the forest. Behind him, the torches muster for the chase and dot the night with their red glows. He might as well be outside the palace at Nri, or in Rome, or Prato, or on the shore of the mainland looking back at the island. The torches of his pursuers are always there, gathering behind him, driving him forward. Who awaits him at the end of his circuit? (1997, 741)

This is the question to which the fiction has been moving. Sign-posted as "not yet," his destination is rapidly becoming "now". And at the end of the novel this can only mean a reckoning with the Water-man, summed up as his past, his inner self, his splintered being, torn between the circumstances of his birth and childhood, the Niklot, and the attempt to re-fashion himself, the Salvestro:

> For Salvestro there is only the Water-man now, and the Water-man is himself, the self he fled long ago when he pulled himself out of the Achter-wasser and stumbled into the forest. He is always there, hanging in the water, waiting to coax him forward down the ramp of ice that leads to drowned Vineta. The ringing in his head is her bells. (1997, 741–2)

Vineta, linked again to Nri, is the noise in Salvestro's head, the wavelength that simultaneously tuned him in to Usse's father's messages and also distorted them. Vineta is also the pre-Christian Kingdom of Salvestro's vanished ancestors. Like Usse, the message of purification, healing and renewal is a suicidal one. All that remains to him, in the absence of a still point or moral centre, through whose Law he could reach adult subjectivity, is to return to Vineta, and merge with the Imaginary drowned Mother, beneath the icy waters. HansJurgen, Usedom's surviving monk, observes how:

> There had been the torches, and Salvestro on the ice, gesturing at them. ...Salvestro was not shaking his fist. He was waving, or beckoning to them. The islanders carried clubs and scythes and they waited for him in silence, not daring to follow him out there. It was as though he were mocking them, for they feared the sea off Vineta Point as they always had, and they feared what lay beneath it. They feared Vineta. ...Eventually Salvestro dropped his arms. He turned and began to walk away, out onto the ice, growing smaller and smaller until the darkness swallowed him and he could be seen no longer. The islanders had waited there through the night as though, in their ignorance and superstition, they thought he might appear again out of the darkness. ...But Salvestro had not come back. (1997, 752)

Hans Jurgen completes the diary narrative of Father Jorg and also concludes the novel—"*He was the last of his kind just as I am of mine*" (1997, 753).

In what way was he the last of his kind? First of all, quite specifically, he is the last of the indigenous Baltic people of that Island, prior to its invasion by the Danes. It is also the age of the Renaissance, a time marvellously captured by Steven Greenblatt's *Renaissance Self-Fashioning*. It is a time of "change in the intellectual, social, psychological, and aesthetic structures that govern the generation of identities" (1). This change, which heralds a loosening of the hold of the religious in favour of the secular is summed up in Greenblatt's epilogue:

> It seemed to me the very hallmark of the Renaissance that middle-class and aristocratic males began to feel that they possessed...shaping power over their lives, and I saw this power and the freedom it implied as an important element in my own sense of myself. (256)

Salvestro stands on the brink of this discovery, but is neither middle-class or aristocratic. He is part of the underclass whose battering at the hands of Popes and prejudice returns them not forward into the modern era, but backwards into a death wish longing for the womb, away from the punishment of the Law of the Father and the Subjectivity it falsely promises.

But, Norfolk is, I think, also saying something to the late twentieth century man, through the echo of his Renaissance protagonist. Like Salvestro's suicidal ending, the explorer urge of a powerful, patriarchal and imperialist masculinity, is in our day as anachronistic as Salvestro's splintered identity was for his. Ultimately, Vineta is none other than the twentieth century scepticism for quests and adventures in far flung spaces. It is a metonymic Vheissu, mythical lost city in Pynchon's *V*. Vheissu begins as one of those privileged dream spaces of masculine escape—it begins as

The Anti-Quest and the Migrating Tale 95

the dream of "outlandish regions where the Establishment held no sway" (Pynchon, 157). Vheissu, for Pynchon's explorer is the tatooed, exotic North African woman

> as if the place were, were a woman you had found somewhere out there, a dark woman tattooed from head to toes. (171)

At first she is gorgeous and utterly alluring in all her Otherness, but

> soon that skin, the gaudy godawful riot of pattern and color, would begin to get between you and whatever it was in her that you thought you loved. And soon, in perhaps only a matter of days, it would get so bad that you would begin praying to whatever god you knew of to send some leprosy to her. To flay that tattoing to a heap of red, purple and green debris, leave the veins and ligaments raw and quivering and open at last to your eyes and your touch. (171)

The white man, who flays and violates woman, black people, foreign lands, is caught in the act of this butchering and rape. And so, this lure of the quest is exposed, but also re-played endlessly in the horror of Conrad's Kurtz—the extraordinary man whose sense of purpose has evaporated in the absence of the quest. In answer to the question, posed by one of the characters in *V*—"What sends the English into these terrible places?" another replies:

> "I think it is the opposite of what sends English reeling all over the globe in the mad dances called Cook's tours. They want only the skin of a place, the explorer wants its heart. ...I had never penetrated to the heart of any of those wild places...Until Vheissu. It was not till the Southern Expedition last year that I saw what was beneath her skin". (204)

In answer to what he saw, Pynchon's twentieth century Kurtz can only whisper his postmodern version the Western male stuck record—"Nothing. ...It was Nothing I saw" (204).

Difference, Demonism and Exploring: Some Conclusions

> "God knows how many Stencils have chased V. about the world". (*V*, 451)

We saw in chapter one how V.Y. Mudimbe in his *The Invention of Africa* illustrated and critiqued the phenomenon of double representation in how the West viewed its African Others, through a painting by Hans Burgkmair. In quite an intriguing coincidence, Burgkmair produced a famous woodcut of the rhinoceros dated 1515. As Bedini explains:

> Whether Burgkmair received a sketch of the beast from a correspondent in Lisbon...or whether he personally viewed the rhinoceros, cannot be determined. ...[However] Burgkmair was in frequent communication with Portuguese traders and voyagers to the Indies, as demonstrated by the series of woodcuts he had produced in 1508 depicting the peoples and domesticated animals of Africa and Asia. (1988, 121)

A reproduction of Burgkmair's rhinoceros actually frames each of Norfolk's chapters and provides the cover of *The Pope's Rhinoceros*. This connection, like the echoes and reverberations of stories and myths, re-told, re-cast in bronze, overheard through keyholes and transported across lands and seas, leads us to speculate as to whether, like the artist Burgkmair, Norfolk reproduces Mudimbe's double representation or whether he breaks the back of this colonialist discourse. To recall, what Mudimbe so resents in the picture Hans Burgkmair created in 1508 and entitled *Exotic Tribe*, is that the black figures depicted have features that distort them into being simply "blackened whites" resulting in the reduction of difference, but in the name of "the *white* norm" (1988, 8). Simultaneously, the tribe is exotic because of fundamental differences between the appearance of the black figures and those same white norms—"namely, nakedness, blackness, curly hair" (1988, 9). What this means is that white culture sets the standard, by which the black, naked primitives can only fail to come up to scratch.

Norfolk's representations are quite different. The blemishes surviving in the novel do not destroy the beauty of its achievements. The centre of white civilization, symbolised most powerfully by Rome, provided no moral standard. Quite the opposite. The white protagonist failed to salvage a moral still point by which he could continue to live, and he dies in his own birthplace, not in an Africa asked to serve the purpose of womb and burial chamber. The overwhelming insight that Norfolk enacted so subtly was the process described by Iain Chambers in relation to quite another context when he threw out the challenge to Western writers to return allegory to its material reality and to recognise that when myth finds itself elsewhere, its re-telling is fundamentally shaped by unequal power and all the travesties and injustices that this inequality musters.

The universalism that the novel partakes of is not based on a white norm. Bigotry, persecution and oppression most certainly can, and do, cut across race and gender and are often class based or belief inspired. The image, for example, of the blinkered, cold and cruel islanders of Usedom, with their torches and hatred is highly reminiscent of the American Klu Klux Klan, albeit that the Klan was based on racial hatred. It is an image that reverberates with Homi Bhabha's impassioned defence of Salman Rushdie's *The Satanic Verses* and his horror of the religious fanaticism that inspired the Fatwa against him:

'Blasphemy' stands for the phobic projections that fuel great social fears, cross frontiers, evade the normal controls, and roam loose about the city *turning difference into demonism*. (226, 1994b, my emphasis)

Norfolk exposes orthodoxy and hates the blinkered 'good' citizens, hypocritical Popes, slavers and rapists and has fathered a novel that spectacularly exposes the Emperor and his Laws.

Norfolk has created in Salvestro an extraordinarily sensitive portrait of a man, who searches for his identity, confronts patriarchy and prejudice along the way, but is not simply re-cast as a new hero in the old mould. In the process, Norfolk confronts the iniquity of unequal power and oppression and acknowledges the culpability of ordinary men, like himself, like Salvestro. White men, who even when their ears are fine-tuned to engage in dialogue, rather than domination, cannot simply hear clearly and speak in new tongues. What he has also done is to weld the life trajectories of individuals to global forces, which set up a magnetic field circumscribing the possibilities open to them. In addition, Norfolk translates socio-economic and historical realities into the language of discourse and looks at the power of the narrative chain as it binds worlds and contributes to the destinies of individuals.

I do not wish to follow with an inevitable 'but' that will subtract from the uniqueness of Norfolk's vision and sensitivity. I wish, rather, to add to the novel's achievements some of the difficulties, which snare it. I had some questions about the consequences for its politics of the portrait of the loony princess and, linked to Usse's prophesies, of the overtones in the novel of the Xhosa Cattle killing.

We have to consider the portrayal of Usse, and the identity between her and Salvestro, with their changed names, fluid identities and noises in their heads. A difficulty here is the stereotype that invariably emerges as she metamorphoses from person into prophetess—African woman as fatal to men and unearthly—"a living ju-ju":

He [Namoke] sensed the force of her through them, how she lay coiled inside the painted body, strong and untouchable like a python's muscle. Her breath filled their lungs, pumping them full so that if she were to hiss and suck they would collapse, fall to the ground as sucked-out skins, Nri taking back their spirits. (1997, 611)

And here we are brought back to the minefields of representing Africa, and using women to do so, on the part of European men. What is missing is the depiction of flesh and blood women. The material body in the form of the clay model may be at the core of the bronze, but it is still the image of the penis, which, need I say, excludes woman in bodily reality. Here lies the double bind for these writers, as articulated by Martina Sciolino when she bemoans the fact that the subject position is still gendered male and "no matter who or what V. signifies, the V. position is always feminine" (160). Writers like Pychon and Norfolk, however, are confronted with the conundrum posed by Sciolino that recurs in all of our chapters—they "deconstruct inherited tropes calling their literary patrimony into question, yet remain dependent on them" (160). This they do because "how does a writer speak beyond the very structures that constitute his cultural repertoire?" (161).

This is also Alice Jardine's point embodied in her concept of "gynesis"—a rather daunting specialised word for which there may be some justification. Her study is based on the premise that "the crises experienced by the major Western narratives have not...been gender-neutral. They are crises in the narratives invented by men" (24). What this has resulted in "within the Master narratives in the West" is "a vast self-exploration...in an attempt to create a new *space* or *spacing within themselves*" (25). What this has involved is a "reconceptualization of...what has eluded [the Master narratives] what has engulfed them" (25). And in the terms of Jardine's study, "this space has been coded as *feminine*, as *woman*" (25). It is a space in the narrative, rather than flesh and blood women, and in that space we see "the transformation of women and the feminine into verbs at the interior of those narratives that are today experiencing a crisis in legitimation" (25). Does this not reverberate with the role of Usse merely as Norfolk's narrative crucible in which stories muddle and mix?

While it may become something negative in the process, gynesis does also hold out the hope of re-making the language, of finding new ways of speaking and writing, which, as we will increasingly see, is crucial to the whole effort to wrest the discourse away from its horrible past. But the tension and potential contradiction is obvious as metaphoric woman is the device for exploding the metaphor of the quest. And the big concluding question is whether Norfolk has broken out of the conventions of Africanist discourse in his depiction of other cultures and landscapes.

I think that he substantially has done so. We should conclude the discussion of the novel on the note that one of its greatest achievements is its humility. It anticipates the difficulties that the white man has in hearing the voices in his head, even when he is tuned in to other people and cultures. Norfolk acknowledges that his white man, Salvestro, is an unwitting player in the tragedy of his mother's murder, a stranger's rape and Usse's insanity, which leads her to compel her community to destroy their livelihood; he is part of the imperial advance guard. What Norfolk is tactfully pointing out is that, with the best will in the world notwithstanding, white men sometimes involuntarily contribute to the exploitation wrought by their kind.

A parting shot to lead us into the next chapter: *Lemprière's Dictionary* is replete with mutating bodies—with the ghoulishly human-like automatons with which the eighteenth century was fascinated, as well as with the cyborgs of the twentieth century imaginary—flesh bonded with machine. The crossovers between the human and animal, between the human and the machine, are wholly sinister in that novel. For example, early in the novel, dog assassins horribly mauled Lemprière's father to death. They had been programmed to do so by a member of the evil Cabbala, who "drew their hates and affections along filaments of steel and sutured their soft brains with silver-wire stitches" and turned them into killing machines—"crude engines" (1991, 237). Norfolk appears to be warning us about the consequences when science and imperialism collude in order to dispossess ordinary people of their gold and their humanity. In the next part of this book we will explore these species boundary crossings more closely, within the tradition of Tarzan, Jane and apes and Africa. Do these mutating bodies, cyborgs, humanoids and strange, new primates, which we are about to encounter, offer up the hope of a new species, freed from the shackles of race, or do they reinforce a pernicious European trope, which links Africans and apes in a porous interchange?

Part Three:
Sons and Apes

CHAPTER FOUR

The Battered Boys of Rice Burroughs: Tarzan and Jane Goodall

Introduction

The subject for this part is to scrutinise what happens when our writers choose settings, which echo Tarzan and include apes in Africa. In this chapter, I will establish the nature of the fictional pond, as our chosen writers skate on thin ice over the cracks and casualties of racist and sexist traditions. The Tarzan inheritance has already been substantially documented and I will look at it only very selectively. Of equal and intriguing significance is the inspiration afforded to fiction writers by the network of women primatologists who observed apes and chimps in the wilds of Africa. The name, Jane, conveniently, if inadvertently, carries the double overtone of Tarzan's woman and these scientists. These women, who studied those primates, inspired two of T. Coraghessan Boyle's short stories—his "Descent of Man" in his collection of that title (1987) and his "The Ape Lady in Retirement" in his *If the River was Whiskey* collection (1989). In the process of examining these stories, Boyle's most recent novel, *Riven Rock* (1998), will come up in interesting ways and conclude the chapter. In the next chapter, we will continue this theme by looking closely at William Boyd's *Brazzaville Beach* (1990), and to a lesser extent, Peter Høeg's *The Woman and the Ape* (1996) and Will Self's *Great Apes* (1997).

The Tarzan tradition can be summed up as one in which black people are savage or absent, their traces appearing in the image of the apes. It is a discourse in which white men are the muscular, intrepid, inherently civilized and superior kings of the jungle and where blond and buxom women are their objectified quests and prizes. We will see these tropes mingle with those from a different tradition, where those blond bimbos in leopard skins have metamorphosed into scholar primatologists in working khaki shorts and whose devastating intellects render our Tarzan flexing his biceps somewhat ridiculous. As Jane of the jungle, metamorphoses into Jane Goodall of the research lab, what happens to the manliness of the Tarzan? And what fictional significance have the writers drawn from the coincidental recurrence of the name of Jane?

As I think about Tarzan, his Jane and the other Jane, Jane Goodall, my questions for the chapter emerge. Have late twentieth century male explorers, Conrad's sons and Tarzan's offspring, seized the space and chartered new and politically radical symbolic universes, as they make their fictional journeys to the so-called jungle? Have white men been liberated from the clone of Tarzan, of the burden of being hunters and wild men? How have these writers dealt with the colonialist discourse associating apes and black people? Have their depictions liberated white women from the stereotypes that imprison them in roles of sexual objects or ball biters? Have these women and local African people been afforded their own autonomy? Have the apes been freed from the manipulative troping of humans, who have little real respect for their rights and ways of living? Can we in the meantime agree to begin with the expectation of good faith on the part of complex, politically aware, writers like Coraghessan Boyle and William Boyd?

There are, in truth, many Tarzans, which is why he survives in the culture's imagination so long after the first book that introduced him to us. There is the reactionary, dominating jungle man, lording it over apes and Africans, lumped together in a degree of denigrating indistinguishability. There is the progressive Tarzan, earnestly seeking who he is, alienated from his white kin, who enslave and murder animals and have no respect for the culture of wild spaces. There is a satirised modern Tarzan limp, inadequate and flabby. There may even be another Tarzan, one who is neither white nor black, and who stands for the migrant cosmopolitanism of our times.

Paul Theroux has declared:

> I do not want to be Tarzan and cannot think of anything drearier or more stupid and barbarous than racism. The last thing I want to be is the King of the Jungle, any jungle, and that includes Boston as much as it does Bujumbura. (39)

Paul Theroux may not wish to be a Tarzan, but the moment he became a white man in Africa he had to work within, or against, the grain of this image, which involuntarily flows over the gendering of every latter day male traveler into Africa. There were aspects of being Tarzan that certainly appealed to Theroux, and may well still make the role attractive—"There was Jane. She aroused me: her enormous breasts strained the makeshift knots on her monkeyskin brazziere" (Theroux, 31).

It is, in fact, Theroux himself, who Mary Louise Pratt gives as an example of the involuntary mastery of foreign, white, male eyes, even after "newly assertive...places and people" have gained their independence:

> Lament as they might, these seeing-men do not relinquish their promontories and their sketch books. ...They are still up there, commanding the view. (1992, 220)

The Theroux of the travel books, of the adventures in far flung places would have little trouble, in fact, identifying with Burroughs's biographer, Porges, who, quite amusingly for us, gives the Pratt scenario, but inverts the politics. He embraces the marvellous possibility of freedom and domination offered by Tarzan. In this he may well be being more honest than the Therouxs who are constrained these days in articulating some of their fantasies:

> The lone man is of course ourselves, the ever-triumphant hero of our daydreams. This Ed understood instinctively, assuming that as he lived vicariously in the role of John Carter or Tarzan, so did others live in their own illusory roles. ...
> There is not a man or woman who occasionally does not like to get away into a more or less primitive wilderness where he is 'monarch of all he surveys'. (133)

Porges may have paid lip service to the possibility of the lone woman, but the reality is that the Tarzan trope, the white man's monarchical gaze over the jungle, is quintessentially about male gendering:

> It is hard to think of a trope more decisively gendered than the monarch-of-all-I-survey scene. Explorer-man paints/possesses newly unveiled landscape-woman. (Pratt, 1992, 213)

I think that an important reason for the survival of the Tarzan trope is that albeit, men like Theroux deny the attraction, Tarzan with his courage and manliness, his muscleman body that wins the gorgeous blond buxom female, continues in quite subtle ways to represent an ideal. This he does in an age when this same white man has lost a lot of ground, body image and sense of identity. Michael Gorra describes his own response to the Tarzan books in terms of "the desire for an Other who is *a perfect reflection of yourself*" (1991, 86, my emphasis). Early on Gorra knew that the Tarzan stories were "Africanist Discourse" that they were about "Africa" in inverted commas and were "set in a sort of generalized jungleland" rather than "a documentary account of African life" and yet he "did not therefore discard them. They satisfied too many of my needs for that" (1991, 87). Those needs include feeling great about your body, your masculinity, your ability to attract and ravish beautiful women, all of which are quite problematic to achieve or even to desire, if you are a white male a hundred years after Tarzan.

Tarzan, moreover, could only be a white hero at the expense of black underlings, who fall into his dazzling shadow and merge into a landscape of brutes, primitives and hairy apes. One of the most problematic and contradictory narrative conventions established by Tarzan discourse is the entwined absence of local African people and the simultaneous implication, sometimes overt, that they are indeed present in the shape of the apes.

Africans and Apes: the Reactionary Tarzan

When Tarzan views 'man' in the form of the local, African inhabitants, he is repulsed by "the low and bestial brutishness of their appearance" (Burroughs, 71):

> Tarzan looked with wonder upon the strange creature beneath him—so like him in form and yet so different in face and colour. His books had portrayed the *negro*, but how different had been the full, dead print to this sleek and hideous thing of ebony, pulsing with life. (Burroughs, 76)

These so-called people are "more wicked than his own apes, and as savage and cruel as Sabor herself. Tarzan began to hold *his own kind* in but low esteem" (Burroughs, 90, my emphasis).

The reality is that these black people, who are rated by Tarzan as lower than the apes, become part of the landscape of Tarzan's jungle and merge in more or less overt ways within tropes based on the Tarzan stories and films.

Apes, gorillas, orang-utans have merged into black Africans in the popular culture and nowhere more suggestively than in the Tarzan seminal myth. As the Jamaican, Neville Farki, insists in his rewrite of the Tarzan story, *The Death of Tarzana Clayton,* the use of apes in Edgar Rice Burroughes's story is a thinly veiled racist metaphor for the Ashanti people, who inhabited that region. This, he says, is "blatant racism" which perpetuates

> the story that Kala was an ape, and the whole tribe of Kerchaki were apes. The idea of a white baby on the breast of the Ashanti woman was to Edgar quite revolting. (32)

Eric Cheyfitz explains that Jane Porter, Tarzan's woman, represents "everything in 'civilization' that must be protected from the *apes and black Africans*" (11, my emphasis). The most resounding unspoken of the Tarzan tradition is this blurred boundary between apes and local, black people. I would suggest that it is impossible to construct enlightened fiction around apes within an African context, without confronting this tradition of blurring the apes and African people head on. This confrontation implies the active obliteration of this fake species marker as well as the illegitimate application of fixed evolutionary scales that are rigged in the favour of Western interests.

These interests, the struggles over lands, wealth and status, are often veiled in the language of universal human histories of evolution. Donna Haraway makes the point about fake universalism, which conceals the European representation of blacks in the guise of apes, when she describes images constructed for a Commonwealth Institute exhibit in London, entitled "The Human Story", as part of the Institute's 1984 Focus on Africa:

> One is a dark ape looking full at the reader, holding a mask in his hand. The mask is of the face of a young white man; beneath the veneer of the white race lies the universal truth of the dark humanoid animal. The eyes that would see out of the eyeholes in the mask are those of the upright apeman, the guarantor of human unity. The story of Tarzan has been evoked by the merest fragments of that important colonial saga. (1989, 190)

The tradition of the buried savageness within and beneath the veneer of white civilization has an inauspicious history. That dark core has been understood metaphorically as the black man/ape—a "dark humanoid animal". We will see the trouble that some writers get into when they retain this paradigm, albeit characterised as something positive, rather than the demonic horror that Kurtz discovers within his own dark heart. In other words, like journeys to Africa, apes, our closest genetic relatives in the animal world, have been used by people to make discoveries about their own makeup. The ape is a catalyst unleashing conscious and unconscious Western associations with universal human origins, race and gender difference, biological and sexual drives, civilization and savagery.

Haraway, building on Edward Said's description of Orientalism, which we discussed in chapter one, coins the term "simian Orientalism" for the ways in which the stories we tell about apes and gorillas frame our thinking about race, gender and imperialism. She suggests that

> Simian orientalism means that western primatology has been about the construction of the self from the raw material of the other, the appropriation of nature in the production of culture, the ripening of the human from the soil of the animal. (1989, 11)

Simians, in other words, are ideal as metaphors for 'primitive' humanity—"traditionally associated with lewd meanings, sexual lust, and the unrestrained body, monkeys and apes mirror humans in a complex play of distortions over centuries of western commentary" (1989, 11). And the humans that they most obviously mirror, these so-called primitive humans, are black Africans, in whose land Tarzan feels free to build his empires, whilst investigating the nature of his own identity.

To sum up and emphasise, if authors suggest this porous boundary between local people and animals, or if novels imply it by not working overtly against the discourse, then they are flawed and tainted.

Is there a Better Tarzan?

Having said this, a question is, what might a better Tarzan, who does not oppress and appropriate, look like? Marianna Torgovnick has some suggestions when she asks us to re-read Tarzan and discover the potentially revolutionary possibilities in his bewildered attempts to assess who and what he is. She suggests we "take Tarzan seriously as an attempt to imagine the primitive as a source of empowerment" (1990, 45). Her argument is that the early Tarzans "expose the shaky basis" of hierarchies, such as "the hierarchy of male over female, white over black, West over rest" (1990, 46). The early Tarzan, "raised in the jungle by apes…quite simply does not know who or what he is" (1990, 47). In this context, Tarzan questions "with shame and confusion…'why don't I look like the other apes?'" and "at moments like these, the Tarzan novels imply that norms and any sense of self and Other are culturally defined" (1990, 48).

Torgovnick is referring to that famous moment of archetypal species confusion in the first Tarzan book. It is the point at which the boy Tarzan sees his reflection in the water and realizes that he does not look at all like his ape family:

> Tarzan was appalled. It had been bad enough to be hairless, but to own such a countenance! He wondered that the other apes could look at him at all.
> That tiny slit of a mouth and those puny white teeth! How they looked beside the mighty lips and powerful fangs of his more fortunate brothers!
> And the little pinched nose of his; so thin was it that it looked half starved. He turned red as he compared it with the beautiful broad nostrils of his companion. Such a generous nose! Why it spread half across his face! It certainly must be fine to be so handsome, thought the poor little Tarzan. (Burroughs, 39)

Torgovnick may be being a little optimistic here. Tarzan may be thrown into identity crisis, but look at the undertow of authorial intervention, where the young, naïve Tarzan's misguidedness is exposed through the mediation of the more knowing omniscient narrator. The reader given a quite different assessment as we are made to picture "the fierce and terrible features of the ape beside those of the aristocratic scion of an old English house" (Burroughs, 39). In other words, we readers are in cahoots with the writer and are less than enamoured of the beauty of "fangs" instead of teeth or of a nose that "spread half across his face".

Torgovnick herself recognises that this fluidity between nature and culture that throws power relations into imbalance and sends the discourse into a spin is a moment only. All too soon "potentially utopian uses of the primitive surrender to uses of the primitive that bolster existing power relations" (1990, 55). What is sadly the case, is that "oneness with animals and with nature is only brief and intermittent in the Tarzan stories and does not drive their plots" (1990, 71). However, Torgovnick does go on to confess that:

> The Tarzan I like best is the doubt-filled Tarzan, willing to learn from blacks and women, willing to ask and examine the question What does a man do? ...For while Tarzan ends by affirming Western hierarchies in his seemingly irresistible urge to rise to the top, he begins by needing to learn what hierarchies exist in the human world and by suppressing his doubts about their inevitability and basis. (1990, 70)

What Torgovnick appears to be suggesting is that what is interesting and meaningful is precisely the instability and contradictoriness of the stories. Furthermore, what she implies is that the stories are compelling and enduring precisely because they work in this tense zone of confusion and disorder:

> The books loath colonialism and imperialism, and yet they valorize ideas that made (and make) Euro-American colonialism and imperialism possible. (1990, 62)

Ultimately—and this crescendos Torgovnick's celebration of the Tarzan oeuvre—"the books are as contradictory and double as our culture is, as confused as Tarzan himself is" (1990, 62). This identity crisis is certainly symptomatic of our times and gives rise to the suggestion that the postmodern Tarzan may be either white or black, part of a new class of cosmopolitans with splintered identities, so much a product of our times.

Michael Gorra, in similar vein, describes Conrad, for whom English was a third language as a "translated man", not unlike Rushdie or Naipaul, and says that in this regard, he is "a forerunner of the postcolonial writer" (1991, 88). To cut race out of the equation, however, is to ignore the power imbalance inherent in the figure of the aristocratic white man, who lords it over savage black people wearing the grotesque masks of apes. This history of racism and expropriation makes Tarzan's journey to the jungle a profoundly different one from that undertaken by African writers and intellectuals to the Metropole, although there may be meeting points along their differing journeys.

I would, rather, like to suggest that in the character of Tarzan, we can identify not the dilemmas of a Rushdie or a Soyinka, but an intriguing foreshadowing of his white sons, some of whom were also born in Africa. These sons of Tarzan also clear the bush and construct a path between England and the interior of Africa and back again, as they write their novels with African settings and translate and interpret this continent for a European audience. In so doing they are on that razor edge between facilitating understanding and betrayal, as Janus faced they look in both directions simultaneously, speak with forked tongues and deny their white fathers, whilst speaking a version of their language.

This confusion will certainly be familiar as we travel with T. Coraghessan Boyle and William Boyd, Will Self and Peter Høeg, back and forth between England, America and the jungle, real and imagined. These journeys, moreover, are charted in quite fundamental ways by the white woman in Tarzan's life. They are journeys whose perils and unpredictable destinations are multiplied by the fact that in our times there is not one Jane, but two.

The Two Janes

There is the original Jane of the Jungle, whose distress enables the heroic Tarzan to fulfil his function as saviour and in the process to display his built male body in all its perfection:

> Jane Porter—her lithe, young form flattened against the trunk of a great tree, her hands tight pressed against her rising and falling bosom, and her eyes wide with mingled horror, fascination, fear, and admiration—watched the primordial ape battle with the primeval man for possession of a woman—for her. (Burroughs, 171)

What has changed is late twentieth century woman—liberated, intellectual and unwilling to be saved by a Rambo, Tarzan or Schwarzenegger. The symbolic shorthand for this new woman in the latter day Tarzan story is Jane Goodall. This is so because she came to Africa, worked with the apes and shares a name with Tarzan's woman. This has not gone unnoticed by writers of fiction, as we shall see.

This female metamorphosis has, of course, had dramatic effects on the self- image of the musclemen of old. And all this is not to say that strains of the old Jane (albeit eternally young and desirable) are not echoing in the fantasy chambers of modern, Western man.

A version of these two Janes mingling into one is put forward by Donna Haraway in her critique of the media portrayal of Jane Goodall's research among the chimpanzees in the Gombe National Park of Tanzania. She suggests that Goodall, and the other famous female primatologists, like Dian Fossey and Berute Galdikas, may have been scientists, scholars and professionals, but they nonetheless played the role of messengers and go-

The Battered Boys of Rice Burroughs

betweens for the white men, who in post-imperial times have been expelled from the jungle. Latter day Tarzans have had enough of the industrialised polluted west and want to return, but have become somewhat out of touch with new conditions in a jungle taken over by black Africans speaking a new language, that of Independence. These women represent the possibility of resurrection:

> She is his surrogate. It is he who has been excluded from 'nature' by both history and a Greek-Judeo Christian myth system; and more immediately, he is being thrown out of the garden by decolonization and perhaps off the planet by its destruction in ecological devastation and nuclear holocaust. It is time to call in *the blond and female* mediator to negotiate the discourses of exterminism and extinction in space and the jungle. (Haraway, 1989, 152, my emphasis)

Or, as Evelyn Fox Keller points out, the indeterminate status of women position them as mediators "between man and nature, and between animate and inanimate" (70). However, these blond, female intermediaries, who retain overtones of Jane of the jungle, have reversed her role. Now, an emasculated Tarzan has to depend upon a new Jane to enable him to embark on his adventures.

Torgovnick contests this image of the old Jane as embodied in the new— "if these women [primatologists] began by being perceived as 'virgins in the forest,' chastely mediating between culture and nature, each in her own way became incompatible with that narrative" (1997, 105). She suggests that Haraway does not give enough credit for the ways in which these women, like Fossey and Goodall, refused the gender roles laid down for them of dependent wives, nurturing mothers and powerless victims (1997, 104).

Most importantly, however, the pivotal difference in Torgovnick's and Haraway's emphases relates to Haraway's insistence that what is crucially omitted from the narrative of primatologists, like Jane Goodall, is the "people of Tanzania" who "disappear in a story in which the actors are the anthropoid apes and a young British white woman engaged in a thoroughly modern sacred secular drama" (1992, 307). In other words, "the white hand obliterates once again the invisible bodies of people of color, who have never counted as able to represent humanity in Western iconography" (1992, 308).

The primatologists are characterised in the media, and represent themselves, as intrepid and brave females, alone in the wilds of Africa, albeit that they were surrounded by black men. The absence of these men is as always present in menacing sexual innuendo. As Jill LeBihan states in her paper entitled "Gorilla Girls and Chimpanzee Mothers" and in which she refers to the writing of these scholars:

> Miscegenation is the suppressed horror within these texts. Whilst the all important contact, the touch, between ape and woman is emphasized, the relationships between the women and their African co-workers are always underplayed. (146)

What is indeed clear from the original Tarzan, is that when Jane is kidnapped by a hairy Other, the danger is her sexual violation by a foreign species, ape or African:

> He threw her roughly across his broad, hairy shoulders, and leaped back into the trees, bearing Jane Porter away toward a fate a thousand times worse than death. (Burroughs, 168)

And in this theme of kidnap, there is another suggestive, albeit coincidental correlation between the two Janes. Jane Goodall, working in Gombe Reserve in Tanganyika, had to close up in 1975 as a result of the kidnapping of four students by guerrillas from Zaire (Haraway, 1989, 167). This real live kidnap on the part of black guerrillas resonates with the Tarzan myth of the seizure of Jane by the apes. We will be watching Boyd's fictional account of this kidnap very closely in the next chapter. And later in this chapter, we will see some interesting fictional role reversals in this escape triangle in which the players are the white man and woman and a dark, hairy humanoid, part ape, part man. This manipulation of the species of ape leads to quite another issue—if the metaphorical merging of apes and blacks is unconscionable, then what also of the literal existence of primates as animals in their own right?

Apes not as Tropes

Torgovnick may be on stronger grounds when she admires the 1984 film of the Tarzan story entitled *Greystoke: The Story of Tarzan*. This is so, I think, less because it portrays a revolutionary Tarzan, than because of its sensitive portrayal of the apes, as beings with their own autonomous lives:

> The most remarkable part of the movie is its opening—long sequences without language that show Tarzan being raised by apes and entering into intimate, loving relations with them. This Tarzan...acts completely within ape norms. (1990, 71)

Of course there *is* language in that opening sequence. It is ape sign language and not English and that is the whole point. The ape norms, which truly prevail, are not human and the film retains a consistent line that this ape society, integrated into and harmonious with its environment, is superior to the rapacious and cruel human, Western and 'scientific' way of life:

The Battered Boys of Rice Burroughs 113

> The movie's turning point...comes when Tarzan finds his stepfather among the apes brutalized in scientific experiments and helps him to escape. When the ape is killed by policemen, Tarzan's commitment to English culture vanishes; knowing this, Jane releases him back to Africa, and we last see him re-entering the forest to rejoin the apes among whom he was reared. This Tarzan has learned the only serious lesson Burroughs was ever willing to draw from his Tarzan series: the lesson that man alone among living creatures kills wantonly and that comparisons between men and beasts often insult the latter. (Torgovnick, 1990, 71)

Apes are not metaphors here, nor are they caricatures of humans. Haraway too insists on giving animals literal existence as social players in their own right:

> I want to use the beady little eyes of a laboratory mouse to stare back at my fellow mammals, my hominid kin, as they incubate themselves and their human and nonhuman offspring in a technoscientific culture medium. (1997a, 211)

Again we encounter the minefield of the metaphoric and the suggestion by Haraway is that what we have to do is to break the chain that links "people of colour, nature, workers, animals—in short, domination of all constituted as others, whose task is to mirror the self" (1991, 177). Rendered undignified and anthropomorphic, invaded in their habitats, these creatures are too often manipulated and abused.

This question of the human attitude to the apes is an area that we will see some of the writers taking up. The difficulty, as always, arises from the narrative traditions that have used and abused Third World people as well as animals in so many different ways that it is dangerous for a novel to situate itself anywhere within this figurative minefield. In fact, I think that the apes are key to what gives the Tarzan tropes their potency and their pitfalls. They are creatures that appear to occupy a kind of buffer zone between the human and the animal. And this leads to a creature of fabulation, a powerful trope of recent times, which has particular resonance in this part of the book, but which will recur. I am referring to the cyborg.

Cyborgs, Mutants and Hybrids

I have been suggesting that the porous boundary between ape and black person is embedded in the Tarzan tradition and is the biggest obstacle to writers, who are battling to resist the entrenched discourse. Donna Haraway would undoubtedly agree. However, looked at from another angle, she attempts to erase the tradition by viewing that space differently. What if Jane willingly coupled with the ape and produced a mutant, a new being, who had crossed over species and prejudice? Haraway herself insists that "I have always preferred the prospect of pregnancy with the embryo of another species" (1989, 377). Can we see a way of developing Haraway's belief in the saving power of the concept of the cyborg, as a mechanism to rescue us from the tentacles of racism and sexism that bedevils and feeds the Tarzan, Jane and Ape stories? She is hopeful that the image of apes and chimps can provide a solution to the horrors performed in the name of so-called ethnic cleansing. This they may do because "primates"

> existing at the boundaries of so many hopes and interests are wonderful subjects with whom to explore the permeability of walls, the reconstitution of boundaries. (Haraway, 1989, 3)

Haraway wishes "to set new terms for the traffic between what we have come to know historically as nature and culture" (1989, 15). Setting new terms for the traffic does not mean, for Haraway, "policing the boundaries between nature and culture—quite the opposite". She is "edified by the traffic" (1989, 377). In other words, if Darwinian theory evoked Victorian terror in response to the suggestion that all species are related, raising the spectre of "interdependence between beauty and beast" and of the possibility of "miscegeny—the frog in the bed" (Beer, 9 & 117), or the ape and Jane miscegenating in the tree, then Haraway invites the frog, the computer chip, the Martian, right into the hotbed of Western prejudice and celebrates the mutants that emerge with new stories to tell us.

Haraway's now famous "A Cyborg Manifesto: Science, Technology, and Socialist-Feminism in the Late Twentieth Century" defines the cyborg as "a hybrid of machine and organism". In other words, cyborgs are "creatures simultaneously animal and machine" (1991, 149) and in so being, they are simultaneously socially real and fictional and "populate worlds ambiguously natural and crafted" (1991, 149). In fact, the code organising the cyborg's changing identities is that of the boundary breakdowns she so admires, of which Haraway signals in particular three crucial examples—between human and animal, between organism and machine and between physical and non-physical, being both real and virtual reality (1991, 151, 152, 153). Moreover, this definition and discussion of cyborgs, far from being a diversion from the concerns of this chapter, will intriguingly follow us through the fiction under discussion as a recurring image, mingling with latter day Tarzans, Janes and Apes.

According to Haraway, as ape transmogrifies into cyborg, that dimension of Western culture, which has been organically implicated in essentialism, racism, sexism, colonialism, plunder and butchery, is offered the utopian dream of regeneration. She attempts to erase the terror of cross species mating evoked by Tarzan and to invent new stories of constructed, hybrid,

The Battered Boys of Rice Burroughs 115

origins from which creatures—vampires, coyotes, tricksters and cyborgs—are born:

> Who are my kin in this odd world of promising monsters, vampires, surrogates, living tools, and aliens? How are natural kinds identified in the realms of late-twentieth-century technoscience? What kinds of crosses and offspring count as legitimate and illegitimate? Who are my familiars, my siblings, and what kind of livable world are we trying to build? (1997b, 211)

The error that Haraway makes, however, is the same one she herself warned us about earlier, of not sufficiently taking into account the history of exploitation, unequal power and expropriation of land. When Haraway constructs a cyborg from an ape and a machine, what emerges all to often looks remarkably like Arnold Schwarzenegger in *The Terminator*, or, even more tellingly for our purposes, like Johnny Weissmuller in any number of Tarzan films. Haraway herself in her Cyborg Manifesto concedes that:

> from one perspective, a cyborg world is about the final imposition of a grid of control on the planet, about the final abstraction embodied in a Star Wars apocalypse waged in the name of defense, about the final appropriation of women's bodies in a masculinist orgy of war. (1991, 154)

This cyborg world is not usually Haraway's, which tends to be gendered black and female, redressing cruel power imbalances and forging alliances with new kin. It is more "the stupefying overstuffed and intransigent figure of former bodybuilder Arnold Schwarzenegger" who is "*both* Barbarian...and Cyborg" (Pfeil, 1995, 30–31). Or, as Katherine Hayles explains:

> The reality is that the cyborg has already been appropriated by multinational corporations as they proceed to implement more de-skilling of human labor, more interlocking of data networks, more development of space weapons, and more uncontrollable defense systems. (284)

Fred Pfeil sums up the dangers, but hints at possibilities, on which I too do not wish to foreclose at this point:

> If, given *the omnipresence of power relations* and our being within historical time, no psycho-social body is ever finally closed, no imaginary ever complete or fully resolved, it is nonetheless possible—and, for radicals, arguably necessary—to be aware *when certain bodies are mutating, and which social-symbolic imaginaries are disturbed and up for grabs.* (1995, 32–3, my emphases)

We will see bodies mutate in the rest this chapter and the next, and we will attempt to understand the consequences of these transformations in the light of the past and present relations of power, within African settings.

Man Descending: T. Coraghessan Boyle's Tales

"I reflected that this was not the Jane I knew and loved". (*Descent of Man*, 8–9)

The title of T. Coraghessan Boyle's collection, *Descent of Man*, (1987) could sum up the core issue of the stories and novels we will be touching upon. For once 'man' does not refer to humanity in general, but the 'descent' refers quite precisely to the downfall of the Western male—"Descent of Man" plays on Darwin's evolutionary scale as the apes move up and human males decline in physical and mental prowess.

We saw in chapter two that Boyle began his novelistic explorations in search of his identity by way of the journey to Africa with Mungo Park and Ned Rise. Mungo may have been searching for the source of the River Niger, but Coraghessan Boyle was seeking his own origins and an understanding of the nature of his masculinity within the context of the many persona that characterised him. Likewise, Boyle may here caricature and parody both the men and women in his stories, stories, which are very funny, but he seriously grapples in them with major issues of gender and identity. Again we will see how he emphasises the ways in which white men and women sand and polish their gender desires, struggles and dislocations against the rough surfaces of black people, of the Other, from faraway places.

The story plots the disintegration of the relationship between the first person narrator and his partner, who works in a primate centre. The partner, who is significantly called Jane Good, is the first of the fictional primatologists that we will be encountering in this and the next chapter, based on the real life Jane Goodall.

Jane "suddenly began to stink" as the story opens (1987, 3). The stench of apes is a focus in both of Boyle's ape stories. Their stench is masculinity in the raw and when Jane begins to stink, "the stink of her, bestial and fetid" (1987,4) is her contamination by her attraction to an ape, in preference to her partner, the first person protagonist of the story. The animal inside this white male is aroused by the stink and bestiality that invades their home and he is visited by the animal instinct to mark out his territory by weeing:

> One evening, just after her bath (the faintest odor lingered, yet still it was so trenchant I had to fight the impulse to get up and urinate on a tree or a post or something). ...(1987, 4)

We will see later that even his ability to urinate is undermined by the ape as Jane becomes sucked into the way of life of the primate. She eats insects buried in her naval, stops washing and eventually leaves her peeved and increasingly belittled boyfriend for the ape, significantly named Konrad.

Before this happens, the narrator goes to pick Jane up at the Primate Center, which was a former school, and steps into what is literally the "BOYS' ROOM" (1987, 5). This setting highlights the physiological transformations in the hierarchy as the narrator struggles to wee in a situation where "the urinals were a foot and a half from the floor" (1987, 5). The chimpanzee, who is short but massively strong

> opened his fly and pulled out an enormous slick red organ like a peeled banana. I looked away, embarrassed, but could hear him urinating mightily. (1987, 5)

By contrast:

> My own water wouldn't come. I began to feel foolish. The chimp shook himself daintily, zippered up, pulled the plunger, crossed to the sink, washed and dried his hands, and left. I found I no longer had to go. (1987, 5)

The silly white man, with his little prick, by comparison with the "enormous slick red organ", is further humiliated by the janitor in a reversal of fortune that is sexual, racial and class-based. In case readers might imagine that the bodily decline of this white man is compensated for by his class and education, we are in for a surprise. The white, intellectual man is being supplanted in every way. The janitor of the Center, forms a friendship and alliance with the ape. They joke and chat together in chimp sign language enabling the janitor to become an articulate intellectual, as he explains to our bewildered protagonist:

> Yo sees, Mastuh Konrad is sumfin ob a genius round here. He can commoonicate de most esoteric i-deas in bof ASL and Yerkish, re-spond to and translate English, French, German and Chinese. Fack, it was Miz Good was tellin me dat Konrad is workin right now on a Yerkish translation ob Darwin's *De-scent o Man*. ...Dis lass fall he done undertook a Yerkish translation ob Chomsky's *Language and Mind* and Nietzsche's *Jensits von Gut und Bose*. And dat's some pretty heavy shit, Jackson. (1987, 7)

The context of the story is that North American men, like our poor narrator, have become reconstituted males. They have relationships with women who are their intellectual equals and who run careers. When Jane decides to invite the ape home to dinner, she leaves a note for her partner instructing him to "vacuum rug and clean toilet" (1987, 12). This manly, virile ape brings out the feminine in Jane and she cooks for him. He eats a massive meal and then sits listening to *Don Giovanni*, whilst sipping brandy. He is the king and although only "four eight and three quarters" in height, weighs "one eight-one" while the diminished narrator weighs only "one forty-three" (1987, 14). The implication surely is, that if men regained their potency and power, their women would once again service their needs and bow to their massive members. The next day Jane moves out.

Boyle uses the fortuitous coincidence that Tarzan's Jane and Jane Goodall share a name. This connection enables him to overturn the Tarzan story of Western culture. The narrator, searching in Jane's stuff for clues to the meaning of her departure, finds her "Edgar Rice Burroughs collection" on her bookshelf (1987, 15). When he goes looking for her at the primate center, he learns that she has run away to the ape, who eventually rescues her from our diminutive Tarzan, who is dumped, demeaned and maybe even dies. In a radical reversal of the original, the ape saves Jane from Tarzan and finally stands even taller than him:

> I grabbed Jane. But Konrad was there in an instant—he hit me like the grill of a Cadillac and I spun across the room, tumbling desks and chairs as I went. I slumped against the chalkboard. The door slammed: Jane was gone. Konrad swelled his chest, swayed toward me, the fluorescent lights hissing overhead, the chalkboard cold against the back of my neck. And I looked up into the black eyes, teeth, fur, rocked-ribbed arms. (1987, 16)

Thus ends the story and leaves the question of why Boyle named his ape Konrad, both in this and the second story, which we will come to in a moment. I would like to suggest that, like the two Janes, whose fortuitous shared name enables connections to be made when they are put alongside each other, there are two Konrads. Spelled with a 'K' it is the Polish version of Conrad's middle name. It is also the first name of a famous scientist, called Konrad Lorenz. Lorenz won a Nobel Prize "in recognition of his development of the science of ethnology" (Editor, *Animal People*, 1). He pioneered the resistance to cruelty and killing in the study of these animals and insisted that most could be learnt by examining them in their own environment and disrupting their way of life as little as possible (Editor, *Animal People*, 2). Thus, his research was the inspiration behind the encouragement of woman field biologists, who were previously "almost unheard of" and included none other than "Jane Goodall, Dian Fossey, and Berute Galdikas" (Editor, *Animal People*, 2).

What is the significance of this double naming? In the sense that this ape is named after the creator of *Heart of Darkness*, he is the unconscious white male terror of the black man's superior sexual prowess and also of the existence of deep, untapped savagery and sexuality within himself. All of this suggests another level at which to read this story. Could it not have arisen as a nightmare, a horrible fantasy of the narrator? He may well find his partner's absorption in her work threatening and competing with the time and energy available to him. He certainly feels unmanned by this new woman, who induces the repressed cultural terrors of King Kong competitors with gigantic penises, and even superior minds.

At the same time, and this qualifier is crucial, by naming the ape in this way, Boyle caricatures the seriousness of Conrad's tale and distances himself from the protagonist of the story, who is held in its sway. Boyle reminds us that what he is describing is part of the discourse to which we succumb, even while realizing that Edgar Rice Burroughs and Joseph Conrad were simply (or complicatedly) story-tellers. In this sense Boyle is making a critique of the power of these stories and how they destroy all who imbibe their archetypes.

If Conrad's tale establishes a dark savageness at the heart of man, metaphorically visualised as Africa, then Konrad Lorenz suggested that this savagery can be socially moderated. Lorenz's seminal work, *On Aggression* (1966), expressed the belief in the innate core of violence, hunting, killing and war-mongering in the male of our human species, but softened this proposal with a degree of optimism about man's ability to change his nature. In other words, Lorenz did think that "present-day civilized man suffers from insufficient discharge of his aggressive drive" (209) but he also believed that "individuals of an aggressive species" could learn "to live peacefully together" (258).

"Descent of Man" illustrates the ambivalence on the part of men like Boyle with regard to the consequences, the wages of virtue, for these reconstituted, new, gentler men who vacuum and clean and then lose their women to the older styled, aggressive, big balled apemen. Furthermore, we will see in the next story that Boyle is of the opinion that these soft men have merely repressed their aggression, which potentially erupts in violent and terrible ways.

This confusion is fuelled, as Boyle is aware, with his Janes and Konrads and echoing Tarzans, by the power of colonialist discourse to continue to peddle its tropes. The culture's big books, the *Tarzans of the Apes,* the *Hearts of Darkness*, survive on dusty bookshelves, and continue, for all the dust, to fuel the nightmares of these hapless males whose unconscious terrors return to haunt them. Animals, abused and manipulated as metaphors for man, as objects of dubious scientific experimentation, find champions among more gentle researchers, both men and women, who recognise the rights of those beady eyed rats to look back and face their laboratory tormentors. All these fortuitously shared names come together in the postmodern pastiche favoured by late twentieth century artists. They develop in their contiguity a symbolic significance reserved in the older days for more meaningful metaphoric links. And all this metonymic splitting and pasting echoes the lack of a solid self-identity that so characterises our millennial moment.

If males are so split, moreover, then this is at least partly so because of their ambivalence towards the transformation that they perceive within women. Given Boyle's complex and ambivalent attitude to the ways in which woman affect their men, however, I think the story expresses his own genuine fears about where men like himself stand within the new roles played by women. The portrait of woman who are themselves the adventurers, intellectuals, explorers and bread winners, do not come off well, as already seen in the portrait of the smelly, distant and cruel Jane Good. This we will see even more clearly in relation to the depiction of "the ape lady," of a different Boyle story, the primatologist who has returned to America from Africa in her old age.

In "The Ape Lady in Retirement", Beatrice Umbo, "the celebrated ape lady, the world's foremost authority on the behavior of chimpanzees in the wild," has "come home to Connecticut to retire" (Boyle, 1989, 194) after forty years in Africa at the Makoua Reserve. ('Beatrice' may have overtones of 'Berute' as in Galdikas). She is utterly miserable and totally unable to relocate—Africa has in a real sense become her home and the chimps, her family.

She encounters a young man in the supermarket, who is a devotee of her work. She is taken with this man because he reminds her of a favourite chimp, Agassiz:

> It was his grin, the way his upper lip pulled back from his teeth and folded over his incisors. He was Agassiz, the very picture of Agassiz. (1989, 194, my emphasis)

Howie, as ape man, is emphasised throughout the story:

> This hulking, earnest college boy, this big post-adolescent male with the clipped brow and squared shoulders, and she beamed at him till her gums ached, wondering what he'd think if she told him he reminded her of a chimp. (1989, 196)

Howie may remind Beatrice of Agassiz, but the ape that figures in this story is our old friend Konrad. To find out more about Howie and his destiny, therefore, we need to examine what has happened to Konrad since the earlier story, given that Konrad is that part of Howie that is an ape, a male animal.

Boyle often uses a device, one that enacts his message, which is to have more than one character to explore the nature of a single split individual. We saw him split himself into his warring parts in a range of characters in *Water Music*. In "The Ape Lady in Retirement", the two characters that together constitute Boyle's portrayal of modern man are Howie and Konrad, the ape.

This should not be understood crudely, however, and there is an aspect to this story that decries the abuse of animals as animals, on the part of humans. Konrad is both literal animal and symbolic of the male of the human species.

Konrad is coming not just for dinner this time, but he has come to stay. He is an old friend of Beatrice. She had described him in the wild and she is now taking him on to save him from the zoo. Beatrice is horrified to find Konrad, when he arrives, is dressed like a human and supplied with American junk food. Konrad, like late twentieth century man, has been domesticated, manipulated and lost his sense of identity.

The double significance of Konrad as both literal animal and metaphoric man, becomes clear in the passionate, un-satirised description of his history:

> Raised as a human, in one of those late-sixties experiments Beatrice deplored, he'd been bathed, dressed, and pampered, taught to use cutlery and sit at a table, and he'd mastered 350 of the hand signals that constituted American Sign Language. ...But when he grew into puberty at the age of seven, when he developed the iron musculature and crackling sinews of the adolescent male who could reduce a room of furniture to detritus in minutes or snap the femur of a linebacker as if it were tinder, it was abruptly decided that he could be human no more. They took away his trousers and shoes, his stuffed toys and his color TV, and the overseers of the experiment made a quiet move to shift him to the medical laboratories for another, more sinister, sort of research. But he was famous by then and the public outcry landed him in the zoo instead, where they made a sort of clown of him, isolating him from the other chimps and dressing him up like something in a toy store window. There he'd languished for twenty-five years, *neither chimp nor man*. (1989, 198, my emphasis)

If Konrad has become partly man, the sad male whose wildness has been domesticated, then the story also takes pity on him as an animal, a wild creature of nature subjected to the cruelty and abuse of humans. In an interview, in fact, Boyle explains that he "might have been a biologist if it weren't for all the technical aspects" as he has "a tremendous love for animals and nature" (in Adams, 55).

However, the overtones of the fate of Western masculinity embodied in the ape as metaphor are undeniable. We have already seen in chapter two that the sixties was a crucial era in Boyle's own political growth and subject formation. This was the era in which males were shaken up in the crucible of feminist liberation and compelled to re-think their domestic roles, their fathering and their macho masculinity. Men like Boyle, who were young at that time are now assessing the longer-term consequences of their reconstitution and not altogether liking what they find. Beneath the benign and infantile love Konrad harbours for cheese nachos and sugar daffies, lies his dangerously repressed masculinity. And in all of this, according to Boyle, late twentieth century woman has a lot to answer for.

And so, what has happened to Jane Good after her long career as primatologist, to Beatrice Umbo, now in retirement? Beatrice, bloodsucker, is described as focusing her gaze on Konrad with her "bright narrow eyes",

> the eyes that had captured every least secret of his wild cousins, the rapt unblinking eyes of *the professional voyeur*. (1989, 199, my emphasis)

Here we have a hint as to the 'Umbo' part of her name. Otto Umbehr, a man, note, otherwise known as Umbo, was a famous photographer working in the late nineteen twenties and thirties. Beatrice Umbo is the butch voyeur, who does not stop watching and judging:

> She was absorbed in the dynamics of the crowd, listening to their chatter, observing their neck craning and leg crossing, watching the furtive plumbing of nostrils and sniffing of armpits, the obsessive fussing with hair and jewellery. (1989, 205)

She is observing this crowd at a public lecture she gives at the State University. She is a miserable, isolated human being. The intellectual woman is shrill, asexual, friendless and critical of humanity in general. She looks at her audience and all she can see are "blank-faced housewives and their paunchy husbands, bearded professors, breast-thumping students" (1989, 205). She has denied her femininity and is unable to make herself attractive:

> She'd debated wearing one of the crepe-de-chine dresses her sister had left hanging forlornly in the closet, but in the end she decided to stick with the safari shorts. (1989, 205)

Beatrice may have rejected the particular kind of experimentation to which Konrad has been subjected, but, as a fellow scientist and a bossy woman, she is culpable in rendering Konrad split and reduced. Boyle, it is true, would probably concur with Beatrice that "chimps had an innate dignity, an eloquence that had nothing to do with sign language, gabardine, color TV, or nacho chips" (1989, 200). The conundrum, however, is that her solution is part of the problem, as the powerful woman dominates and dictates to her man—"she was determined to restore [his innate dignity] to him" (1989, 200). She will ration his television viewing and his junk food consumption, like the good mother she is. Her sentiments regarding Konrad's animal rights are fine, but the problem is that she colludes with his domestication even as she rejects it, in her imperious sense of ownership over him—"she wouldn't have one of her chimps responding to human language either, as if he were some fawning lapdog or neutered cat" (1989, 203). She refuses him his junk food and he is utterly dejected, and, note, infantilised, "pinning Beatrice with an accusatory look, a look that had nacho chips and Fruit Roll-Ups written all over it" (1989, 208). She, however, is firm:

> They'd make him *schizophrenic*—neither chimp nor man—and if there was pain involved in reacquainting him with his roots, with his true identity, there was nothing she could do about it. (1989, 208, my emphasis)

No longer a fantasy embedded in the unconscious of the latter day Tarzan, he is that diminished splintered, schizophrenic late twentieth century man himself. Again, woman is also debased in this descent of man. Beatrice describes herself in the process also as feeling schizophrenic, missing Africa as she does (1989, 208).

At this crucial point, Howie arrives to fulfil his offer of taking Beatrice up in his Cessna plane. He cannot say "no" to the domineering female, the *manvrou* Beatrice, who decides to bring the chimp along for the ride, although Howie clearly has his reservations (1989, 209). Howie, in other words, is in the thrall of the dominating woman and what the story makes clear is that modern man himself is in an identity crisis, neither wild nor domesticated. There is great ominousness in the air created by the cocktail of ape stench and euphoria.

Konrad and Howie end up fighting for the controls of the plane, in a gross male power struggle in which Konrad is "gibbering and hooting and loosing his bowels in a frenzy" (1989, 211). Howie, meanwhile, "was working up a frenzy of his own" (1989, 211). In a gorgeous line, comedy gives way, as only Boyle can make it do, in a moment of horrific clarity on Beatrice's part—"Howie hit [Konrad] again and Beatrice knew she was going to die" (1989, 212). More horror follows as bits of Howie are torn off. Then a rather wonderful, peaceful, utterly macabre kind of suicide pact between the dislocated woman and the fractured chimp/male brings dignity to both at the climax of the story. Instead of the emasculating voyeuristic gaze of the female, the ape becomes the viewer—"Konrad was looking into her eyes" (1989, 212). There is five hours of flying time and Beatrice makes no effort to learn to land the plane. Konrad at this point discards the undignified human behaviour he has been taught. Cigarettes forgotten, sign language abandoned, he speaks to Beatrice in his own language "'*Urk*'" (1989, 212) and she replies in like manner—the story ends—"She reached out and touched his hand. '*Urk*,' she said" (1989, 213).

This ending is a tragic paradox. They can discover wholeness only by dying and taking Howie with them. And trailing, nibbling away at the wise understanding of the abuse of animals in experimentation is Konrad as a man, finally bringing his woman to heel, taking charge and thereby healing them both of their schizophrenia. This the new man in Boyle knows to be a fantasy and one into which he only partially buys.

Furthermore, Boyle's recourse to fantasy solutions of spiritual recovery in a faraway place called Africa carries political penalties. Beatrice Umbo can only be healed by way of a surrealistic, kamikaze act identification with a mythical Africa, which has become her true home and where she had not been schizophrenic. Only flying wildly in the aeroplane, reminiscent of her flights in Africa can she begin "to feel almost whole for the first time since she'd left Makoua" (1989, 210).

We will encounter flying in planes as a significant symbol again in the next chapter. We have already seen in chapter two how Boyle's persona, Ned Rise from *Water Music*, opted never to return to London from an idealised life close to the soil of Africa. We will see again in another part of this book, a similar tradition within gay fantasies. This transference onto a mythical Africa, which is not dark, but lit up with the utopian resolution of the tensions of Western life, is as problematic as the heart of darkness. It does not break the paradigm of Africa as manipulated figuratively to serve Western desires and it denies Africa's concrete and diverse existence.

Simultaneously, in another order of splitting, Konrad is this time an abused laboratory rat animal much more fully than he was in the previous story. If the story has any hope or solution, it is not in relation to the problems besetting masculinity. It is in terms of the treatment of animals, whose dignity has been eroded. This is the only way to understand the significance of the ending of the story when Konrad returns Beatrice's gaze and they speak in his language.

What this story illustrates is that both men and women in America in the late twentieth century have become schizophrenic, in the popular (and medically incorrect definition) sense of the word—that is to say, split personalities. Neither wild animals nor fully domesticated, they are estranged from themselves. In this motif, this story anticipates Boyle's most recent novel, *Riven Rock* (1998).

Schizophrenic Man as a Riven Rock and Some Conclusions

Riven Rock fictionalises the true-life story of Stanley McCormick, a schizophrenic, for whom any contact with the female species is utterly disastrous. Schizophrenic Konrad, the ape, anticipated this novel that explores man's split personality in the image of the rock that is riven in two. Another interesting link between the story and the novel is that Agassiz, Beatrice's favourite ape in "The Ape Lady in Retirement", is named after the famous biologist, Louis Agassiz, who explained the formation of an atypical rock fragment "that differs from the local bedrock," as an *erratic* (*Britannica*, no. 4, 548). Man's erratic/schizophrenic behaviour likened to a rock implies that the core of man's deepest nature is being dangerously altered, split and deformed. This quite problematic and essentialised metaphor, taken from nature's landscape, is buttressed by the use of apes, evolution and biology, to express the fractured condition of people in the late twentieth century.

Riven Rock is not set in Africa, but deals so substantially with all the issues of masculinity, apes, splitting and the new woman, who is invariably a biologist, that it does bear brief treatment here. Stanley, like our new men, hates and despises traditional, macho males,

> men, with their hairy wrists and bludgeoning eyes, their nagging phlegmy voices and fetid breath and the viscid sweat that glistened in their beards and darkened their shirts under the arms. (1998, 4)

However, given that Stanley is also a man, this horror of men results in self-hatred and loss of identity. At the acute stage of the onset of his illness, he looks into the mirror "and there was nothing there. No one. No person" (1998, 219). Dr Hamilton, who sets up a bizarre colony of apes within the huge estate, Riven Rock, in which Stanley is incarcerated, seeks a cure via the comparison between human and primate behaviour. Ape book open, he explains that Stanley's mind "has been split down the middle" (1998, 59). It is clear that the riven rock of the title is a metaphor for Stanley's insanity— "the massive slab of sandstone girding the tree was split in two" (1998, 125).

Stanley's split, once again in Boyle, is linked his repressed manliness, the "dark place inside him" that hates his man's anatomy and regards "his penis" as "some terrible uncontainable thing" (1998, 116). This dark place is the raw ape-like sexuality of the man. Chapter seven, echoing Burroughs, is entitled "STANLEY OF THE APES" (1998, 128). In this significant chapter, which ends the first part of the novel, Stanley is seen escaping from his room—"clambering down the drainpipe with all the agility of a, well, of a *hominoid*" (1998, 154). Eddie, his keeper, searches for him, amidst the stench and fucking of the monkeys and with uncharacteristic delicacy Boyle hints that he finds him in a tree coupling with Julius. There is Stanley, the "naked one, white as any ghost" and the ape, "the shaggy hunkering split-faced one, and their hands moving each at the place where the other's legs intersected" (1998, 158).

If Stanley is Konrad, the ape, the wild, schizophrenic side of the human, then Eddie is Howie, the human male, whose own violence towards women and splintered personality is more concealed. Boyle uses Mungo Park, Ned Rise, Howie and Eddie, among many others, in order to explore his own masculinity. What is telling is that while Stanley and Katherine are given their true-life names in the novel, Eddie, who is "presumably modelled on

McCormick's real-life attendant, Kenneth McKillip", is "one of the only characters in the novel whose name has been changed" (Kurth, 2). And that fictional name is Eddie O'Kane—of Irish background and an abuser of alcohol—sure signs of Boyle's autobiographical identification with this character, as discussed in chapter two. He even shares a version of a name with the *Water Music* character, Ned Rise.

Eddie too is split between his human kindness and compassion in his job of caring for the mentally ill and his repressed ape-male sexuality that makes him a philanderer and even a rapist. For example, Eddie is getting drunk in a bar when he sees the woman with whom he had cheated on his wife back home. Eddie has no claim on this woman to whom he has no commitment. She is there with another man, who "had his arm around her shoulder" (1998, 142). A jealous, territorial, sexually aroused Eddie, walks up to them "and tore the arm off Giovannella's shoulder as he might have stripped a dead limb from a tree" (1998, 143). His glare is "lunatic" (1998, 143)—like the mad Stanley's? His voice lowers "to a primal growl"—like an ape's? And the woman "fought him every inch of the way" as he abducts her and rapes her. The primal, male force in him makes his hands "unconquerable" and "there was no power on earth that could stop him now" (1998, 144). And "she had to understand that, and finally, after he'd been rough with her, maybe too rough with her, she did" (1998, 144).

In being vanquished, we have the cliché that Giovannella becomes content and the next time "when he pulled her to him, he didn't have to force her" (1998, 145). Incredibly, after raping her, "he was swelling to the point of bursting with something else altogether, something that felt dangerously like…well, *love*" (1998, 145).

What is Boyle saying here about what is, but never properly named, a rape? He appears to be adhering to the age-old patriarchal myth about an unstoppable, savage, male drive and, worse, a deep receptiveness in the female to this manliness, notwithstanding an initial resistance to it. The problem seems to be when this virile, male thrust is repressed, resulting in insanity and violence. Boyle has a lot of ambivalent sympathy for the alcoholic, confused Eddie, whose background so resembles his own as described in chapter two. And if anyone has destroyed Eddie's manliness and dignity, it is Stanley's wife, Mrs. Katherine Dexter McCormick, who is rich and educated, a biologist with overtones of none other than Jane Good, Beatrice Umbo and Ailie Park. Katherine and her ilk are "pants wearers. She-men" (1998, 296).

Katherine is a scientist and a suffragette. She despises "the average man" as

> an overgrown playground bully distended by nature and lack of exercise until he fitted his misshapen suits and the ridiculous bathing costume he donned to show off his apelike limbs at the beach. He was unreliable, loud, demanding, clannish, he defended his prerogatives like a Scottish chieftain, and he expected the whole world to bow down to him and fetch him his pipe and newspaper and coffee brewed just the way he liked it, with cream and sugar and the faintest hint of chicory. And why? Because men were the patriarchs and providers of the earth and obeisance was their due, and that was the way of things, ordained by God, Himself a male. (1998, 67)

This portrait is given partly in sympathy and partly in parody of such affluent, privileged women, the bane of poor Eddie Kane or Stanley, or even Boyle, for that matter. Boyle satirises feminist women as much as he distances himself from sweaty armpitted macho men. The feminists sink into comfy chairs, while "the kitchen staff piled a table high with cold cuts, toast points and caviar, plums and raspberries from the orchard" (1998, 169).

These wealthy, unaware, childish women are as barbaric in their own way as the horrible "hurricane of testicular howls" (1998, 167) emitted by ape-like men in opposition to these women. And in a final reversal of the Tarzan tale, with yet another Jane, the stereotypical hint is that Katherine and fellow suffragette, Jane Roessing, are lesbians:

> Jane was sitting right beside her now and she could smell the exotic rich dampness of the roots of her hair and feel the warmth of the thigh pressed to hers and somehow Jane's arm was resting on her shoulder and Jane was rocking her. (1998, 173)

Jane remains her constant companion through the novel—not Tarzan but Katherine gets her Jane in an even more sweeping reversal of the old Tarzan, Jane and ape triangle than we have seen up until now. If Katherine, moreover, feels attracted to manliness again, she soon learns her lesson when she takes Julius, the orang-utan, and symbolic male, to a posh hotel on an outing into town. Julius has already been associated with her husband and Boyle underscores the point on this fateful outing when she strolls with him "as if she were on the arm of her husband" (189). This apparently tame animal asserts his manipulating male power in a humiliating incident. Julius traps Katherine in the revolving door of the hotel and she is exposed to a view of his horrible brute genitalia "inches from her face, the long dark organ in its nest, the meaty bald testicles, the maleness at the center of his being" (1998, 190).

From metaphor of modern repressed man, back to abused animal, like the Konrad who has been fed and then denied nachos, Julius's punishment is that "after the Potter Hotel incident," he is "sold for a song to a travelling circus—on Katherine's orders" (1998, 196).

Stanley may be mad, but in his split personality he stands for all the fears and abnormalities, distortions and anomie that the writer Boyle grapples with as he explores the meaning of his own manliness. Out of the maelstrom, in which the Law of the fathers has been swept away, arise gross, distorted and punishing voices—the Judges speak to Stanley:

> the Judges shouting him down with their lips writhing like a spadeful of earthworms through the black gnarled ape's beards that covered their mouths and their screaming wet cunts. (1998, 127)

No subjectivity is possible in this condition of crisis. The Judges are a hybrid of animal, male and female parts, a syncretism between the unacceptable rapacious man and the equally blood sucking and demanding female. Squeezed between the old style man and the new style woman, the schizophrenic late twentieth century explorer has nowhere to go except into the manic ramblings of his own lunacy, signalled by Boyle's use of italics and loss of the full stop that separates thoughts and constructs meaning in language. Instead he remains merged in the infantile Imaginary where he cannot be "*a man a real man a he-man like his father the president and his brother the president and harold the vice president*"(1998, 422). He "*didn't win the race or drive the ball over the fence*" (1998, 422). And he tries to blot out Katherine's sexual and maternal desires and domesticating demands—"*but no more no more and never again make me a baby stanley make me a baby*" (1998, 422). This recalls the work of Gilles Deleuze and Felix Guattari, (chapter one), who posed the existence of a kind of schizo dimension as the alternative to the Law of the father and the 'sane' language of his good citizenship (1984, 351). Stanley's babble, his refusal to become his father, the president, or be his brother, the trainee president, is characteristic of our times.

We saw in chapter two a tormented Mungo Park, pinned to the house by the enslaving fecundity of his insatiable woman, whose drive to produce babies is precisely her weapon against his instinct to adventure and discover new worlds, rivers and skies, the great freedom from domestic confines. Ultimately, these women in their white lab coats, with their aching, desiring wombs, are just as bad, voyeurs and vampires all:

> Now the best she could do was watch her handsome husband through a pair of binoculars like a field biologist studying the habits of some rare creature in the wild. (1998, 185)

This leads us directly to William Boyd's *Brazzaville Beach* where primatologist, Hope Clearwater, yet another Jane Goodall clone, has come to Africa to observe the chimps in the wild, one of whom is called—wait for it—Conrad.

CHAPTER FIVE

Chimp Wars, Guerrilla Wars and Gender Wars: William Boyd's *Brazzaville Beach*, Will Self's *Great Apes* and Peter Hoeg's *The Woman and the Ape*

Archetypal Africa: Introduction

The protagonist of William Boyd's *Brazzaville Beach* (1990) is a woman, Hope Clearwater, another of our Jane Goodall clones. We are still in the space of the jungle triangle of Tarzan, Jane and Ape and grappling with their new roles and old baggage. Hope is in Africa at the Grosso Arvore Research Centre, where she is also an observer, watching and filming the behaviour of the chimps. She had come to get away from England, where she had been married to the difficult, manic-depressive John Clearwater, mathematician, failed genius and eventually suicide case.

At Grosso Arvore, further disasters befall Hope, resulting in her virtual expulsion from the research center. These disasters arise out of what she observes among the chimps and out of the civil war that is plaguing the country. The novel opens in Africa, on Brazzaville beach, where Hope attempts to unravel her past.

This is the linear structure—England to Grosso Arvore to Brazzaville Beach. The reader, however, receives all the planes of the novel simultaneously in a temporally and spatially re-ordered universe. Experience, in other words, flows seamlessly between continents and chronologies, such that events comment on each other and have consequences and implications across the bounds of historical time. This invites one of the problems we have encountered before —the sense of mythical, universal time within the contradictory framework of the historical novel, where some of the events in Africa are based on identifiable historical realities.

These realities include the fictional portrayal of the famous Louis Leakey—Mallabar, director of Grosso Arvore in Boyd's book. As Donna

Haraway explains, in real life, it was Leakey who suggested that Goodall study the wild chimpanzees at the Gombe Stream Reserve, in Tanganyika, in 1960 (1989, 164).

In addition, there are reverberations between the real and the fictional chimp relationships. Haraway, in the context of Goodall, describes how "Flo had failed as a mother; Flint had remained much too dependent on her and was unable to accept weaning and the birth of his sibling, Flame" (1989, 84). In *Brazzaville Beach*, "Rita-Mae's son was Muffin, an adolescent, a nervous, neurotic chimp who was only happy in his mother's presence and who had been deeply upset by the arrival of her new baby, Lester" (1990, 32).

There is also the kidnapping section of the novel—Gombe, in fact, closed in 1975 as a result of the kidnapping of four students by guerrillas from Zaire (Haraway, 1989, 167). There is even the banana feeding station, which although Jane Goodall initiated it and the fictional Hope Clearwater disapproves of it, the bananas create echoes of history, even as history is transformed into fiction.

This sense of the mixture of history and myth is heightened by reference to recognisable African countries and yet the country of the novel's setting remains unclear. The Africa of the novel is, in fact, a fictional conglomerate, with its overtones of Tanzania, Zaire, as well as the Portuguese ex-colonies of Angola and Mozambique. Commentators come up with diametrically opposed suggestions—Sean French posits that the setting is East Africa, possibly Mozambique (38), while Anita Brookner informs us that the novel is set in West Africa (38); Thomas Edwards feels that it "sounds like Angola" (33–4) and Stephen Wall insists that Boyd has taken us to neither the east nor the west of the continent, but to "the centre" (19).

Perhaps the most apt description of the setting comes from Hope herself:

> We could be almost anywhere in Africa, I recognized. The scene was at once typical and banal. A pot-holed road running straight through low scrubby forest, a scatter of decrepit huts, a strange dry smell in the air of dust and vegetation, a big red sun about to dip below the treeline, the plaintive chirrup of crickets. (1990, 327–8)

An archetypal African setting carries many dangers of essentialised representation, notwithstanding that its banality undercuts exotifying the big red sun or demonising the strange smell and run down huts. Boyd is, I think, attempting to do here what he admired in the writing about Africa of the Polish foreign correspondent, Kapuscinski. He says that the "essence" of [Kapuscinski's] approach is "not about historical analysis; it is about feelings, sensations, the vividness of the singular moment" (1992,178). In other words, "what strikes one is Kapuscinski's feeling for the quiddity of a place, a person or a moment" (1992,178).

The minefield is manifest. Capturing the emotional, the sensual, tragic or funny substance that delivers the visceral feel of a place is the stuff of the best journalism or fiction. Within the context, however, of the representation of Africa, the search for a kind of authentic symbol, potentially falls back into lack of respect for the concrete reality of the people and the place, for the autonomy of the particular African moment that is being fictionalised. It potentially reverts to stereotype and generalisation, rendering a homogeneous Africa the playing field of European tropes, quests and inner journeys. The entire novel, in fact, is written on this razor's edge of Africanist discourse. I will be demonstrating that if its strength lies in its unraveling of male gender constructions, then its weakness is its refusal of engagement with the historical and political contexts of its setting. To illustrate this, let us go straight to the guts of the novel where both chimps and Africans go to war.

Man and Ape Merge: Chimp and Guerrilla Wars

A white writer, who sets his novel in an African country, in which both the local inhabitants and the chimps are fighting internal wars, within the racist paradigm that equates Africans and apes, is taking an enormous political risk.

The chimp war is given detailed treatment in the novel. Hope had been invited to Grosso Arvore by its Director, Eugene Mallabar, to document some strange and sinister behaviour that had begun among the chimps. In the final stages of writing his book, Mallabar had observed that "there had been a mystifying schism in the chimpanzee tribe". Hope's job is "to observe this small breakaway group—the southerners, as they were known" and to try to find an explanation "for their untimely departure" (1990, 30). Mallabar using "a rare moment of anthropomorphism describes this Southern group as 'family'—"'we would like to know why they left us and how they are getting on'" (1990, 30). The moment is rare because the chimps are not supposed to be described in human terms, and yet, we hear about this schism among the chimps within just over a page after we learn about the civil war in the country, making the comparison between the warring animals and humans inevitable:

> [Mallabar] had chosen the wrong country. The civil war which began in 1968 brought massive problems, not to say occasional danger. Happily, the fighting that took place was always at a safe distance, but there remained always the threat of sudden upheavals and breakouts from enclaves. The crude violence employed by the four armies contesting power, and the unpredictable nature of their fortunes, meant that the old days of glossy magazine stories, cover features and TV documentaries were over. (1990, 28)

Like the mysterious outbreak of hostilities among the chimps, there seems to be no rational, political or socio-economic cause of the civil war.

The sporadic, crudely unpredictable outbreaks of indigenous hostilities echo the strange schism in the chimp band. This appears to play into the bad old imagery of Africa as a site of savage, irrational bloodshed and violence. In the same piece about the journalism of Kapuscinski, Boyd divulges his own perspective on the nature of the African continent and its wars:

> No one writes more effectively of the sweaty cafard, the brutal contingencies, the hilarious and terrifying randomness of events, of the blithe, cruel anarchy of African countries in chaos. But at the same time no one conveys better that seductive allure of the continent, the captivating, tenacious fascination for the place that is always present despite the irritation and dismay, and no one better testifies to the stoicism and the dignity that prevail despite the most shocking and casual atrocities. (1992, 175)

Boyd admires and respects aspects of the culture he finds and experienced in Africa. But his sense of its random cruelty and chaos flaws his novel. Quite early on Hope becomes suspicious that the chimps are killing and eating their own kind. The atmosphere is charged, given how totally radical and monstrous this would be, were it true, to say nothing of contradicting Mallabar's previous books and current research. Eventually, Hope witnesses the infanticide and cannibalism herself as Rita-Mae attacks Bobo, Lena's baby, and together with Rita-Lu, eats him. The description is grisly, ghastly and grotesque:

> I looked round. Rita-Mae was eating Bobo. She tore into his belly and pulled out his entrails with her teeth. She flung his guts away on to the rocks. Rita-Lu, meanwhile, climbed out of the tree, circled round Lena—who started to scream, loudly and monotonously—and rejoined her mother. They both fed on Bobo's body while Lena screamed vainly at them. (1990, 130)

These behavioural aberrations relate to the scary and altered behaviour of the Northern Chimps as they go to war against the Southerners. Again we are treated to the utterly gory and horrible portrayal of the chimp war and the dreadful attack on Mr Jeb:

> Then Darius grabbed both his legs and dragged him violently to and fro along the ground, running backwards and forwards. In the course of this, Mr Jeb's head hit the trunk of a date palm and gobbets of blood spurted from his nose. Darius stopped at once and licked and slurped at the blood that dripped from his nostrils. ...
> Pulul approached, sat on Mr Jeb's back and started twisting his leg round and round. I saw, rather than heard, the break. All natural tension suddenly went from the limb. Pulul then gnawed at the toes, biting one of them off, and nearly severing two others. Mr Jeb made no sound while all this went on. (1990, 176–7)

Boyd, through Hope, searches in the novel for scientific explanations for apparently random, spontaneous and unpredictable events. Although the precise link between the infanticide, cannibalism and war is not spelled out, Hope proffers a reason for this atypical, bewildering chimp behaviour. One of her colleagues at the camp, a rather pathetic and inadequate character, Ian Vail, has written a paper in which he suggests that

> It is not the alpha male that gives the group its cohesion, it's a female. A dominant female. It was Rita-Mae that led the group south, not Clovis. (1990, 52)

Hope feels that Vail's paper holds a clue to what she is discovering—that the northern males are fighting the Southerners to get Rita-Mae back (204). They are, moreover, described as doing so in the most consciously cruel manner, making demonic parallels between human and chimp behaviour and linking sex and violence in the deepest psyche of both humans and animals:

> "They attacked two chimps, quite deliberately, completely unprovoked." I paused. "They got one and they killed him, trying to cause him as much pain as possible. It was horrible." I thought again. "Actually, I almost said inhuman. In fact it was all horribly *human*, what they did. They wanted him dead and they wanted to hurt". (1990, 204–5)

The fact that both the people and the chimps were at war, in reality, in different parts of Africa is a coincidence, as is the shared name of Jane Goodall and Tarzan's Jane, or that "guerrilla" and "gorilla" are phonetically indistinguishable. It is a link, however, that others found significant before Boyd fictionalised it, which is precisely how popular culture builds on received stereotype. Haraway, in fact, referring specifically to these historical events, describes how in the 1984, the third, National Geographic film of Goodall, entitled *Among the Wild Chimpanzees*:

> The news of warfare, infanticide, and cannibalism among the chimpanzees emerges. This was not just the comic competition over bananas, but the systematic attacks of one band of chimpanzees by members of another 'community.' The infanticides were the result of the awful systematic behavior by one mother and her daughter, Passion and Pom, who killed and even ate the infants of other mothers in the community. (1989, 184)

Haraway explains that what all of this meant was that:

> Gombe 'no longer reveals the gentle noble savage.' That dream was lost not only at Gombe, but in the entire post-colonial western imaginary and its bestiaries and ethnographies. 'Now we see unexplained violence.' This world holds the seeds of 'terrorism' and guerrilla warfare. The dream of beginnings has been devastated. (1989, 185)

As the Empire not only writes, but fights back for its independence, we witness the representational evolution from the gentle ape and noble savage of colonialism to the murderous cannibalistic chimp and terrorist—the blood hungry black man. 'Bestiaries and ethnographies' buttress the focus on the unexplained horror and violence. What we need to clarify is whether Boyd is reflecting that post-colonial National Geographic imagination, or making a critique of it, or writing a tense mixture of both. In other words, does this novel emerge out of the familiar crucible of innate, gruesome human savagery visible in all its horror only in the light of the tropics? Or does it break away from that paradigm?

What I have been implying is that William Boyd's novel teeters most dangerously when he links the chimp war to the civil war raging in the country. At the same time, his guerrillas and their leader are not who and what we would expect, when we view them up close, as Hope ends up doing. Reminiscent of the real kidnapping of some students attached to Gombe, Hope and Ian Vail get kidnapped in the Land rover by a bunch of UNAMO guerrilla fighters, consisting really of some harmless boys and a rather intriguing Dr Amilcar. This brings us to the question of the depiction of the civil war itself.

What is striking is that if Boyd's description of the chimp wars, its grisly bloodshed and violence, is graphic, then his observations of the civil war are muted and understated. What we are given is Hope's memory (in italics) of a description of the Biafran war that someone had given her, a memory jogged by her kidnap. A key explanation for the outcome of that war is 'superstition'—the execution of a fetish priest, causing the morale of the Biafran side to collapse. Furthermore, a statement about the chaos of war concludes this digression and is given in the language of science, which is significant in this novel:

> In mechanics, systems that lose energy to friction are known as dissipative. In most systems that loss is gradual, measurable and predictable. But there are other dissipative systems that are ragged and untidy. The friction grips, and then suddenly eases, only to grip again. If you consider life as a dissipative system, you will understand what is meant. The most dissipative system anyone will ever encounter is war. It is violently uneven and completely unpredictable. (1990, 274)

The use of the reality of Biafra, with its associations of spurious violence and horror, becomes a shorthand description of *Brazzaville Beach*'s fictionalised war. Reverberations, moreover, between the animal and the human wars are quite explicit. In one of the very few descriptions of the human violence, Hope, Amilcar and the young soldiers come across a village that has been attacked and burnt:

> Three dead bodies blazed there, tall, pale yellow flames wobbling along their length. The corpses were swollen but already charred sufficiently to make sex or age or manner of death impossible to determine. The smell coming off them seemed to pour down my throat—porky, nutty, sour and mineral all at once—like a foul medicine. (1990, 324)

In assessing how this happened, Amilcar deduces that "it must have been a patrol" (1990, 324). This same word, "patrol," was used to describe the Northern chimps who send such a "patrol" to prey on the Southerners. Furthermore, in the relative absence of any analysis of the war, it is inevitable that the graphic and gory description of the chimp war stands as a shorthand language filling in the gaps. And given Hope's curiosity, her seemingly boundless capacity for observation in the quest for knowledge, her patent disinterest in the underlying reasons for the human conflict bears some thinking about. Only after the kidnap does she express frustration at her ignorance and she does not find a way of answering these questions she poses, either then or later:

> I felt frustrated and angry with myself. UNAMO. UNAMO…Who were they? What were their objectives? Hadn't Alda told me they had been defeated by an alliance of the Federal Army and FIDE? There had been a big battle, Alda had said—it seemed like years ago now—so who was Dr Amilcar and where was he taking us? (1990, 286–7)

We are told that the Musave River Territories declared their independence in 1963 and "unilaterally seceded from the republic" (1990, 307) again with its overtones of the Biafran war. But we do not understand the basis of the secession or what is at stake or how this situation came about historically.

What we do learn a great deal more about here is the character of Amilcar, albeit that we are not particularly enlightened about the war, for which he eventually gives his life. The nature of this character is important, given that he stands as the one local person who is afforded any importance in the novel. Hope's assistants, in the tradition of the writings of the famous female primatologists, are given little fictional attention.

Amilcar is a courteous, sophisticated intellectual, gentle and kind, notwithstanding that he has kidnapped Hope and Ian. He is simultaneously represented by Boyd as an extremist in his radical, left wing ideological commitments—Hope refers to Amilcar as a "zealot" who "saw the world in this simple way, devoid of any connection to the evidence on hand" (1990, 327) and later, in the authoritative mode of the italics, she refers to his "*mad moral certainties*" (1990, 332). However, the portrayal of this character is quite contradictory. Countering this image, he has studied medicine in

France and in Lisbon and worked in UNAMO field hospitals prior to joining the guerrilla army (1990, 290–2) and when he is not being a guerrilla, he is a volley ball coach, and his soldiers, the initially terrifying kidnappers, are no more than boys, dressed in the T shirts of their volley ball team.

A model for this gentle revolutionary can be traced to his namesake, the Guinean activist, Amilcar Cabral, who also died for his beliefs, as will Boyd's Amilcar. Perhaps even more powerfully, Amilcar is based on the life of Boyd's friend and fellow writer, Ken Saro-Wiwa, who he had met in the eighties. Boyd writes:

> I have described Ken Saro-Wiwa as an African Gandhi, and though he would, with typical modesty, reject the comparison, it remains valid. Ken is the bravest man I have known. He was wholly aware of the forces arraigned against him and that the stakes were very high. He gave up a comfortable and successful life and vocation to engage in an explicitly non-violent struggle for a cause he deeply believed in. (1995, 22)

The emphasis is equally on the courage, commitment and also the non-violence. Boyd respects political passion, even if he is unable to identify fully with revolutionary zeal. We will see, however, that Boyd agonises about the brakes on activist intervention in Africa that should characterise a committed *white* man's behaviour. This particular agony will become very significant as the novel develops. It is quite ironic that the real life kidnapper actually was Laurent Kabila (Jane Goodall, in interview with Claudia Dreifus, 6). While Boyd most probably did not know this at the time, it does highlight the dangers of his composite and ambiguous depiction of a revolutionary who has the intellect and commitment of his namesake, Amilcar Cabral, and the suicidal courage and conviction of Ken Saro-Wiwa, but also the fanaticism of the manic Laurent Kabila, his unwitting real life model.

Amilcar dies in this war when he is hit by a randomly fired "spray of bullets" (340). This death crescendos the problematic association between African men and the chimps. Conrad, one of Hope's most human-like chimps, also dies in the civil war of the animals. Boyd repeatedly emphasises Conrad's humanity—"Conrad was an adult male, whose eyeballs around the iris were white, not brown, a feature that gave him a disconcertingly human gaze" (1990, 32 &124). Amilcar too is a gentle, male creature caught in the cross-fire of a bad war. For all the sensitivity of the portrayal of both the man and the chimp, associating them in this, or any, way evokes the damaging trope of a porous boundary between African man and ape.

What is clear, however, is that, key to Boyd's political aspirations and his muted identification with Amilcar in the novel, is his choice of a female protagonist in the form of Hope Clearwater. This character, in fact, has many roles to play in the novel.

Two Janes become Three Hopes

> Morgan pounded his chest, "Aaah-ooah-ooah, ooah-ooah!" he bellowed, adding in a throaty basso profundo: 'me Jane'. (*A Good Man in Africa*, 125)

"Me *Jane*"? Boyd's humour very often resides, as it does in *A Good Man in Africa*, in male characters, who are unable or unwilling to live up to macho stereotypes. Being overweight and syphilitic rather than agile and hunky and being Jane rather than Tarzan, Morgan Leafy, Boyd's rather endearing and caricatured good man in Africa, embodies Boyd's awareness of the power of the Tarzan trope. In *Brazzaville Beach* the protagonist, through whom the novelist speaks, is the white woman. If Tarzan has become Jane, however, has Jane become Tarzan in a simple role reversal? In fact, who exactly is Hope Clearwater?

> My name is Hope Clearwater...Or, "Hope Clearwater is that tall young woman who lives on Brazzaville Beach." It is not so easy. Which voice do I use? I was different then; and I'm different now.
> I am Hope Clearwater. She is Hope Clearwater. *Everything is me, really*. Try to remember that, though it might be a little confusing at first. (1990, 6, my emphasis)

What precisely should the reader remember? The novel switches between first and third person narration, between Hope, first person participant, telling her own story and an apparently omniscient narrator, Boyd, telling his story from above. I say 'apparently' as what Boyd, via Hope, is warning the reader to do, is to be aware that it is Hope, rather than her creator, who is manipulating the voices. This is so whether the language is "I am Hope" or "she is Hope". We have to remember that "everything is me, really". This bewildering narrative device alerts us to the crisis of authority regarding who can speak, who can act, who has political credentials and who must hold back. White males today watch in awe as Tarzan of old has no such qualms. He is not only a player in the jungle wars but the main part, the man who sorts out the locals and wins the girl. It is appropriate that more informed and sophisticated men like Boyd understand that this role is no longer available to them. But if someone like Boyd no longer wishes to be Tarzan, he is unclear as to how to become a player at all, rather than be an inept bystander.

I think that Boyd has written his male desires into a female part as an attempt at a political solution to his problem of finding a relevant role for himself, as a white man. He has also written into that female part the now familiar love/hate relationship with the white woman, who has partly supplanted him and who has partly remained the object of his quests and desires. Far from being the clear waters that the hope signifies, we are in very murky narrative swamps as two Janes multiply into three Hopes.

There is, firstly, the Hope, who acts out Boyd's own, male desires for a meaningful, active and political role. There is, secondly, Hope as Jane Goodall, the voyeur, the steely intellectual liberated woman, who has supplanted Tarzan and occupies his space on the top of the tree. There is, finally, the more traditional, feminine Jane, or Hope as Penelope, or as Boyle's Ailie of chapter three, wife of Mungo Park, the woman who keeps the hearth warm until the white man can return to his rightful place.

The first Hope, Boyd's alter ego, takes chances, makes choices and acts upon what she believes, freed from all the constraints and history of the white, male coloniser. She comes about as a result of Boyd's sensitive awareness that a white man

> can all too easily see himself as a heroic, semimythic figure, a pseudowarrior, one who has been through hell and back, with his sweat-stained fatigues and grim countenance, trudging through the earth's trouble spots with a world-weary, yet indisputable macho swagger. (1992, 176)

Hope, as a woman, on the other hand, is allowed to become a soldier enlisted into Amilcar's war and to act decisively in the war between the chimps as well. Amilcar asks for her help in the war and she agrees and lays a couple of land-mines (1990, 337).

I am suggesting that in helping Amilcar to wage his guerrilla war, Hope is acting out Boyd's desire. Look at the bodily identification between Hope and Amilcar, the description of which immediately precedes Amilcar's request for assistance in the war:

> The cluster of bites on my neck itched. As I scratched them I realized they were in exactly the same position as Amilcar's curious scar. I thought if we had more time, and the occasion was right, that I would tell him about my port-wine mark, splashed across my skill.
> "Hope," he said suddenly, "would you help me a little?" (1990, 337)

In one of the novel's labyrinthine twists in the struggle for identity, if Hope is Boyd and if Hope is also Amilcar, then Boyd is Amilcar, the black brother, Saro Wiwo, whose struggle he can only enter through writing about it after the black man's execution. This is not the first, and will not be the last, time that these white writers fantasise about being black, or linked to an African blood brother. We will see the mark on the body, linking a black and a white man again, in Adam Thorpe's *Pieces of Light* in chapter nine, for example.

Likewise, in this mode of living out Boyd's dreams of relevance, Hope is able to play a part in ending the aggression between the chimps and in relieving the pain of the wounded animals. Hope is more or less dismissed from Grosso Arvore. On her way out by Land Rover, she "suddenly knew exactly what I wanted to do" (1990, 379). She goes off to search for the poor remnants of the besieged Southern chimps, "to search the areas where Conrad had last been seen" (1009, 380). She has no definite scheme and, beyond a nostalgic goodbye, she doesn't know what she hopes to achieve by "hatching such a preposterous plan" (1990, 380). Coincidentally, in a rather contrived plot moment of the wishful thinking of dreams, just at the time that Hope happens to be watching, the Northerners silently arrive for the kill, totally outnumbering the Southerners in a gory, terrible final battle.

This time, Hope does not merely observe but she participates in the fighting, opting on the side of the gentler Southern chimps against the vicious Northerners, like Pulul, Darius, Sebastian and Gaspar. We see her toting her gun in the male, phallic role:

My first shot caught [Pulul] in the chest, high on one side, and knocked him spinning off his feet. Then Darius leapt across the stream and galloped towards me. I shot him full in the face when he was about six feet away. I saw shards of his disintegrating skull fly up into the air like spun coins. I turned and fired at Sebastian and Gaspar as they fled, but I missed. Then they were all gone, bounding away out of the valley, screaming in panic. (1990, 391)

Then she looks for Conrad, the special, most human of the chimps, who is horribly wounded and mutilated, in order to put him out of his misery:

I found him twisted and bloody under the mesquinho bushes. His right hand had been torn off at the wrist, and he waved the stump at me in parody aggression. His face was red and pulpy, minced by Darius's fists and nails. But his brown eyes looked at me as directly as ever. Accusing? Pleading? Hostile? Baffled?

I crouched round behind him, so he couldn't see me, and fired once into the top of his head from six inches away. (1990, 392)

While she is shocked and shivering, she achieves a degree of inner peace:

I felt much better. I was glad I had killed Darius and Pulul. I was glad I had been there to end Conrad's suffering. I recovered my nerve and calm quickly. I knew my conscience would never be troubled, because I had done the right thing, for once.

The chimpanzee wars were over. (1990, 392)

The novel leads us to compare the two killings. Hope intervenes in the human war to help Amilcar, out of friendship. She fails. She equally intervenes in the chimp war, where she rather spectacularly succeeds—the "wars were over". If Boyd cannot see his own way clear to making an intervention in the politics of Africa, then he can make a difference in the realm of his writing. The putting of Conrad out of his misery is a discourse murder. It is Boyd's sense of manipulating the heart of darkness trope and producing something different, not least of all in his sensitive portrait of Amilcar.

All of this is not to say that this role given to the white woman is unproblematic as a solution to the white male dilemma. First of all, it elevates the white woman into a false innocence, as if she did not collude with, and benefit from, the colonising enterprise in certain ways. Furthermore, the concealed male hand, guiding all of Hope's choices reinforces male ascendancy, even as it effaces itself in a disguise.

This explains what Anita Brookner observes when she points out that Hope's "attitudes are more masculine than feminine" (38). Or as Sean French puts it (perhaps a little harshly) with regard to Boyd's "drag act as Hope Clearwater":

> I can think of no contemporary novelist so preoccupied with genitals—male, female and animal. In this novel the preoccupation is taken to an extreme and, when Boyd describes Hope fondling her own body or observing various male penises, we must read this in the knowledge that it is a man who is fantasising it. (39)

The female as male in disguise, flows into the next Hope persona. In being the one who wields the gun, who surveys everything from the lofty treetops and who makes the definitive intervention, does she not also become the threatening new woman, the emasculating, voyeuristic Jane Goodall clone, Tarzan in drag? Boyd, like Boyle before him, has tremendous ambivalence towards such women.

The depiction of Hope as a scientist, a primatologist in the honourable tradition of Jane Goodall or Dian Fossey, rests on her seeing eye, that eye that these male writers find so threatening and unfeminine. She scientifically watches the most appalling and gratuitous violence in Africa. In the same way as she observes the chimps, she had scrutinised her husband back in England and probably contributed to the splintering of his mind. Like Stanely McCormick, John Clearwater has a powerful, female scientist on his tail. Note how she charts, marks and watches John's attitude to his work and his mental deterioration:

Chimp Wars, Guerrilla Wars and Gender Wars 143

> Apart from his new alcohol-free life, there were no other significant changes in John's life that Hope could easily discern. ...Covertly, *she observed and analysed him*. (1990, 65, my emphasis)

When she finds evidence that he is having an affair, the plan she makes is "she would watch John in secret, covertly, over a weekend" (217). Hope, moreover, envies him:

> That was it: John had secrets and she envied him. ...She envied him his secret knowledge, but it was, she saw, an envy that was strangely pure, almost indistinct from a kind of worship. He was at home in a world that was banned to all but a handful of initiates. (1990, 72)

Why worship? Note the confusion here between John's and Hope's own ambitions and mathematics and particularly the explorer simile:

> And this, I suppose, is every mathematician's secret dream. To have a function, a number, an axiom, a hypothesis named after you. ... It must be like being an explorer on a virgin continent, naming mountains, rivers, lakes and islands. ...There you are on civilization's intellectual map. For ever. (1990, 133–4)

Furthermore, the explorer image in her envy of the mathematician is extended into a place, the archetypal Tarzan site of domination in the sun at the top of the tree:

> An ordinary numerate person could, by dint of hard work, go so far up the mathematical tree. But then you stopped. To go beyond required some kind of faculty or vision that you had to be born with, she supposed. Only a very few occupied those thin whippy branches at the extremity, moved by the unobstructed breezes, exposed to the full fat glare of the sun. (1990, 73)

This flows into Jane as Tarzan and Jane Goodall simultaneously— woman simply becoming bad, ambitious man:

> Though she was reluctant to admit it for a long time, Hope was in thrall to a vision of the future in which her name glowed with lasting renown. (1990, 244)

This she 'hopes' to accomplish by coming to Africa where she will fight Mallabar for this recognition and where she will literally play the archetypal role as Tarzan, victorious participant in jungle battles, the male body still present in the form of her powerful gun. Is Boyle saying that all that feminism is about is Jane's desire to be the one on top, mistress of all she surveys? When she observes the chimps, not unlike how she watches her husband, will it be in order not only to uncover scientific truth, but to oust Tarzan/Mallabar, who has all the recognition, fame and glory, from that position? The satirised good man in Africa may beat his podgy chest intoning "Me, Jane" but does not the fierce and serious Hope, his alter ego, respond with a "Me, Tarzan"?

In other words, if male behaviour is being scrutinised and problematised in this novel, then it is once again done so ambivalently, filtered through the steely, ambitious observing female gaze. But this is not the whole story. Hope splits yet again into a third role, that of more traditional female, subservient to the man in her life. By definition, in order to appreciate the nature of this third Hope, we first of all have to understand one of the male characters not yet discussed—Usman Shoukry, Hope's lover. Let us keep the third Hope in reserve as we focus on this enigmatic Egyptian.

The Cyborg, the Lie and the Beach House

I would like to suggest that the key character of *Brazzaville Beach* is a minor one, in line with Boyd's frustrated sense of the necessity of sidelining of male aspirations. If Boyd used the female protagonist to express his desires, then the man with whose life the novel ends is not only marginal by virtue of his minor status in the novel, but also because of his role and his race as an Egyptian mercenary in the African war. I am referring to Usman Shoukry, who leaves Hope his beach house, the one from which she ponders the meaning of life at Brazzaville Beach.

Usman is Hope's apparently very casual lover, encountered on her occasional visits to the town, to purchase supplies for Grosso Arvore. Usman is "an Egyptian and in his early forties, I guessed" (1990, 93), a mercenary pilot in the civil war (1990, 95). Usman's role as mercenary is not really developed in a novel, which is not too concerned with the political and historical realities within its unnamed archetypal Africa in which an equally archetypal, endless civil war is being fought. Usman's plane goes missing after one of his engagements and he is presumed dead.

Usman Shoukry may be Egyptian, but to Boyd he is an Usman, an Everyman, the hope and future for Boyle himself, with his own chequered cultural past, in which, like Tarzan, he was born in Africa. In chapter one, we saw the significance of David Caute's rewrite of Salman Rushie as an Egyptian, given Caute's own Rhodesian background. Egypt is a hybrid border zone between Africa, Europe and the East and through Usman, Boyd imagines his own late twentieth century hybridity.

The fact that Boyd was born in Ghana differentiates him from writers who do not have this connection with the African continent and yet who use it metaphorically in their fiction. Boyd's life history is, in fact, quite varied. Of Scottish background, he was educated at Gordonstoun, and then at the universities of Nice, Glasgow and Oxford, rendering his "'Scottish formation'...of the kind that could be could be called diasporic" (Dunn,

151). While we should not take the analogy too far, the Tarzan myth must have particular resonance for Boyd. Like Tarzan, he too was born in Africa, far from his family's roots and cultural background. He too goes back and forth in his fictions, depicts characters, who are culturally dislocated, and is ultimately recognised as a British writer, notwithstanding his birthplace in Africa.

This point is emphasised in A. O. Scott's review of Boyd's latest novel, *Armadillo* (1998), where the main character, Lorimer Black, encounters a minor character, Francis Home, and

> Noting Home's olive complexion and "dark crinkly hair," Lorimer wonders about his background: "Cypriot? Lebanese? Spanish? Egyptian? Syrian? Greek? Like himself, Lorimer knew, there were many types of Englishman". (1998a, 10)

Note also, of course, in this realm of cyborgs and mutants, that an armadillo is both an armed man and an animal whose body is has a hard, protective covering. This double meaning is relevant to the nature of the main character of that novel, which we cannot go into here, but also to all the guises and masks that Boyd dons through the many personas of this book, not least of all the Egyptian, Usman.

I suggested earlier that there are dangers in taking the Tarzan myth too far, in relation to black writers, who come from backgrounds that experienced colonisation. This link was made by Gorra and is being suggested here in a further comment by Scott:

> And indeed, many of the most inventive British novelists of recent years—Salman Rushdie, Hanif Kureishi, Caryl Phillips, Kazuo Ishiguro, James Kelman—have reinvigorated the idioms and widened the scope of English literature by, in effect, colonizing it. (10)

The link may assume too much in terms of the power imbalance between white and black writers, but it is certainly suggestive in relation to Boyd's fiction, which is shot through with characters whose cultural displacement is writ large. As Dunn has it, "Boyd's cosmopolitan reach is one largely of a comic restlessness—round pegs in square holes, unlikely people in unlikely places" (152).

Three intriguing puzzles in relation to Usman may provide keys to the novel as a whole. Firstly, what is the meaning of the miniature cyborg 'planes' that Usman invents? Secondly, and linked to the first, what is the significance of the lie he tells about his life? Finally, what is the significance of Hope's inheritance of Usman's beloved house on the beach, given that the relationship was apparently very casual? This last question will bring us directly back to the nature of the third Hope persona.

Usman's cyborg planes, part live horse-fly, part inorganic, have been intricately designed and Hope was duly amazed when he had demonstrated them to her on one of her trips from Grosso Arvore:

> He reached out and carefully picked one from the air with a delicate plucking motion, and held it out to me. It was like a tiny precise glider, fragile, rather beautiful, made from doped tissue paper and slivers of matchwood. The wingspan was about two inches. Beneath the wing, in a meticulous harness of glue-stiffened threads, was a horse-fly, its wings a hazy blur of movement. (1990, 209)

We have already seen that aeroplanes and flying are significant in the adventurer colonial genre. The view from the top resonates with Tarzan's bird's eye and stands for colonial conquest. It is not by chance that the film version of *Out of Africa* makes so much of Robert Redford and Meryl Streep in Redford's plane, to the strains of extraordinary music, sweeping over the landscape of Kenya in a glorious act of freedom and ownership. We saw Boyle's version of that moment with Beatrice, Howie and Konrad in their flight from hell, taken in memory of Beatrice flying, Karen Blixen style, with her husband back in Africa.

Flying as an image, outside of the colonial context, has been an important one for Boyd before and stands for the male urge for adventuring in faraway lands, for establishing fame and fortune and for abandoning the claustrophobic confines of the domestic. Man dreams of being free, out there in the elements, be they sky for Boyd or water, the River Niger, for Boyle. In a later Boyd novel, *The Blue Afternoon* (1993), a character, Pantaleon, exhibits an obsessive passion for building and flying a machine in the early part of this century. He confides his passion to his friend, Salvador Carriscant, a pioneering surgeon:

> His face was alive and mobile, joyful. "Honestly, Salvador, I've never experienced a moment like that. I felt…" He paused, he could not think of the exact word. "I don't know. On the verge. *Like an explorer, I suppose, discovering a continent*, an ocean. Something like that. Everything ahead is blank and I am going to take a step into the void, part a curtain, if you know what I mean". (1993, 220, my emphasis)

Again there is the link between these endeavours, be they mathematical, medical or aviational, and the simile of exploring so called empty continents that await discovery by these adventuring men. The joy of flight is bonded to the driving ambitions of men, desperate always to reach the top, ambitions about which Boyd is ambivalent. Usman's invention is fuelled by his desire for an entry in the world book of records. The evidence for his having achieved "the smallest powered aeroplanes in the world" (1990, 209) is that Hope must capture their image on film—"'I need you as a witness'"(1990,

209). Once again Hope is observer, but now Usman holds the camera and Hope is in the support role for male achievement:

> I stood there while Usman took several flash photographs. I held my hand as close to the planes as possible to convey the scale. (1990, 210)

The woman's body may "convey the scale", but the irony of Boyd's demonstration lies in the reduced scale of man's ambitions, given that adventuring in the old Tarzan style is no longer appropriate or possible for late, weary twentieth century men. The plane is now tiny and the trapped and suicidal insect pinned to the wood and paper is surely the reduced and ineffectual man we have come to recognise. No longer pilot and powerhouse, this insect of a man is on a set course to extinction:

> "Can you set them free?" I asked.
> "No. They're glued in place." He smiled. "They're pilots for the rest of their life."...
> "What now?"
> "They die in combat," he said. He picked up a can of fly spray. PifPaf it was called, a yellow can with crude red lettering. He pointed it at one of his aeroplanes and enveloped it in a cloud of spray. ...
> For a while the plane flew on as normal, but then it began to judder and sideslip and in a second or two it fell fluttering to the floor like a leaf. (1990, 210)

Was Usman himself on such a suicide mission when he took off in his plane and did not return? We must remember, however, that if Usman is the insect trapped in the glue, he is also the artist, who has constructed these little marvels as well as the male, ambitious for recognition and acclaim. Can he be understood in terms of a lie he had told Hope?

Usman had said that he "had trained for many years to be an astronaut". His chance came when the Russians had "opened up their space programme to certain third world countries" (1990, 215). He describes how he had come really close to being the one selected from Egypt to go up into space, his dream nearly came true:

> "You see, it was my dream to go into space. I talked to the others who had been, who had looked down on the world. I saw the photographs..." He smiled, sadly. "I think that was my mistake. The photographs were so beautiful, you see." He screwed up his face, wincing at the memory of their beauty. "I stopped being the perfect technician. I even began to write poems about the earth, seen from outer space. I think that was my mistake."
> "So they chose the other one."
> "I was there right up to the blast-off. In case something went wrong with him. But it didn't."
> "That's sad." I felt full of love for him, then. (1990, 215)

This is one of the few moments that Hope expresses something for Usman beyond convenience and a good time. It also attempts to explain, and even to rationalise, his choice to be "here...fighting someone else's war" (1990, 216) and yet, the whole story is a fabrication:

> I bought a book...a history of the exploration of outer space. On reflection, I should not have been that surprised, but I have to tell you it came as something of a shock to learn that there were no Egyptian astronauts. Not one. ...But Usman's lie does not really bother me: the dream enchanted for a moment, which gives it a kind of validity, I would have thought. (1990, 395)

Is it truly the case that Usman's lie does not matter? Finding out the truth surely utterly changes our view of the suave Usman and renders his little flying cyborgs as desperate and also rather pathetic as the receptacles of their creator's displaced and fabricated, ambitions. Furthermore, Usman becomes one of his insects as we observe these silly little men in their flying machines, with their delusions of grandeur and their longings to rise higher and higher into space.

If Usman is so reduced in his manliness, however, it is Boyd, his creator and alter ego, who is recognising that the old style of masculinity is problematic. Boyd is being courageous and self-critical in recognising the false basis of male claims to fame and glory and is exhibiting the kind of diffidence and humility that we found so sensitively built into the narrative of Lawrence Norfolk.

Moreover, after the dust has settled on the lie, a fine residue of skill and talent survives and the male shrunk to size may yet have something to contribute. Usman's intricate horsefly plane design, which Hope hangs up in the Beach House, is the mark of true scientific and artistic creativity.

However, in this tense novel of transformation of old stories and their scarring survivals, the cyborg design hanging in the beach house is also a sign of Usman's proprietorship. And this continued ownership, even in his absence, brings us now to the third Hope, who has been waiting in the wings. Ultimately, one of the Hopes embodied in the name of the woman is that she will hold fort, keep those wretched home fires burning. The female facilitator of Usman's designs is reincarnated as Mungo Park's and Boyle's Ailie, waiting for her missing man to return and regain residence of his house:

> I have my own strong intuitions, and a curious feeling that one day the former owner of this beach house may pass by to check on the renovations.
> And, strangely enough, everywhere I go now, I think I see him. (1990, 396)

Chimp Wars, Guerrilla Wars and Gender Wars

This Hope is the primatologist of Haraway's nightmare, intermediary for the white man, who has been expelled from Africa, and whose foothold she continues to secure.

Finally, in this novel's desperate search for meaning, if the white man is to have a role, which the white woman enables, it rests philosophically on our common humanity, which becomes the bedrock upon which *Brazzaville Beach* sits at its conclusion:

> Hope sits in her bright, loud house and looks out into the darkness towards the sound of the waves. It seems strange, but not inconceivable, that Clovis should have had a sense of his life passing by—a finite sequence of present moments—just as she does. (1990, 322)

Light and dark images are loaded in fiction about Africa. The contemplative thoughts in the bright house relate to our common bonds with those characterised as Other—here Clovis the poor, butchered chimp, and, a bit later, two old women from the village, who Hope, as always, is watching—"*Yes, it seems to me we share the same invariants. The differences between us are superficial*" (1990, 366).

But what is the darkness into which Hope looks if not the savagery of the bad apes and the violent illogical war in which Amilcar lost his life? Conrad has it seems not died after all and the metaphor for our common human shadow is the African darkness beyond Hope's bright house. And this gives us Usman's lie in a different light. If the lie appears not to matter, it is because the novel has a higher truth up its sleeve, a truth that renders history and politics, the here and now of Africa or anywhere else, redundant. The hybrid man, who is black and white, African and European—Egyptian—is our common humanity.

And with this truth, these little cyborgs also stand, among their other meanings, for involuntary drives and instincts, for the animal in humans, along with their creativity and their talents. They offer a kind of certainty in our uncertain times. They provide the split and doubling Boyd, with his masquerading and unveiling, a degree of predictability, given that their routes are controlled by instincts that avoid collision:

> Their fly instinct, I guessed, controlled their movements; they seemed to avoid each other easily, and they altered course whenever they flew too close to a wall. (1990, 209)

These cyborgs syncretise cultures, pin flesh onto metal, and construct a pastiche of horsefly and paper, but in the end use new materials to discover old, universal truths. In this sense, the lie turns out to be a red herring, as it did in *Heart of Darkness*, where Marlow has discovered the truth about

Kurtz. The lie Marlow tells Kurtz's 'intended' is merely a chivalrous, Tarzanic style gesture to a silly little Jane, who needs to live in her bubble of ignorance. The lie Usman tells Hope and which she, new woman, uncovers through her researching his story, endears him to her in the light of their common, flawed humanity. Within an obliterated local reality, we are left with the truism about human nature, discoverable only back in the cradle of civilization, on the African continent of origins, apes and black people. And this is the crucial point. The gesture to human universals only becomes dangerous on this site of apes and instincts, within this discourse of dark hearts and vicious apes linked to local war-mongers.

Boyd's *Brazzaville Beach* enacts a process whereby the drag artist slowly strips ultimately to reveal his maleness. This male body, however, bears the marks of the discarded costume. The wings of the exposed man have been clipped, reduced and miniaturised and his ambitions, desires and lies cease to carry the same old power.

The male quest in the late twentieth century is not primarily for unknown rivers, for gold or lost tribes, for fame and fortune, but for meaning, certainty and a role in society that can provide reconstituted white men with a solid identity. Late twentieth century males, like Boyd, are weary of the macho mantle and the pressure on them to produce Tarzanic feats. They are nonetheless wary of the female, who appears to have supplanted them in this role. What they are indeed most weary of is their own ambivalence in the face of the difficulties of throwing off old grails and rewards, an ambivalence they couch in the language of satire and irony, in the device of female protagonists and forked tongues.

Boyle's and Boyd's men are mainly insane, dead or missing by the end of their encounters with Africa, apes and primatologists. Hope and Usman, however, liberate their little insect planes and although they are doomed, like Konrad and Beatrice, they have their moment:

> We stood at the threshold of the bungalow and launched the little aircraft into the night. At first, away from the inhibiting cube of the room, they seemed perplexed and flew to and fro in tight trajectories of three and four feet. But then one of them very suddenly climbed up and away and we soon lost sight of it as it flew beyond the glow from the bulb above the front door. The other continued to zigzag for a while longer and then it too, perhaps caught by a gust of wind, seemed to bank off and up, and soared away into the huge expanse of the night. (1990, 210)

These insect planes, with their live and mechanical parts, for all their reduced, cruel and ambivalent symbolism, seem to hint at a solution to the traps confronting modern masculinity. This solution takes us back to Donna Haraway and the suggestiveness of her cyborg boundary crossings and forward to the fiction of Peter Høeg and Adam Self.

Mutations: More Apes, "Insectoid Men", Cyborgs and Hybrids

With two more novels to touch upon, what has emerged is that this entire book could have been called the chapter title—"The Battered Boys of Rice Burroughs: Tarzan and Jane Goodall". But then it would have been a very different book. The minefields inherent in the Tarzan tradition of superior white men and apes with echoes of indigenous people, set in a mythical African so-called archetypal jungle, are laid wherever we look. While *Weary Sons of Conrad* is a book about serious novels and re-constituted men, they are hard pressed in this part of it, not to become shipwrecked and sabotaged on their journeys.

We are still in the age of uncertainty. Identity is fluid, splintered and up for grabs. We continue to see how many European men have lost confidence in their roles as patriarchs, providers and Law-givers. They have not carved out new and comfortable roles to replace these traditional functions. They have difficulty with professional and powerful late twentieth century women, who seem to emasculate them and to invade male strongholds. "Emasculate" is a keyword. The apes and the spectre of Tarzan are bodies, great rippling, hairy muscles, belittling and taunting modern atrophied European man.

The mutating white male body is at the core of Will Self's *Great Apes* and we will see how many of the themes of this part of the book will coalesce around this body. Simon Dykes, the protagonist, appears at the beginning of the novel to be a human being, an artist. His artistic vision is primarily of "bodily disintegration" (137). In his paintings, "the human bodies would be scarcely visible" (24). His vision is remarkably reminiscent of Boyd's, as humans are compared with "massed termites". They are, echoing Usman's creations, "insectoid humans—all carapace, all exoskeletal" (24).

K/Conrad dies many deaths in his multiple guises as our ape ancestor, rejected Father Author of primal Master texts. The narrative killing of the Father, as we know only too well, continues to re-visit the sons in their dreams and nightmares. Simon has a terrible nightmare fantasy of central London "dumped upon by a giant ape":

> A post-imperial Kong who smashed the windows of the department stores and pulled out wriggling handfuls of humans, twined them between his digits and caught *like the termites they were* in the cable-thick fur on the back of his huge hands. (26, my emphasis)

This great post-imperial Kong with the powerful body, signifies the demise of Empire and embodies those poisonous overtones linking the ape with the uprising of indigenous black people and of the decline of civilization, of language and the Law:

> He flexed his mighty arms, drummed on the roof of Hamley's and let out a massive 'HooooGraaa!', which seemed to mean: I am body. I am *the* body. Sod the Father. Sod the Son, and piss on the Holy Ghost. (26)

In other words, this highly satirical novel, where everything is tongue-in-cheek, is nonetheless involuntarily reproducing overtones of Africanist discourse of post independence chaos and disintegration. This huge new force from the periphery shits on the Centre, understood as Oxford Circus itself. Kong is on a rampage:

> finally squatting in the very centre of the Circus itself to strain, push and deliver a turd the size of a newspaper kiosk, which wavered, lengthened from stub to cigar, before plummeting fifty feet from Kong's arsehole. (27)

In the midst of these nightmare visions transposed into paint, Simon wakes up one morning in a transformed world in which it is the apes, which have won the evolutionary battle and rule the earth. They keep humans in the zoo and all the rules, taboos and laws by which humanity defines itself have been overturned. In this new world, Simon, too, is an ape, but he retains the "delusion" that he is human and has to learn to find his ape identity and to return thereby to psychic health.

In attempting to make sense of this terrifying metamorphosis, Simon considers the possibility that his "delusions of the bestial masking the human" were linked to his artistic vision of the disintegration of the human body:

> What, after all, were the apes, if not distorted versions of the body? That they were all body—all *embodiment*, was the only certainty. (183)

When Tarzan presided over the apes, the white male body was in fantastic shape. The link between a strong imperial power and a white male muscular body machine is an integral part of the Tarzan discourse. As Richard Dyer puts it, "the built body and the imperial enterprise are analogous" (165). He enlarges on the nature of the analogy:

> The muscle hero has landscaped his body with muscles and he controls them superbly and sagely; the lands of the muscle film are enfeebled or raw bodies requiring discipline. The built white male body and colonial enterprise act as mirrors of each other, and both, even as they display the white man's magnificent corporeality, tell of the spirit within. (165)

The spirit within is displayed through these bodies because:

Chimp Wars, Guerrilla Wars and Gender Wars 153

> The built body is an achieved body, worked at, planned, suffered for. A massive, sculpted physique requires forethought and long-term organisation; regimes of graduated exercise, diet and scheduled rest need to be worked out and strictly adhered to; in short, building bodies is the most literal triumph of mind over matter, imagination over flesh. (153)

In the post-independence age, the white man's weight lifting burden has horribly metamorphosed and these wonderful bodies have shrunk. Ironically, writers like William Boyd or Coraghessan Boyle utterly reject imperialism, but are nonetheless hard pressed to find an alternative to the old style of male domination. Boyle's narrator, remember, cannot even manage to wee through his little penis and Boyd's great aviators are reduced to tiny insect cyborgs, like the massed termites of Simon's paintings. Simon himself is in body crisis, neither ape nor man.

In the heady days of Empire, the built white body established protective boundaries against domesticity, powerful women and even black men—"only a hard, visibly bounded body can resist being submerged into the horror of femininity and non-whiteness" (Dyer, 153). We have seen some of the invasive horrors of liberated, post-imperial femininity. Apes may dominate Simon's new universe, with all their arse-licking, shit drinking and copulating, but intellectual women, especially primatologists, remain dour, sexless, suspect beings, even in their chimp incarnations. Jane Goodall and Dian Fossey are mentioned by name in *Great Apes* (219, 262, 329, 375). The Jane Goodall clone in this novel, however, is drawn fictionally along identical lines to Boyle's Beatrice Umbo. She is Ludmilla Rauhschutz and is billed as one of Jane Goodall's ex-field researchers, who split from her and "managed to bribe the Tanzanian government to allow her her own research station in the Gombe region" (375). As always, these, now ape, 'women' have lost all their female sexuality:

> Rauhschutz was a striking figure, so obese as to be almost a ball of dark-brown fur. Her muzzle was disturbingly flat and animal for a German chimp, and her close-cropped head fur didn't help matters. Nor did the hideously patterned shortie mumu that flared around her shoulders like a perverse material garnish on an unappetising dish. The mumu unobscured the non-object of desire that lay between her lanate legs. It was easy to see why Rauhschutz eschewed a swelling-protector—she had no need of one. When in full oestrus her welling must have been a paltry affair, for now, in a fallow period, her perineal region was barely noticeable. (388)

Within this scenario of terrifying, intellectual and sexless women creatures, of the political and physical ascendancy of apes and, it is hinted, blacks with great bodies, the possibilities invested in the new creature, the cyborg, again raises its head. The concept of the cyborg is a receptacle for all the acute contradictions that sear this part of this book. Apes signal a porous boundary between the human and the animal and deliver a dire history of racial politics. Robocop Schwarzenegger, who represents technological advances embodied in his mix of metal and flesh, is a late twentieth century Tarzanic cyborg. Most importantly, the concept itself is politically unstable, moving as it does between the reincarnated macho man and the enlightenment of species and boundary crossing. For all these reasons, the cyborg recurs in the fiction occupying this particular site of apes, primatologists, Tarzans and Janes, new and old.

For example, the drug company, whose product may have been responsible for Simon's hallucinations and bodily confusions, is suggestively called "Cryborg" (270). And as Simon recovers, the healing, which *Great Apes* appears to be promising, is that of some kind of hybrid between the physical body of ape-ness and the sensibilities of the human. His movements are both ape and human. He is described as "the ape man," redolent of Tarzan, as he swings himself out of his bunk (237) but he "was still forcing himself to walk upright on the level" (237). In response to a big, hostile ape, Simon feels

> the fur at the nape of his neck stiffen and bristle—a sensation which he had never consciously experienced before. He too began to utter a series of aggressive barks, while drawing himself up to his full height. (291)

Simon learns, as an ape-man, to express himself like "an enraged wild human, and yet suffused with a weirdly visible, essentially chimp meaningfulness" (313). This brings us to another satire on humanity, not dissimilar from *Great Apes* in that it, too, constructs a fantasy world of boundary crossing between ape and man. I refer to Peter Hoeg's *The Woman and the Ape*.

* * * * * * * * * *

> "What do you call yourselves?" she asked. "I mean you don't say 'apes,' do you?"
> The ape thought this over, trying vainly to reconcile two incompatible languages before coming up with an acceptable compromise.
> "'People,'" it said. "We call ourselves 'people.'"
> "And us? What do you call us?"
> "'Animals,'" said the ape, "is what we call you". (*The Woman and the Ape*, 171)

A similar problem, with a now familiar solution, is posed by Høeg's novel, which is translated from the Danish and set in London. The novel opens with the smuggling of an ape into London from some faraway place and, like Conrad, Boyd's *Brazzaville Beach* ape, this one is also unnerving, thanks to the look in his eyes, which is totally human (1996, 6).

The ape escapes, only to be re-captured into the ambit of the sinister Adam Burden and his creepy sister, who had been responsible for the illegal capture and smuggling of the animal in the first place. They are ambitious, with horrible schemes for enlarging London Zoo. What they do not reckon with, is Adam's beautiful, Danish wife, Madelene, who, at the outset of the novel, is an alcoholic rapidly on the road to self-destruction. This is because of the pitiful state into which 'Man,' her husband, archetypally named 'Adam,' has descended, or so it is implied.

Adam's parents had been part of Colonial Africa—Kenya—archetypal site for big white hunters, predators and imperialists. The shed is full of their hunting trophies. Their object in life had been "to shoot, collect and exhibit". However, "the world had changed" (1996, 46). The post-imperial age, in other words, made their way of life in Kenya anachronistic and so they attempted to export it into the heart of London.

No longer hunters, big white Tarzan figures at home in the jungle, Adam's 'burden' is to continue to have power over wild creatures, but he cuts a rather ridiculous figure in London, toting his anachronistic gun (penis?) which fails to function at crucial moments. Like Tarzan, or Adam, first man in the Garden, he is still King of the Jungle, when Madelene first meets and falls in love with him:

> In his body resided his cricket, his javelin throwing and a veritable succession of physical victories over other males; in his hide the requisite arrogance and essential resources and in his voice when he reached her a richness possessed only by those with a roar that comes from the gut, together with the kind of polish acquired only at the most expensive private schools and universities. Around him, like a mane or an aura, hung an awareness of having practically no natural enemies. (1996, 38)

However, the humanised ape, whose name is Erasmus, ironically after the sixteenth century Dutch humanist, the renaissance man, who signified the ascendancy of man, wins Madelene away from her husband and exposes his lion's mane as a mask of his inadequacy. Madelene helps Erasmus to escape, dressed as a human in disguise. Adam, who thinks she has run away with a lover,

> found that the Adam Burden he thought he knew had been given his marching orders. Over him and through him and out into the night thundered herds of runaway elephants and enchanted swine. He was incapable of moving a muscle and not until day began to break and his inward bellowing died down to be replaced by a kind of lethargy, was he able to drag himself across the floor and lift the telephone receiver. (1996, 117)

Again the white man, the proverbial Adam, finds himself expelled from the garden. Again too, the white woman is not expelled with him, but joins up with the new dominant and hairy species, which has given Adam his marching orders. In other words, there is much escaping, recapturing and escaping again, but like Jane Good in Boyle's "Descent of Man," in a stunning reversal, it is the ape who saves the girl from the crushed Tarzan, whose ineffectual bullet misses its mark and signals his bodily impotence. And along with his descent, the metropole, London, Hampstead Heath, is also diminished, echoing Simon's vision of its being shat upon by an almighty Kong-ish turd:

> The next instant a surge of murderous jealousy shot through Adam and out of his index finger, and he squeezed the trigger.
> Too late. The white-hot projectile sped out into the world, never to find its target. It flew whistling across the southern side of Hampstead Heath then, over the Vale of the Heath, it began to waver and rotate and lose height, before falling impotent to earth. For by the time Adam pulled the trigger the ape had already, a moment before, wrapped an arm round Madelene, lifted her off her feet and leapt off the balcony. (1996, 149)

Hardly able to speak, his impotent gun lowered, flaccid, he acknowledges the victory of the ape:

> Then Adam Burden put down his rifle. Madelene and the ape retreated towards the door. Adam followed them, unarmed, awkward. He stopped in front of the ape.
> "I would like...to wish you good luck," he said. (1996, 226)

Once more, and this point is crucial, Erasmus is not just an ape, but rather another hybrid of the man and the ape. His dental chart points to the fact that the animal can't be an ape—its dental arch indicated that it is "humanoid"—in fact, it is the chart of a "of a non-existent creature" (1996, 49). In the vet's analysis, in genetic terms, Erasmus is more a human being than an ape (1996, 193). Here the solution for white men, who feel diminished, appears to be that the ape's the virile body should be syncretised with his. Erasmus, in the late twentieth century, offers the hope of the Renaissance flowering of strength and creativity, of the human. Furthermore, like Boyle's Konrad, with overtones of Lorenz, the man who suggested that aggression could be tempered, Desiderius Erasmus believed that

> With strenuous effort the very stuff of human nature could be moulded, so as to draw out...peaceful and social dispositions while discouraging unworthy appetites. (*Britannica*, no.18, 490)

In a rather regressive piece of male fantasy, we see the body returned to the male creature in a mythical, elemental description of the love making between Madelene and Erasmus, that would rival Rice Burrough's imaginative powers:

> She bit his ear lobe, gently but deeply, until on the tip of her tongue she felt the first metallic hint of blood and her nostrils were filled with a scent, a savannah of scent, a continent of scent, of animal, man, stars, glowing embers, air beds and burning rubber. (1996, 155)

Like Adam and Eve, or Tarzan and Jane in the African bush, Madelene and Erasmus find themselves in St Francis Forest, a prelapsarian paradise in the heart of London:

> Sitting there, in the sun, his hairless buttocks looked like two halves of a honeydew melon, only twice as large. At that moment Madelene realized where they had landed. That it was to the pornographic Garden of Eden they had come. (1996, 159)

With clear overtones of ape as Other from faraway places, within the discourse that enables traffic between African and ape boundaries, there is an echo of suggestion that the white man needs the mythical advanced sexuality of the black man, the potency of the savage man, to bring him back to speed. This cyborg man, resurrected Tarzan, can once again rescue Jane/Madelene and fly away with her. She recovers her femininity in the process and discards her sexless khakis and reverts to Jane of the Jungle. Madelene wears

> nothing but a bit of cloth around the top half of her body and another bit of cloth around her bottom half. Outwardly they look like two displaced apes—for Madelene, too, could pass for an ape. Erasmus rarely carries her now, she can manage on her own, even 70 or 80 feet above the ground. (1996, 181)

Erasmus warns them that after they are gone, they must remember "how hard it is to tell, in each one of us, where the part that you call human ends and the part you call animal begins" (1996, 216). The cyborg rainbow possibility is reinforced in the final words of the novel, which pans to a new age image of an angel in the sky, an angel which is "for all we know...one-third god, one-third animal, and one-third human" (1996, 229).

It is by now abundantly clear that any implication that the way back to their great bodies is for white men to infuse their beings with the reputed sexual power of blacks hybridised with apes, is political dynamite. Haraway was right in contesting purity, racial separation and cruelty to animals. But her cyborg solutions appear to forget the minefields that certain species crossings carry as part of their baggage.

In conclusion, the fuse is set and I suspect that the detonator is the ape. It is extraordinarily difficult, I would like to suggest, to produce fiction freed of the history of colonialism and the Tarzan myths linked to it, twinned with the ape story of evolution and the gender story of kidnaps and rescues.

This may appear to be a pessimistic and prescriptive conclusion. Irony and satire, experimentation with old stories to produce new tales and monsters is surely the stuff of the writer's autonomy. It is indeed, but old tales and monsters enter the imaginative crucible and create unstable political mixes of which the writer may not always be aware, or fully in control. Nor may they simply cover their tracks, as does the joker, Will Self. His psychiatrist ape suggests to his patient, Simon Dykes, at the very end of *Great Apes*, that "your conviction that you were human and that the evolutionarily successful primate was the ape was more in the manner of a satirical trope" (404). This flippant flirtation with the mask of the postmodern love of stories conceals the quite painful search for a new male identity.

But what is also clear is that when identities are splintered, when solutions are being sought, when race and gender are being interrogated, when cyborgs are being born, then what may be possible is not a foregone conclusion. We should remember Fred Pfeil's suggestion that "when certain bodies are mutating" and disturb the "social-symbolic imaginaries" then, given that "no psycho-social body is ever finally closed" and "no imaginary ever complete or fully resolved" then something new and radical may be "up for grabs" (1995, 32–3). I am still looking for novels with Apes, Janes, and Tarzans that make a genuine reversal of the discourse.

There is another angle on the cyborg story, one that leads to the next part of this book, when gay men will be embarking on their fictional travels. Haraway acknowledges, in her celebration of the progeny of the computer chip and the frog that the vision is heterosexual:

> The story of compulsory reproductive sexuality is never far in the background in primate visions. ...Not for a moment does all the boundary crossing—of species barriers, machine-organism barriers, language barriers, earth-space barriers—relax the injunction to be fruitful and multiply, heterosexually. ...The progeny are cyborgs, creatures with ambiguous and permeable boundaries: monkeys, apes, and humans, all entwined in a compulsory reproductive politics. (1989, 146)

What alternative stories to that compulsory heterosexuality are some of the white, gay sons telling and why do they journey to Africa to tell them?

Part Four:
Sons as Gay

CHAPTER SIX

Secret Sharing: The Closet and Empire

The Sublime of the Closet

> If the idea of 'homosexual writing' is useful, it probably applies best to the period when homosexuality was criminal, and hence when the fictional treatment of same-sex love had to be implicit, indirect, deflected, latent. (Lanchester, 11)

Fiction lends itself to devices of concealment—decoys and smokescreens, dense forests of metaphor and unreliable narrators masking authorial moral points of view. All of these, and many other mechanisms, were close to hand when homosexual writers at the turn of the nineteenth century fictionalised their forbidden desire, desire that might not have dared not speak its name out loud, but found poetic codes, nonetheless.

Two questions follow from this that concern us here, and in the next chapter. Firstly, what are the consequences when those dense, figurative forests are none other than the African bush, or when the concealing mask reveals an African person, through whose services 'difference' can be coded and transferred from a sexual to a racial identity? Secondly, what happens to 'homosexual writing' at the turn of the twentieth century, when being gay has a name, an identity and, certainly by comparison with a hundred years ago, a freedom enshrined in law? Has it, paradoxically, lost its power and purpose?

The compelling nature of the exquisite pain, urgency and danger of concealment, as well as the rather delicious challenge to readers to break the codes, I would speculate, helps to answer the question Eve Kosofsky Sedgwick, priestess of "the epistemology of the closet", asks in her path breaking book of that title:

> I've wondered about my ability to keep generating ideas about "the closet," compared to a relative inability, so far, to have new ideas about the substantive differences made by post-Stonewall imperatives to rupture or vacate that space. (This, obviously, despite every inducement to thought provided by the

immeasurable value of "out" liberatory gay politics in the lives around me and my own). (1990, 63)

While Stonewall dates the beginning of gay militancy when homosexuals resisted being raided by the police at Stonewall Inn, New York, 1969, it did not make gay secrecy redundant. Or as Cesare Casarino puts it— "one has always wondered about the pleasures of the closet", pleasures "steeped in danger" (1997, 202). Not only danger but

> one has at times felt in the closet an incommensurable intensity of enclosure, a joy of infinitely finite and crammed spaces, a claustrophiliac ecstasy of the flesh. (1997, 203)

Casarino is emphatic that "the sublime of the closet" of his title "is *not* a coming out (1997, 203), which is "not to underestimate the immense power and necessity of coming out for any queer politics" (1997, 203). The concept of "the sublime of the closet" establishes the paradox of the closet as an exquisite prison, a paradox whose riddles, both narrative and spatial, I will be attempting to read against the politics of race and Empire.

Later, Sedgwick raises a different issue from the dangerous pleasures of concealment, that ensure her continuing fixation with closetedness, when she points to its continuing relevance today, notwithstanding gay liberation— "even at an individual level, there are remarkably few of even the most openly gay people who are not deliberately in the closet with someone personally or economically or institutionally important to them" (1990, 68). Even Will, the protagonist of Alan Hollinghurst's novel of "out" gay culture, *The Swimming-Pool Library*, which we will examine in some detail in the next chapter, and who is a totally liberated, young gay man, finds himself at the opera with his grandfather:

> The three of us in our hot little box were trapped with this intensely British problem: the opera that was, but wasn't, gay, the two young gay friends on good behaviour, the mandarin patriarch giving nothing of his feelings away. (1989a, 140)

Sedgwick sums up that the reality is that "the epistemology of the closet has given an overarching consistency to gay culture and identity throughout this century" (1990, 68). This tradition, plus that continuing necessity for closets, but of a distinctively, fluid, virtually real, now you see it now you don't, late twentieth century design, is the framework of my own investigation. In this way, the challenge is to take Sedgwick further and attempt to avoid the risks she herself identifies, "risks in making salient the continuity and centrality of the closet, in a historical narrative that does not have as a fulcrum *a saving vision...of its apocalyptic rupture*" (1990, 68, my emphasis). This we will be doing in the context of foregrounding other risks, risks that relate to the tradition where the closet was a continent.

In focussing on two recent gay novelists, then, we will wonder whether they have recognised and discarded the attitudes and prejudices of their ancestors that became enshrined in the literary traditions of homosexual secretiveness. We will examine the nature of what Dellamora calls a "cultural gap" between E.M Forster's generation and that of gays, who fostered and furthered gay liberation. We will ask with him what precisely are the connections "between a man whose lifelong response to homosexuality was affected by his terror, at age sixteen, of what happened to Wilde, and the young men and women who, in the immediate aftermath of 1967, were inventing gay liberation?" (1993, 158–9).

I will not presume in this chapter to judge the politics of concealment or 'coming out' as they have been hotly debated, for example, around E.M. Forster, and his posthumous publishing instructions. What it is certainly my brief to consider, is the extent to which the fictional codes and narrative devices, which protected and nurtured homosexual writing, did so at the expense of the real lives and lands of colonised people. Furthermore, I ask, have the stains of colonialist discourse survived in the more recent fiction?

The two novels that are my primary interest and focus in the next chapter, are Alan Hollinghurst's *The Swimming-Pool Library* and Patrick Roscoe's *The Lost Oasis*. I will, however, be touching on a short story by each of these writers in this chapter, as I establish more clearly the spatial and narrative contours of the tradition of concealment, known in shorthand as 'the closet', but specifically within the historical context of Empire. Furthermore, in order to acquaint ourselves with these sons, we will have to re-visit some fathers, although with a selective and narrow focus in mind. There is always Conrad, but here the key text is not *Heart of Darkness*, but *The Secret Sharer*; E.M. Forster's overtly homosexual writing is of great interest and particularly a short story set in Africa; And of course the architect of the archetypal image of the terror of the exposure of the secret is Oscar Wilde.

Finally, in the next part of this book, in chapter eight, I will return to Hollinghurst and his latest novel, *The Spell*, when we move from the enclosed space of the closet to the open spaces of landscape. The significance of Hollinghurst's return from settings in Egypt, Kenya or the Sudan to the English countryside of Dorset will be read in the context of his awareness of the pitfalls and minefields of adventuring to other places, in order to map his own politics, aesthetics and sexuality. But in 1983 when his first piece of fiction is published, and his only short story to date, Hollinghurst sets it in Egypt. What is he doing there? To find out we have once again to undertake a sea voyage into tradition with the ever-present Joseph Conrad, this time into a cabin-closet occupied by secret sharers.

Secret Sharing: Re-visiting the Fathers

Cesare Casarino, in his doctoral dissertation, focuses upon "an investigation of spatial discourses" and in order to do so, he refers to Michel Foucault's concept of "heterotopia" (1994, 20) and their applicability to homosexual imaginative geographies. What are heterotopia? They are privileged, potent spaces within Western culture in the twentieth century. The characteristics of heterotopia, as described by Foucault in his paper entitled "Of Other Spaces", are as distinctive as they are difficult to pin down. As Foucault puts it, they are "real places—places that do exist" (24) but as a kind of "counter-site" in relation to all the other spaces within the culture. In other words, "they have a function in relation to all the space that remains" (27). They enable the culture to define itself against the grain, as it were, of such spaces; they contest or invert the mainstream social sites and are "outside of all places". But in being outside, they act as a mirror held up to the society; it is "a sort of shadow that gives my own visibility to myself" (24). Heterotopia are spaces where deviants live, where "individuals whose behaviour is deviant in relation to the required mean or norm are placed" (25). If they are places where the Law is thrown into question, then they are also unstable and hold out the promise of the resumption and reinforcement of mainstream authority.

Foucault suggests that colonies are a type of heterotopia and this we have already seen elsewhere, and will encounter again, in this book. Even Foucault buys into the exotica of a treasure island trope in his enthusiasm for this role ascribed to other places and people:

> Brothels and colonies are two extreme types of heterotopia and if we think, after all, that the boat is a floating piece of space, a place without a place, that exists by itself, that is closed in on itself and at the same time is given over to the infinity of the sea and that, from port to port…it goes as far as the colonies in search of the most precious treasures they conceal in their gardens, you will understand why the boat has not only been for our civilization, from the sixteenth century until the present, the great instrument of economic development…but has been simultaneously the greatest reserve of the imagination. The ship is the heterotopia *par excellence*. In civilizations without boats, dreams dry up, espionage takes the place of adventure, and the police take the place of pirates. (27)

The question is what is the outcome of the superimposition of the heterotopia of Empire with those sacred homosexual spaces of closet concealment? What when the boats carrying the adventuring colonisers and jolly Roger pirates double up as closets, as the secret cabin spaces in which men consummate their illicit, illegal attraction to other men? Foucault tells us categorically, without substantiation, that "we live inside a set of relations that delineates sites which are...*absolutely not superimposable on one another"* (23, my emphasis). We will see that some kind of superimposition is indeed effected, as imperial expeditions and homosexual concealment create a palimpsest of text and subtext, on deck and below, with all the murky maelstrom of politico-cultural consequences. Nowhere is this more visible than in Joseph Conrad's novella, *The Secret Sharer*.

The Secret Sharer plots an incident in the life of a young sea captain, who is a stranger to both his men and his boat as he takes up his new command. He makes an unusual decision to keep watch himself and out of the sea emerges a naked man, with whom the captain establishes an immediate "mysterious communication" (1961, 240). Leggatt is his name and he is escaping from his own ship, the *Sephora*, where he killed a man. The legitimacy of this action is never in question. The murdered man "wouldn't do his duty and wouldn't let anybody else do theirs" and was, in fact, an "ill-conditioned snarling cur" (1961, 242), a lowly type our captain recognises all too well:

> And I knew well enough the pestiferous danger of such a character where there are no means of legal repression. And I knew well enough also that my double there was no homicidal ruffian. (1961, 242)

The Secret Sharer is a story of same sex desire couched in secrecy. Leggatt is referred to as his double, mirror reflection, own self on almost every page of the story. This is itself a concealing device, a narcissism, that will hint that Leggatt is a figment of the captain's imagination, his reflection in the mirror rather than a flesh and blood male, for whom he feels powerful, forbidden desire—"it was...as though I had been faced by my own reflection in the depths of a sombre and immense mirror" (1961, 241). Sedgwick explains narcissism as concealment when she develops her concept of the glass closet in relation to Oscar Wilde, later in this chapter. The concealment is always partial and the bodily reality of the other man punctures his immateriality as ghost or self-reflection. The Captain "took a peep" at his double and the fluid sensuousness of his heaving chest is unmistakable:

> His arm was still over his eyes; but his chest heaved; his hair was wet; his chin glistened with perspiration. (1961, 253)

The language of 'normal' interaction is prohibited in the light of the necessary secrecy—they are silent by day and whisper by night—"it would not have been prudent to talk in daytime; and I could not have stood the excitement of that queer sense of whispering to myself" (1961, 256). We will witness again and again this recourse to secret alternative communication systems, for example, when a Hollinghurst's character learns Arabic, or a boy of Roscoe loses the power of speech almost completely. Conrad emphasises and repeats the significance of the secret whispering—"at night I would smuggle him into my bed-place, and we would whisper together" (1961, 268). In fact they would only ever hear each other's whispered voices—"the time had come to exchange our last whispers, for neither of us was ever to hear each other's natural voice" (1961, 279).

How and why does this parting come about? The captain protects Leggatt from the skipper of the *Sephora*, who comes searching for him in order to give him up to the law. It becomes clear, however, that the hiding of Leggatt cannot continue, not least of all because the captain is torn between his duty above board and his secret below:

> I was not wholly alone with my command; for there was that stranger in my cabin. Or rather, I was not completely and wholly with her. Part of me was absent. That mental feeling of being in two places at once affected me physically as if the mood of secrecy had penetrated my very soul. (1961, 266)

Leggatt himself proposes that he should be marooned, and in a dangerous manoeuvre, which takes the ship perilously close to the shore, this is achieved. Leggatt has to disappear as stealthily as he materialised in order for the captain, somewhat smugly (albeit uncertainly, given what we have seen) to revel in the now "perfect communion of a seaman with his first command" (1961, 285). Leggatt turns out to have been but "a 'breathless pause' in the discourse of the law" (Casarino, 1997, 214). Casarino, with more than a hint of affront, describes the ending as a "staggering betrayal",

> the deafening fanfare of the restoration...of normative order. Virtually everything in this narrative—each and every whisper, glance, and secret understanding between Leggatt and the narrator; each and every expression of their desire—is here effortlessly hollowed out of any import and indeed obliterated in the face of the narrator's final reunion with his long lost and first love: the (hetero) eroticized female body of the ship. (1997, 241)

This is, of course, not the whole story, and Casarino himself concludes that:

> Ultimately, this text unleashes far more desire than it can process and than its narrator can abjure. ...For no acrobatics of homophobia can ever take back the claustrophiliac ecstasies of these two male bodies and the spectacle of their secret sharing. (1997, 243)

Beyond the question of what is sexually repressed and also revealed in the use of these boats and tall sea stories, always looms the question of how these writers dip into the Western cultural arsenal in order to construct and conceal their sites of "claustrophiliac ecstasies". Conrad veils his story of forbidden sexuality within the very contours of the narrative shape itself, within "a boy's tale of romance and adventure" (Casarino, 1997, 229). And nowhere are these boys tales more evident than in colonial expeditions begun on the high seas.

Marlow begins *Heart of Darkness* by telling just such a tall tale to a community of men. This tale describes his hypnotic attraction to Kurtz, a power far greater than that portrayed between Kurtz and his insipid 'intended'. If Kurtz's "horror" linked to human depravity pushed beyond the limit, is translating, at least in part, Conrad's buried sexuality into a metaphor of African savagery, then the European quest for safe closets, is surely a version of the Imperialism that we know so well? And if this seems far-fetched, let us return with Casarino to delve a little deeper into who enables those divine whispering moments between our secret sharers.

Casarino asks a startling question with regard to the man that Leggatt had murdered:

> But who exactly is this third man who...is absolutely indispensable for the narrator's and Leggatt's romance to take place as it is precisely his murder that brings them together...? (1994, 254)

Conrad does not include him as a character in the story and had dispensed with him, "the snarling cur" (1961, 242), in a moment of dismissive representation through Leggatt's eye and the Captain's sympathetic concurrence. But Casarino, in a deft critical ploy, brings him back in the flesh by way of a character that Conrad indeed describes in a different work—"For one has surely met him before. His name is Donkin. His ship is the *Narcissus*" (1994, 254). And what does Donkin, taken from *The Nigger of the Narcissus*, represent?

> Donkin is at once the personification of an urban lumpenproletariat in social ascent via its increasing involvement in the politics of unionism and socialism. ...Thus Donkin...resurfaces at the entrance of *The Secret Sharer* so as to be promptly sacrificed as a body of aberrant masculinity on the alter of a consecrated male-male romance whose spectacle is about to unfold (1994, 255)

And again, no sooner is it clear that the politics of class are fundamental to what is shared by the secret whisperers, than Casarino forces another issue, by returning "one last time to Leggatt's murder so as to begin to tell yet another story, which should have been perhaps the story all along" (1994,

261–2). This story he recasts, not from fiction, but from history, as he explains that Conrad had used a real event as his inspiration for *The Secret Sharer*—that is "the murder of a sailor by an officer aboard the *Cutty Sark* (1994, 262):

> In Conrad's rewriting of that event, though, there is a crucial omission: *the murdered sailor was black.* The fact that the enabling and foundational moment of a narrative of romance between two white men is thus constituted by the murder of a sailor who is not only the embodiment of the antithesis of (Conrad's definition of) the laboring male body but also a resistant black man—such a fact marks the coming-into-being of same-sex desire in *The Secret Sharer*. (1994, 262 – 3, my emphasis)

We are discovering closets within closets as Conrad represses the historical reality of the murder of a black sailor, as the spur to his tale of the collusion between two white men in suppressing the crime. This Casarino rightly calls a foundational narrative moment. Conrad's tales, more than any other writer's I think, provide the symbolic shorthand congealed in the culture's archive of ways and means of Othering the lands and people from countries that were colonised.

Closets as boats, a painting, a white horse, a hut in the bush, the Pyramids, the North African desert or even the shape of the fiction itself, will make themselves visible in the rest of this chapter, for all their diversity, in their similarity as "the paradox of the open secret" (Casarino, 1997, 234) and their unstable politics of both gender and race.

Egyptian Antiquities, Closets and a Thieving Boy

> The number of gay and bisexual male writers and artists who have travelled through North Africa in pursuit of sexual gratification is legion as well as legend; Andre Gide lost his virginity on the dunes of Algeria in 1893 (where Oscar Wilde served as his procurer two years later), and E.M. Forster on the beaches of Alexandria in 1916. Morocco has also served as a mecca for the gay and bisexual literati vacationing in North Africa—many clustered around Tangier's famous resident Paul Bowles. (Boone, 1995, 90)

It was while on holiday in Egypt that Alan Hollinghurst had an idea for a short story that was published in 1983 as "A Thieving Boy". Here are the bare bones of it. Tim's parents are killed in a motor accident and friends of theirs, a bland, benevolent couple, who are the narrators of Tim's story, adopt him. He succeeds at school and wins a scholarship to Cambridge, which he suddenly throws up and then he disappears and his foster parents lose touch with him for some years. On retirement, this unadventurous, elderly couple surprise themselves and go off to Egypt on holiday, where by

Secret Sharing 169

sheer chance they bump into Tim, who is living in Cairo as a teacher of English. He invites them to his apartment, where they encounter, Mustafa, his Nubian servant, and where they begin to piece together that his secret, and the key to his flight from England, Cambridge and them, is that he is a homosexual. He arranges to take them to the Pyramids and later they read in the local newspaper that while they had been on this expedition, Mustafa had robbed Tim of all his valuable possessions.

Why Egypt for Hollinghurst's first bash at fiction? North Africa is mapped out by Joseph Boone as falling within "an imagined terrain of male [homosexual] desire that has specific geographic coordinates" (91). This spatial reality pegged to fantasy sites satisfies Foucault's definition of heterotopia quite precisely and according to Boone it stretches "from the North African countries of Morocco, Algeria, and Tunisia to Egypt and thence to the Syrian-Arabic peninsula" (91). In fact, "of all the regions of the Near East, Western writers most readily associate ancient and modern Egypt with the spreading "contagion" of homosexuality" (Boone, 93). Egypt as a privileged space emerged at the outset of this book, in chapter one, where David Caute re-wrote the life of Salman Rushdie into an Egyptian setting. In addition, when William Boyd in the last chapter sought a character who could represent his own hybrid origins and identity, his Everyman, Usman Shoukry, was Egyptian. What we have already discussed, and Boone highlights here in this new context, is that Egypt occupies a quite specific interstical zone between Africa and Europe. It is not Europe's Other, precisely, but a bridge, "a conduit between East and West, Europe and Africa, the familiar and the foreign" (Boone, 93). And in this capacity, "Egypt has come to represent in the Western imagination an intermediate zone" (Boone, 93).

More specifically, what is the special significance of Egypt, and North Africa more broadly, for homosexual writing? When Hollinghurst crafted his first closet, his hiding place for the secretly gay Tim, who sought refuge from parents and Establishment, he sent him off to Egypt because in fulfilling this fantasy function "as a realm of nonfixity", Egypt "has become a ready-made symbol for that *interior world* of the polymorphously perverse" (Boone, 93, my emphasis).

The story, which is a parable of "coming out", is structured around symbolic closet interiors on larger and smaller scale—Tim's little flat, the tiny cage-like lift to reach it and the awesome pyramids. The story Hollinghurst tells, in fact, is not so much of the boy exiting the closet, as of the parents entering it and finding him inside. The conduit into the concealed space is the lift the couple enter in order to reach Tim's flat, a lift with an ominous mirror that fails to return their image as they approach a space with different rules and practices:

> It was of French construction, a little rattling cage of fancy ironwork; inside was a full-length mirror that had almost faded into total darkness and showed one looking more anxious than ever as one strained to see one's reflection in it. ...Unlike civilized lifts it did not cushion one's arrival by a gentle slowing as it neared the required floor, but accelerated to its maximum velocity and then stopped instantaneously, leaving one feeling rather shaken and foolish. (1983, 103)

No cushioning of the arrival into foreign territory, this 'primitive' cage of exotic filigree erases their solid sense of Englishness and in an already shaken state, they arrive inside Tim's space to find him cross-dressed as an Arab in "voluminous white cotton trousers and shirt" (1983, 104) and, to their great surprise, also able to speak Arabic (1983, 105). It is in Egypt that he has been able to make himself into another person and the key to this new person is that inside this little flat, within the "Cairo townscape" (1983, 103), they encounter Tim's "servant", Mustafa, the blackest possible Nubian boy:

> As we entered the room a black boy was arranging, rather than simply placing, some bowls of the delicious Egyptian roasted peanuts on the low white table. He wore a long white gallabeyah, and his appearance was intensely striking, his skin the blackest it could possibly be. (1983, 104)

Like the decorative lift, the boy appears aesthetic in his exotic dress, his artistic arrangement of an Egyptian delicacy on a low table that suggests intimacy. He is a beautiful man-child, "quite six foot tall, slender and aristocratic looking" and "one's conviction of his handsomeness grew second by second" (1983, 104). The impassive "one" viewing this boy's body so lovingly is, of course Hollinghurst, who is in some difficulty here with his passive, parental spectators. I will return to the question of narrative point of view in a moment. For now, the question is whether Mustafa is angel or demon. Tim says he is his saviour, getting him food very cheaply from the market (1983, 105). Is he lover or servant, saviour/angel or thieving boy, we wonder? The description of Mustafa's hair sums up our perplexity in reading the signs—"a huge fine fuzzy black aureole, sticking out three or four inches" (1983, 105). Like a halo, yet black instead of golden, this hair is contradictory in every way—fuzzy and high like an Afro, it is also fine. This ambiguous, beautiful boy is part man, part child, part servant, part aristocrat, part "rather sympathetic" with his "immediate and effective charm" and part menacing.

The menace emerges in a small, yet quite shocking, incident, which becomes enormously significant as a code for reading off the consequences of the violation of the closet on the part of the well meaning yet also threatening foster parents. As they are about to re-enter the lift in order to return to their world, they hear smashing glass and Tim goes to investigate.

Secret Sharing 171

Suddenly we feel the sinister currents of repressed violence and spilled secrets. Mustafa has dropped the tray. The shattered glass is reminiscent of the mirror that is too dark to reflect an image as fragile identities, newly forged, are shaken and smashed. Tim attempts to retrieve the privacy of his space and shuts the door on the parental pair, shielding Mustafa and himself from their curious, startled gaze, but not before they have caught a glimpse of the back of the naked Mustafa. And here Hollinghurst's narrative posture of telling the tale through their eyes, rather than his own or Tim's, takes strain again as they lovingly describe, on behalf of Hollinghurst, the "hooped, black, muscular curve" of this back view of this body as "unforgettable". What they also observe is "his long and elegant fingers holding between their tips a bright shiver of glass" (1983, 107). Mustafa's behind may be exquisite, but the live, quivering glass in his hand is ominous and scary.

This repressed chain of violence, sexuality and ambiguous servility will be fortified in *The Swimming-Pool Library*, as we shall see in the next chapter. What is clear and understated here is the significance what they saw as they left, which induces Tim to explain his situation more explicitly. This Hollinghurst does on Tim's behalf in the most delicate and concealed language, never naming homosexuality in the story. This telling occurs, note, on the way to Gizeh to visit the pyramids:

> It seemed obvious, and he admitted it in a matter-of-fact way, genuinely untroubled about it, but having preferred, if it had been possible, to spare us a discovery which might upset us, however harmless it was morally and in itself. This was consideration rather than cowardice, and we appreciated it as such (1983, 107).

In an interview with David Galligan, Hollinghurst was asked "as a boy, did you discuss your attraction to other boys with your parents?" (1997, 4). He answers:

> No. It took me a long time. I didn't come out as such to my parents. I sort of seeped out, really. My fear of their censure and disapproval was quite strong. I didn't really come out until my final year at university when I was twenty. That's one reason my student life wasn't very happy. I felt very locked into myself. (1997, 4)

Hollinghurst went to Oxford and saves Tim from the experience of his unhappiness there, locked into his secret, by having his first fictional character refuse to go to Cambridge and by sending him instead to North Africa. The link between the shape of Mustafa's body, its "muscular curve", and the necessity of the journey to North Africa is made quite explicitly:

> We saw it all: Tim's whole course assumed a direction, his long route *curling* towards Egypt as we could see it in our mind's eye on a classroom map, a snake-like progress which was the inevitable pattern of his life. (1983, 107, my emphasis)

The curve of the black, male body is like snake, creature of poison and betrayal, agent of expulsion from the garden and the Law of God the Father. The ambivalence towards the necessity of abandoning that Law, which necessitates entry into the snake pit and the den of thieves, is built into the liminal position of Egypt on the British and also gay mapping of the globe. The snake is an African creature, whose body outlines the journey on a map in an English classroom. The venom of the parental 'seeing it all' is buried just beneath the honey of calm, English narrative reasonableness. The understatement of the parental reception of the revelation of their foster son's sexual orientation is belied by what is implied were the consequences of their visit to the flat. While Tim is doing the dutiful son stuff, taking his foster parents sight-seeing, Mustafa burgles the flat, having clearly been thrown off balance by the visitation of Tim's family, who have brought home the reality of his own servility and of Tim's foreignness, for all his Arab dress and knowledge of the language.

What is the significance to all of this of the Pyramids to which they are speeding while Tim is "seeping out" to his foster parents as gay?

> Despite the unthinkable weight of it all it was fresh and cool, and Tim showed us the ventilation-holes hundreds of feet long which bring air into the very heart of the pyramid. You could feel it stirring.
> The emptiness too seemed quintessential, and it was after all only for a short period that the Pyramids, or the tombs we were to see in the south a few days later, had been full. Tim explained to us the irony of corruption whereby those most trusted to keep the secrets of the tombs had given them away, the priests were in league with robbers and vandals, and what had been planned to preserve the dead intact for ever had served only to lose them and all their possessions at the first opportunity. (1983, 108)

The Pyramid too is ambiguous space—strong and weak, morally challenged by associations with Pharaohs, theft and betrayal. There is the contradictory power and also vulnerability of this space and the safety and secrecy it only partially affords. Pyramids as heterotopia stand for Egypt itself—eternal, conqueror of time and in that sense, invulnerable. But, overlaying its associations with eternity, origins, the inscrutability of the desert and the mystery of Africa, is its symbolism as archetypal closet. Buried in its entrails were unimaginable treasures, secreted there for safekeeping. Its hidden passages and interiors are not claustrophobic, but have been designed to admit life giving air and ventilation. Their impregnability, however, is a desert mirage. Just as the parents have entered the flat and stolen the treasures within, so the crooks and vandals, both local thieves and Western robbers, stole African treasures, and have entered and plundered the pyramid's wealth. And yet, the possibilities contained within their ability to endure all onslaughts remain their wonder:

> They remain startlingly beautiful as well, those titanic, crumbling triangles pitched together at the edge of an almost limitless desert. (1983, 108)

Like the paradox of the closet made of glass, the eternal pyramids, like their desert home, are limitless in their capacity to survive, albeit that they are "crumbling". We have ourselves entered the symbolic interiors of lift, flat and pyramid. There is a fourth, intriguingly absent present space, which falls outside the frame of the story, but which inspired it, as Hollinghurst himself explains the interview with David Galligan:

> I'd been to Egypt for three weeks with some friends. It was at the beginning of 1980. I was twenty-five. *The idea of the story came to me when we were looking at the Colossi of Memnon.* I came back to England and the next week, I made a sketch of it one day and wrote it over the following two days. ...It's the only story I've ever written. (Galligan, 1997, 7, my emphasis)

The Colossi are all that remain of the mortuary temple of Pharaoh Amenhotep 111, which was violated and obliterated by subsequent Pharaohs. Hollinghurst substituted the Pyramids for the Colossi as the massive and symbolic closet interior that has survived, as well as having also been plundered. What would Hollinghurst and his friends have seen when they observed the amazing Colossi? Not husband and wife, the giant statues are both this Amenhotep—not the Pharaoh and his Queen, but two images of the Same, the Narcissus, the mirror, forcibly exiled from the safe confines of the ancient temple and exposed to the elements on which they gaze.

That gaze suggests another possibility. Still speculating, perhaps the Colossi that remain in the ruins are not the exposed homosexuals, but the massive parental couple, the granite Law of the Father that endures and survives against all odds. Perhaps it is both of these, as robbers double up as the robbed and Hollinghurst explores his own murky terrain as both oppressor, white man and master and oppressed, gay, closeted and locked into himself by his parents' stern, enduring gaze.

Every player in this story, in fact, is a double agent, oppressor and victim in a complex interplay of gender, race and imperialism, which Hollinghurst will develop to sophisticated heights in *The Swimming-Pool Library*. It is only at the most superficial plot level that Mustafa is the thieving boy. Concealed in the deceptive title of the novel are the thieving parents, who like the pyramid robbers of old, have entered the sacred spaces, temples and sanctuaries and enabled the violation of their buried inhabitants.

And yet, they are the ones who have the last word in the story, which ends with their perception of Tim's betrayal of them, by which, however, they are perplexingly "enriched":

> Perhaps he [Tim] was less upset by it than we should have been, or was too young to feel as we did, returning to England incredibly enriched and ready to talk of our experience forever, how much we learn from those who betray us. (1983, 109)

Even here, their betrayal by Tim is echoed by Mustafa's betrayal of Tim, a Tim, who has also, presumably been hugely pleasured by Mustafa, the boy who has stolen all his possessions. And throughout, the story signals the narrative duplicity involved in its telling as the absent presence of Hollinghurst himself secretly accuses his parental narrators of complicity in crimes committed.

And this is the political razor on which Hollinghurst skates in his story. Mustafa's riveting blackness, Cairo and the desert pyramids are those magical fetishized places of European, gay imagination, which unleashed Hollinghurst's creative powers. The exotic North African tropes which are ready to hand, however, have simultaneously been confronted by Hollinghurst, who attempts to invert robber and robbed within his own self conscious critique of imperialist plunder. But his adoring gaze on the objectified black body is only partially obscured by way of the device of the bland parents, who do the looking. Note the quite interesting narrative dilemma here. Hollinghurst has chosen narrators with whom he does not identify at all, but it is they who describe Mustafa. What we have in this short and simple story is yet another hiding space, but this time within the narrative cage itself.

The story is framed by collusion between the heterotopia of faraway Egypt and the conventional, heterosexual English parental monolith, behind which Hollinghurst conceals his authorial omniscience. Cairo, the exotic foreign place, enables this couple to be themselves and not themselves simultaneously as their ability to describe what they see and what it means is stretched to breaking point:

> How guilty he did feel about us we never actually found out—and whilst we were in Cairo we were able to observe what he had done, how he had broken away, with a suspension of the judgement we would feel when we got back to England. For a few days we found ourselves *willing collaborators in what was in some respects a conspiracy against ourselves.* (1983, 103, my emphasis)

We will see in the next chapter that Hollinghurst dumps them in *The Swimming-Pool Library* and 'comes out' narratively by telling his story through the first person eyes of Will, his promiscuous, gay protagonist, who also loves to look at, and to fuck, black men, with all the political minefields that carries. For now, we are still in the space of concealment.

Patrick Roscoe, Dorian Gray and a White Horse Closet

In a story entitled "The Beginning of the World" Roscoe furtively creates a variation of the Dorian Gray parable. In so doing, he announces his own gay sexuality, but in code. The story is part of the collection, *Love Is Starving for Itself*. The stories in this collection are set in Mexico, in a small village. What is suggestive about this setting, and links it to the North Africa of the later novel, is that familiar sense of liminality, of a border zone, this time between North and South America. These stories are mainly about the heterosexual love affairs of the village inhabitants. Concealed beneath the surface, however, in some of them, are hints of the homosexuality, which will, slowly and painfully, come out in *The Lost Oasis*. For now, Roscoe is contained within the narrative structure of his closet.

The world begins in the story with the arrival of the stunning white horse into the village, an animal that the villagers surmise comes from "the modern world" (1994, 10). The extraordinary thing about the horse is he "did not appear to grow older" (1994, 13) and "remained young and strong despite time's passing" (1994, 18). One day the villagers notice, to their great amusement, that the boy, Salvador, has fallen in love with the horse. This unnatural love, so redolent of a homosexual decadence, is not tolerated by Salvador's father, so familiar as the punishing hand of the Law:

> As a last resort his father took to tying Salvador to the avocado tree in the back yard. The boy would sit quietly with the thick rope fastened around his waist until his father's heart softened. Receiving his son's promise never to go near the white horse again, the father untied the binding knot. The moment he was free, *the lover* ran off again. (1994, 20, my emphasis)

The horse does not return this passion and "appeared as indifferent to Salvador as he had always been to others" (1994, 20) quite precisely fulfilling what Hollinghurst describes in his Oxford thesis as the sense of the pathos of unrequited, unreciprocated passion, which is "distinctly homosexual in tendency" (1980, 23). Salvador's spirit, however, merges with that of the horse and as he becomes more like the animal, he loses the power of speech:

> The boy's tongue became clumsy with disuse, and it grew difficult to understand the few words he offered when addressed. People ceased speaking to him, then forgot

he could talk at all. In his eyes lurked the dark, dreamy look often seen in dumb animals. An aroma of grass and dead leaves drifted from him. Sometimes people would frown upon feeling the old sensation that the white horse stood behind them like a spirit. Turning, they saw only Salvador. (1994, 21)

The loss of language, of human socialisation, signifies the extent of Salvador's fall from society and "his parents came to think of Salvador as gone, lost, dead—even when he walked right past their door" (1994, 21).

The white horse disappears from the village, whose "world grew older" (1994, 21) and "the aged sat still and silent within dark doorways" and were "forgotten or at least ignored by the young" (1994, 22). One day, however, a young man enters the village with the still splendid white horse—"its coat was sleek and shining; muscles swelled beneath its skin" (1994, 23). We suspect that the youth is Salvador, also eternally young, and still without clear human speech, given that he "mumbled with a tongue thick as though with drink" (1994, 23).

In a quite shocking climax Salvador consummates his love after a fashion, thereby destroying the horse and his eternal youth, as surely as the knife to Dorian's heart exposes him for all his aged ugliness:

> The young man stroked the white horse lovingly, longingly. Its coat slowly darkened like the sky losing light, until it was the common colour of any horse. While the townspeople fled this sight in fear, tears fell from the young man's eyes and stained the dimmed coat with darker patches. (1994, 23)

The young stranger disappears and the people harness and domesticate what is now the common brown horse and put him to work, thus putting the finishing touches to the annihilation of his power and magic:

> However, as soon as it was harnessed, the animal aged. With astonishing rapidity its muscles vanished and its coat dulled. Within a month the horse was a bag of bones unable to pull a plough even one yard. (1994, 23)

The capture of the body and flesh of the white horse boomerangs on the town where all hope of love and light is banished. Even the Law itself, God, disappears from a darkened universe:

> God closed His eyes forever, and under a starless sky the children groped blindly, seeing only with the weak eyes of their feet. They clung to the old brown horse, which appeared a blacker shape in the darkness. They were reluctant to wander far from it, for fear of cutting themselves on the sharp wire fence. "Where are we?" they cried in the dark. (1994, 24)

The bleakness of this vision is contained in the double whammy of unreciprocated passion and the destructiveness of acting upon this doomed love in fleshy, bodily touching. And within this sad story are many layers of concealment. There is the use of the genre of fantasy and myth. According to Hollinghurst, with reference to Firbank and Forster, but relevant to Roscoe as well:

> It is in this margin between naturalism and fantasy—between responsibility to observed life and to the imagination—that the subversive and unstable element of homosexual concealment flourishes. (1980, 9)

In fact, Hollinghurst suggests, "homosexuality entails a special *way* of writing" which "only prevails if homosexuality itself is not discussed" (1980, 47). Furthermore, within the concealed parable of homosexual yearning and fall from grace is the language of Camp, which enfolds the florid colours and landscapes of Mexico. Here again we have the interplay between the secret language that has been appropriated by homosexual writing, whose alphabet is places like Mexico and Egypt, places which serve as Western gay Camp codes of repressed sexuality. I have been alerting us to the fact that this interplay carries political consequences sometimes unforeseen by writers.

The Language of the Glass Closet

Philip Core suggests that Camp "originated as a Masonic gesture by which homosexuals could make themselves known to each other during periods when homosexuality was not avowable" (9). Homosexuals, in other words, "whose desire to conceal something and to reveal it at the same time" developed particular styles of dress and décor, speech and mannerisms. Camp, in other words, "was and remains the way in which homosexuals and other groups of people with double lives can find a *lingua franca*" (9).

By definition, there is some difficulty in describing in words a 'language' that is primarily about performance, theatricality and exaggeration—"a sensibility (as distinct from an idea) is one of the hardest things to talk about":

> Indeed the essence of Camp is its love of the unnatural: of artifice and exaggeration. And Camp is esoteric—something of a private code, a badge of identity even, among small urban cliques. (Sontag, 515)

In the light of Camp, we are able to re-read the code when returning to the moment in "The Thieving Boy" when the intensely black Mustafa in his "long white gallabeya" is arranging the "delicious Egyptian roasted peanuts on the low white table" (1983, 104). The parents observed that "there was something so aesthetically calculated about his presence there that the idea could only have sprung from the imagination of a white person" (1983, 104). Or, as Sontag would have it:

> Camp taste has an affinity for certain arts rather than others. Clothes, furniture, all the elements of visual décor, for instance, make up a large part of Camp. For Camp art is often decorative art, emphasizing texture, sensuous surface, and style at the expense of content. (517)

Like the touch of Salvador, however, the chill eyes of the Parents, who break the code in Hollinghurst's story, dismember the artifice.

This is the context in which Salvador's loss of language speaks to those who are able to read the code; this is the loaded significance of the whispering secret sharers, who will never hear each other's 'normal' speaking voice. Sedgwick suggests that "in the vicinity of the closet, even what *counts* as a speech act is problematized on a perfectly routine basis" (1990, 3). She enlarges, without referring to Camp by name, but capturing its nature quite precisely, that "'closetedness' itself is a performance initiated as such by the speech act of a silence" (1990, 3).

The crucial concealment, however, which is so partial as to be transparent, is that Roscoe's story is a version of *Dorian Gray* and in the telling of it, he has built himself a a closet within the closet—a story encased in the coded story of Oscar Wilde's archetypal parable. And in revisiting the site of that ghoulish painting which conceals the flesh and blood of Dorian's debauched body, we come to what Eve Kosofsky Sedgwick, in her *Epistemology of the Closet*, refers to as the "glass closet", the contours of which are paradoxically revealing even as they strive to keep a secret.

The gay fathers, white and privileged though they may have been, lived and wrote under the cloud of the criminalisation of their sexual preference, a criminalisation that called for narrative strategies that could both provide an outlet, but also a hiding place:

> For Wilde, in 1891 a young man with a very great deal to lose who was trying to embody his own talents and desires in a self-contradictory male-homosexual terrain where too much was not enough but, at the same time, anything at all might always be too much, the collapse of homo/hetero with self/other must also have been attractive for the protective/expressive camouflage it offered to distinctively gay content. *Not everyone has a lover of their own sex, but everyone, afterall, has a self of their own sex.* (Sedgwick, 1990, 160–1, my emphasis)

This ambiguity was also built into *The Secret Sharer*, but the nature of this concealment, however, is only partial and coded, visible to those who know where and how to read it. For if the desire were perfectly concealed, the writing would fail in its moral, aesthetic and therapeutic purpose, but if it were frankly exhibited the cost could be fatal, as Wilde indeed was to discover. The excitement, moreover, of the forbidden desire would falter if exposed too directly to scrutiny. This ambivalent space, the "open secret", both visible and invisible, protective and dangerous, has been referred to by Sedgwick as the "glass closet" (1990,164):

> *The Picture of Dorian Gray* occupies an especially symptomatic place in this process. Published four years before Wilde's "exposure" as a sodomite, it is in a sense a perfect rhetorical distillation of the open secret, the glass closet, shaped by the conjunction of an extravagance of deniability and an extravagance of flamboyant display. (1990,165)

If the concealment is partial, then so is the Narcissistic love, in that self-hatred laces the desire of homosexuals, like Wilde or Forster, given when they lived and how much danger and ignorance surrounded same sex love. And if the reflection, the adored Self, is also an abomination, then a metaphor was close to hand to capture the dark, dreaded and degraded desire. In other words, the beautiful blond boy that Dorian appears eternally to be, hides the loathsome toad, the shadow, the dark side from which the blond has seeped away—up in the attic or schoolroom, there is a dark and savage, threatening presence.

The figurative name given to that self-hatred varies—painting, attic madness, but most significantly also, Oriental opium den or black African savage. To further complicate matters, that dark, loathsome savage self is also both loved and hated. It is made flesh in the person of the beautiful black boy, the Mustafa, who is snake and thief, as well as beautiful angel and saviour. It is Lord Henry's observation in *Dorian Gray* that:

> the bravest man amongst us is afraid of himself. *The mutilation of the savage has its tragic survival in the self-denial that mars our lives.* We are punished for our refusals. (Wilde, 27, my emphasis)

But we are punished also for our embraces. That Wilde has an archetypal and stereotypical Caliban in mind, moreover, to express this hidden, hated desire, is unambiguous. Speaking in his own voice in the italicised preface, he depicts the ambivalence of the taste of the age through the rage of Caliban:

> The nineteenth century dislike of Realism is the rage
> of Caliban seeing his own face in a glass.
> The nineteenth century dislike of
> Romanticism is the rage of Caliban
> not seeing his face in a glass. (ix–x)

The rage of Caliban signals the deepest inner desires, which rage because unfulfilled and which are identified with the Self, with identity, as the Subject struggles with the glass, with the search for a glimpse of the true self, metaphorically inscribed as mirror. This elusive inscrutable self, that rages unseen, or else throws back a horrible, unwelcome visage, is therefore, paradoxically and crucially, also Other. This self as Other is recognisable as none other than a version of the racism that Chinua Achebe identifies when he slates Conrad's African savage heart as Europe's inner darkness. This is the same syndrome when Wilde, in depicting Dorian's inner evil and depravity at their pinnacle, takes him into a space that is the dark and Orientalised London of the opium-dens—"the way seemed interminable, and the streets like the black web of some sprawling spider". It darkens and "as the mist thickened, he felt afraid" (291). Inside the filthy and debauched den, "some Malays were crouching by a little charcoal stove playing with bone counters, and showing their white teeth as they chattered" (293). Debauchery is signified by race—not the Caliban of the pure unsullied instincts, but "a half-caste, in a ragged turban" who "grinned a hideous greeting" (296). The fallen woman smiles crookedly "like a Malay crease" (296).

The intersections between the intimacies of sexual desire and fantasy, and structural and historical questions of sexual politics, nationalism, imperialism and race, are buried beneath a kinetic labyrinth. What seems to be the case, is that gay writing, within a colonial and postcolonial context, is enmeshed in an even more opaque web as allies and foes, Self and Other, oppressor and oppressed play their own game of musical chairs, where to lose out, is at best to cease to write, at worst to suffer public shaming and premature death. However opaque and labyrinthine these relationships are, while none "of these accounts will be simple ones to render—even to render visible", Sedgwick warns us that we need to attempt them in order to plot "the eroticized borders" in our "mapping of the national body" (1992, 244). Unless we do so, unless we confront the symbiosis between the gay codes and the politics of race and Empire, we will collude with the Law of the Imperial Fathers. The gay sons, in their search for a subversive space concealed by the use of the familiar exotic metaphors of the Fathers, may find that this mechanism is potentially treacherous.

To sum up, in re-visiting the gay literary tradition a quite particular quest is ours as we appreciate the performances, the drama of Masonic, Camp moments and simultaneously have to bring to bear political and moral judgements in a fictional theatre in which black actors and foreign landscapes are the letters of the secret language.

Sadly, this is totally out of keeping with the spirit of Camp. My dilemma in this book is that I wish to celebrate the aesthetic playfulness of the codes, to recognise the dire necessity of homosexual concealment historically and also, and by no means least of all, the sensuality and acute pleasure it generates. But organic to the politics of this book is another agenda, based on the history of abuse of the African continent and its inhabitants. When Philip Core includes "Little Egypt" and "Arabs under 21" in his list "of things and people, about which there is nothing to be said, which have become Camp to admire, collect or discuss" (298), what alternative is there to exposing and rejecting the politics of this extraordinary statement? All of this is context for the conflicts, agonies and concealments of E.M. Forster.

"The Golliwog that Lies Within": E.M. Forster and Race as Closet

E.M. Forster "was in his mid-teens during Wilde's trials" and he "appears to have been permanently affected" (Dellamora, 1994, 83). What this meant is that Forster, like Wilde, or even more so, given Wilde's tragic fate, had a need "both to express and to dissemble a special interest in male intimacy" (Dellamora, 1994, 85). While Forster's fiction concerns itself, politically, philosophically and aesthetically, with a great range of issues and dimensions, and should not be reduced to his homosexuality, I think it is fair to say that all of these preoccupations operate within the structural space carved out precariously by the "glass closet".

The glass closet, remember, is a contradictory space in two senses. Firstly, it conceals and displays simultaneously. Secondly, it is a reflecting surface into which the paranoid Narcissus gazes with both love and self-hatred. Bearing this in mind helps to explain the puzzle that Christopher Lane explores in his analysis of E.M. Forster—that of the gap between Forster's professed "liberal-humanist commitment to interracial friendship" and the fact that such friendship "often falters in his fiction" (146). What Lane wishes to understand is why "Forster's narratives consistently frustrate" homosexual encounters between "men of different races, classes, and nations...by wounding or destroying the protagonists who attempt to fulfil them" (147).

What Lane also wishes to do is to understand the linked gap "between his [Forster's] 'public' novels about friendship and his 'private' and posthumous stories about sex between men of different races" (146). Lane's own analysis, I think, explains this puzzle. He describes the symbiotic and enabling connections between the public and the private fictions, a symbiosis which oils the hinges of the closet and which separates the politics from the fiction. Lane describes how Forster's fiction negotiates his "literary and sexual ambivalence" by having as its "underside" a "supplemental narrative", that of the secret, overtly homosexual stories, published posthumously as *The Life to Come* (165).

The story, "The Life to Come", which gives this collection its title, is set in Africa. What this suggests, as Christopher Lane puts it, is that "a shift in geography was the condition for homosexuality tangentially to re-emerge in Forster's texts; he transposed the problem of homosexuality onto race and colonialism". Exile, then, becomes "the condition through which an otherwise impossible homosexual drama could fleetingly emerge" (152).

What I will be tracing in the following pages is the way in which the transference of sexual preference onto race is the oil on the hinge of Forster's glass closet. This transference enables him to move from private fantasies to public novels and from political to fictional writing, albeit that his journeys from one to another dimension are fraught with tension, mishap, pain and violence. This central point, in fact, underlies this chapter as a whole. In the coded closet language of forbidden desire, in the glass cabinet of the public fiction, cross-racial friendship conceals and signifies the scandal of same-gender sexuality. In the unpublished fiction, where the writer emerges from the cupboard, secretly at night, cross-racial friendship between two men attempts to be sexuality consummated. The freedom from closeting, however, is imaginary. Narcissus escapes from glass only to discover the paranoia of the entrapment in the mirror of self-hatred and even of buried racism. The men who transgress are meted the ultimate fictional punishment for what is homophoebically portrayed as their sins and at the end of a long night, E. M. Forster ceases to work in the medium of fiction for the remaining years of his life.

"The Life to Come" begins in a "dark" and "vast", "wild region", the African forest, where two men have made passionate love in "a small African hut". The wick of a lamp reveals that the one is our familiar, white and golden haired young man, while the other is black, with "pagan limbs". The landscape may be archetypally dark and wild, but it is contradictorily described in the terms of an English pastoral idyll, that is very rapidly shattered, all within the space of the first page:

> A stream sang outside, a firefly relit its lamp also. A remote, a romantic spot... lovely, lovable... and then he caught sight of a book on the floor, and he dropped beside it with a dramatic moan as if it was a corpse and he the murderer. For the book in question was his Holy Bible. (65)

The Law of civilization, of the bible, has been violated in the heterotopia of hut and African bush. The white man is a missionary, Paul Pinmay, who was sent in the faint hope of converting the other man, called Vithobai, to Christianity. Vithobai was "the wildest, strongest, most stubborn of all the inland chiefs" (66). Pinmay succeeds where other missionaries have failed, as Vithobai, who falls in love with Paul, misunderstands Christianity to be the religion of love, the means to the fulfilment of his desire for the European man. How this had all come about is that after he had earlier publicly spurned Pinmay's advances in his ancestral stockade, Vithobai had come to Paul's hut secretly that night and Paul had read to him from the holy bible and:

> spoke of the love of Christ and of our love for each other in Christ, very simply but more eloquently than ever before, while Vithobai said, "This is the first time I have heard such words, I like them," and drew closer, his body aglow and smelling sweetly of flowers. And he saw how intelligent the boy was and how handsome, and determining to win him there and then imprinted a kiss of his forehead and drew him to Abraham's bosom. And Vithobai had lain in it gladly—too gladly and too long—and had extinguished the lamp. And God alone saw them after that. (67–8)

Vithobai and his people, on the strength of that union, embrace Christianity, facilitating, amongst other things, the great rise within missionary hierarchy of one, Paul Pinmay, whose success in this conversion is much marvelled at and so "the new district naturally fell to his charge" (69). As Paul's fortunes rise, so those of Vithobai, who has been Christened Barnabas, decline. By allowing Christianity into his life and that of his community, he opens the doors to the Church's ally, imperialism, and he soon finds his lands, livelihood, power and status, dignity and culture, disappear along with his name. The forest, site of heady love, is destroyed to provide wood for the mines, the one place apparently that Christianity allows men to be unclad. Irony thickens the page in this conversation between Pinmay and Barnabas:

> "How much of the timber is earmarked for the mines?" inquired Mr Pinmay, in the course of the conversation.
> "An increasing amount as the galleries extend deeper into the mountain. I am told that the heat down there is now so great that the miners work unclad. Are they to be fined for this?"
> "No. It is impossible to be strict about mines. They constitute a special case." (74)

Barnabas/Vithobai, however, still lives in the hope that Paul will fulfil his promise and come to him again as a lover. The horrified Paul brutally tells him that that will never be. Paul is sickened by the thought of the 'unspeakable' act he had committed in the forest, and determines to purge his desire, repress his sexuality and never to repeat the abomination. His guilty secret and self-hatred, predictably arouses over the years acute and deflected hostility and revulsion in Pinmay towards Vithobai. He despises "the dark erotic perversion that the chief mistook for Christianity", and is repulsed by "the cold voice of the somewhat scraggy and unattractive native inviting him to sin" (76–7). He therefore orders the auspicious hut, in which the act had taken place, to be pulled down. Eventually, some years later, Pinmay does not really even feel much sorrow when he hears that "the unfortunate fellow was dying" of consumption, a disease, the ironic narrator tells us, brought in by "one of the imported workers" (77). Barnabas put up no fight against the disease—"his heart seemed broken" (78). Mr and Mrs Pinmay pay him a final charity visit. The conversation between the two men and the outcome of this visit are startling, dramatic and violent, redolent with the cacophony of Forster's conflicting values, alliances and desires.

Vithobai had been carried up onto the roof, where Paul Pinmay ascends alone. The dying man is "stark naked", shod of shabby European adornments, such that Paul involuntarily calls him by his original name, Vithobai. It is only now, when it is too late, at the point of death, that Vithobai rebels and struggles for his dignity, his self worth and his past. When Pinmay protests that he is lying on the bare roof and not even on a mattress, Vithobai replies:

> "It is my own roof. Or I thought it was until now. My wife and household respect my wishes. They laid me here because it is not the custom of my ancestors to die in a bed."
> "Mrs Barnabas should have known better. You cannot possibly lie on hard asphalt."
> "I have found that I can". (79)

The magical symbolic talisman, which signifies Vithobai's return to the source of his cultural past, is the only object on the roof—"a curious skein of blue flowers threaded round a knife", blue "the colour of despair in that valley". This provokes some terror in Paul that Vithobai is "going back to all your old false gods" and he pleads with him to "forget those wicked flowers" (79).

Vithobai, however, is only aware of the theft of all that was his and for which Paul Pinmay was culpable. It is now Vithobai who speaks with the authoritative voice of the narrator:

> Mine are this little house instead of my old great one, this valley which other men own, this cough that kills me, those bastards that continue my race; and that deed in the hut, which you say caused all, and which now you call joy, now sin. (80)

Paul becomes desperate for Vithobai's forgiveness and lays his head on his breast, while the other "raised a hand painfully, and stroked the scanty hair, golden no longer" (81). At this point, the true visage of Forster's narcissus begins to emerge, with all the Wildean overtures of imminent revelation, punishment and death. Paul utters fatal words, again provoking a

Christian misunderstanding, unleashing the narrator's irony concerning the forked tongue of religion and explaining the title of the story:

> "God's mercy is infinite, and endureth for ever and ever. He will give us other opportunities. We have erred in this life but it will not be so in the life to come."
>
> The dying man seemed to find comfort at last. "The life to come," he whispered, but more distinctly. "I had forgotten it."
>
> "The life to come," he shouted. "Life, life, eternal life. Wait for me in it." And he stabbed the missionary through the heart. (81)

The moment left to Vithobai before death is one of supreme sensual, moral and vengeful delight as their fortunes are again reversed and Pinmay is destined to blaze the trail to the other life as servant to Vithobai, supreme chief again:

> He had scarcely the strength to push the body onto the asphalt or to spread the skein of blue flowers. But he survived for a moment longer, and it was the most exquisite he had ever known. For love was conquered at last and he was again a king. He had sent a messenger before him to announce his arrival in the life to come, as a great chief should. "I served you for ten years," he thought, "and your yoke was hard, but mine will be harder and you shall serve me now for and ever". (81)

The authorial mix of emotions is palpable. Even as we rejoice in Vithobai's just vengeance, we mourn Paul's agony and punishment for his illicit urges; we simultaneously identify with Vitobai's dying outrage at the wrongs he has suffered and we shudder at the savage violence that erupts beneath the superficial Christian veneer of civilization. The skein of blue flowers doubles up as poetic despair and horrible native fetish. The story's extraordinary climax has Vithobai mounting Paul once again, but this time in an exhilarating and glorious unity of sex and death:

> Mounting on the corpse, he climbed higher, raised his arms over his head, sunlit, naked, victorious, leaving all disease and humiliation behind him, and he swooped like a falcon from the parapet in pursuit of the terrified shade. (82)

Sex and death may unite, but their fusion embodies authorial ambivalence. Ultimately both Paul and Vithobai are the losers. This is Forster's homosexual self-hatred, but it is also the coloniser's ability to deflect historical reality into personal and symbolic inward journeys. In other words, at one level, the story is extraordinarily radical in its understanding and critique of Christianity, which is bonded to imperialist economic interests. The "civilizing mission" is exposed for what it is in the light of the exploitative mines, which lay waste to the woods, the European import of fatal disease and the appropriation of land. However, for all this perceptive critique of imperial plunder, the story truly begins and ends as an exploration of fleeting homosexual pleasures paid for with the punishment of eternal damnation. An embattled sexuality wears the closeted garb of race and plays on the field of colonialism. Or, as Lane has it:

> In his determination to retain Pinmay's and Vithobai's intimacy—a determination that went hopelessly awry in the narrative's execution—Forster could not conceive of homosexual desire without accompanying elements of violence, slavery, and distress. Thus we might argue that Forster's expectation of redemption precipitates an astonishing burden on his texts, forcing them to buckle under the strain of reconciling impossibly conflicted sexual and racial desires. (170)

The sexual constructs its closet by hiding behind the racial. This is why Lane's suggestion that Forster, for all his ambiguity, ultimately chooses to align with the white character (173) is less than true. But it is also more than false. What Forster chooses to suppress is his homosexuality and in so doing, he uses black, colonised people to carry the metaphorical burden of that love/hate relationship. This metaphor is waiting to hand, however, because of the buried racism in even the most committed of liberal humanists. See, for example, Lane's description of Forster's friend and fellow novelist, J.R. Ackerley, who characterised "the unconscious in palpably racist terms":

> "However honestly we may wish to examine ourselves we can do no more than scratch the surface. *The golliwog that lies within* and bobs up to dishonour us in our unguarded moments is too clever to be caught when we want him". (172, my emphasis)

In other words, "for Ackerley, as perhaps for Forster, the ego is a white man as the unconscious is a black man" (Lane, 172). The demon of racism, the golliwog that lies within, emerges out of the relentlessly prejudiced Western cultural arsenal, despite, or perhaps as part of, liberal and humanistic ideology. The European man once again annihilates the reality of history, of colonialism, of the real aspirations, pain and oppression of African and Indian people, as they serve a figurative purpose in the inner explorations of agonised white men.

June Perry Levine pinpoints a version of this scenario in her description of how in Forster's posthumous homosexual fiction there is a recurrent motif of

> the tame in pursuit of the savage, oscillating within a field of attraction and repulsion. Although the strangeness is repugnant, the tame pursues the savage because conjunction will be completion. (72)

The tame man has the power of "Forster's own tradition"—public school, Oxbridge, income and social position. The 'savage', however, has "sexual potency" and "its representatives are either foreign—Mediterranean, Eastern—or working-class English" (Levine, 72). What Forster does then is to represent these qualities symbolically, separated out into different fictional characters, representing either timidity or savagery. This results in essentialisation of the dark skinned man, who invariably plays the role of the sexy and savage. These people are then manipulated as devices of concealment, as figurative tropes, as signifiers for inner and unruly dimensions within the psyche of the privileged, white and gay character.

By transferring sex to race, within this pervasive culture of deeply embedded racism, where the self-hatred of the homosexual is metaphorically painted in colour, the Imperialist ethos is unwittingly reinforced by means of this figurative opportunism. However, while this reverberates with the discourse of the African as the European dark side, it also departs from this seminal paradigm. This is so because true joy and completeness and loyalty to their own natures occurs for these British protagonists only by way of the fleeting moments with those black boys, before all the other snakes enter the garden. It is so because the closet hut houses the true being of the protagonist, who is himself destroyed by the necessity of concealment.

This buried prejudice ensures that the transference to the site of the African hut does not serve the liberating function that the 'other geographies' were supposed to deliver. These other geographies may enable the fantasy to develop up to a certain point, but ultimately it climaxes in a cacophony of sex and death because the golliwog within bobs to the surface unbidden.

Forster attempts to broker and mediate his political, personal and aesthetic ambiguities by way of ingenious narrative strategies, which enable him to speak with his forked tongue, to contain his political confusion, to code his sexuality. In other words, the narrative structure of the fiction itself is a vehicle of concealment. This occurs both within the published fiction where it adopts the guise of friendship between men, as well as in the secreted and posthumously published work, where it is overt. So careful is Forster of his secrets, so terrified of the shame of discovery, that even these overtly homosexual stories enact complex texts and hidden sub-texts within their narrative structures. They resemble nothing so much as fictional Fort Knoxes of security checks and balances, which protect the inner sanctum. For example, Levine suggests that buried in the language of "The Life to Come" the depressing ending of the devastation of Vithobai's two-pronged act of murder and suicide is contradicted by the choice of words:

> The vitality of expression in the verbals and verbs of the last sentence—"mounting," "climbed," "raised," "leaving," "swooped"—almost obscures Forster's implicit meaning. (85)

The language undercuts the action and brings us back to the code of Camp. Forster builds his narrative strategy precisely on the failure of narrative, as in language, where the unspeakable becomes the spatial, in which masculine fantasy seeks outlets for desire.

The Closet and the Law

These ambivalent spaces of homosexual desire may structure the narrative, but those structures are vulnerable when built on the foundation of inflicting loss language and of meaning onto colonised puppet characters. It may well be that that Wilde's *Dorian Gray* encourages "masculine desire to surface at points where the narrative strategy fails" (Lane, 85), but whose desire is facilitated and at what cost? Salvador, who loses his heart to a horse, is a Mexican cardboard creation, whose lost tongue enables Roscoe to speak from within a Camp closet made of glass.

The glass closet is a powerful structuring principle in Forster's narrative design. The Marabar caves in India or the hut in the African forest are echoes of the primal space of the glass closet. And with the loss of language as the marker of social Subjectivity is the threat of barbarism, and up bobs 'the nigger within' suggestive of going native, of being forever frozen in the infantile Imaginary, of the hell of the African afterlife, insanity, incoherence, irrationality and violence. Those ambivalent spaces are also the site of the only true sexuality that the benighted protagonists fleetingly enjoy. They, in addition, are also the last stop before the chaos and babbling, but only as long as they remain hidden, enabling the semblance of British propriety to be desperately retained outside of a securely bolted closet.

As long as the man occupies this closet, he can belong to his wider cultural reference group. At the same time, however, the moment the man enters the closet with another man, he is vulnerable to discovery and to social and cultural excommunication. In this sense I understand Lane's reference, again in relation to *Dorian Gray,* to a "cultural hinge between allure and danger" (87). This hinge, I would suggest, is crucial to the construction of the closet, enabling entry and exit. The cultural hinge, in other words, accommodates movement between legitimate and criminalised activities; it attempts to negotiate a compromise between social, cultural and moral expectations, and the urgencies of forbidden desire. It regulates the "nebulous distinction between culture and anarchy" (Lane, 87). These spaces are the sites of narrative disorder in the face of the disarray of the Law, the Law of the Fathers, infringed by these gay men.

There is a cautionary note to be sounded, however, about that Law, which could have been only in partial disarray. As we have seen, the likes of Wilde or Forster may have been outside of the Law in their sexuality, but as privileged British males, who enjoyed mobility, holidaying in the colonies, in North Africa or India, where they could fuck young, black boys with joyous abandon, they also simultaneously reinforced that Law. This we saw reflected in the contradictory politics of their stories.

All of this sets the political parameters against which to read Hollinghurst's and Roscoe's novels in the following chapter. Hollinghurst's poem, entitled "Dry Season Nights", will take us there. This poem is rendered in a mixture of realism and fantasy as Hollinghurst dances on the tightrope of race, sexuality and history. The poem mingles Camp and seriousness with the allure of other places and black bodies of Caribbean boys:

> Slick, shuffling demons of the carnival,
> the Jab-Jab boys have bodies black with oil;
> they grab you if you do not give them coins.
> Half-scared, you gave too much, and then regretted,
> not giving but not having been abused
> by devils whose worst weapon is a hug
> (such liquid blackness, blackness that comes off,
> daubed handprints on those tropic cottons ...). (1989b, 54)

Those black bodies will surface in London in *The Swimming-Pool Library* and will give the blond narcissistic protagonist more than a hug. How does Alan Hollinghurst juggle questions of race and sexuality, Empire and oppression, in his first novel?

CHAPTER SEVEN

Out of the Closet?
Alan Hollinghurst's *The Swimming-Pool Library* and Patrick Roscoe's *The Lost Oasis*

The Closet Viewed and the Viewpoint of the Closet: Introduction

In the previous chapter, I posed the following question: "What happens to 'homosexual writing' at the turn of the next century, when being gay has a name, an identity and, certainly by comparison with a hundred years ago, a freedom enshrined in law?" Alan Hollinghurst's *The Swimming-Pool Library*, in charting the relationship between the young, blond and beautiful Will Beckwith, and Charles Nantwich, who is of his grandfather's generation, quite precisely addresses the nature of the historical transformation of gay ways of being in the world. He does so, moreover, within the historical context of Empire and its aftermath, as well as the gay literary tradition discussed in chapter six.

In the novel, the young protagonist, Will, encounters another character, the elderly Lord Charles, in a public lavatory in Kensington Gardens, where the old boy was clearly up to a bit of harmless no-good of peering and gazing. However, he is frail and equally clearly not up to it, in every sense of the word, and passes out, in front of Will, who revives him. Like Will, only two generations earlier, Charles is an ex-Winchester boy and an Oxford graduate. Charles eventually begins to hand over his papers and memoirs to Will, in the hope that he will write the story of his life. The critical point, for our purposes, is that Charles is also a former colonial officer and his journals document his experiences in Africa and the sexual appetite nurtured there for young black men. This history contextualises Will's own attraction to black men, along with his desire for working class boys.

In addition to the history of colonialism, Will recovers the history of gay oppression through the journals. The criminalisation of homosexuality in Charles's time starkly contrasts with Will's freedom to act out his every desire. More than that, Will uncovers the startling information that his own grandfather, on whose largesse his privileged life of leisure and luxury depends, was himself one of the prime architects of this criminalisation (1989a, 325). Even worse, it was none other than this grandfather, who had been responsible in the nineteen fifties for the imprisonment of Charles himself, on charges of homosexuality.

Although Charles and Will enjoy the same privileged, aristocratic perch, their generational experiences of being homosexual, and therefore their lifestyles and perspectives, are also profoundly different. The Chinese box structure of Hollinghurst's novel may be best understood in the context of the nature of the site of the closet, raised in the previous chapter, and also in terms of Sedgwick's reading of Proust's *A la recherche du temps perdu*. Taking us back for the moment into the closet of the past, Sedgwick finds in Proust the suggestion that "an ability to articulate the world as a whole" may spin around the tense "axis between two closets". This turns out to be one closet, viewed from two differing angles:

> in the first place the closet viewed, the *spectacle of the closet;* and in the second its hidden framer and consumer, the closet inhabited, the *viewpoint of the closet.* (1990, 222–3)

Out of the Closet

> coming out…not as a vacuum or as the blank it can pretend to be but as a weighty and occupied and consequential epistemological space". (*The Epistemology of the Closet*, 77)

It is quite precisely that coming out space that is made spectacularly visible in *The Swimming-Pool Library*. Hollinghurst takes that space and constructs it in time by making his two views of the closet as separated by the generations. The older generation—the life and times of Charles Nantwich—is the closet as viewed by Will Beckwith. This space is fleshed out around Charles's home, his artifacts, the concealed Roman baths beneath his house and the narrative, the story within the novel, of Charles's journals and photographs, written and set in Africa. The second space, the one occupied by Will himself, is the "out" space of the late twentieth century liberated gays. This space, in which Will functions, and from which he observes the life history of Charles, is a fluid, highly sexually charged zone, where gay men enjoy apparently limitless sexual possibilities, and explicitly act upon them. While this site occupies different actual places in the novel, it is symbolically centred on two swimming-pools, which together provide a particular history of gay coming out. The particularity of this coming out relates to the social privileges of the actors—it is an aristocratic charmed circle that Hollinghurst chalks up for us, and the first of the two pools is the swimming-pool library itself, a public school place of adolescent experimentation and discovery of sexuality.

At this posh school, prefects were known as librarians in their area of special responsibility—"so there were the chapel Librarian, the Hall Librarian, the Garden Librarian and even, more charmingly, the running and Cricket Librarians" (1989a, 163). In Will's last term there, aged a pubescent thirteen, he was appointed the swimming-pool librarian. And the changing room, leading to that swimming-pool, becomes the heterotopia, as defined and used in the previous chapter, the charmed, magical space, where powerful adolescent gay sex was first learnt and enjoyed. As the older Will, nostalgically recalls:

> Sometimes I think that shadowy, doorless little shelter—which is all it was really, an empty, empty place—is where at heart I want to be. Beyond it was a wire fence and then a sloping, moonlit field of grass—'the Wilderness'—that whispered and sighed in the night breeze. Nipping into that library of uncatalogued pleasure was to step into the dark and halt. Then held breath was released, a cigarette glowed, its smoke was smelled, the substantial blackness moved, glimmered and touched. Friendly hands felt for the flies. There was never, or rarely, any kissing—no cloying, adult impurity in the lubricious innocence of what we did. (1989a, 164–5)

In an interview, Hollinghurst has this to say about the origins of the title of the book:

> My friend Andrew Motion and I used to send each other postcards of paintings to which we attached silly captions. He sent me one of a Will Roberts picture of Christ driving the money changers out of the temple, which has hunky, square figures wearing only long bathing drawers, carrying their big ledgers, running out of the picture with the Christ figure waving his arms behind them. Andrew retitled it "The Removal of the books from the swimming-pool library." The phrase "swimming-pool library" stuck in my mind because *it suggests both the scholarly/literary/ contemplative life as well as the active life.* At that time, I divided my own life between swimming and sitting in the library, so I decided I was going to call the book by that name. Then I had to rationalize the decision by inventing all this about the swimming-pool library. It was all dreamed up to justify the title. (Galligan, 1997, 3, my emphasis)

The "active life", we are left in no doubt, is both sporty, the exercise of swimming, and sexual, the exertions of fucking, indistinguishably entwined in a seminal, chlorinated pool. It is, however, also profoundly linked to a quite different kind of activity—the scholarly pursuit, that is also at the heart of Hollinghurst's identity. He may trivialise his title as a dreamed up invention, but it spoke to him so loudly because the contemplative, intellectual, moralising life of this writer entwines with his sexuality, his desires. And it is from this plaited twine that Hollinghurst weaves a complex narrative platform from which he views both Will in his sensuous swimming-pools, and from which he enables Will to view Charles.

It is therefore no coincidence that the adult swimming-pool heterotopia, the site on which the novel centers, the Corinthian Club, is situated in Great Russell Street, heart of the great libraries, bookshops and universities of London. The Corry, as it is known, is a loaded space, both 'out' and concealed, another country, where race plays a central role, reminiscent of Forster's imaginary India or Africa. The "pool lighting had been redesigned", which gives a "suggestive gloom":

> Small, weak spots let into the ceiling now give vestigial illumination, like that in cinemas, over the surrounding walkway, and throw the figures loitering or recovering at either end into silhouette, making them look black. Blacks themselves become almost invisible in the bath, the navy blue tiles, once cheery, now making it impossible to see, even with goggles, for more than a few feet under water. The luminous whiteness of the traditional swimming-pool is perversely avoided here: the swimmers loom up and down unaware of each other, crossing sometimes in the soft cones of brightness.
> All this makes the pool seem remote from the rest of the world. (1989a, 15–16)

In the pages that follow, I will be building up links between buildings and interiors, with the special significance of closets and maimed bodies, between narrative structures, language, the arbitrariness of the sign and the disappearance of fathers and grandfathers, true and false. Black and white bodies meet partly secretly, holding out a hope for a new bonded humanity, but under a broken pediment, within the suggestion of Roman Imperial conquest. There is a

> broken-pedimented doorway surmounted by two finely developed figures—one pensively Negroid, the other inspiredly Caucasian—who hold between them a banner with the device 'Men Of all Nations'. (1989a, 12)

The Corinthian Club is a kind of continuation of the public school, where race and Empire entwine in a coded Camp chain of damaged buildings and simultaneously beautiful and damaged bodies. Its pastiche of history and pornography, the explicit and concealed, also provides the narrative thread of the novel. These connections, between the ruins of Empire, its plunder and its cross race desire and also destruction, will become even clearer when we enter Charles's house and examine its peculiar architecture and the art objects Charles has collected.

The Closet Viewed

This paradoxical and morally elusive chain that binds all the various the actors in the drama of Empire, is visualised by way of the images, the photographs, artworks, effigies, mirrors and magical objects that anchor the novel. On his first visit to Charles's house, Charles shows Will some of his precious objects and paintings. The tone is auspicious, the objects redolent with meaning and Will's responses appear to be a kind of test as to whether he qualifies for the job of writing Charles's memoirs. The first of the "icons" that he is shown is a stone of three heads of the Egyptian King, Akhnaten:

> Looking again, I could see, reading Arabically from right to left, how the wide Pharaonic features were modified, and then modified again, elongated and somehow orientalised, so that they took on, instead of an implacable massiveness, an attitude of sensibility and refinement. ...
> "It's wonderful," I said. "Where did you get it?"
> "In Egypt before the war. Made my trunk pretty heavy...I was coming back from the Sudan for the last time."
> "It becomes more wonderful the more you think about it." I could not have delighted him more.
> "I'm so glad you see the point. For a while it was quite an icon to me." The point, as I saw it, was that you could take an aesthetic decision to change shape. The king seemed almost to turn into a woman before our eyes. (1989a, 90)

The European plunder of African treasures here signifies the same feeding off other cultures and classes. The heavy trunk, containing the stolen Egyptian artefact, carries overtones of the secret spaces, plundered from the cultural arsenal of faraway lands and creating the possibility of reconstructing a fortification back home. Will's attitude to the sculpture is contradictory—the stolen object is described in stereotypical terms, both of race and gender as a kind of evolution from the thick African features to the more delicate Oriental and of the male to the more delicately female. However, the inspiration of fluidity of identity, the possibility, through art and endeavour of changing who and what you are, in the different stages, rituals and rites of passage of a complex life, is magnificently captured by Will's description of the inspirational icon. It captures the hybridity of identity of late modernity.

The other icon that Charles proudly displays to Will on that first visit, is a painting of "an eighteenth-century colonial servant" and exemplifies the interweaving of race, servitude and boxing:

> From its mandorla of gilded oak leaves a livery-clad negro turned towards us. A sky of darkening blue was sketched behind him, and the showy form of a palm-tree could just about be made out. He appeared to be an eighteenth-century colonial servant; evidently a favoured one. ...
> I stood up to look more closely at the pugnacious brown face with its thick lips, flat nose and short curly hair. It frowned ironically from the crimson and gilt of the high-necked footman's coat. (1989a, 91)

Nantwich explains, and this is central and the link with the first icon, that "he was a man with several lives: first of all he was a slave, then he got brought back to England by a General whatsaname in the War of Independence. ... The General trained him up as a boxer" and "When he'd done with fighting he just carried on in service" (1989a, 90). Highly reminiscent of Johnson, Mungo Park's guide in Boyle's *Water Music*, (chapter two) here is servant, boxer, black man, slave, all heavily aestheticised.

This painting is a sign pointing to Charles's forays into working class areas, where as benefactor and also voyeur, he sets up recreational facilities, such as boxing for "rough boys". In this, with all its sexual and moral ambiguities, he is part of a long tradition (Koven, 365). Aristocratic gay men, in other words, ostensibly "came to heal the wounds of a class-divided nation, it seems probable that many were also driven by the need to come to terms with their own sexualities" (1989a, 373).

Later, Will and Charles descend into the cellar, where there is a remnant of Roman London, in the form of fragments of ancient baths. The walls "had a continuous frieze running round" and when glanced at appeared "tastefully classical", but "were homosexual parodies when inspected close to" (1989a, 93). The floor, "uneven, pitted in places, was a mosaic" (1989a, 93). In one image, "a gleaming slave was towelling down his master's buttocks" (1989a, 94). But the most significant image is of the two boys running toward the water, or already in it:

> They were intensely poignant. Seen close to, their curves were revealed as pinked, stepped edges, their moving forms made up of tiny, featureless squares. The boy in full-face had his mouth open in pleasure, or as an indication that he was speaking, but it also gave a strong impression of pain. It was at once too crude and too complex to be analysed properly. It reminded me of the face of Eve expelled from Paradise in Masaccio's fresco. But at the same time it was not like it at all; it could have been a mask of pagan joy. (1989a, 94)

Pagan and Christian, pleasure and pain, passion and loss, the image is meaningless and featureless when viewed from afar, but again, viewed close up, it yields its varied meanings. And encompassing all our readings and interpretations is Hollinghurst's warnings about crude closure, given that what survives into the present, as fetishised object, is an incomplete fragment, that will retain its enigma for successive generations. Most significantly for our purposes, however, its intimations of paradise soon to be lost, remind one of the transitory nature of Imperial power, no less true of the British Empire, of which Charles was a functionary, than of this Roman.

The King Akhnaten image and the painting of the colonial servant, the hidden Roman baths, the photographs of Africa and of the martyrs, can be interestingly understood as other instances of the fetish as "compromise object", as defined by McClintock at the end of chapter two. Charles is positioned in a maelstrom, as aristocratic coloniser, with a driving passion for his black servants that turn them into his masters; he is a male explorer, with homosexual desires; he is at the pinnacle of the British social ladder, with his club and his title and he has a prison record for indecent behaviour. The fetish, then, as magical object, attempts to resolve these contradictions, to comfort and order the discrepancies and rough edges. McClintock, remember, defined the fetish as "the displacement onto an object (or person) of contradictions that the individual cannot resolve at a personal level" (184). The fetish object was seen as "inhabiting the threshold of both personal and historical memory" (184). This intersection between personal lives and historical memory structures the entire novel. The images—art, photographs, icons—negotiate the hazardous and opaque terrain, which moves through Empire, via the gay past, from love, sensuality and yearning, through pornography, cruelty and oppression.

Dellamora's reading of images such as this one emphasises their symbolic function in the arsenal of colonising powers; the mosaic, for example, was part of the intricate design that contributed towards the reinforcement of the Roman colonising power through the production of material monuments that would naturalise their rule and symbolise their power, through the impressive presence of material manifestations. In this sense, the baths represented "invented tradition" calculated to consolidate the coloniser's power (1994, 189). This invented tradition, with its material exhibitions of symbolic power, characterised African colonialism as well, and Dellamora points out that it was Conrad himself, who drew this parallel:

> If one adopts the view of Roman invaders that Conrad takes in *The Heart of Darkness*, then they, like many Victorian colonists in central Africa, were surplus members of "an extended governing class," redundant at home but needed abroad. Like cricket grounds laid out in Kenya or South Africa, the baths in a Roman context signify the superior civilization that justified the invaders' inroads. ... In this reading, the images signify not ecstasy but cultural dominance. (1994, 189)

The images of cultural dominance, however, are themselves splintered by the erotic allure of beautiful, black house-boys, who compromise the domination of gay colonisers. During Will's second visit to Charles's house, however, a strange and creepy incident will cast its shadow over all the other viewing of the splendid, sensual objects on show in the house. It will remind us, moreover, of the razor edge between sexual liberation and racial oppression, between the Slave's bonds and his ability to hold the needy, homosexual Master to ransom, to which we were introduced in Hollinghurst's "The Thieving Boy", of the previous chapter.

On this second visit, Will finds Charles locked up in his dressing room by his black servant, the weird and sinister Lewis. Here master is turned prisoner in some macabre and cruel sexual game that the two of them play. Will frees Charles and assists him to his bed, where the intrepid Lewis has made an effigy of Charles:

> Actually in the bed, its wide featureless face absurdly crowned by a panama hat, lay a full-sized human effigy. It was only the rudimentary dummy that schoolboys make to suggest their sleeping forms in the near-darkness of an abandoned dorm, but in the light of a summer afternoon the bunched-up bedding and clothes of which it consisted were revealed as glaringly offensive. Its lolling pillow of a head was meant not to deceive but to warn. ...Red rose petals were scattered artistically around, and where the heart of the effigy might have been there was a rust-red stain on the white bedspread that did resemble the colour of long-dried blood. I reached for a little bottle on the bedside table: it was vanilla essence. (1989a, 106–7)

When white men engage in black magic, we are in the cultural tradition of Kurtz's horror, of white men, as Conrad would have it, succumbing to the primitive urges buried beneath the veneer of culture, art and civilization. As Charles himself had many years earlier put it in his journal, in which he documents his experiences as a colonial functionary:

> There was a tendency to treat Africa as if it were some great big public school—especially in Khartoum. But when you were out in the provinces, and on tour for weeks on end, you really felt you were somewhere *else*. If you'd had the wrong sort of character you could have gone to the bad, in that vast emptiness, or abused your power. (1989a, 282–3)

Will comments that "'it sounds like something out of Conrad'" (1989a, 283). Here Hollinghurst is alerting us to the discourse of the Fathers, of the generation of Charles, from which he feels, perhaps too confidently, separated. It is by the light of the creepy events of that second visit that Will reads Charles's journal and examines his photographs, photographs that Will believes "although enigmatic" would be "the *keys or charms to open the whole case to me*" (1989a, 111, my emphasis). Here is no murder mystery to be solved. The keys to the case are the ways into the enclosed box of

Charles's secret sexuality. The photos are mainly from the African years and most of them

> showed groups of natives, largely or wholly naked, standing round under dead-looking trees, gazing at flocks of goats or herds of cattle. In some Charles appeared, in shorts and sola topi, flanked by robed, shock-headed men of intense blackness. There was one heavily creased photograph of an exquisitely soulful black youth, cropped at an angle, where presumably another figure in the picture had been scissored off. After the scene in Charles's bedroom this gave me a mild unease, as if it might be a magical act of elimination. (1989a, 111)

The photographs have become signs of illegitimate boundary crossings into alien and dangerous rituals. They link to the homosexual imaginary of Empire and its aftermath, which constructs boats and caves, tents and pyramids, wherein illicit desire and illegal practices mingle with the discourse of voodoo, savagery and blood letting. That this is still the case for the aged and battered Charles is demonstrated by the bizarre goings on in his strange, museum-like house containing fetishes and threatening servants.

And all of these weird occurrences only make sense in terms of the history of Empire and Charles's former life as a District Officer. This life, that history, and the closets that Charles constructed around them, we view mediated through Will's reading of Charles's journals—"then I settled down to read about Charles's doings long ago" (1989a, 125). In other words, the narrative structure takes us through the thresholds of a narrative within a narrative, as we read Charles's perceptions of African people and landscapes, as read by Will. Charles loves the young adolescent bodies of the naked Nubian boys and he observes that:

> The beauty of the men is so openly displayed that it seems a reproach to lust. I felt anger & something akin to remorse last night when I thought of how this noble, graceful people has, until so recently, been stolen into slavery or mutilated into eunuchry. (1989a, 126)

The ambiguity of gay collusion with, and distaste for, imperialism emerges in the "remorse" and is consolidated in the life and fate of Taha, Charles's houseboy. Within the maelstrom of baffled desire, dedication to duty and lust, within the contradictions of power, authority and yearning, Charles falls in love with Taha, who returns a great trust, loyalty and tenderness, but who is not himself gay. There is an extraordinarily poignant scene, which Will reads in Charles's journal, when Charles nurses the youthful Taha after he has been stung by a scorpion and which captures all the dangers, paradoxes and inversions of power, love and authority, filtered through an Orientalised African landscape. Charles tells Taha the story in his "painfully correct Arabic" from *Thousand & One Nights* of Prince Ahmed, which he acts out with props, which causes Taha to laugh "with that delight which children show at certain well-worn jokes" and Charles

> capered around, squatting on the mat, peering out of the window through the binoculars—though I saw not the Princess Nur-al-Nihar but birds coming down into the nim-trees, a stupendous sunset above the rocks, a girl loping home with a dog at her heels. (1989a, 247)

Always peering, looking and capturing. The African landscape is as aestheticised with its nim trees and sunsets as the Eastern tale Charles is embellishing, to the delight of his young Arabic, African listener—master turned ambivalent father, with overtones of incest. During the telling

> the most exquisite thing happened. Taha slid his hand shyly across the blanket & clasped my own. I scarcely faltered as I spoke of Ahmed's arrow...but I felt a squeezing in my chest & throat & hardly dared look at him as, all unconsciously, I made our two hands more comfortable together, interweaving his long fingers with my own. (1989a, 247)

Master turned lover and victim, Ahmed's arrow squeezes painfully in Charles's chest, foreshadowing, for all its exquisiteness, the terrible wounds that his love for this boy, then adult, will inflict on Charles. Taha returns to England with Charles, as his manservant, after Charles's stint in the Colonial service ends. Taha marries and raises a family. However, "his loyalty was unaltered" (1989a, 301). Back in England, both Charles and Taha will be violated. Charles's sanctuary is invaded and plundered by the Law and he, like Oscar Wilde, is thrown into prison for his sexuality. Then in a most spine-chilling manner, Taha is cold bloodedly murdered by fascistic English young racists while Charles is incarcerated—"they showed no mercy: stones and dustbins were used as well as knives" (1989a, 302). This is matched by the brutality with which Charles is informed of this grotesque tragedy by the prison authorities.

Taha and Charles share different kinds of oppression—one murdered and the other imprisoned. This partially cuts across their master/servant or coloniser/colonised differences. This is less so with regard to the generations that follow. Taha's son, Abdul, inherits from his father a more lethal cocktail of paternalism, exploitation and violence, as a black Briton. On his release from prison, Charles assumed responsibility for Abdul, finding him employment as a waiter in his exclusive London club. But this kindness is redolent with menace and exploitation, as Abdul is sucked into the gay sub-culture, which turns him into an object of the gaze of old Queens and sets him on the ambivalent path of "love and dedication to prurience"

(Dellamora, 1994, 178). And the most sinister of all of these Queens is the photographer and filmmaker, Ronald Staines.

The Closet Viewed as Grotesque: Late Twentieth Century Secrecy and Pornography

If Charles skates on the razor's edge between philanthropy and exploitation, between victim and oppressor, then a character, who is stripped of ambiguity, who is Charles reduced to the pips of the decadence and domination of his class and privileges, is the photographer, Ronald Staines. We first encounter Ronald Staines at Charles's club, Wicks, where Charles is treating Will to lunch. Our first examination of Ronald is filtered through Will's appraisal of him as a slimy and decadent self-constructed man:

> He was dressed entirely properly, but there was something about the way he inhabited his clothes that was subversive. He seemed to sliver around within the beautiful green tweed, the elderly herringbone shirt and chaste silk tie which plumped forward slightly between collar and waistcoat. His wrists were very thin and I saw that he was smaller than his authoritative suiting. *He was a man in disguise.* (1989a, 50, my emphasis)

Spider catching flies into his fine, artful web of gay pornographic desire, Staines dresses beautiful black and working class boys up as biblical figures to titillate gay sexuality in his fictional photographs. Charles, apparently benevolent grandfather and philanthropist, collaborates with Staines in luring the sexy young working class waiters, and Abdul, the black chef, all from Charles's club, to be 'actors' Ronald's pornographic video production. Will

> was surprised to remember that Charles had told me there was no dining at Wicks's on a Sunday evening. But I was staggered to think that he—and Staines—could actually lure the staff elsewhere and make them act out those fantasies which they must have fathered in sly glances over their fatty beef, soapy veg and boiled school puddings. What bizarre transactions and transitions must have taken place. The whole thing had that achieved bizarrerie which made it normal to the participants, *demonic* to the outsider. (1989a, 219, my emphasis)

False fathers, they seek exotic pornographic escape to satisfy their lust, a lust that Will defines as "demonic". These randy old white men and their dirty movies, are blood sucking parasites. To Will's horror, a horror that sends him scurrying away, he sees Abdul's scarred nakedness, his body 'stained' and mutilated. This image builds up the implication of the destructive and wicked abuse of these black and working class "film stars":

> His flat stomach was crossed by the longest scars I had ever seen, as though long ago, and with the crudest means, someone had removed all his insides. With his

scarred black skin inside the thick black fur he struck me, who adored him for a moment, like some exquisite game animal, partly skinned and then thrown aside still breathing. (1989a, 220)

At the same time, on the first occasion that Will had met Abdul, reminiscent of Mustafa with the glass shard, of "The Thieving Boy", discussed in the previous chapter, who was both victim and perpetrator, Abdul "stood abstractedly sharpening his knife on the steel and gazing at me as if I were a meal" (1989a, 49) – both butchered and butcher.

Will's abhorrence of the pornographic videos of Staines is more characteristically Hollinghurst's, who stretches the narrative voice of his protagonist a little beyond credibility as the hedonistic Will, in an uncharacteristically high moral tone, declares that "I didn't need the decadent secrecy of Charles and his pals" (1989a, 221). For a moment:

I had seen myself, with weird detachment, in the society of corruption: the baron, the butcher, the boozed-up boyfriend, *and most corrupt of all the photographer.* (1989a, 222, my emphasis)

In interview, Hollinghurst explains how his first two novels "had to be written in the first person because their first personhood is very much what they're about" (Galligan, 1997, 5). They are also very much what Hollinghurst is about as he emerges from the protective secrecy of the imperfectly masked third person narration of the stolid parental eye, to which he had resorted in "The Thieving Boy" and into an open gay politics of representation. When asked by Galligan: "Have you ever thought of yourself as being a political writer...?", he replies: "One intention I do clearly remember formulating with the first book was that I wanted it to be told from a gay point of view, completely and unself-consciously" (Galligan, 1997, 5).

Hollinghurst deals with the problem of stretching our credibility with regard to the hedonistic, yet moralising, Will in two ways. Firstly, he acknowledges that Will as judge is uncharacteristic in that he is undergoing a momentary and temporary change, and was (although, sadly, briefly) "quite exhilarated by that grand illusion, that I could make myself change" (1989a, 222).

Secondly, and more realistically, it is the secrecy that the late twentieth century Will, with Hollinghurst's approval, abhors. Will revels in being out of the closet and sees the perverse secrecies of the likes of Charles, and particularly, Staines, and their blue movies, as the sick remnants of closetedness. It is the concealment that Hollinghurst defines as pornography. As Will puts it, he didn't need *the decadent secrecy* of Charles and his pals—and as I had left Staines's house I had thought of putting the whole thing behind me. Why be encumbered with the *furtive peccadilloes of the past*, and all the courteous artifice of writing them up? I wasn't playing the same game as that lot. I looked forward to clear July days, *days of no secrets*, of nothing but exercise and sun, and the company of Phil. (1989a, 221, my emphases)

The huge store that Hollinghurst sets on being 'out' in the open as gay is tremendously important to the affinity he shares with his first person narrator, along with the distance from him, which we will come to in due course. Will loves to walk arm in arm with his lover, "to insist out loud that he was mine" (1989a, 227). The break between the generations, however, on that spinning axis of the view from the closet and the closet viewed, is also not absolute. If there are moments in the novel when Will has to be closeted, as in the 'box' with his grandfather at the opera, referred to in the previous chapter, there are also times when the older generation may now 'come out' in public. Will describes "a frisson of shock into pleasure" when he encounters a "hopelessly old and refined" couple who linked arms in total "openness" (1989a, 228) leading him to assert that "I wanted men to *walk out* together. I wanted a man to walk out *with*" (1989a, 228).

What is incredible here is that for Hollinghurst, this gay freedom is always linked to the acknowledgement of freedom bought at a price in relation to colonial history. The heterotopia of North Africa in general, and Egypt in particular, emerges through the inspiration afforded by this old refined couple. Will

remained, leaning on Phil's bunched shoulder, one flamingo leg drawn up, and spoke quite seriously about the British Museum, outside whose black north entrance we were standing. On a huge pillar above our heads a poster advertised the Egyptian galleries, with a number of aproned, broken-nosed pharaohs standing stonily, but rather pathetically, in a row. (1989a, 228)

This brings to Will's mind "Charles's relief of Akhnaten" (1989a, 228). The crumbling architecture of Empire frames gay bodies, whose delirious sexuality is shadowed as much by the broken architecture as by the creeping horror of AIDS, which this novel refuses to name. We will encounter again this link between maimed bodies, Empire and broken buildings in Patrick Roscoe's *The Lost Oasis*. For now, Egypt, with its links to Empire and the racism that accompanied it, brings us to Hollinghurst's distance from his narcissistic, blond and beautiful Dorian-like narrator, with whom he only partially identifies.

The Closet, Empire and the Law Re-visited

If Hollinghurst distances himself from Will, how does he build that distance into the structure of his labyrinthine novel? Here is the nub of its politics. Where does Hollinghurst stand in relation to the representation of black bodies, Empire and gay sexuality? Does the novel collude in part with the history of colonial violence and racism that are simultaneously being interrogated and exposed? Perhaps it is true that the fiction is itself stained, even as Hollinghurst distances himself from Staines, his creepy photographer, in his disguise of impeccable, creamy suit. This Hollinghurst himself appears to confess, via Will's love affair with the sexy, youthful, black Arthur, where authorial approval for the boundless sexual energy between the golden and the black boys is marred by the more sinister undercurrents:

> I was eight years older than Arthur, and our affair had started as a crazy fling with all the beauty for me of his youngness and blackness. Now it became a murky business, a coupling in which we both exploited each other, my role as protector mined by the morbid emotion of protectiveness. *I saw him becoming more and more my slave and my toy, in a barely conscious abasement which excited me even as it pulled me down.* (1989a, 38, my emphasis)

Ultimately, the question that is being asked here is the extent to which the magnetic pull of these black bodies, with the abasement that is so destructive, is not the old and ghastly metaphor of the dark side, here the absent presence of the scourge of AIDS, to which all that unbridled sex is going to make the Wills so tragically vulnerable? Hollinghurst is fully aware of this problem, but only partially distances himself from it. Will's friend, James, who is a doctor and so much more serious and sober than Will, and who receives tremendous authorial approval and empathy, goes for magazines, which have "secret and illicit power" over him, and which are "put out from Chicago by the Third World Press" which "specialised in blacks with more or less enormous cocks, and in leaden titles like *Black Velvet, Black Rod* or even *Black Male*" (1989a, 251).

Kobena Mercer when first he viewed Robert Mapplethorpe's photographs of black bodies had similar reservations. In his paper, entitled "Looking for Trouble", Mercer argued that at first he had assumed that Mapplethorpe had fetishised the stereotype of the enormous black penis, by casting it as magical object of terror and desire of the white, homosexual male. By fixing, framing and capturing it within this stereotype, the White, gay man assumes the familiar mastery over the object, (1991, 187) turning the black man into a "juju doll" (1991, 191).

What worried him was that the fetishised black body "lubricates the ideological reproduction of 'colonial fantasy' based on the desire for mastery and power over the racialized Other" (1991, 187). This, Mercer reminds us, was pointed out by Frantz Fanon as "the fantasies of his white psychiatric patients" which "summons up from the political unconscious one of the deepest mythological fears in the supremacist imagination: namely, the belief that all black men have monstrously huge willies" (1991, 188).

Mercer re-views the photographs and, to some extent, has a change of heart in that he becomes undecided about the politics of Mapplethorpe's representations of black bodies. He realizes that the photographer/writer was aware of this exploitation of black bodies. What if he was employing devices and strategies in his art precisely to expose and contest, rather than to collude with, the power of the Oppressor? What Mercer concludes is that the photographs are full of masks, of "jokey irony" (1991, 188). This is, of course, dangerous and is fraught with the possibility of betrayal. Photograph can turn boomerang as your regular dirty old man peers lustfully at Mapplethorpe's beautiful black men with their big penises. The conundrum with which Mercer leaves us is that the politics of the pictures is "strictly undecidable" and that the photographs are "open to a range of antagonistic political readings". This is, of course, a "risky business" (1991, 197). This is so

> because Mapplethorpe's photographs do not provide an unequivocal yes/no answer to the question of whether they reinforce or undermine commonplace racist stereotypes. (1991, 189)

This observation reverberates with a reading of Hollinghurst. The connection between him and Mapplethorpe is real, rather than merely suggestive. In 1983, Hollinghurst flew to New York to spend "several days at Mapplethorpe's studio" (Galligan, 1998, 10). In answer to Galligan's question as to "what is his [Mapplethorpe's] brilliance", Hollinghurst replies that "it was partly his introducing a particular kind of sexual subject matter into relatively high art with an absolutely undeterred, unhesitating forwardness" (Galligan, 1998, 11). In response to a further question, Hollinghurst elaborates:

> DG: Your novels are horny and hot and full of passion and obsession and excess and extreme. At the same time, your vehicle, like Mapplethorpe's, is cool, detached, classical, traditional, reserved. It's form versus content.
> AH: That was what I hoped to bring off. That's what good art tends to be like. It contains passion in particular forms. One wants to feel that the artist is exercising a supreme control over the material; at the same time, the material itself may be wild and passionate. (Galligan, 1998, 11)

But is this not precisely what his photographer, Staines, does? The novel emphasises both Staines's supreme artistry and his explicit homosexual content. The key is that Hollinghurst distances himself from the exploitativeness of a Staines and injects into that classical, analytical form, the politics of opposition to racism and imperialism. In other words, the authorial voice distances itself from the decadent Dorian Grayness of Will Beckwith; the authorial voice is that contemplative, scholarly and moral position of Hollinghurst himself, whose books occupy library space in the sensual liquidity of the liberated-from-the-closet swimming-pool.

Hollinghurst has a very minor character, with an important message in this regard—the young Argentinean Gabriel, a sexy, young and debauched gay man. He may not be a mythical and ethereal angel from God, but he is nonetheless a demonic messenger bringing a crucial warning about Western domination, about the paradox of Desire, and about the relentless, shameful and continuing existence of racism, deeply embedded inside European Culture. Will picks him up at the very hotel where he has come to see Phil, his lover, who he supposedly adores. Not only is Hollinghurst implying a critique of the shallowness of some gay loyalties, in the relentless pursuit of new sexual encounters, but, and perhaps more significantly, this incident with a Latin American exposes Will's own prejudices:

> His lips curled back in a friendly primitive way, and gave an unexpected animation to his dully beautiful face. I realised he reminded me of one of the sketches of Akhnaten on Charles's stele—not the final inscrutable profile, but one of the intermediate stages, half human, half work of art. (1989a, 318)

Will stereotypes the features of the Latin American, who is objectified, linked to the Egyptian artefact, de-humanised and primitivised. As always, however, there are the overtones of danger to Will from this foreign stranger and the ambiguity of this perch of power from which he views and solicits—"I followed my conquest—my conqueror?—out" (1989a, 319).

The scene is actually very funny, in that painful, serious way that the best humour can be. Gabriel has been entirely sucked (literally as we shall see) into the global capitalist sexual economy, as he speaks the language of "crudely dubbed American porn films":

> 'Yeah,' he would croon, 'suck that dick. Yeah, take it all. Suck it, suck that big dick.'
> I took a pause to say, 'Um—Gabriel. Do you think you could leave out the annunciations?' But it wasn't the same for him without them, and I felt unbelievably stupid appearing to respond to them'. (1989a, 320–1)

Because Gabriel cannot function sexually, without his American style lingo, he tries something else and spends some time in the bathroom and emerges

> completely naked except for his cock-ring, the pale gold wafer of his watch and…a black leather mask which completely covered his head. There were two neat little holes beneath the nostrils, and zipped slits for the eyes and mouth. (1989a, 321)

Significantly, part of the horror of this new guise for Will is that

> Close to I could see only his large brown pupils and the whites of his eyes, blurred for a split second if he blinked, *like the lens of a camera*. (1989a, 321, my emphasis)

Part of what Will dislikes is that in assuming the mask, Gabriel, the half-human, Egyptian art object, reverses the power balance and becomes the photographer, with Will as his object. In this way, the omniscient Hollinghurst turns the tables on his arrogant protagonist.

The distance between Hollinghurst and his thoughtless, hedonistic protagonist explains the ending of the novel, where Will is off " to have a swim: one must keep the body if not the soul together" (1989a, 336) and the last words of the novel reinforce the fact that Will has not recovered some deep sense of moral purpose—"and going into the showers I saw a suntanned young lad in pale blue trunks that I rather liked the look of" (1989a, 336). We may see the world through the unconstrained first person narration of Will, but Hollinghurst's distance from his protagonist is constructed in the secret language of Camp, the theatrical gesture of his ending, where his character has not grown in depth through experience and understanding. Even as he invokes this coded language, however, Hollinghurst subverts it with moral purpose, so alien to Camp stylishness. He exposes his distaste for outside the closet selfishness, promiscuity and historical amnesia. If Charles ambiguously continues as Master and Slave owner, if Ronald Staines is unambiguously revealed as spider, ensnaring the poor and the ex-colonised in his glittering web, then even Will, golden naive boy, ignorant of Empire and its trappings, will continue the unsavoury and unstable traditions of oppression.

In other words, Will may view the closet through Charles's life, but Hollinghurst views the politics of late twentieth century gay promiscuity and selfishness through his distance from his protagonist, the side of Hollinghurst that is so undeveloped in his character—the life of contemplation, seriousness and books. The politics is in the distance and the distance is as much moral as historical. As Hollinghurst puts it in the interview, which I will quote in detail as it gets to the nub of the fraught relationship between sexuality and imperialism:

> *The Swimming-Pool Library* shows Will exploiting people over whom he has various kinds of social advantage. He still exemplifies the old-fashioned English pattern of upper-class people being sexually attracted to working-class ones. One of the things the book deals with is this old truism that gayness enables people to make contacts across barriers of class and race because gays are drawn together by sex. This is all fine and dandy except that it is also a liberty that can be exploited or corrupted. It's in Will's nature to use black people and working-class people as sexual objects. (Galligan, 1998, 11)

Hollinghurst has written a novel of homosexual desire, which he traces back to its part in the colonising venture and forward to its morally ambiguous traces in London, where to be black or working class is to be prey to the old white men of Empire and the amnesiac, young but still predatory white men of breeding and means. His novel abounds with objects, photographic images and fetishes that acknowledge the morally ambivalent history of gay oppression and imprisonment within the frame of imperial plunder and racial domination.

In this, Hollinghurst differs from Wilde, Conrad or Forster. These closeted 'fathers' reinforced their safe hiding places with recourse to their privileged positions in both race and gender terms. These may have been attacked and made vulnerable by their illegitimate and illegal desires. But ultimately, be it Conrad whose secret sharer is abandoned, or Forster whose black imagined lover turned into the 'golliwog within', they tended to rescue at least the letter of the Law of Imperialism and Race. What this collusion amounts to is none other than the smug conclusion to Conrad's tale whereby the Law reasserts itself as it banishes and maroons the outlawed secret sharer. Thus Sedgwick, by reference to Proust, describes how "the establishment of *the spectacle of the homosexual closet*" becomes "a presiding guarantor...of authority—someone else's authority—over world-making discursive terrain that extends vastly beyond the ostensible question of the homosexual" (1990, 230). In other words, "it is around the perceptual axis between a closet viewed and a closet inhabited that a discourse of the world takes shape" (1990, 231).

And at this point, with the intrusion of the Law, with its tablets on which so many decrees are written, Sedgwick, highly uncharacteristically, loses courage. She realizes that within Proust's text "so many other, in some ways more electrified filaments of meaning are knotted around that signalizing thread of the sexual subject" (1990, 247). She is, however, reluctant to allow these many threads to light up our understanding—"let me tell you why I have waited until so late to broach this pluralizing of the novel's subject, and even now barely mention it, and only with serious misgivings" (1990, 247). What are her misgivings? She is afraid that "it can de-gay the novel" (1990, 247).

This is a very strange reservation on Sedgwick's part. It has surely been her point all along that gay writing, as much as gay desire, entwines in complex ways with multiple forces, histories and politics. It is the touchstone of Hollinghurst's novel and of this book itself that if homosexual history and that of Empire are not seen as imbricated, then homosexuality runs the risk of oppressing, even as it is itself oppressed. In foregrounding the Law as receptacle of the culture's dominant values, how can Sedgwick not consider the nature of those values and the extent to which different classes and races buy into them? And this, I must repeat and emphasise, is where Hollinghurst most significantly parts with his literary and homosexual forebears, in that he acknowledges a chasm in the Law, which cannot easily be breached. As he says in interview:

> There probably are deep questions about the way life is depicted in the fiction of, broadly speaking, my generation of writers who are, again broadly speaking, not believers anymore. We're all wondering where authority can be fond, where values can be derived from. The preponderance of sexual subject matter in the last twenty years, the way novels are almost obliged to have a lot of sex in them, is partly to do with that. The body and sexual life take on an unconstrained urgency because that is where people are looking for value and significance, not to some handed-down code of values. There is something lawless and desperate about it. (Galligan, 1998, 10)

And with the alienation from the Father and the search for an alternative Law, we come to Patrick Roscoe's *The Lost Oasis*.

Coming Out in Slow Motion: Lost Fathers and the North African Desert

> Jose kisses my eyes and I see pink flamingoes take flight above Lake Nakuru, scatter across Kenyan sky. ...Eyes turned heavenward, silent, a man and three children hover around a white Peugeot parked beside an empty, badly paved road, with brush stretching in all directions. ...There is still more travelling to do, Mitch and the desert demand, more of that curious motion, backward and forward simultaneously, that lies beyond chronology, outside itinerary. (40)

At the opening of the novel, Richard has just learnt the news that Mitch, his father, is lost somewhere in the desert of North Africa and he is realizing that he has to journey there to discover a lost father and a fractured past.

Richard is the protagonist and the youngest of those three hovering children. The eldest, also a boy, is known simply as MJ and the middle child, a girl, is Lily. Much of their childhood was spent travelling in the African bush through empty and unmapped roads with their strange and unreliable father and absent, schizophrenic mother.

Richard is also the bearer of authorial viewpoint, of Patrick Roscoe, who is divulging his fictional device where *The Lost Oasis* formally enacts its refusal of historical time by taking us back and forth into present, past and possible futures as we take the twisting path with Richard on more than one journey, sometimes in opposite directions simultaneously. One of the journeys is into memory as Richard excavates and examines his almost unbearably painful childhood of emotional deprivation, insecurity, nomadism and bewilderment. The years in Africa came closest to providing a sense of home, but one that is so partial and peculiar as to exacerbate the children's foreignness when on visits to their biological roots and family in a small town in Canada called Brale.

This journey of childhood rememberance is criss-crossed by another as Richard in the present searches for his father and travels through a succession of increasingly seedy and crumbling rooms, then into the desert of North Africa. If the one journey is the more conventional one of searching for psychic health through remembering what was painful and repressed in the unconscious during childhood, then the other appears to be of the slow coming out of a gay man, who has been hiding in enclosed spaces, who exits from these into an intermediate zone of African desert and thence into full, healed and alternative subjectivity. And this metaphoric, evolutionary trip through Africa, healing though it might be, carries enormous dangers.

Appearances, however, can be deceptive. For the moment, what interests us most in that apparent slow motion "outing" is the evolutionary scale of progress from closeted Morroccan interiors into the intermediate zone of the North African desert, the interspace, where a civil war is being fought. At first sight, it appears that only by surviving this desert may Richard take the flight back to Spain and the safety of a European harbour. Africa may be being manipulated again for European psychic needs and desires. African civil wars, moreover, as we saw in chapter five, carry their own particular representational minefields.

However, in subjecting this novel to a second sight, a mixed and complex possibility emerges, which is that, at the same time, *The Lost Oasis* itself confronts and explodes the Questing in Africa trope. If the Father must be found in the journey into childhood memory, then he must remain lost in the coming out, which is not forged through the Symbolic gateway of the Law of the Fathers, but through more interesting exits, including a problematisation of the discourse through which Africa has been represented in the European imagination. And always, between the different possible readings is the razor edge along whose dangerous contours our writers wobble and sometimes wound themselves, their fictions and the concrete lives and lands of African people.

Out of the Closet? 211

Quests, Discourse and Language

When Richard becomes aware that he has not only to search for his lost father, Mitch, but to conduct the search in Africa, he realizes

> that to search for him in Africa would be more difficult, and painful, than to search anywhere else. I had scrupulously and successfully avoided returning to that dark continent during my adult travels; the ghosts of MJ, Lily and myself, slight shadows still haunting the Ngondo hills, waited to be rescued, and I knew I was not strong enough for that task. Why Africa? I asked Jose again and again in the days following Ardis's telephone call.
> And especially why the desert, when I had been dreaming fearfully of sand and dunes for so long, so often imagining in sleep their difficult demands that perhaps the force of my unconscious field influenced Mitch, without his knowing, to seek the Sahara and to slip from the globe there. (1995, 84)

The dark continent is only the most obvious of the metaphors. The return to beginnings in Africa is potentially a metaphoric grand journey undertaken within the tradition of the great explorers, adventurers and big white Questers. Why indeed should the father slip from the globe precisely at the Sahara desert? We are left in little doubt that this is a meaningful, symbolic point of disappearance, construed within a figurative paradigm.

We have discussed, more than once in this book, how dangerous the metaphoric stranglehold is, in its potential to buttress stereotypical representations of Africa. W.D Ashcroft, in an intriguing paper called "Is That The Congo? Language as Metonymy in the Post-Colonial Text", suggests "metaphor has always, in the western tradition, had the privilege of revealing unexpected truth" (3). He quotes Paul deMan as suggesting that "'the inference of identity and totality that is constitutive of metaphor is lacking in the purely relational metonymic contact'" (3). Bearing in mind the discussion of the two poles of language in the first chapter, what we will see in the pages that follow is that if Roscoe sends Richard on a metaphoric journey back to "the dark continent", he will return him to Europe and ultimately to the safe haven of his lover's arms, by exploding the metaphor. However, the bits of metaphoric shrapnel will wound his brave novel. Nevertheless, in the process, Roscoe realizes that he must learn to speak a new language, one that could have endowed an identity to his silent Mexican boy, who was unable to speak for love of the white horse. But first, to "the dark continent" of childhood beginnings and the Quest for the lost oasis.

Childhood as the Metaphoric Dark Continent

The novel begins with the Prologue, in which Richard tells us that in 1971 "Mitch told me about the lost oasis" (1995, 1). We are not enlightened as to what precisely Mitch told him, but we realize that this lost Oasis, which gives the novel its title, is the space where Richard hopes to find his lost father. What we also realize from the outset is that Mitch was an unreliable storyteller:

> But already, by now, MJ and Lily and I were beginning to doubt the truthfulness of our father's stories, though *we still couldn't challenge...his famous view of history as metaphor.* (1995, 3, my emphasis)

At this time, the family had been living in a Tanzanian town, Morogoro, for three years, and were now travelling through Europe. Even during those three supposedly settled years in Africa, the three children had been lugged around on "at least half a dozen trips", including "five days in Istanbul, a long weekend of *siestas* on the Costa Brava, several *midis* in Marseilles" (1995, 3). As Richard's Quest metamorphoses from finding a lost father, to challenging that father's metaphoric view of Africa's history, so Roscoe will find a way of writing against the grain of the dark heart. Or at least partially. In the process, Richard's gay sexuality will find its own version of 'coming out'.

The return to Africa takes Richard back in memory into that childhood of endless motion with a feckless, unreliable father and a deeply mentally ill mother, who is utterly incapable of providing emotional nurturing. Richard's growing subjectivity represses the desire for the love of the mother into an unconscious where it metamorphoses into African lepers and beggars. We are back in familiar territory with the bad, sick and diseased innards of the European being understood *metaphorically* as African, as the children are constituted as maimed, needy and fractured subjects. The beggars in front of the greengrocers

> reach out hands, they whimper and moan to me; though we speak a separate language, and they have moved beyond words anyway, I understand what they want: we need the same thing. Their limbs melt in the Tanzanian sun, shrink before my sight: shortened fingers, toeless feet, bare rounded bones like handles of old walking-sticks smoothed by constant touch. They could be male or female, young or old. *Leprosy*, Ardis has told me. (1995, 22)

The metaphoric link between the lepers and the children is made overt:

> Ardis emerges from the store. ...We stretch out hands to her, we whimper and moan. All we want is a single coin, small and round and flawless, to hide within our rags. We have learned not to ask for much; give us only a token of pity, please. Now I am missing one ear, a nose; this is only the beginning: one day my soul's straitjacket may disintegrate with divine disease, my heart lose it cage of bone. Ardis glances indifferently down. (1995, 23)

As the children enter their own, isolated Symbolic zone, through the gates of the Law of these strange, eccentric and unreliable Parents, they accumulate a weird religion. The schizophrenic Ardis worships Judy Garland—"'Judy Garland died'" she [Ardis] finally remarks, flatly. "'She died to save us all'" (1995, 24). Richard and his siblings acquire a strange language in the process of being constituted as distorted subjects. Like the Father, who speaks in metaphor, the Mother too turns the African landscape into a symbolic zone of idiosyncratic meanings and connections:

> Ardis is infected with the power to transform terrain into *symbols which speak its truth*. The baobab beyond the wall, the armies of ants which file relentlessly through the garden, the mica glinting upon the road: what do these things mean beyond themselves? (1995, 25)

Richard's sexuality which will become deviant and for which Roscoe may be seeking an explanation, is entwined with the contagion passed on by the lepers:

> Before sleep I chant my prayers to Judy Garland and Jesus, then in dream lipless mouths open to impart essential information into my waiting ear. The surrounding world requires interpretation; five senses are not enough. From the eroded ovals, however, emerges only moaning. I waken to realize this is really the painful sound Ardis and Mitch make together in the dark. (1995, 27)

The mangled vowels of the lepers, pouring their infection into the boy's unconscious as he dreams, entwine with his developing body and knowledge of adult sexuality. In such a world, where Jesus and Judy Garland unite as spiritual pillars, the regular five senses of normal kids are not enough. And indeed, when these children visit their aunts and cousins back in the little, suburban Canadian town of Brale, they "didn't know how to make friends or join clubs, become members or fit in" (1995, 163). The language of their classmates "was as incomprehensible as Swahili, their behaviour as strange as a Massai tribal dance" (1995, 163). In fact, constituted as they are through the Law of Judy Garland and Christ, with souls of lepers and the secret language of their parents' eccentric metaphorical universe, their bodies are contaminated and permeated by the excesses of an imagined Africa:

> I always thought, during those Sunday dinners, that an unpleasantly pungent odor, composed of dust and overripe papaya and the decaying flesh of mutilated monkeys, clung to us, and festered upon the antiseptic skin of every Brale room we entered; it seemed to no avail that the three of us had, since 1974, taken to showering a dozen times a day—and Lily even more often—until our skin possessed a permanently scraped, raw aspect. (1995, 164)

Those scraped and raw bodies are the emotionally and mentally wounded creatures they are, made manifest:

> Despite a battery of tests and medications, [MJ's] headaches were never diagnosed or treated with success. ...MJ was unable to heal and rise;...At eighteen he disappeared on his way to Montreal, where he was headed to look for work. I think he couldn't stand for us to see the veins still throbbing with angry blood beneath his brow. He needed to lose Africa, to lose us. *I continued to believe that a dark continent lay hidden just beneath our skin;* with a sharp knife you could peel away a layer to discover the rich taste of mango, the smells of charcoal and dust and rotting fruit, the mocking laughter of hyenas in the night.
> Perhaps Lily was searching for these things when she used the razor on herself. (1995, 108, my emphasis)

If Africa is the metaphor for the sickness of soul of Richard's siblings, then so it is for him too, with his wounded sexuality, which resulted in ten years of his life as moving from one room, (one closet?) to another in all the capitals of the world in a totally meaningless meandering. He warns us against the temptation to place meaning, adventure and experience into those metonomyic years of monotonous nothing:

> Paris and London
>   California and Mexico
>   Berlin and Rome.
>   Crete, Ios, Formentera.
> *String the names together and it sounds glamorous. ...*
> When they had ended, I thought of those ten years as a lonely, wandering dream from which I had finally woken. (1995, 244, my emphasis)

Returning to Africa is painful because in this landscape Richard is the diseased body writ large, wrested from safe hiding in unconscious wandering dreams—"if this bloody search lasts long, I will eventually have to sleep, wrapped in a filthy blanket, on a piece of cardboard in the shelter of a doorway, *with the other lepers and beggars*" (1995, 89, my emphasis).

The search for the father, in fact, turns out to be a decoy, concealing in the narrative guts of the novel the true quest, which is for Richard's gay identity to be liberated from the seedy closeted enclosures, which echo his childhood nomadism from one hotel room and one continent to another. In this story of quests within quests, this secret search emerges in a dream, where the lost father is of a very different kind indeed. The wish fulfilment dream is told in the narrative style of the Mexican stories referred to in the previous chapter. The dreamer is Richard cross-dressed as a local North African villager, who describes how "we all grew up with mothers' dire warnings that if we were not careful the tattoo artist would etch hideous, permanent pictures upon our sleeping skin" (1995, 144). This dream quest is for a different father entirely. It is for this renowned master tattoo artist, who, it is also reputed, has the power to change the path of one's life forever, if only one can find him (1995, 143). The dreamer does find him and desires to have from him a unique mark, the nature of which lies with the imagination of the tattoo artist, except for the "one thing I knew for certain: it should be imprinted upon my heart" (1995, 146).

The mark of Cain, given by God the Father, is reproduced in a mingling of stories, Mexican, Arabic, African, Christian and Camp. The cursed brother, who displeased god, transgressed one of His commandments by killing Abel, his brother, and is destined to wander nomadically bearing the tattoo of God as a sign on his body. An ambivalent sign even in the bible, one which protects Cain and his like, but which also marks them out as different and disorderly. This is the coded language, so different from Hollinghurst's explicitness, describing being marked out as gay. This mark, this difference, is initially a blessing on the body. It "seemed at once to suit me and to describe me" (1995, 147). Later, however, the mark becomes the sign of the curse, which isolates him from his fellows—"now I was lonely, and separated from those around me" (1995, 148). He closets himself—"I tried to keep my tattoo hidden" (148). In the secret code of the Mexican story, glimmers of homosexuality are revealed embedded in the dream—"'I hope you got what you wanted,' my mother said, as another wedding procession wound past our door with its bright song of union" (1995, 148). The dreamer searches for his double, his Narcissus, the reflection of the same, so redolent of gay meaning, the buried, closeted counter-quest of the novel:

> In this way my long journey began. First I roamed the town itself and then the towns nearby in search of someone with the same tattoo as mine. ...It had to have a twin. (1995, 149)

The existence of a 'secret sharer' would erase the mark, the tattoo of difference, secrecy and isolation: "my mark would vanish beneath his gaze as his would dissolve under mine, and we would no longer each feel the same constant pain" (1995, 149).

The Lost Oasis secretes this homosexual Quest behind the search for the lost Father. Sedgwick describes this deceptive maneuver of hiding the true quest behind another more visible one in Proust. The clever writer, in making the viewed closet visible through its glassed substance, thereby diverts attention from his own secret, shameful desires, which remain concealed, blocked up, occluded. The difficulty that this poses for Sedgwick in reading Proust, is that the reader is sucked into a concealing conspiracy with the ambivalent, closeted narrator. The spectacle of the closet, which we view along with Proust as *"the truth of the homosexual"* (1990, 231), makes it "one of the most difficult problems of Proust-reading *to find a space...in which the other homosexual desires in the book can at all be made visible* (1990, 231, my emphases).

We saw the overt quest for the source of the Niger metamorphose into another in Boyle's *Water Music* in chapter two. The emergence of these sub-quests which become dominant are crucial for the politics of the novel's representations of Africa. How does this pan out in *The Lost Oasis*? Ultimately, Roscoe's goal is to find that Oasis space, freed from the secrecy of metaphoric codes and glass closets. So blockaded is this sexual secret that the novel, refers, doubly obliquely, in a dream sequence where Richard has become a North African, to the white horse story, which we saw in the previous chapter was Roscoe's version of Dorian Gray. There we saw how the touching of the beautiful white horse resulted in the loss of its unique colour and with that loss, of all the beauty and colour of the world. Likewise, this dreamer, cum Richard

> continues to roam from place to place in hope of discovering someone marked like me. The tattoo still burns above my heart; I have not grown used to its ache. *While the colors of the world have faded*, and stars dimmed with my faith, the tattoo flames as brightly as in the beginning. Now it is many years since I have been to my town, and I do not know if my family and friend still live. (1995, 149, my emphasis)

This is still the world of allegory, Quests and symbols, where Cain is marked by God, the Judaeo-Christian father, within the narcotic fug of North African stereotype. The space in which homosexual desire can find release is here extraordinarily elusive, by contrast with *The Swimming-Pool Library* just discussed. We are given quite precise clues as to the existence of the buried Quest by way of the repeated injunction, again linked to a Mother figure, but this time speaking the truth, right at the outset of Richard's journey: *"Don't look for your father. You've already found him. Go back"* (1995, 87). Who he has already found, as we saw from the outset, is his gay lover, Jose. We will return to the mysterious stranger, the woman who issues this advice, when we come to look at Richard's mother a bit later.

Roscoe flags an awareness of the duplicity inherent in the focus on metaphoric Quests, coded in the language of adventure and exploration, when later, possibly in another dream, Richard encounters a man who asks him:

> "And has monsieur found the tattoo artist?"
> "Monsieur is not looking for the tattoo artist. Monsieur is looking for Palmolive and Crest". (1995, 189)

And if the significance of the insistence on the search for the trivial, concrete and literal, as opposed to the symbolism of questing has escaped us, the chapter ends – "'Palmolive and Crest', I think, walking from the *quartier portugais* towards the brightly lit streets and cafes and stores" (1995, 193). Soap or washing powder, metonyms supreme, cleanse the African landscape, for the moment at least, of its European symbolic manipulations. The contradiction, however, that the novel constructs for itself, lies with the irony that the mechanism to dismantle the metaphoric cleansing is none other than the return to basics, as in being stripped of all 'civilisation', language and culture. And where else, invariably, does the European enact this stripping down than in Africa in general and in the African desert, in particular?

Going Native as Metaphoric Cleansing: Contradictions Abound

If Richard dreams himself an African subjectivity, he begins going native in reality, starting with some cross dressing as he swaps his coat with a North African youth for an inferior one:

> His hands grasp my jacket, slip it off my shoulders, from my arms. Quickly he takes off his own jacket and hands it to me. He puts on my coat as I put on his. Slightly too large for me, the garment feels thin, worn, shabby—unlike my denim jacket lined with soft red cotton, with a warm red hood. (1995, 199)

As he goes more and more native, starting with entering the life of a village boy in his dreams, to swapping clothes and bodies, Richard struggles to unlearn the language of his father's metaphoric version of history, which is also the white man's language of power and colonialism, given that "[in Africa] a man's white skin carried a certain built-in power" (1995, 44). In other words, his mind empties of words and hits on random sights and smells, which chance to come his way:

> The desert radiates a silence difficult to break; the idea of speech grows pointless. What is there to say? inquires the desert. What? demands the infinite, glassy sky. (1995, 216)

In fact,

> It is becoming difficult to think at any length of what took place an hour ago; my mind slips instead to the sounds of flutes and bells, to the smell of the nearby desert. (1995, 259)

Crest and Palmolive, the sights and sounds that happen, by chance, to occur, are devoid of the memory that translates such flutes or desert smells into meaningful encounters with the landscape. With the dissolution of memory and writing, time itself disintegrates:

> I glance at the wall where my row of scratches—my discontinued calendar—has been covered with soot. I have no idea of the date. (1995, 297)

And here is the rub. As Richard descends into the mythical time of metaphor, as opposed to the concrete realism of metonymy, as he immerses himself in the process of obliterating his father's historical distortions, he invokes new symbolic meaning. Blackness of soot, of black skins, of African darkness erase his writing and transform him into a chameleon, into a creature who changes colour:

> Moonlight transforms my skin and the sand into nearly the same colour. I feel camouflaged.
> Chameleon. (1995, 299)

But in the very process of unlearning, he is implicating the bodies and landscape of Africa, and contaminating his text with classic tropes of African Orientalism at the very moment that he is struggling to cleanse it with the amnesia of happenstance:

> The sound of drums grows louder; this is its source. Dark shapes shudder around flames. I smell perfume and animals, smoke and cooking meat. ...The dancing bodies twist and flail, inhuman song winds above the drums, kneeling camels cough. (1995, 300–1)

The howling, inhuman gyrating savages on the shore, viewed by Marlow from the safe distance of his slow sailing boat down the primordial Congo River, are all too familiar. Richard's disintegration crescendos with the emergence of a sick and deformed androgynous creature:

> From a distance it looks like a crippled animal, perhaps a dog or a cat, crawling beside the road. ...A kind of desert creature I have never seen before? Gradually, it becomes evident that this is a human being of sorts. It pulls itself through the dust with its arms, legs dragging lifelessly behind. ...I can't tell if beneath its rags this is a man or a woman. (1995, 335)

Horrible, deformed creature, it is reminiscent of the beggars and lepers of his inner life, albeit that:

> The sores on its hands do not indicate leprosy, but flesh scraped raw from clawing the ground. One leg is exposed beyond the rags. It is swollen as large as this being's torso, and ends not in a foot but in an even thicker, rounded shape.
> Elephantiasis. (1995, 336)

Like the ambivalence of the mark of Cain, which both protects and singles out the cursed, and like the savage, which is both primitive and pure, this creature will carry him along in the perilous African desert. And, of course, this creature is none other than Richard's diseased unconscious, his shadow, his soul, his inner being, forged in deformity in Africa. It is simultaneously his saving core and his burden:

> I feel myself drawn forward. In a few steps I have caught up. I walk slowly beside the crawling figure, almost in slow motion. ...Its form travels over the ground beside me like my shadow made solid, my shadow made without light. Allah's reflection of my soul. (1995, 337)

Just as we are gloomily preparing to indict Roscoe for his irretrievable demise in the quicksand of the discourse, something rather shocking happens to make us re-focus our thinking. Soldiers emerge on the scene and, shockingly, kill off the maimed creature:

> The bullet entered the back of the cripple's head. It does not make a clean, neat hole. It rips a large, ragged tear in the rags covering the head. A messy smear of pink and white has splattered through the rip. ...
> The lame legs stop jerking as the shot's blast fades into silence. The sound rolls across the dunes; probably it can be heard for miles. Probably, like the loud laughter of the soldiers. ...the driver and three soldiers in the front of the truck are also laughing. None of them appear to notice me. (1995, 346–7)

Exploding the Quest Paradigm?

What is the meaning of this apparently brutal slaying? Is this yet another example of Afro-pessimism where savage, grinning soldiers are always gratuitously violent and monstrous? Are we back in the zone of Boyd's warring chimps, that eat their young and kill their disabled? The description of the shooting buys into those familiar portrayals. But something does not quite fit. Why do none of the soldiers appear to see Richard? What if the maimed creature were a figment of Richard's thirst-mad hallucinations, much like one of his drug-induced dreams? Furthermore, what if this creature were the leprous, beggarly soul of his tormented youth, which he drags back to Africa with him? What, most interestingly, if the realities of Africa's history, struggles and issues facilitate Richard's battle to kill off, to break the dreamy, metaphoric, Orientalist paradigm, which simultaneously drains his sexuality? Finally—and a lot hinges on this question—is it possible that instead of an act of gross cruelty, the soldiers, in reality, performed an act of humane kindness?

> As I begin to walk away, I notice something on the road. It is what the soldiers threw from the truck. A canteen of water. I swallow a warm mouthful, then sling the canteen over my shoulder and softly laugh. (1995, 348)

After the shooting "the desert is safer" and what appears now to be missing, "left behind" is "my strong, crippled spirit" which had been crawling across the sand (1995, 348):

> As dusk turns to evening, I begin to feel lighter. More light than ever before, as if unnecessary weight has been shed. As if I were a shadow on the sand. Only spirit, not flesh. (1995, 348)

With the shedding of his maimed body, begins the process of growing a healthy sexuality, based on self-love. But first, Richard is the spirit and the beautiful, sensual Jose is the flesh—"Jose walks slowly beside me. I am the shadow falling by his side, the shape of his soul floating across the ground" (1995, 366–7).

Furthermore, with the throwing off of the burden of the leper, the beggar, the elephantisistic creature, the false Quest after a lost father is revealed as a delusion and a mirage, of the same order as his father's crazy paranoid imaginings, his spy thriller versions of history. Richard becomes convinced that his father was "one of those delusionists convinced that the gum-snapping Safeway checkout girl is an underground operator of the IRA" (1995, 241) and ultimately had over many years "filled fifteen daybooks with notes for the plot of a thriller he planned to write but at some point began to live instead" (1995, 241). Finally, and crucially, Richard realizes and informs the absent father—"It would take more than any bodyguard, more than any Jose, to protect me from you (1995, 345).

Here is the major discovery, which is the necessity for distancing from the Father, from his paranoid symbolic view of the universe. This leads to the wonderful, funny anti-quest anti-climax of the novel. Richard arrives at the Café Oasis. This is an ordinary little tearoom. It could have been called anything; it is a metonymic bathos, which explodes the metaphoric significance of the search for the lost oasis, which is the code name for the lost father—"I am prepared to understand, in the end, that I will never know for certain what happened to him" (1995, 356).

Crucial, moreover, to this breaking of the symbolic/metaphoric paradigm is Roscoe's realistic description of the guerrilla soldiers and the war, breaking down Mitch's idiosyncratic troping. These descriptions are couched through the telling and writing of local people, rather than filtered through the dreams or delusions of the European imagination, and show the fruits of research on the part of Roscoe. Ahammed, who comes quite specifically from the northern edge of the West Sahara, quite reluctantly explains to Richard, the foreigner, about the war:

> Still with reluctance, Ahammed continues to explain that for more than fifteen years a dispute has simmered over the territory, once dismissed as barren, that lies south of Morocco. Phosphates, he says. It was because of rich reserves of phosphates that Hassan 11 invaded the abandoned colony in 1975 and seized control of its northern two-thirds.
> "Many of our people moved down there," Ahammed goes on to say. ... "But Mauritania wanted the area's southern third. And the Polisarios, the guerrillas, wanted to make the whole place an independent Western Sahara state. Algeria and Libya supported their struggle and the war began". (1995, 155)

Or, as a pamphlet which Richard finds explains:

> A lone speck of a Spanish colony surrounded by French territory, Sidi Ifni was held by Spain after the rest of Morocco achieved independence in 1956. For thirteen years it remained a Spanish enclave, though to force this situation's end Morocco eventually blocked all entry points by land, sealing off the town except by water, allowing only that Atlantic access. For three years the town was more deeply isolated than ever. Finally, in 1969, Spain acceded to Moroccan pressure and gave up Sidi Ifni. (1995, 226)

Finally, we will see in the next section that this metonymic, realistically described history, with dates, places and powers concretely named, along with the soldiers, plays a similar role to that of the mysterious blond woman and explains the otherwise puzzling connection between them—"a poised blond woman has materialized into a stern, dark soldier" (1995, 332).

Blond Mothers, Dark Soldiers and European Homecomings

If the quest for the Father turns out to be mirage rather than oasis, then equally the search for love and nurturing from the sick, incapable mother has also to be abandoned. We saw, in fact, that the origins of Richard's sickness of soul, his leper rotten core, lay with his cold, blond, splintered mother, from whom he futilely begged for recognition and love. Sedgwick, in fact, goes so far as to suggest that it is "the figure of the mother", who is central in gay tradition of grappling with the constraints imposed by straight Law. She is the "extreme or even ultimate power", and who is the person "who *can't know*" (1990, 248). In fact,

> This topos of the omnipotent, unknowing mother is profoundly rooted in twentieth-century gay male high culture, along the whole spectrum from Pasolini to David Leavit, by way of, for instance, James Merrill, whose mother figures in *Divine Comedies* as the all-powerful blank space in the Ouija-board alphabet. (1990, 249)

Remember Richard's dark shadow as beggar/leper pleading for love from a distant, uncaring mother. Remember his hallucinating dream search for the tattoo artist in which the envious mother, who issued "dire warnings", remarks to the isolated son, who is different from other men, "'I hope you got what you wanted,'...as another wedding procession wound past our door" (1995, 148). There is, furthermore, an intriguing metaphoric connection between the cold and distant mother, the colonising power and interiors in *The Lost Oasis*:

> *Rambo IV* is playing at the Cinema Le Paris. In the streets off the square wait the Hotel de Lyons, the Hotel de Bordeaux, the Hotel de Marseilles. In these names, and in the architecture of the older, more impressive buildings, sound echoes of a former colony's mother, plaintive attempts to summon near a parent sometimes disinterested, always distant. (1995, 91)

Rambo, American dream quester, male adventurer with the fake, great body, occupies the screen named after the capital city of the colonising mother country, as are the succession of hotels, with their endless rooms in which Richard has been closeted all his life. The "plaintive" colony, beggar like Richard, seeks the attention of the parent, who is always unavailable. The links between these colonised interiors and the Rambo dream quest is contained within the metaphoric paradigm of Fathers with delusions of grandeur. If it is true that "containment, order, closure are associated with metaphor" and that "surplus, collapse and openness with metonymy" (Tsomondo, 86) then the crumbling of those interiors simultaneously signifies the disintegration of the power of the colonising mother and the 'coming out' of the repressed colonised/gay subject.

And then we have to ask again, whether in linking his destiny to the trajectory of the struggle for national liberation on the part of African countries, Richard is not admitting via the back door his father's deluded, metaphoric view of history, where the Polisarian guerrillas are, at the end of a long day, fighting for the psychological liberation of a white gay man? In other words, is Roscoe falling into this trap at the very moment when he so perceptively perceives that individual freedom cannot be won without the dismantling of the edifice of an oppressive history? Let us investigate this link between the Mother country, Subjectivity and metaphoric Quests.

Crucial here is the strange, repeated warning on the part of a creepy, mysterious blond woman, who is associated with the mother but is not mother and who is ultimately a stranger. At the very outset of his journey, Richard encounters this "a waxy icon of warning" (1995, 86) against the journey, a warning, which is repeated in italicised emphasis throughout the novel. It echoes like a childish intonation:

> *Don't look for your father. You've already found him. Go back.*
> The train jerked into motion, my head banged the wall behind my seat, the space across from me was empty.
> *Don't look for your father. You've already found him. Go back.*
> Were those the last words of a dream—words which in fact woke me—or were they words spoken by a woman as she rose, stood before me, then turned into the shadows?
> *Go back.* (1995, 87)

The chapter culminates in the repetition of the warning, to the rhythm of the train and linked to the metonymic meaninglessness of jingles, names and ultimately of quests for lost fathers or even mothers. *"Go back"* punctuates the page as in a chorus, twice, until:

> *You've already found him.*
> Said a blond woman on a southbound train in the North African night.
> Call her Dagmar or Anke. From Frankfurt or Munich or Bonn.
> Does the name matter? (1995, 88)

She appears and vanishes throughout his journey, in fleeting chance encounters. He sees her out of the corner of his eye (1995, 114) and the singsong returns to his mind:

> Dagmar or Anke or Ardis
> You have to call her something. (1995, 115)

There we have it—Ardis—this figure, this stranger, may as well be the mother, who had always herself been "a stranger" (1995, 22) to her children, with "blond hair" (1995, 61). And if the name of the mother may cease to matter, then the son may be able to free himself from his desperate neediness.

In other words, progressing from being a figure, whose withholding of love and approval maims the body and soul of her children, the cold, blond woman becomes anybody and therefore nobody. As Mother becomes increasingly associated with metonymy, she becomes the antithesis of Parent, guarding the gateway of the symbolic entry into a hostile, imperialistic and homophobic consensus. By becoming the randomly named stranger, the bonds of neediness are loosened and the magnetic power of interiors, of secrets, closets and metaphors is weakened. And like the words linking a sentence, this refrain embeds the anti-quest, even as Richard appears to be focussed on his search:

Don't look for your father.
You've already found him.
Go back. (1995, 188)

Remember that the Prologue is the novel's present. It sits on the cusp between past and future. It is the moment at which Richard, living in Spain with Jose, receives the news of his father's disappearance, and makes the decision to return to Africa to search for him. It is at the very outset of this journey that the strange blond woman issues her warning and it is already in the Prologue that Richard has begun to transform his mother from the powerful figure of his boyhood yearnings, to the person who happened to chance into his life. The novel indicates this change through a preference for metonymy, Roscoe's now familiar syntactical device. Ardis is losing the link between words and their meanings and see how Richard has come to terms with his mother's limits:

She wants to know what day or year it is. She wants to know how old she is. She wants to know her middle name. ...
   My mother and memory.
   I try to imagine what it must be like not to remember your middle name or what you wore on your wedding day or when your first child was born. (1995, 32)

This leads Richard to speculate and Roscoe to italicise:

Does the name matter?
You have to call it something. (1995, 34)

The answer appears to come from the mother herself, in distancing her loss of meaning from the father's paradigm:

Ask your father what matters.
He's the man with all the answers. (1995, 34)

Just when this mysterious woman looks as if she will herself become a new Quest, a metonym turned metaphor by dint of the sheer slipperiness between the poles, Roscoe concretises her. By giving her a mundane name and making her genuinely into a happenstance stranger met on a train, she becomes insignificant in the long term of his life. Landing up in hospital after his brush with death in the desert, Richard regains consciousness to find the blond woman beside his bed and the sing-song is involuntarily invoked— "Dagmar or Ankee. From Frankfurt or Munich or Berlin" (1995, 368). Her name is Alice Murrow and stripped of the symbolism of the earlier manifestations, she is simply an embassy bureaucrat, eager to get rid of him, back to Europe as quickly as possible to avoid any embarrassment, which

Out of the Closet? 225

could be caused by wandering Europeans in African hotspots. Still in the persistent metaphoric alphabet of places, but without implicating Africa, Richard refuses to go back to cold Canada and insists on a world in which colour and love are restored. That world is Spain, Spain where the white horse is reincarnated in the flesh and blood of Jose, his secret sharer, who has a tattoo like his. And so, he is ready finally to exit the closet:

> I look around this room in the Hotel Royale, then turn my eyes to the sky beyond the window. A door opens in the sky as it changes from grey to blue. Another room appears through that door. It is a room I haven't seen before.
> "Are you ready?" asks Alice Murrow. She steps into the hall. I gaze towards the sky and through its blue door and into its upper room. A sense of loss sweeps over me; swaying, I reach for the bedside table for support. Stabbing loss turns into something gentler, something bearable. I smell the heavy bleach on my clothes and feel the unfamiliar shoes pinch my feet. My fingers touch the cross around my neck.
> Am I ready? Of course not.
> That doesn't stop me from turning from the window and stepping from the room. (1995, 375)

Jose had given Richard his silver cross on a chain as a good luck charm for his journey—the mark of Cain is excised as the tattoo is erased and replaced by the love token. This is the moment of "stabbing pain" of giving up the fatal tattoo, the hotel room, the closet, the fake search for his father, the un-usable past. The strange, borrowed clothes link to the earlier jacket exchanges and splintered identities as a stronger, surer Richard exits the closet and takes us to the last part of the book, which is called "**The Upper Room**":

> "There is always one moment...when the door
> opens and lets the future in". (1995, 377, quote from Graham Greene)

And so, finally, "the ancient web of threads...that has always connected me to Mitch and Ardis, MJ and Lily...has loosened around me" (1995, 380). It's still there but he can now breathe and welcome the newer thread, which is the lifeline to Jose. Jose, dressed in brown and blue clothing are the sand and sky, but most significantly, the blue pool of water, the Oasis (1995, 381–2). The quest for lost fathers is exposed for the cul de sac it always was and the oasis is located, not in Africa, but in the body and flesh of Jose, soul mate and sharer, no longer secret, however. The truth was always there, repeated in the nursery rhyme lingo of a stranger:

> Go back.
> You've already found him.
> Before me, the magic door opens in the sky. (1995, 383)

The warning may have been to go back, to abandon questing in Africa, yet tenaciously the understanding contained in this message, appears dependent upon the baptism of African desert sand storm, which lifts the veils from Richard's eyes—"Yes, everything looks different" (1995, 321). And so, stains of the survival of the metaphor of Africa as the site of the European unconscious stubbornly remain. This is so notwithstanding that the bedrock of the novel's discoveries is the attack on that metaphor itself. Or, as deMan says, the "double bind" of Proust's *A la recherche du temps perdu* is that it is "the narrative of its own deconstruction" (77). The difference, however, is that while Proust, according to deMan, appears to assert the superiority of metaphor over metonymy, whilst secretly undercutting that preference (16), Roscoe attempts to enact the superiority of metonymy and simultaneously falls partly into the trap of the metaphoric Master narratives. Like Proust, however, I think one can say with deMan that Roscoe's *The Lost Oasis* "asserts and denies the authority of its own rhetorical mode" (17). And with this African desert space as privileged Western baptism by heat and light, we come to the final part of this book and to weary sons of the soil.

Part Five:
Sons of the Soil

CHAPTER EIGHT

Crossing the Great Desert Void

> Argan trees contain the startling vision of goats who somehow manage to scale the thorny branches to feed on leaves. Glimpsing animals in the air, I feel that from this point the scenery will become increasingly strange and unexpected; soon, perhaps, there will appear camels flying above the dunes, or fish walking along the road.
>
> —Patrick Roscoe, *The Lost Oasis*

The Deep Grammar of Lost Fathers in North African Desert Spaces

The African desert—source of European imaginaries run riot—was at the centre of Patrick Roscoe's dilemmas in the previous chapter, where the desert was the pivotal point at which he simultaneously exploded and reinforced Western metaphors. This chapter will take that discussion further. It will continue to investigate the intriguing and elusive links between African landscapes and quests and between that land, gender and rhetoric.

The title of this chapter is taken from a story by Walter Abish—"Crossing the Great Void"—a story, which also centres around the search for the lost father in the African desert, this time on the part of a character called Zachary. It is taken from a collection suggestively entitled *In the Future Perfect*, a title whose pun glues together history and grammatical tense, a welding, which is central to Abish's project.

Malcolm Bradbury, who provides the introduction to Abish's collection, gives us some background to the writer, who he sees as something of a nomad:

> It may well be misleading to locate Abish as an American writer at all. He was born, of Jewish background, in Austria and grew up in Shanghai, China, as the old system was disintegrating. His international and polyglot background, which very much shapes his writing, continued; he lived in Tel Aviv and trained in the Israeli army, but he now works mainly in New York City. (ix)

Zachary lives with his mother in America and is obsessed with deserts because the Great North African Desert is "where his father disappeared on a mission behind enemy lines in 1941" (1977, 98). Zachary makes the link between the blank page and the blank African Desert:

> Zachary stares at a blank piece of paper. As blank, he thinks, as the Great North African Desert on a map. Somewhere within that blankness stood his father, patiently waiting to be found. (1977, 98)

Are we witnessing once again the desert as the privileged European space of emptiness and potential discovery, which simultaneously denudes Africa of people with culture, history and lands? No, Abish is as critical as I am of these assumptions and will distance himself even more unambiguously from his protagonist's quest than we saw Roscoe do in chapter seven. Even before he embarks on his quest, Zacherey's English teacher, alias, Abish, takes issue with him:

> Zachary, why do you keep harping on deserts in every essay you write, his English teacher had wanted to know. For one thing, deserts are not quite as empty and blank as you seem to believe. For another, *as metaphors, they leave a great deal to be desired.* (1977, 99, my emphasis)

Not only do we become distanced from Zachary, but we are also immediately skeptical of his father's heroic status in the boy's mind, given that we learn, with some shock, that this father had been fighting on the side of the fascists—fighting for Il Duce. In fact, his father "was a distant relative of Mussolini's second cousin, Fabrino Melchuz (1977, 103) and had interrogated British Prisoners (1977, 102). Now the family lives in America and Zachary works as a motor mechanic. This fascist family history results in an absolute divide between quests and big moral causes and foregrounds the link between African landscapes and Master text metaphors.

The catalyst propelling Zachary away from his essay writing and into the journey to the desert to find his lost father, is a woman, allegorically called Track, in part two of the story. She tells him that:

> Since you appear to be so intrigued by North Africa, you'll be interested to know that the map of Blitlu, an oasis in the center of the Great Desert, is tatooed on my back". (1977, 105)

Passive, pathetic man, with his maimed body—Zachary is deaf—can only begin to formulate a quest if guided, put on the Track, by a woman and his sexuality, which is bound up with this enfeebled questing drive, is entwined with the map of Africa and its vast desert. What he is "infatuated" with is her knowledge of North Africa and her stories about it (1977, 106). We are in little doubt that this journey will not deliver great insights and discoveries:

> Many people still seem to think that by undertaking an arduous journey they are also going to discover something about themselves they have never known. Zachary felt disinclined to tell Track that, as far as he was concerned, discovering anything entailed listening to what people had to say, and until a better hearing aid was perfected he did not have great expectations of discovering anything new about himself. (1977, 106)

Alice A. Jardine whose book, *Gynesis: Configurations of Woman and Modernity*, we referred to at some length in chapter three, is also intrigued by Abish's story. She suggests that:

> Modern Man does seem to be crossing some kind of Great Void. There is a Track to be followed and he has been told that the map to the Oasis is inscribed on her Body. (64)

She is none other than Vheissu, Pynchon's dark, Moroccan woman in *V*, who is tattooed from head to toe (Pynchon, 171) and also encountered in chapter three. What Jardine questions is whether it is a matter of Zachary finding Truth and Meaning, as embodied in the Symbolic zone of the Law of the Father and "as a prelude to a new Messianic Era", or

> does Zachary know that, deaf and blind, *his Quest is already historically amiss*, and that, always already Oedipalized, he would not recognize the Image of his Father at *any* crossroads? (64, my emphasis)

Zachary is not up to the job of explorer—the batteries of his hearing aid run down (1977, 109) and his increasing deafness ensures that he would not know it, even if he found his father. Indeed, at Birsut he encounters an elderly man, who we are sure *is* his father (1977, 112) because of a photograph described to us earlier in the story (1977, 104). However, Zachary himself does not recognise him. Like the café Oasis in Roscoe's novel, finding the father is total anti-climax, a surreptitious knowledge shared by writer and reader, in the ignorance of the protagonist/quester.

What Abish is problematising is the stereotype of the landscape of Africa as nullity, absence and emptiness, as a core feature of Africanist discourse, a feature which we saw Simon Gikandi use to distinguish it from Orientalism in chapter one (Gikandi, 169).

Edward Said, in *Culture and Imperialism*, warns us against looking at landscape only in terms of what the tropes and metaphors tell us. He insists that underlying representations of space is the reality that

> Territory and possessions are at stake, geography and power. Everything about human history is rooted in the earth. (1993, 7)

We return to the necessity of undercutting metaphors, representations, tropes, with the knowledge that these imaginaries are linked to real places and the livelihoods of real people. What Said's book attempts is "a kind of geographical inquiry into historical experience"—space added to time (1993, 7). He goes so far as to suggest that "Britain's cultural identity...imagines itself in a geographically conceived world" (1993, 52). And, "the actual geographical possession of land is what empire in the final analysis is all about" (1993, 78).

If one way of doing battle with the deep grammar of describing faraway lands is by means of an onslaught on metaphor, then another way is quite simply to return home imaginatively and to cancel the flights of fancy to Africa or India. This brings us back to Alan Hollinghurst and his, deceptively light, latest novel, *The Spell*, which has, I think, been quite wrongly described as having "very slight subject matter" (Jensen, 25). I will offer a very different interpretation of this novel, which is set partly in London, partly in the picturesque countryside of Dorset and minimally, yet crucially, in a desert, although not of Africa.

Deserts, Dorset and Breaking Spells

The first chapter of *The Spell* is set in Indian territory in the desert of Phoenix Arizona, and focuses on Robin, one of the major characters, who is a young man at this stage of the novel. The rest of the book is set in England, a generation later, when Robin's son has already grown up. The desert beginning looks as if it is the metaphoric map of the novel, its lodestone. Like Roscoe and Abish, however, Hollinghurst is suspicious of metaphors and of the history of Empire that spawned them.

The young Robin is searching in Phoenix for sites of the buildings, now in ruins, designed by the famous architect, Frank Lloyd Wright. Desert landscapes resonate with Egypt and symbolic pyramid shapes. Robin is only twenty-three and, at this stage, he appears to be bisexual. We actually had assumed he is gay, given his obvious attraction to his young Indian guide. We are shocked, therefore, to discover that he has a girlfriend and that she is pregnant. This invests the structures and landscapes of the first chapter with the ambiguity of Robin's (at least partial) closet and fractured sexuality. As with *The Swimming-Pool Library*, the foreign place, although more miniaturised here, plays a vital role in how to read the serious depths of Hollinghurst's funny, sensuous, satirical and sexy writing.

Robin is in this North American desert as a budding, promising architect, with his camera and notebook, among what are now the ruins of one of

Wright's houses. Note what is left of the house "was the rough bulk of the hearth and the chimney-stack, *a little tower of boulders*, the bluntly symbolic heart of the place" (1998, 2, my emphasis). How reduced are our great pyramids in the ruin of this grand house! And if Wright was a great genius, then here he is also portrayed as an architect of North American appropriation of the land of the Indians. In the context of the ruins, the desert sand storm that blows up in Robin's face is "like a hungry and offended spirit of the place" (1998, 2).

It is here that we can unearth one of the references to the title, which is bound up entirely with the Other, in a throwaway reference to "the unfriendly reflective men who lived in *the spell of the desert*" (1998, 2–3, my emphasis). This desolate, sand swept desert is a microcosm for other colonised and impoverished places:

> He touched the blackened stones and thought of other lonely places—roofless cottages on Welsh mountains, pissed-in pillboxes squatting in the fields at home; and there was something of the outpost in this ruined site, of duty and homesickness. (1998, 3)

There are triangles within triangles. The little mound of stones within the hearth of the house is replicated in the bigger picture of the landscape and when "he straightened up and saw the view" (1998, 3) he sees the triangular structure within the desert. Note, however, the postmodern emphasis on copies, rather than on the extraordinary wonder of the world of the original Egyptian pyramid:

> He had a copy of Wright's plans in his knapsack, and a single photo of the finished house, leached of detail by sunlight and reproduction—*a copy of a copy of a copy*. From here he could see *the vestigial triangle* of the layout, and, matching a distant mountain with a grey shadow in the picture, admire the defiant caprice of the project. He hoped he had shown a similar spirit coming here. (1998, 3, my emphases)

Robin is the adventurer, with echoes of the young man in Hollinghurst's first story, who travelled to Egypt and the Pyramids in search of something, and whose talent and hopes are invested in these projects and places.

But note how ominous are the ruins and copies with which Robin is travelling. He will turn out to be another failed explorer. *The Spell* will wonder, moreover, as to whether this is altogether a bad thing. What the novel so interestingly enacts is the draining away of the spell, the *un*doing of the significance, power and glory of such places and what the likes of Robin can make of them. What we will witness again is the writer attempting to undo the metaphoric and invest his world with literal, material and fleshy reality. We will trace this undoing, in part, by way of an object that Robin finds and pockets and which through the course of the novel becomes a fetish in reverse—*un*fetishised:

> A little way off from the concrete standing he scuffed over something white and squatted down to pick it out of the dust. It was a rough piece of sanitary porcelain, about three inches square, with the letters SEMPE on it, perhaps part of SEMPER, forever. …With a quick suppression of ethical doubt, he opened his knapsack and dropped it in. (1998, 4)

The ethical doubt reminds us that European travellers always plunder and remove, but this is made ironic here by the fact that this particular "treasure" is an old piece of toilet. It re-surfaces in the novel when Robin is exactly twice the age he was at the novel's opening. Danny, his son, in fact, is turning the age his father was when he had pinched the object. Robin, now divorced and openly gay, had returned to live in Dorset where he grew up and where the object now sits on his desk:

> Of course he hardly noticed it any more, it was a sort of paperweight; but there were times when he remembered *its tenuous accidental* story and the quivering light of the day he stole it, or picked it up, which was the day he learned he was to become a father. All he told Lars was, "It's a bit of an old bog from a house in Arizona that I went to when I was a student. When I was Dan's age". (1998, 132, my emphasis)

Lars is the young man with whom Robin is flirting at the party, because his own partner, Justin, is so volatile and emotionally unreliable. Triangles as fleshy sex replace sacred pyramids and magical fetishes:

> It was a three-legged Frank Lloyd Wright chair [Lars] was sitting on, with his thighs apart, following the suggestion of the triangular seat. (1998, 133)

Wright's chair is now merely a framework on which legs are spread out with the aroused penis as the third point on the triangle. The magic has leaked away from the desert place and the surviving spell is embodied in sex—"the crotch thing…the packet" (1998, 44). Robin has become an antiquester—a mediocre, ageing man, engaged in renovations, copies, of old houses, rather than in creating something special and new with the genius of a Wright. Justin, his partner, with Camp spite, but more than a grain of truth, says of Robin:

> "Robin doesn't actually build houses. He could be the Frank Lloyd Wright of the whole Bridport area, but mostly he just tarts up old queens' dados. It's called a country-house practice, darling. Of course, no one builds country houses any more

unless they're neo-classical pastiche by Quinlan Terry, so it tends to be repairs and turning them into flats". (1998, 23)

There are additions and pastiche—postmodern collage and copy—instead of the creation of something bold and adventurous of Robin's promise of the first chapter. But is this such a bad thing for the white man, who needs knocking off his high perch? We should read Robin's life trajectory in the light of two different houses—Robin's own country cottage and the "Victorian loony-bin" (1998, 23) belonging to Tony Bowerchalke, who is one of Robin's clients.

Robin's little house is his pride and joy and is described by Hollinghurst in self consciously parodied pastoral:

> [The cottage] was almost too much, it was the ideal of a cottage tuned close to *the point of parody*, the walls of gold-brown rubble patched with bits of chalk and brick, the straw fantail pigeons on the crest of the roof and the real ones that sidled on the slope of thatch below, the white clematis and yellow Mermaid rose trained tumblingly above the small dark windows, the air of stunned homeliness. (1998, 15, my emphasis)

In a novel of spells induced by sex and drugs as much as by landscapes, the "stunned air" is drugged by nature's excess:

> The air was drugged with the sharpness of flowering hawthorn and cow-parsley and the lushness of the grass in the heat after the shower. Wood-doves made their half-awake calls, and at the edge of hearing there was the trickle of the brook. (1998, 16)

It is this landscape, where Robin was born, and this house that enables him to put down roots with the pride and dignity of not being the interloper in the desert. With a significant metonymic spin on "spell", we learn that the house had been a "shell"—Justin's words, echoing and parodying Robin's in the nursery rhyme style of the mockery of meaning:

> "It was a shell when he bought it," said Justin, in a grim sing-song that mocked Robin's evident pride in the place. (1998, 21)

Proud and rooted he may be, but we are left in no doubt that Robin's cottage is small and cramped, a miniature of the big journeys and vast vistas that adventuring "Kings of all they survey" command. The Niger that Mungo Park 'discovered' in chapter three is reduced to the trickle of the brook nearby the tiny house and the Pyramids of Egypt, one of the world's wonders, is metamorphosed into a strange family mausoleum on Tony Bowerchalke's land.

Buildings, Broken Bodies and Anti-Quests

Tony's house is mentioned on the next page—contiguous with these comments on Robin's house—ensuring that we read them together in the metonymic grammar of the novel.

Robin, his lover, Justin, his son, Danny, and Justin's former lover, who is visiting for the weekend, visit Tony's house. If the opening chapter in the desert of Arizona was replete with landscapes, pyramids and fetishes, then this house, a generation later will signify the cold lack of spirituality and meaning. On arrival, the party focuses

> on the central feature of the gravelled circle, a bare stone plinth on which *some welcoming deity* or tall, nasturtium-spilling urn *might once have stood*, but which now presented them with *nothing but a short rusty spike*. (1998, 52, my emphases)

The house is a grotesque, enormous sprawl architecturally, referred to euphemistically by Robin as "rogue Gothic" (1998, 52). Robin is supposed to convert part of the house into two flats, to help Tony afford to keep up the rest, and, more intriguingly for our purposes, he is also supposed to repair Tony's grandfather's mausoleum, situated in the woods, a mausoleum which is none other than a pyramid.

This pyramid is situated, not in a vast desert, but in an alien, but again miniaturised, landscape, drawing our attention, if that were needed, to the links between this pyramid shape and colonised faraway places—"the wood had an unusual abundance of lichens and epiphytes, which gave it the look of a *dwarf* rain-forest" (1998, 56, my emphasis). The mask over the door of the pyramid is another damaged icon. It is

> an impassively staring Roman face that had been vandalised into noseless Egyptian flatness; Robin at least was never sure if it was a man or a woman. (1998, 56)

This image of the mask of indeterminate gender, but simultaneously as the decline of the life of the spirit and likened to a descent in the scale of evolution from the classic aquiline Roman to the pug nosed African is highly problematic. We last encountered this same image in *The Swimming-Pool Library* in chapter seven, an image which is quite at odds with the general drift of Hollinghurst's politics. What is also interesting is that in that earlier novel, the Egyptian sculpture was an icon, a fetish, which played a crucial and meaningful role in its owner's struggle for identity. Here, however, it is damaged and ruined and signifies only the decline in meaning. The links in the narrative chain of this novel are between the pyramid, AIDS, death and the lack of inspiration or spiritual comfort afforded by this bleak, damp, cold structure. In this way, it also contrasts with the desert landscape of the first chapter:

> He didn't like this building, and had a clear image, a tiny loop of film, in which it fell in on him. He found *its lack of religious assurances surprisingly bleak*. It was over a year since they'd buried Simon, but he was chilled and troubled by literal-minded imaginings, standing within a few feet of a dead body that must be withered and grinning after more than a century of unbelieving rest. (1998, 57–8, my emphasis)

Simon, Robin's previous lover, had died of AIDS and Robin is supposed to be finding a way of mending one of the buckling brick arches, sustaining the pyramid, which is collapsing. Broken buildings, broken bodies and compromised landscapes form jagged pieces of dislocated meaning and splintered identities. Like the crumbling hotels and movie houses with their "echoes of a former colony's mother" of Roscoe's *The Lost Oasis* of the previous chapter (1995, 91), Tony's decrepit house and the collapsing mausoleum of his ancestor, signify the demolition of an age and of the beliefs and quests, Laws and sacred objectives, attached to it. The ridiculous, built body of Rambo, playing in Roscoe's Moroccan *Cinema Le Paris* (chapter seven) underlined the anachronism of the white, male, Tarzan body on display.

Simultaneously, and paradoxically, there is something very positive to be discovered in the ruins of these collapsed, exposed and open structures. They are associated with metonymy, excess and opposition to the quests, order and containment of the big monuments and fixed artefacts. And being ruined in this way, they are full of promise. The spell is broken, or at least transferred to (sometimes drug induced) pleasures of the flesh—the vulnerable, ageing physical body itself. This is perhaps all it ever was:

> [Robin] was embarrassed to hear Danny saying something about opium. Tony had once confided in him, as if it were still a problem, that his great-grandfather had been an addict; and Robin had mentioned to Danny his theory that the pyramid, and perhaps the house itself, was an attempt to realise the architectural phantasmagoria of an opium dream. (1998, 58)

At the end of the day, the spell is nothing more than "the sight of Justin from behind" (1998, 59) and "[Danny] had an impression of life as a party, as a parade of flash-lit hugs and kisses, in *a magic zone* where everyone was young and found to be beautiful" (1998, 71, my emphasis). Ultimately, like the draining away of meaning from the icons, Danny, ironically, "wondered if there was some equally effective spell for making your dick go down"

(1998, 224). Even the second rate creativity invested in this bleak landscape is snuffed when Tony dies

> and the plans had all come to nothing. Robin spoke about all his wasted work as though that were the real tragedy of the thing. (1998, 253)

The wasted work and crumbling icons may be set in rural landscapes of one kind or another, but the loss of spirituality that they signify saturates late twentieth century English culture. When Alex visits the Royal Academy in London

> he looked around at the detritus of old religions, *vessels of exhausted magic*. In front of him was a mask of blistered bronze, paper-brittle and azure with age. For a moment he remembered the broken-nosed mask on Tony Bowerchalke's pyramid. (1998, 66, my emphasis)

This reminds us of Robin's reduced vision, by comparison with all the adventuring promise of his youth spent travelling and researching in desert spaces faraway. It is symbolically captured by his sore eye at the end of the book, covered with a patch, a patch totally distinguished from that of the dashing Captain Hook by his domestication. He is cooking in his cosy country kitchen—"a short apron over his jeans, and a patch over his left eye" (1998, 252).

The other side of this story of reduced, miniaturised and impaired vision, a side we have to keep on re-visiting, is what liberates Hollinghurst's characters from the imprisoning discourse of Empire and its surviving tropes. The gay sons discover a new quest—that of taking possession of their own country and its landscapes. The heart of British self-identity lies in the English countryside. The politics of *The Spell* lies in turning away from voyages of discovery and desert pilgrimages and towards occupying this rural heartland and in so doing, transforming Britain's cultural heritage to incorporate gay men.

Dorset, of course, is Thomas Hardy country and the landscape is fertile with the cultural canon. The bunch of gay friends have been expelled from this Eden and may no longer drink in the historic old pub, one which figures in Hardy's famous novel:

> "We'd been going there for years, of course," said Robin. "It's a nice old pub. Hardy mentions it in *Tess* as a well-known stopping-place on the old road from Bridport to Weymouth. Tess was looked after by the landlord. Unfortunately, relations with the present landlord are rather less cordial since Justin got very fresh with him, which didn't go down well, and then relieved himself in the back porch. So lunch there really isn't a possibility."

Crossing the Great Desert Void

> "Does Hardy also have a bit about the lavs being the smelliest in Wessex?' said Justin". (1998, 61)

Like the "bit of bog" salvaged from the wreck of the Wright House in the desert, the pub is drained of its literary pretensions by way of smelly 'lavs' and gay violations. Justin's peeing in the porch, moreover, is an elemental image of marking out territory. This reminds us of the animal instinct, suddenly aroused in Boyle's threatened male in chapter four, whose urge becomes to pee on his patch as a mark of taking ownership. In this context, we witness the onslaught of the gay men into Dorset, when they arrive from London for Robin's son's birthday party:

> Among the few Saturday commuters, local kids and dun-coloured hikers there was a swishing *little posse of metropolitan muscle and glamour.* ...Robin watched them for a few droll seconds as they collected under the Gothic arch, looking careless but a little abashed by this alien place. ...Robin had put on, almost unconsciously, his sexiest old button-fly jeans, and George was wearing leather trousers, which rather confused Robin with their hot attractive smell. He couldn't help thinking they must look like a pair of affluent queens who'd hired a whole chorus-line of hustlers for the weekend. (1998, 116, my emphasis)

Under the structure of the village arch, in this strange place, these men do not fit in, with their sexy leather among the backpackers and simple locals. This party does not endear Robin and Justin to these locals. As Justin puts it they are "hideously unpopular" and while before the party "they weren't mad about us", now "they loathe us" (1998, 156). Hollinghurst makes it clear that it is the fact that they are gay that alienates them from the villagers. It was not just that they made a noise at the party—"it was homosexual noise. That's what they don't like" (1998, 156).

Robin has no need any longer to be Tarzan gazing out from his tree top perch. In a glorious, theatrical Camp ending, Robin and Justin, with their gay party, which is not idealised and includes former lovers, friends and also foes, go on an outing. They drive along a narrow lane:

> The banks were high on either side, and the hedges above were festooned with the soft swarming stars of traveller's joy, already turning grey and mothy. (1998, 256)

There is a subtle irony in the plant, which happens by chance to be named "traveller's joy", a joy which Hollinghurst is contesting, a joy which was full in the first chapter of Robin's youth, and which is grey and old by the novel's end. The others reach the summit without Robin, who decides to "run the last mile" by himself. The panorama is described through Alex's eyes (Justin's former lover):

> Alex looked aside and saw the whole panorama inland come steadily clear, the line of ascent from the valley bottoms, the silage-heaps weighted with old tyres, little fields overgrown with alder, up past sheltered farms under hanging woods and low bald pastures, and on to the open hilltops, the windwalks and long ridged heights. (1998, 256)

The fields may be little, the farms sheltered and the pastures bald, like some of these middle aged men may already be becoming, but the road leads to its own heights from which the view is spectacular and Robin, who has run his course, joins the gay group, which stands arm in arm, like the stage encore at the end of the performance. They survey the local landscape, but from a new angle. This is the countryside of Robin's birth and his ownership is his birthright, from which being gay has sought to exclude him. Scarred, compromised, some givers, some takers, they are different and also the same, as part of the sexual sub-culture they share. Their taking ownership can be likened to the desert inhabitants of Phoenix, with which the novel began, whose spirit throws up a desert storm. The last lines of the novel read:

> For a minute or two they watched the inky zones of the sea-bed, as the small could-shadows sailed across them; then the sun dropped westward, the surface of the sea turned quickly grey, and they saw the curling silver roads of the currents over it. (1998, 257)

The view is not land, but landscape, a painting, a cultural tradition of pastoral, of Thomas Hardy, which this new gay writing is simultaneously interrogating and appropriating in the construction of a new canon and literary heritage. Susan Sontag, in her "Notes on Camp" suggests that "nothing in nature can be campy...Nothing rural, either. Campy objects are urban" (518). Hollinghurst defies this tradition and re-defines Camp in Dorset, thereby moulding its language to his designs and constructing a landscape painting dotted with gay inhabitants.

But is the only solution to stay at home? With the return to Dorset, we bump into another writer, whose land also turns into landscape painting, whose fictional countryside of Ulverton is similar and right nearby, but whose roots also lie in Cameroon—Adam Thorpe.

Land, Landscape and Clearing the English Bush

> a long-haired graduate who wrote, and ran
> a little company with puppets, whose dreams were rural
> in an urban century... (Adam Thorpe, *Mornings in the Baltic*, 53)

Adam Thorpe published his third novel entitled *Pieces of Light*, ten years after the publication of the poetry collection in which these lines occur. What is of great interest to us is that this novel, unlike the previous two, is fundamentally concerned with Africa, with Cameroon, where the author spent some of his adolescence, having also had a brief, but impressionable boyhood period in the Congo (personal correspondence, 2001). This third novel is, moreover, organically linked to the first, which charts the history of rural England over the centuries as played out within one small village called Ulverton, which gives that first novel its title. *Ulverton* begins in 1650 and takes us to its fictional present—"Here"—1988. What is so intriguing is that, with another poetry collection and novel in between, Adam Thorpe re-visits Ulverton, his rural England, and examines its nature, its forests and village life, its culture and future, through the lens of alternative African landscapes.

What pitfalls and minefields lurk within this scenario! There is the danger that the worst excesses of the romances of Pastoralism might link hands with the distortions and stereotypes of Africanist discourse and produce an idealised escape from urban fatigue. For example, one reviewer, Justine Jordan, describes how

> the characters in *Pieces of Light* suffer from a yearning to return to or reconfigure a time before trauma. As Hugh's war-ravaged father continues his colonisation of the primordial jungle, his equally shell-shocked Uncle Edward fosters the 'wildwood' at the bottom of his garden, hoping that it will one day cover England again, as it did when the climate was African. (25)

African primordial jungles, apparently reverberating with English wildwoods, which originate in African time, do not bode well for a symbolism able to break out of the confines of stereotype. All of this, however, is well understood by Thorpe himself and his readers may be in for a few surprises as we trace the life of Hugh Arkwright in *Pieces of Light*.

Hugh is born in colonial Africa, in the Cameroons, where his father, James, had been sent as a District Officer to a remote outpost. He spends his most formative, free and happy years there until his parents, anxious that he is "going native", send him to his uncle and aunt, who live in the English village of none other than Ulverton, where he grows up through an utterly miserable and isolated adolescence.

Although published separately, six years apart, with other projects in between, *Ulverton* (1992) and *Pieces of Light* (1998) yield most by being scrutinised together, as if the latter were planned as a sequel of the former.[1] This is a re-writing of the actual process. A close reading of the two novels together, then, has to be understood in the context of the lack of a big, originating plan on Thorpe's part when he produced his first fictional visit to Ulverton (see interview with Hagenauer, 8). The big project may have been

---

[1] My page references to *Ulverton* are taken from the Vintage edition, published in 1998.

inadvertent but is certainly what we end up having. Irreverence, moreover, is in the spirit of Thorpe's eccentric, experimental techniques, which invite his readers to travel along time warps, to re-read, re-write, to re-visit and re-look at all his settings in different and transforming lights. At the same time, this raises questions about the nature of the second novel as well. What was happening in *Still* that gave rise to this detailed return to Ulverton via Africa? In fact, in bringing into joint focus all three novels, I will be following Charles Lock, who suggests:

> Though neither written nor presented as a trilogy, each of Thorpe's three novels gains from the presence of the others; and a coherence emerges that in some sense forms a work, an *oeuvre*, that contains and enfolds each book, turns each book into a part. (25)

In this spirit, I would like to begin with the end section of *Pieces of Light*, where I discover a clue to the whole enterprise. Although it appears as the final part of the novel, it is set prior to the birth of the main character, Hugh, and is the novel's earliest time. It consists of the first letters, written by Charlotte Arkwright, Hugh's mother, to her brother, on her and her husband James's first arrival in Cameroon. She describes their house as being crammed full of

> tea-chests, broken chairs, legs of tables, rolls of canvas, empty whisky bottles, shards of glass, books—even half-finished paintings, done on planks of wood. *Our first task, then, was to clear a path, not through African vegetation, but through European dross*. (1998b, 439, my emphasis)

I will have a lot more to say about paintings. For the moment, the interesting point is that the first clearing operation was not that of the African forest in order to make way for the colonial road, but through all that English litter. And so, we too have to undertake that clearing operation and travel to the fictional village of *Ulverton*, Thorpe's first novel. We will be making brief stops on the film set of *Still*, Thorpe's second novel, along the way. What I hope to demonstrate in the process is the uniqueness of Thorpe's endeavour to bring an enlightened understanding of landscape into a global canvas. I use the term "canvas" advisedly. Thorpe's central preoccupation is with the lack of innocence in the traditions of representing places and he writes into his novels his interrogation of the politics of these conventions, especially as they have been used to describe nature.

Pastoralism, Africanism and Pieces of Narrative

> Adam Thorpe's extraordinary first novel, *Ulverton*, laid the past down like sediment, each chapter a slice of time, beginning in 1650 and ending 'Here', and in that way producing a wholly convincing village history in which distant events continue to reverberate through folk memory and legend, delicately but distinctly echoing in place-names and local rhymes. (Jordan, 25)

What Jordan has admirably captured in her assessment of *Ulverton*, is its unity of purpose. What needs equally to be emphasised is the novel's attempts to undermine, problematise, damage and even to murder conventional narrative structures, along with some of the characters. There is no conventional narrative tightness, either between or within the so-called stories, for want of a better word. We will, however, see that there are loose connections and associations between them that become more important by the end where, in a somewhat belated gesture to narrative closure, the suspected murder, which occurs in the first, is confirmed by the discovery of the skeleton in the last.

It is not quite a novel, nor are the bits really short stories. Interestingly, a better word to describe the components of *Ulverton* occurred to me in the light of the third novel. I find referring to them as 'pieces' very useful and for me *Pieces of Light* provides the key to the dappled structure of *Ulverton*. This involves reading the novel sequence backwards and with hindsight, an altogether illegitimate critical practice, entirely appropriate to Thorpe's *oeuvre*. The links between stories are little pinpricks of memory of places and people that went before.

Each piece is separated from the previous one by the different and changing media with which people communicate. These relate to different classes and their relative access to wealth and, linked to it, to language and the evolving technology of the centuries. The pieces thus take many and different forms—diaries, letters, depositions, fictional paintings and photographs, BBC broadcasts and a finale with a film script for a television documentary, in which Thorpe himself appears. Furthermore, within many of these, there are gaps and erasures, stutters and incompleteness. All of this further exposes the constructedness of what we can only describe in scare marks as "the novel".

What we have is a rural cacophony without beginning or end, except for bits of connection via the links between the generations and the land itself, as farms, fine country houses, woods and landscape. All of these endure, along with the superstitions, tales, legends and myths that have emerged, among the people and embedded in the land itself.

Why a cacophony? What is striking is how much tedious farming detail Thorpe includes in many of the pieces. Buried, easily missed, within the weight of the daily grind of tasks, are penlight moments of narrative information, by whose dim illumination a story of a kind emerges. This technique has, I think, two linked goals. The goals are to explode conventional narrative and expose the constructed nature of stories. Secondly, the detail regarding how the land is worked separates the image from the pictorial quaintness that transforms working land into landscape. And in this, Thorpe is placing himself unambiguously in an anti-pastoral tradition. Terry Gifford, in his book, *Pastoral*, describes the poetry of Virgil as establishing two quite different traditions originating in *Eclogues* as opposed to his *Georgics*, the latter being "a practical guide to vegetable and animal husbandry" (18). The *Eclogues*, by contrast, establish the myth of Arcadia in which shepherds engage in song competitions:

> Arcadia is significantly an alpine region that is cut off on all sides by other high mountains. It was the perfect location for a poetic paradise, a literary construct of a past Golden Age in which to retreat by linguistic idealisation. In contrast to the *Georgics*, the Arcadia of *Eclogues* is abstracted from the reality of a working country life. (Gifford, 20)

The difference between the two reminds us of the contrast between metaphor and metonymy, which has been useful in thinking about how to confront discourses of power and oppression. The myths and symbols of pastoral are exposed by the realities of the random literalness of everyday farming work. Already in his poetry Thorpe had provided ample evidence of his anti-pastoral stand. In a wonderful, funny, ironic poem entitled "PARADISO", from the *Mornings in the Baltic* collection, Thorpe places the poet in such a poetic paradise and begins:

> It was Heaven alright:
> we gambolled vaguely about
> the first few days, plucked apple-blossom
> and wondered where our fat had gone (1988, 64)

> Food and sex are in abundant supply—

> and before I could lick
> the honey off my chin
> from the night's repast
> (no fixed time for meals, it was all
> hunter-gathering)
> someone giggled and the lot
> tumbled on top of me, everything swinging. (1988, 65)

However,

> Actually, it was a little
> too much. A sort of glut
> of all the film-stars you've ever fancied (1988, 65)

which turns into a nightmare in which

> I began to pine for my bed-sit
> the High Street in Edmonton, the dog-shit
> and drizzle. (1988, 66)

Things get worse

> (and I gambolled unconvincingly
> until I broke
> down, weeping (1988, 67)

To his great joy, the poet is dropped down into hell:

> A few rather tawdry-looking shops,
> a high-rise in a drizzle, an old
> woman and a rolling bottle
> and religious graffiti
> (God's a Dosser, Sod Off God). (1988, 67)

The rural world of Ulverton, then, is not an Arcadian pleasure dome, but a working land in which we are given a hard, factual avalanche of detail around husbandry. Coupled quite intriguingly with this, there is all the relativity of stories, viewpoints and differing lights from which to view events. The narrative exposes the innards of its working. Fictional letters, paintings and photographs turn this working land into landscape. These are the canvases framing the whole and providing the key to these readings. I will be demonstrating that Thorpe uses some of the devices of postmodernism, with its concern with mediations, method and intermediaries and love of pastiche, but is not himself a postmodernist. I say this because he uses these devices in order to expose a fundamental truth about white, male stories as master narratives linked to the power of property, of the big estates, of the imperialist drive for wealth. Narrative unreliability is exposed by the vested interests of the narrators, interests which turn their stories into rationalisations of their fuckings, thievings and murderings, as they jostle for position, property, sex, heirs and power.

The first piece is particularly important in setting up the style, method and preoccupations of *Ulverton*. Entitled "Return" I will focus on it, not wishing to delay us too long from the story of Africa and the character of Hugh Arkwright, who is also in a sense returning to Ulverton, like the ill fated Gabby, whose return begins the many diverse chronicles of *Ulverton*.

Dated 1650, Gabby, impoverished farmer turned soldier, returns from Cromwell's war. The story is told by the old shepherd, who knew Gabby as a boy and who knows that Gabby's wife, Anne, assuming he was killed in the war, had re-married a rather sinister no-good character called Thomas Walters, or so we see him through William, the shepherd's eyes. Only William, busy minding the sheep, witnessed Gabby's return and when he disappears without trace, William suspects that Anne and Thomas have murdered him. William, meanwhile, has not had sex for twenty years because his pious wife, Ruth, believes that sex is only for procreation. William keeps quiet about his suspicions and ends up having regular sex with Anne in as a kind of subtle form of blackmail.

"Return" provides an example of the use of unreliable narrators, beneath whose, neuroses, ignorance and interests, we as readers have to dig for the answers, or lack of them, as the case may be. William is a fundamentally flawed interpreter of events because he writes from the standpoint of his own frustrated sexuality in desperate search of release.

This first story, moreover, provides further, less obvious, threads in a novel without conventional narrative structure. It does so via the myth that arises out of the story of Anne, who becomes a witch in legend and the rock, which sheltered her and the shepherd, becomes a landmark of potency and folk significance. A different, but equally laden rock emerges in *Pieces of Light*, and it is with such rocks in mind that Simon Schama could have written that:

> our entire landscape tradition is the product of shared culture, it is by the same token a tradition built from a rich deposit of myths, memories, and obsessions. The cults which we are told to seek in other native cultures—of the primitive forest, of the river of life, of the sacred mountain—are in fact alive and well and all about us if only we know where to look for them. (14)

Already by the second story, the events of the first have been transformed into legend. Three stranded men find themselves, to their horror, forced to take shelter under the rocky protuberance, which turns out to be "none other than that place where certain of the spiritually distracted in our grandparents' time fell into unspeakable depravity and cavorted lustfully in nakedness upon its flanks and that is called thereby the Devil's Knob" (1998a, 29).

Multiple genres, styles, forms of English and forked tongued narrators generate reader skepticism regarding versions of reality. This is powerfully reinforced by Thorpe's emphasis on ways of seeing linked to technology that manipulates the light. The foremost of these is our eyes—eyeballs close up, blind eyes, misinterpreting eyes—all punctuate Thorpe's fiction. Linked to this is his preoccupation with painting, photography and film.

The intersection between the use of colour within a pastoral tradition and the pillar of darkness within Africanist discourse, buttressed by an understanding of interests, privilege and oppression, provide Thorpe with an opportunity to make a profound and global critique. The interesting point is that the pastoral tradition has used blackness to signify the threat and ugliness of poor people, which feeds into racist Africanist discourse in interesting ways. This point has been popularised by John Barrell in his significantly entitled *The Dark Side of Landscape: The Rural Poor in English Painting 1730–1840*. Barrell points out that "a basic rule of landscape composition in the eighteenth century...is that the rich and their habitations must be illuminated, and the poor and theirs be left in the shadows of the 'dark side of the landscape'" (22). What happens is that:

> This division has the advantage of marking the differences in status and fortune between rich and poor, while showing that the unity of the landscape and of the society it can be seen to represent is dependent on the existence of both, which combine in a harmonious whole. As the landscape could not be structured without the natural contrast of light and shade, so the society could not survive without social and economic distinctions which are thus also apparently natural. (22)

It is in this context that Thorpe's preoccupation with the ideological effects of light and dark imaging within fiction becomes so important. This preoccupation crescendoes in *Pieces of Light*. Already in *Ulverton* and *Still*, however, Thorpe's technique of making his critique of the exploitation of the rural poor, through an understanding of the interests invested in the art and culture, is apparent. For example, Ricky in *Still*, in filming the Victorian servants, is aware that "they're the problem visually" and he determines to "put a filter on and gild them. Why not? I don't want the group bleached out" (1996, 109). In so filming them in the light he makes them heroic and thereby turns the tables on the social hierarchy:

> The guy at the front, the young one with the broad hat and slop jacket and corded breeches, he's hung on to his rake and he leans on it. It looks good, the tangs are *catching the sun, there's a touch of flare*. (1996, 109, my emphasis)

Later he describes how this man, who would normally have been filmed in the shadows of imposing structures and important people, had "worked his back to a dent raking and tying and digging and pruning in the grounds of Randle College for fifty-five years". Ricky feels that "this man is the only really heroic guy I've ever known" (1996, 111).

In an *Ulverton* piece entitled "Deposition", set in 1830, light and dark recur as the framing images in this period in which rural workers rise up in rebellion against their poverty. They are subjected to the Riot Act in response to their destruction of property. People are starving and yet, obscenely, great dinner parties are held by the rich, who manage to stuff themselves with

> capons boiled in their bladders, roasted venison with a marinade of veal, fried ducklings, a complete little cygnet from the Lake, Westphalia ham and a calf's head hashed with larded liver, with ice cream and blancmange as an afterthought. (1998a, 157)

At one such dinner, the painter, Mr. Constable, is present and through him Thorpe expresses his disdain for rural romanticism:

> Mr Constable broke into an exceedingly admirable discourse on opticks, and the lustre of wet grass, and the calm white edges of moving clouds being his soul—or the wet grass was—or both at once—leastways he ended by stating that Paradise was a slimy post in a ditch, or some such, which provoked all present into peals of mirth. (1998a, 159–160)

The rural poor as dark and threatening are linked in this way to black people. The peasants seem "alarmingly swarthy, as tho' rubbed in charcoal" (1998a, 155) or "they had blackened their faces with soot" (1998a, 158); they are "ragamuffins (all of the most swarthy hue, like sweeps—it appears to me this whole village is inked in dirt)" (1998a, 161).

The point that Thorpe is emphasising, and one that will be relevant to the question of why he took his fiction back to Africa, relates to the link between cultural representation and social movements. Thorpe understands fine art, film or literature and developments like the Enclosures in terms of Britain's role as an imperial power. The last is very often forgotten. Ann Bermingham, in her *Landscape and Ideology: The English Rustic Tradition, 1740–1860* underscores both of these points. She indicates that "the emergence of rustic landscape painting as a major genre in England at the end of the eighteenth century coincided with the accelerated enclosure of the English countryside" (1). What she is therefore attempting to do, is to "illuminate the relationship between the aesthetics of the painted landscape and the economics of the enclosed one" (1). She insists, moreover, that the process of enclosure of land "once held in common" and acquired by landowners was accelerated in the late seventeenth century "in the context of nascent imperialism and mercantilism" which required "an agrarian countryside to serve the expanding markets of the towns and colonies" (9).

"Shutter", set in 1859, is another piece where this intersection between representation and social change on a global scale is powerfully demonstrated. It takes the form of a commentary on a selection of photographs, rather than a narrative at all. These visual representations of landscape and portraits comment directly on the pastoral tradition and critique it, but again via an unreliable commentator. The photographer is clearly extraordinary—a woman with a lot of insight, but also with class prejudices. She has complete faith in the veracity of what the camera's eye sees and when her own unwitting comments belie this faith, much of her observation is rendered via the ironic lens of the author. This is how her narration is demonstrated as unreliable. Again I emphasise this because the undercutting of his narrator's voice is such a key to Thorpe's narrative methodology, which draws attention away from individuals and to the landscapes they construct.

Plate XXV11, for example, is a commissioned photograph of "*The Household of Sir Humphrey Chalmers, M. P., At Ulverton House*" (1998a, 170). She insists that all she has done is to render "the facts visibly and honestly, and improved nothing" (1998a, 171). However, it is clear that she has quite carefully engineered the scene around Sir Humphrey Chalmers's interests, on whose commission she depends. So, the household of servants are photographed as evidence of the wealth and prestige of Sir Humphrey:

> On the either extremity I have turned the ladies (parlourmaids only) inwards, so that the eye is drawn to the centre of the group, thence to the magnificent copper beeches behind, and so to the house. (1998a, 170)

Note that this entire, constructed composition is designed to ensure that "the weighty stature of the house supersedes all else" (1998a, 170). In other words, both the figures and the fine house have to be placed theatrically in the right proportions to serve as an indictor of the status, power and prestige of Sir Humphrey. The result is the kind of social order and harmony that Barrell so aptly described in relation to the use of light and dark.

What Thorpe manages to sneak in, however, is the potential for art to undermine these interests even as it reinforces them—"I do not know what the faint figure in the extreme rear of the picture was doing, for I did not notice him at the time" (1998a, 170).

Thorpe's global perspective is again in evidence here where the next series of plates are taken in Egypt, which recurs as a thread in *Ulverton*. The photographer accepts an invitation to join an excavation to an Egyptian tomb complex and quite unthinkingly assumes the right of the British to plunder the tombs and remove the spoils—"I must refrain from disclosing [the site] lest the riches therein be garlanded by other than the British Museum" (1998a, 183).

European plunder of animals, as in the butchering and trophy collection of hunters, or of lands, as in colonialism, become central themes in *Pieces of Light*. The First World War becomes in this context an organic link between exploitation and murder at home and the consolidation of imperialism abroad. This war provides the answer to a key puzzle in *Pieces of Light*, as we shall see, and is a central issue in Thorpe's earlier novels. In *Ulverton*, in the piece called "Treasure", ordinary peasants are enlisted as canon fodder for this war by the pompous squire, who calls on jingoistic sentiment, itself scaffolded by his economic hold over the workers. And in *Still* the rather demented narrator, Ricky, another unreliable old loon, very reminiscent of Hugh's later protagonist in *Pieces of Light*, refers to a filming of a First World War scene entwined with ironic references to the great painters, like Constable:

> There are Monet mornings and Constable afternoons and Claude Lorrain evenings, OK? There's gaslight, there's fog, there's the big wide chalk country and there's the trenches. (1996, 158)

We are brought up short, out of the world of paint with a cameraman whose eyes have been blasted away and with the words "wasted, wasted. So many wasted" (1996, 158). We must remember this War and its shell-shocked victims, Empire and painting, especially of Constable, later, when puzzles have to be solved in *Pieces of Light*. We must remember what Stephen Daniels is suggesting in the following observation, when Hugh's mother appears to practice her final vanishing into the African forest by disappearing first into a Constable painting in an English village. Daniels says that "by the First World War, the *Hay-wain* was upheld as an epitome of the country it was worth dying to defend" (1993, 6).

Ulverton concludes in the present with "Adam Thorpe himself as a named character in a documentary film on Ulverton. We will conclude this "dross clearing" exercise" by looking more closely at the eco-politics of our "long-haired graduate" poet puppeteer "whose dreams were rural…in an urban century" (1988, 53).

Film, like photography, is a technology of light and therefore preoccupies Thorpe in his fiction. This documentary is a day in the life of Clive Walters, property developer. It is clear that he is much hated by the author and his self-promotion and exploitation of the countryside is relentlessly satirised. Thorpe, the author, has great difficulty making any of his characters too authoritative, so he presents us with a stuttering, stumbling Adam Thorpe in a rather contrived attempt at effacing himself. 'Adam' is affiliated to the Ulverton Preservation Society and that he is billed as "Local Author & Performer" (1998a, 330). He has this to say about Clive Walters:

PAN ACROSS TO
CLOSE-UP THORPE THORPE:
  Well what I wanted to say is—
  is that er, he's a difficult
  character, he's—he's a toughie,
  basically, and em, I think it's
  ... (*sighs*) I mean look at that,
  er, estate up at er—in Bursop.
  Saddle Stone Yard. Now he
  Won er, on that one. Got away
  with absolute murder. (1998a, 330)

This artificial attempt at effacement is not all that successful, given that the voice of the real Adam Thorpe resounds finally as authoritative and critical of property developers, their materialistic greed and disregard for the lives of rural people and the earth. All of this is made abundantly clear by the ironic use of photos and of "shepherd's pipe music" and "old sepia photos of Ulverton" (1998a, 317) and "swan on lake" (1998a, 320). Midst the "close-up bumble bee", the "leafy oak-tree" and the cornfield, however, are also poppies as sneaky reminder of the war dead, midst this fake scenario (1998a, 334).

It is therefore a fundamental misreading on the part of John Bilston when he imagines that "nostalgia" is what drives *Ulverton*:

> Thorpe conveys regret at the passing of the old ways (the blacksmith's shop, the unfenced land, the horse and cart and the clop of croquet-mallets) and in doing so aligns himself with English pastoral/imperial tradition. (20)

How could such a gross misreading occur? Is it simply that the reviewer is unable to understand the irony? Thorpe's anti-pastoralism is unmistakable in his writing, as reinforced by his own comments in the Hagenauer, in which he says that he was "trying to subvert the whole pastoral tradition" and that "in so many ways [*Ulverton*] is anti-pastoral" (6). Not just that, however,—"I was trying to do new things with the pastoral" (6). What kind of things? Later on in the interview he expresses delight at the use made by an English organisation called "The Council for the Protection of Rural England" of parts of *Ulverton* in their publicity. He thinks that someone on that Council:

> picked on these particular passages as expressing something about the English countryside that we need to react politically to—to save it or to preserve it, and preserve it in the right way. That made me realize that novels are of course read by people in positions of power or influence, and even if *Ulverton* made a politician

wake up the next morning thinking five percent more about rural England, about the need for conservation, then that's very, very important. (7)

What is certainly true is that Thorpe loves the countryside and does so precisely within a critique of the negative effects of pastoralism on that land and its workers. In other words, there is an organic connection between the love of nature, the respect for those who work the land, the repugnance for human disregard for the protection of the environment and the rejection of idealised pastoral traditions, which Thorpe satirises again and again in all of his work.

Or as Terry Gifford puts it, "the difficulty" or one might say the challenge, "for the anti-pastoral writer" lies "in finding a voice that can be celebratory whilst corrective" (134). This is precisely the voice that Thorpe seeks and it underlies all of his experimentation with narrative technique. In this, moreover, he is part of a politically radical tradition of conservationist radicals, including the authoritative Raymond Williams whose *The Country and the City* was first published in 1973. In it, Williams grapples with the politically slippery issue of pastoral conservatism versus commitment to conservation. Williams contrasts what he calls a "retrospective radicalism", which while it opposes the "new moneyed order" (36) does so by reference to a mythical golden age, "an earlier and happier rural England" (35), with what Williams calls "a precarious but persistent rural-intellectual radicalism", one which is

> genuinely and actively hostile to industrialism and capitalism; opposed to commercialism and to the exploitation of environment; attached to country ways and feelings, the literature and the lore. (36)

The crucial difference between "retrospective radicalism" and "rural-intellectual radicalism" rests with the person's attitude to history. If that golden age becomes the benchmark, that illusory rural paradise where sheep and shepherds endlessly 'gambolled' about then it becomes reactionary:

> As in every kind of radicalism the moment comes when any critique of the present must choose its bearings, between past and future. And if the past is chosen, as now so often and so deeply, we must push the argument through to the roots that are being defended. (Williams, 36)

We saw Thorpe prefer an urban wasteland to a life in the illusory paradise of a rural golden age. Or as he puts it in *Still* referring cynically to "this Third World Thoreau Iron John thing", which made him "pine for my Magimix and my electric toothpick" (1996, 193).

If Thorpe can be classified as a "rural-intellectual radical", which I think he can, then what must be added to the definition is the global perspective of anti-imperialism, strangely underplayed in Williams. While this dimension is certainly stated unambiguously in Williams's book, it is tagged onto the last two chapters, rather than integrated into his analyses throughout. He may state that "the country-houses which were the apex of a local system of exploitation then had many connections to these distant lands" (280) but this is the first we have heard of it. He eventually points out that rivalry between "the rising industrial societies, for markets, raw materials and areas of influence" which "was fought out in their European bases, in the First World War", had such an effect "on the English imagination" that "every idea and every image was consciously and unconsciously affected" (281). This had its roots much earlier, of course, and yet these were hardly touched upon until the end of Williams's study. By contrast, Thorpe takes the global context as his framework and he attempts to weld together complex, superimposed landscapes without illusions.

This imperial element is almost entirely absent from Terry Gifford's otherwise lucid and accessible study entitled, simply, *Pastoral*. Bringing us more up to date than Williams's early study, he can be interpreted as enlarging upon Williams's "rural-intellectual radical" with his concept of the "'post-pastoral'" (150). The "post-pastoral" is aware of the conventions and illusions of the pastoral (149) and consciously seeks a "language to outflank those dangers" (149). This is surely precisely the point we have been making about how to attack the conventions of Orientalism or the Africanist varieties, a perspective lacking here. What is "fundamental to post-pastoral literature is an awe in attention to the natural world" (Gifford, 152). Gifford understands this "ecocentrism" in political terms only when he belatedly defines one of the elements of the "post-pastoral" as the "realisation that the exploitation of the planet is of the same mindset as the exploitation of women and minorities" (165).

This political dimension within a conservationist agenda is fundamental and includes issues of gender as well as of class, where rural workers are afforded the dignity of their issues and ways of life being taken realistically, rather than poetically and metaphorically within elitist pastoral fantasy. Stephen Daniels is helpful in our attempts to place Thorpe within this politics. He entwines his discussion of the imagery of landscape intricately with national identity and thence with the buttressing of such images with the power of Empire and its imperialist ideology. Let us return to his comment about Constable's *Hay-wain* in a fuller context:

> The very global reach of English imperialism into alien lands, was accompanied by
> a countervailing sentiment for cosy home scenery, for thatched cottages and gardens

> in pastoral countryside. Inside Great Britain lurked Little England. At the same time in the 1880s as Greenwich was taken as the Prime Meridian, as the British public gazed at global maps centred mathematically on Britain, with dominions coloured red to show an empire on which the sun never set, and margins illustrated with exotic human figures, fauna and flora, so the very picture of rustic England, Constable's *Hay-wain*, entered the National Gallery and, through reproduction, the national imagination. By the First World War, the *Hay-wain* was upheld as an epitome of the country it was worth dying to defend. (1993, 6)

The point about inclusiveness of race, gender and class, in a radical appraisal of the ways in which humanity uses and abuses the planet is fundamental as Daniels emphasises when he suggests that "the very images of dominion, of power in the land, may be identified as such, then reclaimed or reconstituted" (1993, 7). Daniels substantiates this by reference to:

> Images like Ingrid Pollard's photographs of Black figures in 'traditional' English countryside put complacent views of national landscape into question. Other landscapes may be culturally re-cast. A day's pony trekking for Muslim girls in the Brecon Beacons reminded everyone of Kashmir and Mirpur where they used to live. (1993, 7)

It is precisely such a reconstitution that fuels Thorpe's fiction and his wonderful irony when he has Ricky in *Still* insist on the authenticity of his Victorian set, which would have to hide "Mr Wu's Fish Bar and Ali's Kebabs" (1996, 257).

I would like to suggest, however, that Thorpe only fully explores his global politics, after *Still* when he re-visits his English village through an African connection, in order to consolidate his anti imperialist perspectives. The uneasy jokes in *Still* are telling Freudian signs of unconscious unease. There is the reference to the stiff upper lips of Londoners "so stiff they'll look like those Africans who put soup-plates in their mouths" (1996, 215). Later we have flippant reference to some poor bloke, who brought disgrace of some or other kind to his family and so was banished to some "hellishly unshaded part of the Empire" where "the poor guy had been skewered by Zulus" (1996, 279). This Empire requires disinfectant, given that it is full of "teeming filth and flies" (1996, 281) and "I've thought about getting my Congo machete and trimming out all that stuff about Zelda's letter" (1996, 569). There are other examples, all jokey and superficial, which dot and recur through *Still*. I think Thorpe confronts his African background in *Pieces of Light* and that he does so with an awareness of the discourses of Pastoralism and Africanism that were there before him and which he has to 'reclaim and reconstitute'.

His unreliable narrators stand him in good stead as Thorpe battles to present his global landscape freed from that all-seeing gaze of the imperial white man. The device of the stammering Adam Thorpe in *Ulverton* is far less effective, I think, than the blustery and eccentric old white has-beens that occupy the spotlights of both *Still* and *Pieces of Light*. Both the peculiar Ricky and the crazy Hugh are dislocated from their biological lines— Richard as the illegitimate son of an upper class boy and the maid—and Hugh, whose strange ancestry will be explored in the next chapter. As Cosgrove puts it in his self-criticism in the introductory essay to the republication of his *Social Formation and Symbolic Landscape*, "the figure of the individual European male, conceived as a universal subject", and thus as "the sovereign subject of history" was "effectively, if invisibly…the hero" of his book (xvii).

In *Pieces of Light* Thorpe de-centres that "monarch-of-all-I-survey" by remaining committed to the rights and wrong-doings of historical reality. He takes an archetypal English beechwood and relates its images to forests far away in Africa. In the process, he constructs a radical hybrid landscape, which acknowledges violence and power instead of fake harmony and rural bliss. What saves Ulverton from the developer right at the very end of *Ulverton* is the discovery of the nearly three and a half centuries old bones of the murdered returning soldier of the first story. Quaint and peaceful rural idylls do not sit well with violence and murder, undercutting Clive's selling pitch. History surfaces out of versions, stories and interests in unexpected ways and crimes of the past can be used in the present towards some goodness. The uncovering of crime is a hard core around which all the differing perspectives, genres and devices ultimately and deceptively are organised, even if perpetrators are not necessarily punished. On this note let also re-visit Ulverton, viewed through *Pieces of Light*.

CHAPTER NINE

Hybrid Landscapes:
Adam Thorpe's *Pieces of Light*

Unconscious Terrors and the Power of the Painting

We return in this chapter to the sad story of the life of Hugh Arkwright, protagonist of *Pieces of Light*. We go back again to the time before his birth, to the clearing away of the rubbish, empty whisky bottles and half-finished paintings, which belonged to the District Officer, Mr. Hargreaves, otherwise known as Sir Steggie, who pre-dated Hugh's father. This is the stuff, remember, that must be cleared out before Charlotte and James, can take over the house, on their arrival in Africa. Charlotte is assisted in the clearing out by Grace Tarbuck, daughter of the local missionary, the good Reverend Tarbuck:

> Grace was an excellent assistant. She dealt with the filthy bed covers, and helped me improvise a bed cradle. ...I am quite sure [Hargreaves] was awake the whole time, with a queer little smile, but the odd man made no attempt to communicate. Odd or crazed—I am not sure which.
> From the paintings propped about the place, I came down on crazed. They were mostly a portrait of something between a knight in a helmet and a rhinoceros. It stared out through piggy eyes in front of a lot of lurid leaves, like tongues of patients with interesting diseases. The oil paint was as thick as dried mud, and half of it had ended up on the walls. Some had a name neatly printed at the bottom: *Sir Steggie*. (1998b, 440)

A painting of a hybrid man cum piggy rhinoceros, light and shadows and a crazed white man watching, are images that represent recurrent themes.

These letters, in which all of this is described, represent the earliest time of the family's sojourn in Africa, albeit that the information comes to us at the end of the book. These letters are given to us unabridged and un-interpreted in this final section. However, we as readers can only receive them in the light of the previous section where we watched an aged, somewhat demented Hugh devouring them in search for clues to his past. If Hugh is an unreliable narrator, as we shall see he is, then we are not neutral readers. And this is precisely Thorpe's point about the need for skepticism when we interpret paintings, narratives, plays and poems.

Having said this, narrative is not abandoned in this novel, to the extent that it is in Thorpe's earlier writing, and in order to unravel its many puzzles and mysteries, we do need to understand the plot. In these letters he discovers that his biological parents were not James and Charlotte after all. They were none other than Grace and Mr. Hargreaves, who it now emerged, struck up a secret relationship right here at the beginning of the domestic bush clearing – "[Grace] then sat with Hargreaves while I supervised the placing of our luggage" (1998b, 440).

Later, Grace will bear the child and then die and Charlotte will raise Hugh. The discovery and clearing away of the paintings are linked to this genealogy of illicit coupling and secret adoption, not by deep symbolism, but by happenstance alongside each other. This is what we have been referring to as metonymy rather than metaphor and is a device that Thorpe will use to great effect throughout the novel.

The novel begins with Hugh growing up with Charlotte and James Arkwright as his parents. The little boy, who has a great imagination and pictures himself as an intrepid explorer, makes a discovery of the crazed paintings already described on one such grand expedition:

> Exploring the North Pole in the horribly airless attic under the boiling-hot corrugated roof, where unwanted things were stored, I found some paintings. ...They were frightening pictures: they were pictures of Normans, coming out of the forest. On the back of some of them was chalked *Sir Steggie*, and on others someone had stuck a slip of paper typed *J.S. Hargreaves, Property Of.* (1998b, 14)

In an intriguing inversion of the stereotype, the primordial origins of nightmare and violence originate in Darkest England. The boy is terrified by the pictures and Hargreaves, or Sir Steggie as he will come to be known in Hugh's nightmares, enters the dark realm of unconscious terror—"Mr Hargreaves floated backwards into a mist of gloomy thoughts" (1998b, 14). Given that this bogey-man of unconscious terror is actually the Father, which portals of Authority will enable Hugh to individuate into a full and healthy subjectivity? The identity crisis is broadened and deepened when this terrifying phantom Father is linked to the origins of the English nation, an

Hybrid Landscapes 259

England in which Hugh was not himself born, although it supposedly comprises his roots.

Hugh interprets the paintings as pictures of the Normans invading out of the forest. He makes a string of arbitrary, boyish connections, which over time will develop into the metaphoric patina of the novel's meaning. Just before the discovery of the paintings, Hugh is warned by his Mother against taking on local African customs and emphasises his difference from other children by stressing that he is "the only white child in the whole of West and Central Africa, that I know of" (1998b, 12). This ghastly thought drives Hugh to attempt to change himself into a black boy:

> That night I experimented with cinders from the stove, rubbing them into my face. Then I tried my father's blacking, the stuff he brushed briskly but thoroughly into his mosquito boots twice a week. (1998b, 12)

All this is to no avail, however, resulting in an attack of self-hatred:

> Anyway, both the cinders and the boot-black bothered my skin, and sweat made white streaks. I was a maggot, an albino, an outcast. The books I looked at were full of ugly little princes like myself, with thin lips and sharp noses, who were bossy and very white. That was England. (1998b, 13)

Not just a skin colour, but a country. Hugh's infantile identity crisis flows into language and he consults the Chambers Dictionary in order to look up 'English'. The boy, still in the mirror phase, from which he never entirely emerges, is searching for identity in a dictionary whose entries are metonymic—based on sounds rather than on meaningful connections—"in my father's dictionary, it came after *Engirdle* and before *Englobe*" (1998b, 7). He does not quite understand the entry and asks, speaking in the tongue of the houseboy, who is his constant companion, "'what does *dat* mean?'" to which his father first replies "'*that*, not *dat*, Hugh'" (1998b, 13). It is clear that his 'father' has little of value to teach him, in this struggle for a sense of self, and Hugh translates the dictionary definition into the African terms with which he is familiar. He lands up with a sinister hybrid African England, invaded by the Normans—the Fathers and Law Givers—who insist that an English boy should not have fetishes:

> Normans were the ones who said you couldn't have a fetish. Normans invaded, like leopards, like tsetse flies, like snakes. They had metal helmets with noses, and cruel smiles. I began to be convinced that Normans were in the forest, waiting to murder those of the English race, then put the blame on the English race. I was one of the English race. (1998b, 13)

The Normans are linked to African leopards and snakes and also to a faraway forest in England, where an Uncle has a house, a lawn and some forests. Again there is a metonymic sing-song repetition of "of the English race" and random connections between the image of the Norman invaders from the forest, Hugh's uncle Edward and his fine house and lawn—"I was bored hearing about this house and its lawn" (1998b, 13).

If paintings and visual pictures recur, then so does archaeology—the digging for artifacts, evidence and understanding. What we have here is a palimpsest of English parentage, over African experience, over English experience, all buried in the Unconscious receptacle of terrors:

> By the time I drifted into hot dreams, I was quite sure that Mr Hargreaves was still alive, roaming the forest in a Norman helmet, ready to feed on members of the English race.
> Sir Steggie, looking in at my window. (1998b, 24–5)

Ominously, Hugh learns to make something unpleasant

> disappear into the deepest shadows of my own mind, where I could not think about it except when it crept out in the middle of the night, as the most powerful of the malign spirits usually did. (1998b, 31–32)

Hugh's discovery of the scary paintings had happened "not long afterwards"—that is to say, next to these discussions about English identity, English landscape, the Norman invasion and the threat of "going native". The metonymic links being reinforced are connections between Normans, Hargreaves, the monstrous invader/murderer, England, being white, having to speak in a certain kind of English and being forbidden to carry fetishes to protect you against vicious attack. The deep unconscious terrors, set up in the boyish Hugh, are English. They are associated with light of the Gospel and the faraway place, which is England, which speaks to Hugh through the pictures, which act as a demonic haunting throughout his life. The light is dappled, pieces of it move kinetically and dynamically through associations of England and Africa. There is no fixed blaze of civilization against the darkness of Africa. There is the thickness of the splattered oil paint on a shifting canvas.

We can add to paintings and archaeology the powerful effects of reading fiction on Hugh's fertile imagination. Hargreaves, who has one eye and a ticking fob watch, which assumes enormous fetish power, enters Hugh's feverish imagination as Long John Silver and Captain Hook, a stew of European adventure stories and tall tales, along with African stories told to

Hugh by the servants. Bible stories "walked between the juju talk and hid some of it" (1998b, 19) And:

> I was reading a lot about this sort of thing, of course, in books by Stevenson, Baroness Orczy, Blackmore, Henty, Rider Haggard. ...And the tales I heard from the servants—of monsters, spirits and snakes with jeweled heads, of witchdoctors and sacred trees, of warriors and gourds and precious plumes—merely heightened my belief in the realness of this world just beyond my own. (1998b, 25)

And always, there is light and dark, the signals of the canvas depicting the landscape of the mind. If Hargreaves symbolises the white man gone horribly native, a pirate in the dark, misty unconscious of Hugh's terrors, then another character plays the role of light in Hugh's arsenal of props for survival. This is Herbert E. Standing, an unfortunate young man, who had come out on the boat with Hugh's parents, but had died of blackwater fever. His purpose in Africa may have been missionary, but for Hugh, his mission was to bring civilization of a quite particular kind, to "spread the game of cricket through the native populace" (1998b, 28):

> *His spirit was dressed all in white*, very tall, and remained at the end of my bed with a straight bat all night and every night, in case Sir Steggie should come. (1998b, 28, my emphasis)

And if Sir Steggie and Herbert Standing vie for Hugh's psyche as guardians of boyish Hell and Heaven respectively, then Africa is the Garden of Eden.

The Brightness of Edenic Africa

Hugh loves the forest—"I was not afraid of the forest. Not, at least, of its animals" (1998b, 6). And the visual image of Africa that he takes with him to Ulverton when he is banished from the garden is formed on "a short bush tour" on which he accompanies his parents (1998b, 32). It is recounted by an older Hugh in his memoir as the single unambiguously happy part of his entire life:

> All around us the forest spoke, and a bright three-quarter moon rose. I made it huge and blinding with my father's heavy field binoculars. There was dancing, and the fetish woman waved feathered twigs at us behind a wooden mask with white eyes. It came down to her belly and made her invisible to evil spirits. The dancers' feet shuffled and stamped, helping the sun roll through the bottom of the earth, waking the ancestors up. (1998b, 35)

Look at all the brightness, both of the sun and moon, against the grain of the conventionally dark landscape of Africanist discourse. The moon is magnified through the binoculars and looking through the mask enables the woman to disappear to the view of evil spirits, presumably like Sir Steggie. Masks, binoculars, rituals, forests, lightness and dark, all provide that rich, confusing mixture of European and African imaginaries, landscape and technology that make up Hugh's earliest dreams. This is, however, the only time Hugh is not isolated, lonely, unloved or crazed. It is the only time that the spirit of Herbert Standing prevails comprehensively against the demonic Sir Steggie:

> I was watched from the corner of a hut by Herbert E. Standing's spirit, accompanied as it always was by the sweet smell of linseed oil. I made a century, and bowled three wickets. ...
> Quiri, sleeping outside, no longer had the fob-watch—but I didn't even think of Sir Steggie marauding beyond, such was my complete happiness. (1998b, 36)

Hugh hates the decision to send him to Ulverton in England and away from his beloved African home. He has a terror of English countryside, which he associates with barren darkness:

> I feared England's cold, suddenly. ...How was I going to survive a season when everything died, when the branches were stripped of leaves and nothing grew at all? The pictures of winter in my books reminded me of my worst dreams of skeletons and ghosts. ...
> *The sun burned again through the mist. Pieces of light appeared in the gloom, as if they were solid bits of a puzzle.* (1998b, 47–48, my emphasis)

Hugh's father may be the road clearer, but the forest is protector and the opposite of menacing. The smells, sights and earth of Africa is remembered as full, light and nurturing and contrasted in the boy's imagination and the man's memoir, with the barrenness of England, its wounding darkness, a place of ghosts, death and evil spirits. This passage is flagged as important with the novel's title within it. The potted gloom, the pieces of light enter Hugh's head as fractured points of guidance through the labyrinth of his difficult life and splintered identity. With his expulsion, the lake and his bliss there are about to become unreal, a landscape rather than a lived experience:

> I looked northwards, towards the Crater Lake, and made the picture—the track, the tangle each side, the huge trees and the spotted gloom under them—enter my head for good. (1998b, 48)

The pieces of light/knowledge, moreover, which tax Hugh to piece together the puzzle of his origins, are specifically related here to his parentage. His mother

cradled my head in her hands and looked at me ...
"Grace. Just that word. Will you always remember that?"...
I can't remember what it means, I thought, apart from saying grace. I'll have to look it up. (1998b, 48)

What his mother is hinting at, and looking for, in Hugh's face, are signs of his beautiful and good biological mother, Grace Tarbuck, before her fatal fall. The bewildered Hugh, however, falls back on the metonymic mode of his beloved dictionary. What Charlotte finds, however, is only the sign of his grotesque, one eyed biological father, the despicable Hargreaves. She notes with a frown "that there was something wrong with my eye again" (1998b, 48) and Hugh tells her that he cannot see properly out of it:

> My mother's slight frown dropped into a look of utter horror. I was so surprised that I backed away, my face slipping from her hands. She was now clasping them together, with that horrified stare fixed on her face. (1998b, 48–9)

Two points. Hugh, like the reader, is puzzled by this reaction and can only fully appreciate this critical moment in the novel if we undertake a second reading it, or have an extraordinarily detailed memory of all its early descriptions. This is so given that hundreds of pages separate this early point and Charlotte's letters in the final section when we learn about whom Hugh's real father is—Hargreaves with the selfsame gammy eye. What Thorpe is highlighting and delighting in, is the constructed nature of fiction and the degree of randomness, of narrative capriciousness.

Secondly, this moment is so crucial because Africa enters his head and acts as a compass for his life direction at precisely the same time of the birth of his adopted mother's ambiguous relationship to him. Here her love for him is qualified by her disgust for his genetic father and the visible manifestations of that father in him.

The Africa that Hugh remembers is an image, a picture, and like a painting, it has a composition—the track runs through bush, neatly positioned on each side of it, with the towering trees providing depth and the bits of light characterising the mood of the picture. He takes this mental photograph, looking in the direction of the Crater Lake. The powerful point here is that at the very moment that Hugh clicks the shutter in taking the mental picture of his Garden of Eden, his mother had that strange reaction in looking closely at him. This casts a shadow over the Garden:

> My mother's strange reaction still strikes me as a watershed; after that moment on the path, we were never quite as close. Sometimes, in England, during those few years that remained to us, I had the strange impression that she was looking at me with a slight shudder. (1998b, 49)

This capture of a mental photograph of Edenic Africa is emphasised:

> The picture I took in my head there is still very clear, however. As it turned out, and unknown to me at the time, it records the very last moment of what I sometimes think of as my golden age, before the Fall. (1998b, 49)

And again Thorpe highlights how finally, sailing across the bay from the jetty, Hugh

> needed to see the forest beyond the buildings, to burn it into my mind so that I would never forget it. I sat down and screwed my eyes shut. I had taken a sort of photograph again: I could see it down to the trees sliding across, shutting it off. (1998b, 55)

Hugh leaves Africa with this image burned into his memory as surely as the mark of Yolobolo, which Quiri, the houseboy and his only friend, had cut into the back of Hugh's neck as powerful protection:

> Because I couldn't see it, even in the mirror, [Quiri] drew it for me: it was a cross in a circle, the four points meeting the rim. He explained that this was the symbol of Yolobolo, the powerful creature in the forest that no one had ever seen. (1998b, 44)

It is ominous that Hugh himself cannot see it, in this novel of watching, seeing and one-eyed marks of degraded paternity. Alternative and partial initiations, the mark and the weak eye, Yolobolo and Hargreaves, are both invisible, yet powerful Fathers, who fracture Hugh's identity as surely as they are inscribed on his body. The African pagan ritual, enacted by amateurish boys, makes the naive Hugh about to be exiled from the garden feel that "whatever might occur to me after my seventh birthday, I was now prepared" (1998b, 44). We doubt it.

Carrying with him his mental photographs, Hugh arrives in a strange and hostile England. Already, however, the pictures are breaking up, shattering and distorting and reassembling—"there were pictures in my head—turned from everything I had known and loved—but continually breaking, like the beads of a kaleidoscope" (1998b, 60). All that remains clear, paradoxically, is the unstable picture of a receding coastline from a wave tossed boat:

> The only [picture] that remained fixed was the last view of our coast beyond the fluttering strip of white that was all we could see of the breakers, the sky loaded with long dark clouds, like logs. (1998b, 60)

Pieces of whiteness flutter against the dark clouds, clouds like dead wood, logs, not the live trees of the forest. When the lived experience becomes aestheticised as pictures in Hugh's mind, like paintings or photographs, he continues the dangerous retreat into the mind, into stories and plays, as more real than reality. What the already battered Hugh sees when he views his new environment is a landscape, an image, which daubs over and transforms the original mental photographs he took of his home. For example, prior to his mother abandoning him to his uncle and aunt and returning to Africa, she and Hugh light a bonfire of autumn leaves:

> The smoke joined the huge umbrella of sky, merely smudging it above the house if one looked carefully. It was queer, how whitish smoke could smudge a darker sky. That night my clothes and hair smelt of smoke, but it wasn't the sharp, sweet smoke of home—of the night-watchman's fire or the drumming villages along the river or in the forest. (1998b, 82)

The scene is entirely pictorial—sky framing it like an umbrella, with whitish smoke smudging the sky and both reminiscent of home, but also different. This construction of his own world is reinforced by Hugh's unhappiness in England. At this point we need a summary of the bones of the novel's plot, alongside the development of its multiple images, symbols and theme.

Diaries, Letters and Memoirs—Jagged Narratives and Splintered Identities

The novel is written in five parts. The first four purport to be written by Hugh and the fifth by his mother, all in modes foregrounding the subjectivity of the telling. The first two are Hugh's memoir of his childhood, the first in Africa and the second in England. The third and fourth are Hugh as old man of seventy, first his diary, then therapeutic letters addressed to his vanished mother, sent from a mental institution. We can only build up the picture Thorpe is drawing for us through Hugh's narration. And what is clear is that we should profoundly distrust it, albeit that we seek to uncover some important realities seeping through his twisted depiction of what he sees, remembers, imagines and deduces.

It is only in the third part of the novel that we realize that from the outset we have been reading Hugh's own version of his childhood, his "childhood memoir". He had discovered it when he had been going through the study—always the discoveries, dross clearing away and digging in attics and trunks, as much as in the earth. He had been writing it thirty years earlier:

Wednesday, 8 September
Clearing the study. Found at Sumerian level my childhood memoir rolled up in a ribbon, like an old map. ...Thirty-odd years ago I was writing about my life thirty-odd years before that—and in thirty years' time? I will be a hundred. (1998b, 140)

Hugh's selves are split and unfocused—even he has difficulty recognising himself in his childhood:

Reading my childhood memoir is like watching a man and his son fishing on the opposite bank. Forty was such an awful age, but then things got going and I didn't think about age until about last week. Did Dr Wolff ever read what I wrote, in the end? Wet, steaming red earth of Africa: smell it as I read. Otherwise, it's all happened to someone else before recorded time. (1998b, 143)

Always imperfect vision—how much can you see or hear from across the bank? And what a strange image for a man, who was so imperfectly fathered, to describe his memoir in those pastoral, chocolate box terms of archetypal father and son intimacy, fishing together. This is totally at odds with what we know about Hugh's boyhood and only makes sense when we recall Hugh's propensity to think in terms of paintings. Linked to this there is the ominous mention of what must be a psychiatrist, a Dr Wolff, another terrifying and potentially false father threatening strange metamorphoses, in the line of Wolf men, Leopard men and Rhino men of Hugh's nightmares. And the only reality, which makes his identity belong to Hugh, to be his life, is the earth of Africa.

As steaming, smelling earth, rivers, fish and fishing are translated from soil into landscape, repressed terrors find a fertile site to re-visit and torment the young Hugh, now in Ulverton. Let us then re-read with the aging Hugh, about his arrival in England and take up the story after the first African section.

African Leopard Societies, The English Stage and Many Forests

Thorpe depicts Hugh's new home by laying it out for us quite neatly and again very obviously in pictorial terms—house and lawn, at the end of which are two different woods and a field of barley:

We entered a wood at the bottom of the garden; there were two woods, in fact. One was what my uncle called a beechwood, and the other was next to it but fenced off with wire. My uncle called this the 'wildwood', saying it as one word, but it didn't look terribly wild to me. (1998b, 73)

Two woods, one, the wildwood, that uncle regards as "the primordial forest" (1998b, 356), is a mysterious zone—"I was absolutely forbidden to enter the wildwood" (1998b, 73). The other was more welcoming to the boy, who longs for the forest of 'home'. He superimposes his image of Africa and what lies before him and sees the beechwood in African terms, depicted in the shades of light and dark, which make up the composition of pictures:

> There was no mist, and *the sun fell into the wood in bright shafts.* ...The trees were oddly thick and most of them curved a bit, finishing not very high above us. I was amazed at how *the leaves, if they were caught in the sun, glowed, like lumps of wood* on Baluti's fire when a gust blew across it. ...Then the trees ended suddenly at the field, which I gazed upon as if I had reached the end of the world. I couldn't believe its size, nor its colour. *It was malachite green with bright spots of red and yellow and blue.* (1998b, 72–3, my emphases)

Later, as they return to the house in the twilight, "the grass" of the lawn, "had turned bluey grey" and "the wildwood was a dark lump in the corner" (1998b, 73). If the leaves in the beechwood glow like the illuminating fire of Baluti, who was the African laundryman, then the wildwood is a dark lump of charred coal, occupying only a corner of the stage of Hugh's life, and a stage is exactly what the Beechwood, quite soon will become.

In Hugh's boyhood, adolescence and young adulthood, the wildwood does not really figure, given that the obedient Hugh seems to have followed the Law forbidding entry. Like Bluebeard's locked room, however, it begs narratively to have its day, and it will. What is ominous from the outset is the overtone between this wildwood and Hugh's unconscious terrors of Sir Steggie, Norman invader out of the forest.

Stephen Daniels, in an analysis of the "political iconography of woodland" suggests that the politics "was articulated in the selection, siting and arrangement of trees in written, pictorial and parkland images" (1988, 43). If we assume, as we might most obviously do, that the Beechwood is England and the dark, mysterious wildwood is Africa, then we would seriously underestimate Thorpe's complexity and the originality of *Pieces of Light*. If landscapes are superimposed upon each other, what emerges is a strange, new and discordant picture, a hybrid rather than a binary. Both woods are simultaneously Africa and England, and in combining become translated into neither one place nor another. Leopards, a leopard skin and leopard men will imperfectly solder together parts of the forest grids buried in Hugh's being.

On one of Mother's first return visits to Ulverton, on leave from Africa, Hugh overhears a conversation between the three adults, mother, aunt and uncle, giving rise to a sequence of ghoulish connections. Charlotte starts telling them about Leopard Societies in Africa and the *borfima*, (1998b, 98) or fetish packet (1998b, 100). She likens the leopard horrors to something her English audience might better understand—lycanthropy—the transformation of witch into wolf, or the pathology whereby a person becomes a wild beast in the imagination. This image provides one of the fastening hooks of Ulverton onto the eye of Bamakum, as humans become leopards or wolves. Hugh explains the connection to Ulverton much later on:

> "Maybe Ulverton used to be Ulvesdun. Wolf Town."
> He looks around him a little nervously. "It probably wasn't full of wolves," I add, "but Anglo-Saxon robbers and murderers. Malefactors, anyway. No-gooders, on the run. That's what someone like that was called then". (1998b, 360)

What we understand from Hugh's description of his mother's story, which is patchy and not easy to follow at all, is that Cameroonian men dress up as leopards, with terrible knives as 'paws', and go out and murder their victims. This they do in order to collect the powerful human parts required for this fetish bundle, the *borfima*:

> "You are," my mother went on, "a handsome boy or pretty maiden strolling back from school, when the bushes stir and out leap what look like leopards. But these leopards have human faces above their spots, and their claws are three-pronged knives." (1998b, 100)

Hugh does not need much encouragement to fuel his already established, unconscious terrors:

> I knew then, as one does know these things that Sir Steggie was in England, making for this house. I had no fetish packet in my pocket; its crumbling form was under my pillow, where I most needed it. But when I thought of my fetish packet, I could only see the nightmarish stuff of a *Borfima*—as I could only think, looking at the cross in the village church, of Benin's slaves hanging headless in a stink of blood. The cellar's invisible stairs were very steep, I knew that; I was not allowed on them for that very reason. There was a maid in the Vicarage who had died falling down the same sort of stairs. Cecil had told me, and he had seen her ghost in its pinny many times, moaning between the cobwebs and bottles of wine. She was there among the leopard men, now, holding a three-clawed knife and grinning. (1998b, 102)

Steggie's darkness fills Hugh's mind and Standing's light is muted. Sir Steggie pursues Hugh to Ulverton from African forests and English paintings. Stories spill and leak all over each other, from here to there and back again. All of this is an extraordinary reminder of Norfolk's tale, told in chapter three, intriguingly also involving the fearsome image of a rhinoceros, and where stories also migrated, mingled and wreaked havoc. Here village maidens are both victims and then horribly transformed into ghosts, who wear prim English pinnies and become evil perpetrators—leopard men with paws of deadly knives. The fetish package under the pillow once protected Hugh from night marauders, now is horribly transformed into the *borfima* demanding body parts; Christianity, in the form of the village church, displays mutilated West African slaves. In this gruesome mélange, borders

Hybrid Landscapes 269

are porous and men can simultaneously be beasts, snow may fall in Africa, leopard societies can flourish in England and werewolves metamorphose into leopard men and maul English maidens. In this Grimm world of superimposed African folk and European fairy stories, there is much fuel for the fire in Hugh's head to ignite along the boundaries of these bizarre transgressions, as it does later on, in Hugh's old age, when there is real, albeit a strange, case of murder in the village. We will come to that later.

When she realizes that Hugh might be overhearing this conversation, Charlotte halts it. This is reminiscent of Eusebia of *The Pope's Rhinoceros*, who overheard snippets of stories, which she wove and re-cast within her own context in chapter three. Likewise, the eavesdropping Hugh hears and sees imperfectly, packing away further terrors to add to his already simmering unconscious. In the meanwhile, the young Hugh continues to comfort himself by remembering his image painting "closing my eyelids and bringing back the picture I had taken on the track a year before, down to the last blot of shade and spot of life on leaf" (1998b, 104).

From the beginning, Hugh sees himself as exiled from 'home', which is referred to as Africa throughout his life. He misses his mother, his uncle and aunt are cold, and he suffers in his stiff, uptight English school, where he is identified as different and fails to make any friends, all of which push him further into realm of stories, images and delusions. A month after the leaf bonfire and his mother's departure

> I stood on my own in the beechwood and watched amazed as a great plundering took place overhead: Flint's treasure chest of doubloons and double guineas and moidores and sequins rained down slowly through the sunlight, as far as the eye could see. No one came to gather it, and I played the treasure hunt on my own—the voice among the trees and the death of Merry and the saving of Jim and Silver, and the counting of the gold in Ben Gunn's cave—until dusk. (1998b, 82)

So, to emphasise, like landscapes, stories entwine, a process set in motion already in Cameroon, remember, where Bible stories "walked between the juju talk and hid some of it" (1998b, 19). The lonely Hugh, drawn to forests from his now nostalgically remembered happy youth, turns the Beechwood into a Shakespearean stage—"I decided where my own stage was, in the beechwood" (1998b, 126) and there, with nature's colours as his stage lights, he turns his loneliness into a fantasy theatre:

> In the soft light falling between the grey trees I saw the air of Sicilia, of Arden, of the park in Navarre; the trunks became the columns of palaces and castles; a toadstooled stump bubbled into a cauldron crouched round by witches played with my fingers crossed. (1998b, 127)

African witches populate Macbeth's drama and the natural environment becomes a set design. All of this sustains Hugh's years of growing up, contained in his memoir covering the first two parts of the novel. This section ends abruptly, as presumably does Hugh's boyhood, with Uncle, in stiff English fashion, breaking the news of his mother's strange disappearance—"'the fact is, Hugh, you're going to have to be a brave chap from now on. Your dear mother has disappeared, into the jungle'" (1998b, 136).

Hugh immediately whisks her into his all too fertile mind as inhabiting his idealised African pastoral:

> She had gone to the crater lake. She had gone to paradise and soon she would be back to take me there, too. I had no doubt about it at all. We would live together on the shore in perfect love and harmony, for there were no crocs in the deep, black water, and England was beyond imagining there. (1998b, 136)

Mother's disappearance is a central mystery that we will attempt to unravel later. Part two ends with Hugh happily falling asleep "plotting the gentle curve of my existence with her in the coming years in a hot, green paradise by the lapping waters of the crater" (1998b, 136).

Part three, Hugh's diary, is very short. It jumps to Hugh as an old man of seventy, who returns to Ulverton and his inheritance of the old house and property after his Uncle and his Uncle's second wife have died (much more about her shortly). This part is like a narrative conjunction, providing the plot filler between Hugh's growing up in Africa and England and his growing old, prior to becoming crazed in the fourth part of the novel. It resembles an accelerated film reel and rushes through the period of Hugh's war activities, his illustrious career in theatre, his Aunt's death and Uncle's re-marriage to Aunt Rachael.

Freudian Fairy Tales, Imperial Plunder and the Return of the Repressed

It is the return to the house of his unhappy boyhood, its attic and contents, its woods and fields, which will trigger Hugh's ghosts. On his return to Ulverton, the village mumming troupe seeks Hugh's advice, given both his Uncle's history in promoting pagan rituals and his own experience in the theatre. A critical prop for their play becomes the leopard skin, which had found its way from Cameroon to Ulverton and had been used for this purpose by the Uncle himself, as pointed out by Malcolm, the Director of the troupe:

He mentioned that in Nuncle's *Harmonies of the Primitive* there's a photo of the Ulverton mumming troupe and the hobby-horse has a leopard skin draped on it. (1998b, 166)

This reminds Hugh of how his father had "spent weeks tanning" the leopard pelt (1998b, 150). He is reminded of African rituals and that the leopard's face on the skin has "no lower jaw, being originally a ritual costume in its untanned life" (1998b, 171). Malcolm secures the skin for his pagan ritual, linking African and European non-Christian belief. Is this a lapse into a Conrad-ian styled linkage between European savagery and Africa's dark heart? I do not think so. The crucial difference is that the skin was tanned, turned into artifact and trophy by Hugh's father and comes to symbolize the opposite of African savagery in that it stands for European plunder linked to invasion, war, and imperialism. There was

something terribly creepy about old animal skins, too bestial by half and completely dead and *vanquished but still grinning*. (1998b, 150, my emphasis)

The leopard may be defeated, but it is grinning in anticipation of its revenge. And if this appears to be assuming too much, let us look at a poem, published in Thorpe's *Mornings in the Baltic* collection and entitled "Zebra, A", again as in a dictionary definition. The first verse reads:

Girded round by loin-cloths,
saved for posterity
by camera, knife, the art
of the taxidermist, it
mounted to the realm of dinner-gongs.

The final verse warns that:

it comes, hunting us at night
with its lips drawn back—
searching for its hooves
in some forgotten drawer, trophies
of *God* and *Empire*. (1988, 58)

In part four, Hugh will describe the scene of his father's tanning of the leopard pelt again. This is the part that takes the form of imaginary letters addressed to an absent mother, who disappeared long ago, as part of the therapy suggested by his doctor from the mental institution, after Hugh's nervous breakdown. This, the longest part, will take us back to the early years of Hugh's adulthood and his one and only love affair. It will also take us forward to a murder. And always there is the image—the light and dark of woods, discoveries in attics and the spots on the leopard's skin, like bits and pieces of a puzzle. In the midst of this fourth, revealing part, Hugh dwells on the curing of the skin:

> Scratch scratch scratch as Father swabs the hide. Quiri is in the door of the kitchen, beyond. He's crouched as if someone is trying to shoot him. I go up to him. Quiri is terrified—not of me, but of what we are doing. He tells me that *the leopard spirit will return and avenge itself*. (1998b, 388, my emphasis)

Before venturing further into the labyrinth of Hugh's mind, let us remember the pivotal question of this chapter—what does the landscape of an English village look like after the ravages of Empire? Who is the crazed figure on the canvas whose one, large revolving eyeball overlays two English woods with a forest of Africa? The African leopard, pieces of light spotting its skin, will now guide us towards some further illumination as we take up the story, as told by Hugh in his old age and hear about his entry into the forbidden wildwood. And here we must simultaneously remember the pivotal device of ensuring reader skepticism and the downsizing of his white men, of which Thorpe is so fond. The bulk of the novel is told via those miserable, crazed letters, penned by a narrator in the grip of mental breakdown. All of what follows, in other words, relating to Hugh's past and present, is described through these letters, until we come to the final section of letters written by his mother to his uncle. What follows reads like an archetypal, distorted Oedipal fairy story.

The aging Hugh describes himself as a young man, falling in love with a beautiful young woman called Rachael. They have sex only once and their intercourse appears to be mysteriously forbidden and ominously conducted in the wildwood—the first time we hear of Hugh transgressing the prohibited boundary:

> So I aimed for the wildwood, Rachel dragging on my hand. 'It's alright! It's alright!' I hissed. Perhaps we would have seemed very intent to anyone looking on—to Nuncle, for instance, as we flitted over the wedge of the lawn separating one wood from the other. I don't know, I can't remember how we arrived, only arriving, plunging into the deeps. Clambering over the chicken-wire and plunging into the deeps.
>   It was so quiet, so shadowy, so safely tangled. Such a safe spot for shy lovers. (1998b, 244)

Again this is unlikely—it is all very creepy and ironic. The overtones of taboo and superstition surrounding their coupling are amplified by the terrain, which has soaked up layers of folk memory and superstition. Reminiscent of the mystical rock of *Ulverton*, of the previous chapter, here is another malevolent landscape witness:

> There used to be a village beyond where the rabbits were, and an old witch called Anne Stile had led the children here to dance to the Devil. When she heard someone coming, she covered the children and herself in stone. But being a forgetful old crone, she couldn't remember the undoing spell. (1998b, 241)

Not only that, the scary leopard, the revenge-seeking wild animal out of the African forest is superimposed here too, in the form of the claw marks on the heathy coomb—"a giant cat had clawed its near side. An enormous beast, the king of all the cats, a big beef the size of a house" (1998b, 239). Landscapes, myths and local beliefs mix and mingle with leopards, leopard societies and Africa, shaken into a Molotov Cocktail in Hugh's feverish imagination via the repressed terrors of his unconscious:

> The Witch Stone. Oh, my God. It was actually leering at me. All its wrinkles were a leer on a face. Hit it before it does harm. Hit it, hit it! (1998b, 241)

I had actually confused the rocks from *Ulverton* and this Witch Stone, as pointed out to me by Adam Thorpe himself:

> The "rock" that you identify as a "sacred" landscape link between the first two chapters of *Ulverton* and *Pieces of Light* is not a geographical one, in fact. What you drew my attention to is the subliminal *literary* link: Fierce [Furze] End/Furzecombe Down, "Anne' Cobbold/" "Anne" the Wobble Stone witch. ...I think your point is almost more powerful if you emphasise the subliminal links above. ... (Personal correspondence, 2001)

Subliminally linked landscapes within England and Africa, echo the transferences between mothers and lovers in a cacophony of mental confusion. Rachael becomes Hugh's vanished mother—both as pearls—Mother as the vanished pearl in the forest of Africa and then "Rachael Katzen began to pearl too, in my head" (1998b, 203). And:

> Rachael lay fast asleep in the narrow bed by the window, her head was turned from me, and her black hair lay like black flames on the pillow. It might have been you, dear Mother, lying there, returned from the shadows of the forest, its bits and pieces of light. (1998b, 236–7)

Rachael even acts out the mother's disappearance in the persona of the British aviator—"Look! I'm Amy Johnson! I'm going to disappear into thin air! Wheeee!" (1998b, 240). In true Thorpian time warp, with overtones of the Hamlet that Hugh would know so well, Rachael becomes Mother after the event, when she betrays Hugh with his Uncle, who she subsequently marries. Thus she becomes Hugh's aunt, with "echoes" of being his stepmother and also his vanished biological mother. The suggestive Hugh manages himself to become confused with all the changing identities:

> My head is in a muddle. You and Aunt Joy are becoming horribly, one person, and somehow running around as Aunt Rachael. (1998b, 183)

The bog, into which Hugh is sinking, thickens as false fathers and false or vanished mothers weave in and out of his mind, like changelings and werewolves. Like everything else, Hugh represses the hurt and splits Rachael into two distinct personas—idealised sensual young lover and repulsive old Aunt—always imperfectly separated and partly gelled together:

> I'm going to have to fill you in, Mother. I haven't filled in anyone else about this. About Rachael, I mean. (Not Aunt Rachael, not Mrs Rachael Arnold. ...It's top secret. It always has been. At least, that's what I thought. Top-hole secret! (1998b, 194)

What is meant by the "at least that's what I thought"? What makes it all come apart is that there was a nasty, leering witness to the primal transgressive sexual act in the person of one of the villagers—Jack Wall, a poacher voyeur:

> I paraphrase, as briskly as possible.
> In 1940, a young poacher by the name of Jack Wall, in the woodland attached to the Arnold property up Crab-Apple Lane, was up a tree when he spotted a couple of naked youths coupling "like Adam 'n Eve". (1998b, 193–4)

Hugh does not need much encouraging by way of unconscious storage for night-time, dark terrors, in which *Hamlet* mingles with *A Midsummer Night's Dream* in a melange of tragedy and comedy turned into nightmare:

> Then I switch the light off: the clock has just chimed midnight. ...This is the first of my bad nights. Jack Wall is at the chink. I wake up, disturbed by the feel of his eyeball and a soft laugh. (1998b, 195)

Pieces of Light is a dense and murky book and following the plot with its threads, that both do and do not tie up, taxes the reader, so bear with me as I attempt to unravel and simultaneously interpret. Events now lead up to the murder of Muck by none other than the seedy Jack Wall's son, John. And this murder is the catalyst, the cinder, igniting the fires in Hugh's emotionally parched and suggestive mind.

A Murder, the Leopard Skin and Strange Becomings

There are two stories that we will now trace as they are played out. There are the events leading up to the murder of Muck by John Wall and the reasons for it and there are also the crazy imaginings of old Hugh as his shards of jagged identity cut and shred his sanity. The trouble begins to accelerate in the pub one dreadful night when Hugh suspects that John had heard about the primal coupling in the wildwood from his father and that he had told Muck about it: "To my horror they are hallooing me and nudging each other and attracting people's attention" (1998b, 307). Muck, Jack's contemporary, might even himself have been there:

> As I am turning away, [Muck] sings, very softly, in a soft drawly harshness, "Tiptoe... through the *raam*sons. ..."
> What? What's that? Na whatee dat ting dere? (1998b, 310)

The ransoms refers to the spot where he and Rachael had had sex in the wildwood all those years ago, which causes Hugh to regress to his childhood language of Africa, of his playmate Quiri, in trying to understand what Muck's evil knowledge means. The garlicky smell of the ransoms wafts into the life-threatening stink of poison gas leftover from the Second World War. This time it is the smells put side by side that exude the metonymic connection between sexual transgression and global crimes.

Like all the terrors that live in Hugh's unconscious, beings metamorphose from one human shape to another, like Dracula, or Jeckyl and Hyde or from human to animal, like werewolves, crocodile witches and leopard men. Muck becomes a mixture of Uncle and Aunt Rachael. Even places drift in and out as kitchen becomes pub or even forest, as all is smoky, dark and threatening, like the wildwood, and all linked up with transgressive sexuality:

> Might Muck have actually *seen* it all? He's impaled me, like one of his pigeons. I'm hovering without the power either to alight or rise. The smoke shrouds him. Aunt Rachael peers through it, as she always did. They talked to each other, bleary-eyed, his cup smeared black with his fingers and mouth, hers concealed in her trembling hand. Chortling chit-chat in the damp dark kitchen, years and years of it. God knows what he knows.
> *The one becomes the other in my dreams*, Mother, over a mug of tea. *That's the true horror.* (1998b, 311, my emphases)

Muck, like Jack and his son, John, are all poachers, who kill the wild creatures in the woods. And this is the fulcrum of the seesawing double stories. It is also the cornerstone linking Thorpe's post pastoral conservationist politics with his anti-imperialism. If leopards and zebras, skinned and plundered, seek revenge, then so do the pigeons and rabbits that the likes of Muck and the Walls murder and steal. And so, paranoid old Hugh becomes impaled victim of Muck's ruthless shooting of the creatures of the woods and Muck metamorphoses again and becomes Aunt Rachael.

In amongst all the masks, disguises, skins and concealments, people also move between being victims and perpetrators, a dominant theme in many of the chapters of this book, as weary sons tactfully acknowledge themselves as involuntary beneficiaries of their countries' imperialist ventures. Hugh gives Muck the evil eye, described in the terms of a spitting wild animal—overtones of the leopard (1998b, 312)—leading towards "revenge, I murmur" (1998b, 313). And the three merge together—Muck, Uncle and not the girl Rachael, but the one who married his uncle and betrayed him. "Revenge" was "the same word" that Hugh murmured on receiving the letter about this marriage—"But I never ever forgave them. Nuncle and this new Rachael" (1998b, 313) and "my hatred for Nuncle went on sharpening itself" (1998b, 313)—like, one wonders, the knives in the "paws" of the leopardmen?

Muck's laugh reminds Hugh of his Uncle's (1998b, 317). His eyes are like Aunt (note) Rachael's—"his eyes are runny. They're horribly like Aunt Rachael's eyes" (1998b, 319). Revenge can only be as a leopard man:

> The two stare at me, apparently aghast. I realise that I have been spitting, and not only metaphorically. My lips have drawn back to reveal my gums. (1998, 320)

Hugh puts it all together as if back in a wood, with pieces of light solving the dark puzzle of his origins, with strange fluid identities between mother and lover in a distorted Oedipal elfin fairy story framework:

> It's all coming together. I'm walking through the wood and the pieces of the puzzle are being carried to me by tiny helpful elves. Avenge you, avenge Rachael. (1998b, 321)

He can do this "as an actor can be a king or a fool or anything, anything! As I can be a man and a beast!" (1998b, 374). Muck is murdered, wrapped in the infernal leopard skin and left up a tree, as if mauled by a wild beast or by a leopard man perhaps. Hugh imagines that he killed Muck for revenge and indeed suspicion falls on him, with his African fetishes and as owner of the skin, which is now missing. Hugh sets about searching for this skin and in the process once again, as on his first arrival, the landscapes of Africa and England merge, with their histories of murder and their myths and superstitions about revenge and retribution. What also merges is *Ulverton* and *Pieces of Light* as a great stone, steeped in folklore, gets sucked into the murder site. Under this English, witchly stone is where Hugh finds one of the glass eyes belonging to the leopard skin. This eye had originated in England, had been sent to Africa, and has returned and embedded in the rock of a syncretic English landscape:

> Flecked hazel, ordered from London in a pair by Father, with instructions for insertion from a Mr. Platting, Taxidermist to the Crown. (1998b, 395)

In Thorpe's vocabulary, taxidermy stands as a symbol for European colonial plunder, an interpretation reinforced by reference to the "Crown". The one-eyed Hugh immediately becomes the leopard:

> The one-eyed leopard. I even picture it with an eye-patch on. Imagine that, Mother. A snarly leopard with an eye-patch! (1998b, 395)

Victim and also murderer, power and identity confusions abound in Hugh's poor head. He becomes the leopard terrified of attack by the leopard men, the difference between them being that the latter are "men who know they are leopard men, not men with leopards so deep inside them they don't know they are men" (1998b, 396), presumably like Hugh himself. We see his transformation into a beast which no longer knows he is a man and remember how the zebra in the poem also drew back its lips as it returned to hunt us in the search for its stolen hooves:

> Then this even stranger thing happens. My lips start to draw back from my teeth. ...It requires effort, it's a strain, but I can just about expose my lower gums as well as my upper gums. It makes you feel very fierce, your whole face stretches and becomes one with this snarl, all teeth. ...It protects you from all those leopard men, all those huge metal claws hidden under their skins. (1998b, 396)

These "strange becomings" are the subject of Gilles Deleuze and Felix Guattari's *A Thousand Plateaus*, which is the second volume of *Capitalism and Schizophrenia* referred to in this book on more than one occasion (1987, 151). What is striking is their focus on schizophrenia, which appears to characterise the splintered identities of our era, where subjectivity is imperfectly constituted through the Symbolic zone. The Law of the Father stutters incoherently in a frozen Imaginary, where any unnatural being, human, animal or insect, may emerge unstably.

Adam Thorpe could have had these "becomings-animal" in mind for his deranged protagonists in *Pieces of Light*, for his mad rhino-men and leopard-men, who have never broken into the charmed Oedipal circle. Extraordinarily, Deleuze and Guattari refer to their "becomings-animal" specifically as in "crime societies, leopard-men, crocodile-men" (1987, 247). They describe:

wolf-men, bear-men, wildcat-men, men of every animality, ...And together they spread contagion. There is a complex aggregate: the becoming-animal of men, packs of animals, elephants and rats, winds and tempests, bacteria sowing contagion. (1987, 247)

Back to Hugh, who eventually finds the leopard skin under the witch's rock within a hybrid landscape, "as if the rock is growing the paw" (1998b, 397). Finally, Hugh is caught with the skin and arrested for the murder. Catastrophe feels like Africa being skinned off him, like the poor leopard undergoing taxidermy and being sent to England:

Arms pick me up, no, pin me down. I'm being impaled like the ring dove, the skin is being tugged away, I'm being stripped of my fur. Africa leaves me, I'm raw like the open downs. (1998b, 402)

The truth of the matter eventually comes out. Until John Wall confesses to the murder, Hugh had begun "to believe that I had sallied forth at night with the leopard spirit in me, and settled an aching score!" (1998b, 406). The truth of the matter, and the truth always will out in Thorpe, is that it is all about someone else's sexual transgressions and about the murder of English animals and the plunder of their skins for taxidermic purposes, linking the world beyond Hugh's delusions and misconceptions:

John Wall got the skins and Muck took them to the taxidermist. There's a roaring illegal trade in skins, you see—badger, fox, rabbit, even otter. And then your leopard comes along. By the caravan next to the wildwood, on the old gypsy plot, Muck made a pass at John, that's what they think. ...John hits Muck, slightly too hard. ...Put the boot in, over and over. Horrible, really. Sort of frenzy. Then he, he rips him up with the leopard claws to make it look as if, as if it was an *animal* as had done it, see. Hies him up the tree. (1998b, 407)

Here in microcosm we see how stories and images flow and mingle and distort between individual lives and illicit desires. What is crucial is that Thorpe's rural politics extend to a perception of poaching as spanning the woods of England and the forests of Africa and it becomes a metaphor for colonialism itself, as the lands of other people are stolen and appropriated for European trophies. In his role as poacher and murderer, in a novel in which masks and skins facilitate metamorphoses between human and animal states, John becomes primal colonial myth of white man, king of apish Africans in their jungle forest. John Wall's mother describes how he "took all his clothes off down to his knickers and put [the leopard skin] on. You Jane, me Tarzan. Silly bugger" (1998b, 188). This takes us back to part three of this book, where sons and apes cavort in memory of a Tarzan, whose jungle kingdom has been overrun by late twentieth century transformations.

Darkening Hybrid Landscapes

These realities, as all the foregoing would suggest, relate to how forests and wildlife translate into pictures, images and stories, with quite concrete social outcomes. I would suggest, and this is pivotal to Thorpe's cultural politics and to this part of the book, that what makes his third novel so interesting is that he attempts to construct a grid, which overlays the perception of African forests, stories, beliefs and history and those of an English countryside. In so doing he presents us with a world whose parts are interconnected.

Furthermore, we will see that those interconnections are historical and unequal and that the resultant picture is far from pretty. Thorpe seems to be answering W.J.T. Mitchell's question:

> Is it possible that landscape, understood as the historical "invention" of a new visual/pictorial medium, is integrally connected with imperialism? (9)

Mitchell goes on to suggest:

> At a minimum we need to explore the possibility that the representation of landscape is not only a matter of internal politics and national or class ideology but also an international, global phenomenon, intimately bound up with the discourses of imperialism. (9)

Mitchell's argument is nuanced and he emphasises that "landscape, understood as concept or representational practice, does not usually declare its relation to imperialism in any direct way" (9). He develops the concept of "hybrid landscape formations", which he defines "simultaneously as imperial and anti-colonial" and gives as his example Dutch landscape painting in the second half of the seventeenth century when the Netherlands was transforming itself from colony to empire (10). In other words, Mitchell's hybrid landscape is a politically ambivalent interregnum struggling to resolve warring historical moments. Thorpe's hybrids, on the other hand, are catastrophic, welding together disparate beliefs, histories and languages within an uncompromising political opposition to imperialism.

Another interesting example of hybrid landscapes within an imperial setting is provided by David Bunn, in his analysis of landscape as depicted in painting, as well as in poetry, particularly that of Thomas Pringle in 1820s Cape Colony. In other words, he is examining landscape as "exported from metropolitan Britain to the imperial periphery" (127).

In a section of the paper, suggestively called "Transitional Landscapes" (136), which Bunn defines, by reference to Pringle's poetry, as the displacement of "one landscape into another" as "a sort of negotiated compromise" (139). In the process, for example, "the sharp yellow blossom of the thorny mimosa is displaced, by memory, into the yellow primroses of a Scottish spring" (139). The keyword is "compromise" and these hybrid or transitional landscapes seek resolution of contradictory cultures and politics. Thorpe seeks no such compromises in his tortured landscapes of disjuncture and fracture.

In fact, what Thorpe is attempting to do is to squeeze the heart of a serendipitous bond between Pastoralism and Jingoism, as summed up by Constable's Hay-wain, described earlier. Or, as Gail Ching-Liang Low puts it:

> The pastoral form, which suggests feelings of lost innocence and nostalgia...is a genre best suited to the poetics of Empire. It achieves the twin tasks of disowning culpability for the destruction of indigenous cultures, and of producing a gendered and... *infantilised* notion of culture, central to the imperialist mythopoetics of the boy's story. (43)

By situating his story of nostalgia within a white boy's African home and then by turning that boy's story into a nightmare of dislocation and lunacy, Thorpe refuses both the romance of imperial adventure and the pretty pride in a chocolate boxed English countryside:

> Now I'm standing by the great stone and my hand is on it. ...There are little holes scattered over it; I know what these are, these are where the roots of palm trees poked, when the climate was African, when the stone was not yet a stone. Before it was rolled by the ice and smashed up. ...
> And the little cupping heath becomes a slurry of ice again. The tundra stretches away, the graveyard of all those warm woods and ferns and African beasts. Hippopotamus, even! Crocodiles! All gone—only the tundra now, the wild icy wind and the sheets of scurrying white. (1998b, 393–4)

The cold, darkness of graveyards and despair overlay Africa and descend on his Eden, as surely as the English countryside has been mauled by leopards and violated by witches and voyeurs:

> I will steam up the river to Bamakum, of which I believe there is nothing left. Because when I close my eyes and travel there in my head, I see only tendrils and creepers hanging from tall trees and the dark swirl of water before them. Nothing else. ... Do you think Father would come, too? The three of us should manage, in silence of course, each as speechless as the trees. We'll keep cutting our way to Odoomi, and then take the ancient paths to your dark lake in the crater. (1998b, 413)

There is no light left for Hugh and for the first time his African landscape is entirely dark and reminiscent of Conrad's archetypal steamboat—the trees, the water, even the lake—is a black hole in a mind that cannot any longer summon up words. In this silent darkness, the picture fades as the curtain comes down on Hugh's final performance. However, it is not Africa, which has been his undoing, but, on the contrary, cold England which has vanquished him.

The last section, which provides some filtered and patchy light on Hugh's origins and the novel's mysteries, is given us by Mother herself. In this way Thorpe re-casts the very beginning at the very end of his text, in a typical manipulation of narrative time. Through Charlotte's letters, sent to her brother, the creepy Uncle Edward, we witness her and James's first arrival in Cameroon, prior to Hugh's birth. And like the murder that is confirmed in the final *Ulverton* piece, we are given some answers that pull the whole narrative together, whilst simultaneously we are left with more questions.

The Riddle of Seven and of the Vanished Mother

In her letters, Mother describes the far-flung outpost in the Cameroons, to which they have been posted as Colonial functionaries, as a kind of Garden of Eden, always as imagined in pictures:

> You only have your first evening in Eden once, so we dragged it out until well after one o'clock. ...And, dear Edward—this *is* our Eden: at least, it eerily *resembles the engraving* in the old Arnold Bible, if you remember it. It certainly has serpents as big. (1998b, 444, my emphasis)

The beast in the Garden, serpent, Wolf and Leopard in one, told in the form of the European fairy tale, is of course none other than Hargreaves, James's successor:

> He was...showing his gums again. He bore a remarkable resemblance, with his round spectacles, to the wolf dressed up as Grandmother Hood. (I *loathe* drunkenness, don't you?) (1998b, 446)

The bared gums, a habit Hugh has inherited, are inadvertent evidence of the letters' authenticity and Hargreaves's paternity. The reference to loathing drunkenness is important as evidence of Charlotte's later defection.

Talking of Charlotte's defection, there are two mysteries, one big, one small. The big mystery is what happened to Mother? The smaller one, which I will take first as I think it leads to the bigger puzzle, is contained on a "tiny slip of paper" that the elderly Hugh finds among the letters from his mother to his uncle. It has a kind of riddle typed on it:

> The centre
> Never gives
> Seven answers. (1998b, 278)

The riddle is, I think, the key out of the labyrinth of representation's tyranny and into the core of Thorpe's political realities. Leaking out of Mother's representation of Hargreaves's twisted mind, we are led, by way of the number seven, circuitously, to colonial greed and the First World War.

What we discover is that if Hargreaves mimics the stereotype of white man gone to the dogs in Africa, then this disguise conceals a shell-shocked survivor. Charlotte has "a few revealing conversations with the poor man", including one in which he asks Mother a question: "what three classes of sin are possible, my dear Mrs Arkwright?" Charlotte "thought hard for a moment" and comes up with three—original, deadly and trivial (1998b, 449). This leads Hargreaves to ask Charlotte if "James had had 'a good war'":

> I said that there was no such thing—but that Africa, for all its discomforts, had not been as horrible as the trenches. He nodded furiously. Then he stood up, as if on parade.
>
> "Flanders was in the second class of sin, Mrs Arkwright. Deadly. Deadly sin. *All seven actually*. Even sloth. Sloth let it carry on and on and on and on and on. I have never ever felt such sloth. I watched a man sink into the slime of a shell hole, and couldn't do a damn thing about it, I was filled up with so much sloth."
>
> Every time he said "sloth", he expectorated a little, making him look even more deranged. I replied that I had treated dozens of poor young men with the same listless condition and that it was called shell-shock, or battle weariness. (1998b, 449– 50, my emphasis)

The European War, originating in the Centre, demonstrated the existence of the seven deadly sins of Western belief, reverberating with the seven terraces of hell and their overtones of Dante's *Inferno*, ironically inverted, as Thorpe is so fond of doing. Unlike Dante's pilgrim, Hargreaves *loses* his Christianity, but not in Africa, rather in the European war of greed and power mongering. If he has become an unnatural animal-man, he became so in that war. Dante's pilgrim

> sets out on the night before Good Friday, and finds himself in the middle of a dark wood. There he encounters three beasts: a leopard (representing lust), a lion (pride) and a she-wolf (covetousness). (http://www.awerty.com/divine.html)

Leopards, wolves and rhinos roam in the trenches of Darkest Europe, turning the discourse of Kurtz and all his pale imitators upside-down. The War taught Hargreaves that "there never was any unfallen garden, Mrs Arkwright. No damn fall to make" (1998b, 450).

It was in these trenches that Hargreaves discovered that there was only Hell and no "unfallen garden" in the first place. It is, of course, this war that explains Charlotte and James's presence in Cameroon at all and presumably Adam Thorpe's own origins in Africa as well. It was the German defeat in

Hybrid Landscapes 283

that war that lead the British and French, collectively "The Centre", to sharing the spoils of German Cameroon in 1919, within the context of the European scramble for African colonies.

Charlotte finds this conversation "oddly distressing" (1998b, 450) and comments to James that she thought "Hargreaves had become an out-and-out pagan" (1998b, 451). At this point, the Leopard Society, which we know by now to be crucial to the novel's imaginary landscape, comes into the conversation between James and Charlotte. James points out that "'as long as he isn't in any secret society, darling, it can be classed as professional interest'" (1998b, 451). This leads Charlotte to explain to her brother for the first time (we have already discussed the second time, in the kitchen of Ulverton with the impressionable Hugh listening at the keyhole) that:

> A secret society, Edward, is exactly like the ones we have at home, only the problem out here is that it can end up very nastily. You must have heard of the Leopard society business in Calabar, which was like the Masons with spots—those spots being slavery and murder-by-leopard (someone disguised, with horrible claws). Tarbuck's [the missionary] lot stamped it out, and they all sing hymns now. But around here, and even deeper in the forest, no one knows quite what goes on. There are even Crocodile Societies, apparently, which makes me physically shudder. (1998b, 451)

This is interesting on two counts. Firstly, we quite quickly learn that Hargreaves is indeed dabbling in such secret societies. Charlotte has a "second conversation" with Hargreaves, still described in this particular letter addressed to her brother alone in which "the subject of ju-ju came up" and "fetishes and spirits and such-like were discussed" (1998b, 452). The power of such juju is illustrated by Hargreaves in relation to a man who had been "pierced through the heart with a spear" and who had survived:

> "It's *the seventh*, and final, test. I am not permitted to tell you the first six, each advancing in degree of severity and risk to life. *Only the seventh is not a secret*. Once passed, only old age can claim you. You are immune. Not even the tsetse fly dares bite". (1998b, 452, my emphases)

Hargreaves's seven tests appear to lead the way to a kind of mortal immunity, and are reminiscent of the burdens thrown off by Dante's pilgrim as he begins to emerge from hell:

> As the pilgrims entered Purgatory, an angel inscribed the letter "P" on Dante's forehead seven times, to represent the seven deadly sins (pride, envy, anger, sloth, avarice, gluttony, and lust). As Dante made his way through the seven areas reserved for those who committed each of these sins, the letters were erased one by one, and the climb became less difficult. (http://www.awerty.com/divine.html)

Hargreaves, in his European Hell of the terrible war that Thorpe critiques so uncompromisingly, seeks a way out of purgatory by way of African rituals, which he, of course, abuses and distorts, given the mental and psychological damage he has already undergone. In other words, if the Centre, Europe, has no answers but only Seven horrible Sins to offer, then at least Africa has seven tests, of which the seventh is an answer of a kind. These are seven stages of self-protection against the blasts, the hand-to-hand combat, the nastiness and injury of useless Wars and a meaningless life. Later, when Hargreaves is discovered to have participated in some grizzly ritual involving the murder of a gorilla by tying it down and smearing it with syrup to be eaten alive by killer ants, it is clear that Hargreaves is searching for a cure for his war terrors through seven African answers. He needs no creosote ointment for a cut lip: "'Keep your bloody creosote. I don't need it. That's the whole point, you idiot. *I don't need it*'" (1998b, 471).

Secondly, and this leads us to the question of Charlotte's mysterious disappearance, her description of the morbidly significant leopard societies almost exactly echoes that of Mary Kingsley in her *Travels in West Africa*. Kingsley refers to these societies as "practically murder societies" (385). Kingsley details the nature of these "Human Leopards", so-called because

> when seizing their victims for sacrifice they covered themselves with leopard skins, and imitating the roars of the leopard, they sprang upon their victim, plunging at the same time two three-pronged forks into each side of the throat. (386)

What I am about to suggest I can substantiate with significant but circumstantial evidence. I think that Charlotte leaves James as the marriage disintegrates in order to take off on her own, as did her inspiration and role model, Mary Kingsley. We are also reminded here of Rachael's impersonation of Amy Johnson and thereby of Hugh's mother. She was another pioneering explorer, of the skies rather than of other continents.

We have early evidence of James's drunkenness, which Charlotte "loathes". This drunkenness, moreover, is the result of James's own shell shock in that terrible war, all of which will contribute to his being less of a husband than Charlotte might have hoped for. When Charlotte suggests to James that "his daily intake of Gilbey's" was "medically ill advised", James "stormed off" (1998b, 453). This letter is still of June 13th 1921 and James's drinking and presumably the fighting, clearly only get worse, as we see him finally ending up a pathetic has-been soak in London much later. Charlotte dwells on this problem, which clearly worries her a lot and relates to James's character. She realised that what he has is "an old African habit" picked up "hobnobbing at the Club" (1998b, 453). His drinking has been triggered by loneliness and "difficulties of matching his ambitions with their realization" and always the war:

> He has nightmares in which he again sees poor Bailey in that tent with black bile pouring from his mouth and screaming with pain. (1998b, 454)

Most significantly this section actually ends with intimations of her desire to disappear, years before the event:

> Everything about Africa *touches* one so—the body, then the mind. Do you remember when you read me *Dracula*, all those years ago, and I said that I would like to dissolve into mist, like those awful red-lipped vampires? Well, here one nearly does. (1998b, 454)

We have firm evidence for the breakdown of the marriage in another of her letters, which Thorpe lights up for us. It is dated much later than the rest, "November 28, 1931" and Hugh finds it on the top of the pile. In it Charlotte describes sending the trunk of Hugh's childhood things, which "James believes" is all it contains. However, Charlotte has included the package of letters and so tells her brother to "look carefully and you will see different" (1998b, 302). What is clear is Charlotte's disenchantment with James, behind whose back she has had to send these letters to her brother because "James finds everything of mine, in the end" (1998b, 302). The claustrophobia and will to escape are palpable.

I have to say that Thorpe does leave Mother's exit as mysterious to some extent. This he does as a further indication that the lives and fates of his individual characters are not what this novel is centrally about. This is another version of the anti-quest, where, as in Patrick Roscoe's *The Lost Oasis*, the missing parent in never found (see chapter seven). However, Mother's identification with Mary Kingsley, a single woman explorer, unencumbered by husband or children, has to be significant in a novel where a woman's child is shown to be not her own and increasingly repugnant to her, and her husband likewise, given that he is an increasingly disgusting alcoholic, weakling. We have plenty of evidence for Charlotte's attraction to the life of Kingsley. Echoing Charlotte's letters addressed to her brother, Mary Kingsley's book's title page reads:

> TO MY BROTHER, C.G. KINGSLEY
> THIS BOOK IS DEDICATED.

In fact, Charlotte tells her brother she will emulate the style of Mary Kingsley in her *Travels in West Africa*. On sighting Mount Cameroon, Charlotte yearns "to climb to the top":

> Mrs Kingsley did it—I'm reading her book on deck, when the sun's not burning. *Travels in West Africa*. What about *Nursing in West Africa*? (1998b, 418)

Hugh had even remembered in one of his 'letters' to his mother—"You kept copies of all your letters, for your planned account of your life on the station" (1998b, 295). Charlotte's description of her first viewing of Africa from the boat, could have been taken from Kingsley's own descriptions, also from on deck:

> I mean the point where the copper-green of the forest runs right down to the water under frightfully thundrous-looking cloud. Left and right it runs, on and on into eternity with only a pencilled line of pale beach and the odd white flash of foam between. You can just hear the roar and crash of the breakers from the rail of the poop deck...but the *smell* is the most remarkable thing. It is of things vegetable, rotting. James is saying...that the smell is of the mangrove swamps, stagnant waters between the roots, full of crocodiles. (1998b, 417)

Kingsley's description is of "crocodiles and mangrove flies, and with the fearful stench of the slime round you" (72). Kingsley is captivated by the peak of the Cameroons, called "the Throne of Thunder" (396) and we can see where Charlotte found her use of colour in Kingsley's description of this mountain:

> Sometimes it is wreathed with indigo-black tornado clouds, sometimes crested with snow, sometimes softly gorgeous with gold, green, and rose-coloured vapours. ...(398)

Early on in her time in Africa, Mother, inspired by Kingsley, decides "to venture beyond the compound's perimeters" (1998b, 462):

> I have, of course, read Mary Kingsley's *Travels in West Africa* at least three times. I have even tried to describe things here in her vivid style (and failed dismally). Now I feel, for the first time, the exhilaration of the explorer. A curious mix of solitude and action (it involves the *reclusive* part of the soul, Edward). (1998b, 463)

She goes on to wax descriptive—again in typical Kingsley style—"such virgin realms before one!" (1998b, 463). Hugh knows intuitively that she has taken off on her own, leaving her husband and him for her own life and adventures. He knows this because there is another, much earlier, occasion in which we are given an echo of Mother taking off. This time it is via Hugh's account, significantly not given in the letters from the asylum, where his sanity is in serious doubt, but in part two of the memoir that Hugh wrote of his early years in Cameroon and his first years in England. These are the most powerful and lucid of his descriptions.

Hugh insists that "the very bad news about my mother certainly evolved, rather than broke" (1998b, 117). He places the beginning of it at the very first time he was left in England, when she went back to Africa—"sometimes I think it began as early as when she first disappeared up the lane" (1998b, 117). There were three more leaves "and each one repeated this disappearing act" (1998b, 117). He identifies, however, the crucial disappearance as much earlier than when we hear about it from her brother—"*the real thing* happened during her third leave in 1931" when Hugh was nine (1998b, 117, my emphasis). What is so interesting in terms of our landscape focus is that the place she disappears to on this significant leave echoes a Constable painting. The exploring mother has another of her itches, this time to walk in Ulverton, like her Kingsleyian expedition into the Cameroonian forest: "one morning she said she wanted to go for a 'stretch'. This meant a decent walk" (1998b, 117). Where she decides to go is to Pottinger's Mill:

> The path went round the front of the mill with a weedy yard between; my mother said she remembered it being full of wagons with fat sacks. I tried to speed up, but my mother was dragging her feet. The mill looked huge. She said she remembered it working as if it was yesterday, it made a big booming noise and now it was quiet. *She said it was like a Constable.* (1998b, 118, my emphasis)

Later, when Hugh "was given the bad news" he "saw her being swallowed up again by Pottinger's Mill" (1998b, 117). If Mother is swallowed by an English landscape, one associated, particularly during the First World War, with English values and jingoistic identity, then she is equally sucked into the African landscape, where Hugh visualises her at the Crater Lake. It is an African landscape from which all light has been drained, as these landscapes skid and merge. And if it is into the fiction of landscape that Mother finally ventures, it is part of Thorpe's design of removing the focus from the male explorer both through the female and through the constructedness of images. Justine Jordan suggests that this device is problematic, by reference, I think, to the residual mystery of what happens to Mother:

> But myth demands closure, and in *Pieces of Light* the symbols tie up where the narrative doesn't and inevitably the discrepancy jars. (25)

I think that the refusal to tie up the ends of the lives of the characters, who make up the cast of the novel, underlines once again Thorpe's emphasis on the structural power of traditions of representation, rather than on the actions of individuals. The damage to the countryside wrought by the representation of it in First World War icons, like Constable's *Hay-wain*, and the trophies bagged by murdering hunters, is the flesh and blood of his radical rural politics.

A little cameo sums up Thorpe's methods. Hugh describes in one of the letters to his absent mother in the fourth part of the novel, taking himself to Windmill Hill on sunny day, in order to read the fateful bundle of letters, which reveal the awful truth of his origins. He draws the attention of "a toddler in a postbox-red jumpsuit" (1998b, 337). The happenstance of this child in a red suit is a signal to us of a chain of metonymic associations of the red coat, which had belonged to his mother, but also of Hargreaves's cherry red terry robe, concealing the wolf of little red riding hood. Like in a painting, these associations are made by colour closeness, rather than by metaphoric connection. The letters, the child he never had, the red chain of contiguity, sets off a rambling train of thought in Hugh. As the child disappears back to its mother, Hugh sees

> her red dot like the complementary dab Cézanne or Renoir or maybe all of them put in to off-set the blue-green, like now. Puffs of turning trees, straw light in the air, autumnal. A poppy or a streak on a roof or just a red something, a splotch of red shadow, or the whole painting would go soft. (1998b, 341)

The red dot may well simply be a device to provide the painting its hard core. But the blood it implies and reinforces by way of the supposedly innocently mentioned poppy, reminds us of a War in which people were butchered in the name of imperial greed.

If Hugh is both the viewer and mental photographer of this novel, he is also the dotted figure on the landscape. As both victim and perpetrator, object and subject, Hugh, in spite of his unreliability, or perhaps because of it, also reflects Adam Thorpe's own battles with his late twentieth century splintered, fluid and unreliable white masculine identity.

One of the questions that has motivated this book, is what happens when the white son looks at his parents and discovers that they are impostors, much like Mudimbe's postcolonials do in relation to their false Gallic ancestors, (1994, 192) touched on in chapter one. What we have seen Thorpe attempting to do in his own rejection of the Authority of those Gallic Fathers, is to turn his focus away from individuals and towards the structural consequences of their actions, as forests become landscapes and the powerful white Masters of old, with their erect pens and all-seeing eyes, become impotent and blind old men.

Like the distorted buzz in his ear of messages from the African ancestors, that gave Salvestro such a headache in Norfolk's *The Pope's Rhinoceros* in chapter three, the world we perceive through Hugh's unreliable eyes is a discordant and violent one. Equally, the Hughs, Rickys and shepherds, who dot Thorpe's landscapes, are crazed, tortured figures, light years away from happy pastoral portraits, with which they do not aspire to compromise.

Kipling, Wordsworth and Patrice Kayo's Last Word
Pieces of Light begins with three epigraphs, taken from Wordsworth's *The Prelude*, Patrice Kayo's poem, *The Song of the Initiate* and Rudyard Kipling's *Just So Stories*, respectively. The Kipling provides the origins of the title:

> "What is this," said the Leopard, "that is so 'sclusively dark, and
> yet so full of little pieces of light?"

The benevolent talking leopard metamorphoses from Kipling's colonial pastoral into the horrendous, hybrid shifting landscape of a leopard man poacher, disguised as Tarzan, who captures not the beautiful Jane, but a sad village drunk with closeted transgressive sexual unhappiness and deposits him in a poisoned and forbidden wild wood. At the end of the day, the darkness of that place reveals very few pieces of lightness. But sandwiched between the pastoral of a Wordsworth or a Constable, and the Africanism of a Kipling is a new and enigmatic voice. Patrice, named no doubt for the martyred, murdered Lemumba, is a black Cameroonian, whose poetry is translated from French. His background highlights the colonial post-war partitioning of his country between victorious French and British powers, wresting it away from an equally corrupt German power, which will attempt to regain its glory in another world killing field. Thorpe gives us the following last lines of Kayo's poem on the frontispiece of the novel, and I think that he would approve of Kayo having the last word:

> The panther's child does not fear the night
> I can dance all the dances
> And my mother eats nothing but the flesh of sparrowhawks.

This child of the panther in another "strange becomings", is initiated in an African ritual, which frees him from Western enslaving and shattered subjectivities and enables him to inherit the earth in a poem entitled *Song of the Initiate*. This initiate, whose song Thorpe does not presume to sing in the body of his novel, this re-born houseboy, Quiri, inherits the stool from his father in the first verse and among all of his father's wives, his mother becomes supreme:

> It is I who have taken my father's stool
> And my mother has become queen. (Kayo, 55)

This contrasts with the emptiness and final darkness of Hugh heritage. Hugh ultimately disintegrates in his life of theatre-turned-house-of-horrors. The cast of leopard men, crocodile witches, skins and masks, changelings, Jekylls and Hydes, Draculas, druids, wolves and witches cavort on a forest stage in Cameroon and two woods in an English village. At the end of the demonic pantomime, what is left is a denuded, plundered and hybrid landscape in which the wild animals have been murdered and the vegetation poisoned with the evil gas from sinful European crimes.

Part Six:
Conclusion

CHAPTER TEN

Sons of the Century

As we reach this concluding chapter, what might I say that could capture the flavour of the weary sons and the late twentieth century in which their novels were written? Lynne Segal, in referring to Achebe's famous comment that the conventional reportage on Africa by Europeans "can tell us little except about themselves", points out that "what they reveal of themselves, however, is well worth pondering" (169). What of interest has been revealed in the foregoing chapters that we should ponder now as we draw to a close?

The purpose of this conclusion is simple. It is to answer the primal question posed at the outset—is it possible for white, non-African men to make the fictional journey to Africa without replicating the shameful history of representation, which served imperial ends and which denigrated the countries and people of Africa? I think it is fair to say that the foregoing chapters have demonstrated that it is indeed possible, albeit difficult and that sometimes these journeys are only partially successful. Two tributary questions have been engaging us. Are these writers capable of contesting, overturning and replacing the plundering tropes and marauding metaphors of Africanist discourse? And, are these men able, in the process, to confront patriarchy and to transform themselves as men? Again, 'yes' on both counts, with the reversals serving to highlight the achievements.

We, undoubtedly, have cause for some celebration as we remember the rich treasure of fiction that comprises the topic of this book. However, it would be banal to imagine that victories are complete and old patterns obliterated with entirely new men moon-walking free of history, family, language and tradition. We have, in fact, found examples in every chapter of great demolition jobs on the oppressive colonial past and simultaneously we sometimes have to lick the wounds of the shrapnel that hits its mark in the explosion.

All of this is to say that I am not quite as optimistic as John Cullen Gruesser in his *White on Black: Contemporary Literature About Africa* when he suggests that one category of white, European authors, which includes Boyle and Boyd, have avoided "the dominant traditions completely" and have thereby reversed Africanist myths (163). The writers themselves are also not quite so optimistic.

The fatigue of these writers, who I have called weary sons, is brought on by their own recognition of their collusion with power and their ambivalence in relation to it. Robbers doubled up as the robbed in Alan Hollinghurst's fiction as he explored his own murky terrain as both oppressor, white man and master, and oppressed, gay man. Just about every major player in his fiction is a double agent, oppressor and also victim in a complex interplay of gender, race and imperialism. And nothing recalled this self-confessed awareness of culpability more searingly than Lawrence Norfolk's *The Pope's Rhinoceros* where he depicted the gang rape. Salvador, his ambivalent quester, may have participated in the crime only in order to save the victim from the brutality of the other men, but participate he did, and it is Salvador's penis, which is still inside of her when she dies. And, ironically, with this acknowledgement of the involuntary power of Western patriarchy, Norfolk produced a politically profound novel and forged an alternative masculinity thereby. This achievement is substantial.

In other words, the writers, who have provided the subject of this book, do not need me to point out the nature of the history of imperial plunder and the tropes, which played their roles on the African stage. These writers have, to greater or lesser extent, understood the past and its survivals and have attempted, by way of their unique and powerful fictions, to redress it. All of these varied novels have harnessed their own devices of plot and theme, language and imagery, to tell their differing and compelling tales. I have therefore allowed my methods and means also to fluctuate and metamorphose, between chapters and writers, to allow for these idiosyncrasies of purpose to emerge from the writers themselves. The tension in this conclusion lies in the necessity to pull some threads together without flattening and draining the richness of the variation. I will be sketching trends and common preoccupations, but only lightly, suggestively and tactfully, I hope.

The Ambivalence of the Anti-Questing Quester

Vheissu was a luxury, an indulgence. We can no longer afford the likes of Vheissu."
"But the need," she protested, "its void. What can fill that?" (*V*, 248)

We have seen writers make the fictional journey to Africa in order quite precisely to interrogate the imperialist questing of their forebears. This is, of course, a risky undertaking—almost a contradiction in terms. In *The Pope's Rhinoceros*, the protagonist, Salvestro, returned from Africa, where the quest for the rhinoceros was caricatured in the form of the triumphal return only of a dead animal stuffed with stale bread. Africa has yielded no treasures or even illuminating archetypal Horrors. Salvestro must go home. His final journey was to return to Vineta, which is the suicidal descent into none other than the mirage of Valetta, the mythical land of nobody's reality, merely the textual father of Pynchon's *V*, the archetypal anti-quest novel of our century.

Like Norfolk, Hollinghurst brought his protagonists home from the questing after the lands and wealth of other people. We saw him view the crumbling, toppling Colossi with equanimity and abandon the closet, along with the secret homosexually inspired expedition to India or Africa of his gay forefathers. He enabled gay men to root themselves on home ground in his *The Swimming-Pool Library*. In so doing, he problematised the Canon of British Greats and re-claimed a heritage in *The Spell*. Hollinghurst insists that no longer will gay writing have to conceal itself in Conradian adventures of sea voyages to unknown parts of a falsely blank, deserted globe. And so, politically aware and radical gay sons found a liberating chain of links between anti quest, coming out of the closet and abandoning the heterotopia of Empire—the pyramid, the desert and North Africa itself. Abandoning the Quest for his lost Father in the North African Desert enabled Roscoe to focus on his protagonist's truer birthright, which was to find open and fulfilled love with his gay partner back in Europe in *The Lost Oasis*. We saw, however, the damage wreaked to the project of the anti-quest by a baptism of African desert storms.

The most radical and uncompromising rejection of holy grails and quests in faraway places, came, I think, from Adam Thorpe. His devastating critique of the politics of British imperialism and plunder, led him to reverse the journey away from Africa in order to interrogate the deeply problematic social and political roots of English art and culture.

T. Coraghessan Boyle, on the other hand, was torn about giving up on the Quest, and conflicted about late twentieth century masculine identity. A treacherous backwash threatens the swimmer against the current, especially if the waters are, say, of the River Niger. Where is life's purpose without the quest? Which quests are safe and permissible and what language exists to describe them that would not have involuntary recourse to older figures and tropes? Or, as Pynchon puts it "so in this search the motive is part of the quarry" (386). The quest is for meaning itself in our age of scepticism and uncertainty.

Nothing could sum up better that treacherous allure of questing than Boyle's re-write of the Mungo Park saga in *Water Music*. Eighteenth Century man holds fatal attraction. He is an adventurer more than the imperialist lackey and lookout of his nineteenth century counterpart. Elleke Boehmer suggests that "Enlightenment philosophical debates established in advance the way in which a late eighteenth-century explorer like Mungo park would represent Africans as noble savages" (49). We saw that Boyle fell, to some extent, into the Enlightenment romanticisation of 'the primitive' as his working class, secretively Irish, reborn hero, Ned, rises among the idealised pygmies. Ultimately, schizophrenia and the babble of the speechless, lace his later fiction of doomed flights nostalgically re-living the freedom of African vistas.

William Boyd, too, was ambivalent about abandoning the quest. He had to cross-dress as Hope Clearwater, or make the racial crossover as Amilcar or Usman Soukrey in order to express the persistent allure of exploration. Amilcar was killed in what appeared to be a futile war and Usman, Boyd's enigmatic, pathetic Everyman, was reduced to lying about his participation in the Russian space programme and caricaturing his own delusions of achievement by way of his trapped insectoid cyborgs.

This ambivalence towards the lure of limitless horizons on the horizontal plane has given rise to a transference onto the vertical plane—of digging deep or the high rise building. It accounts for Thorpe's interest in archaeology and perhaps here lies the key to the late twentieth century passion for architecture as a ladder to the moon. The splintered subjects of our Age of Uncertainty are denied the view from the tree-top of the African jungle, a view which bathed their Enlightened brothers in the glow of reason, two hundred odd years earlier. They have, instead, discovered the Urban landscapes of their own cities, with their tall buildings holding out a different possibility.

Fredric Jameson identifies this postmodern "appetite for architecture" and correctly surmises that it "must in reality be an appetite for something else" (1991, 98). I have been suggesting that what this something else is, is the drive to discover radical and different grails, quests and monuments. The postmodern fascination for architecture, linked to male identity and compromised quests, in fact, often took quite a radical form in the novels we have been looking at. This is so, given that this fascination was linked to an understanding of the relations of unequal power between the West and the parts of the world it once colonised. The young Robin began *The Spell* with his research on sites of the buildings designed by the famous architect, Frank Lloyd Wright. We traced the transformation in his identity through his career as an architect, in that he withdrew from the allure of the monuments of other people. In this, Hollinghurst built on *The Swimming-Pool Library* where deep subterranean pools, with their postmodern architectural pastiche became the site of the novel's search for the relationship between Empire and sexuality. In fact, from the outset of *The Spell*, Frank Lloyd Wright's buildings have crumbled. Broken buildings, broken bodies and compromised landscapes formed jagged links on a chain of dislocated meaning and splintered identities. Tony's decrepit house and the collapsing mausoleum of his ancestor, signify the demolition of an age and of the beliefs and quests, Laws and sacred objects, attached to it.

Then again, there was Adam Thorpe, with his persistent digging deep into the soil, a fascination for archaeology as part of his complex network of counter explorations in darkest Europe. Or Lawrence Norfolk, with his sinister, secret headquarters of the East Indian Cabal, who conduct their greedy machinations in the bowels of the flesh turned fossil, under the streets of London in *Lemprière's Dictionary*.

And if not high rises, or deeply dug holes, then the image of flight, which recurs. Some of the writers were aware of the impossibility of what David Savran refers to as the "Icarus-like exploits" of the new fantasies of the white men of the late1970s, 80s and 90s (140). Where writers are ambivalent, their flights may be suicidal, their wings fake, miniaturised and programmed to self-destruct, their buildings and monuments in ruins, like the crumbling hotels and movie houses with their "echoes of a former colony's mother" of Roscoe's *Lost Oasis* (1995, 91).

And out of the ruins, rises an affinity between the writers focussed upon in this book and the so-called postmodern masters, with their big books and pastiche of devices. The anti-imperialist cultural politics of these writers distances them from the postmodern. At the same time, our writers share a critical affinity with the project of the dismantling of the Master Text of the quest of the powerful, colonizing white man.

Thomas Pynchon signified the beginning of what I am referring to here with his sixties monster of a novel, *V*, which profoundly and directly influenced Norfolk's *The Pope's Rhinoceros*. Don DeLillo, another such turn of the century guru, has his *Underworld* protagonist, who is thinking about a club situated "up on the forty-second floor of a new office tower", muse that:

> leaders of nations used to dream of vast land empires—expansion, annexation, troop movements, armored units driving in dusty juggernauts over the plains, the forced march of language and appetite, the digging of mass graves. They wanted to extend their shadows across the territories. (787)

Archetypal, ancient Egypt with its infinitely metaphorical pyramids, has become a mountain of waste in the sceptical diminished goals of our times.

Nick, a waste disposal specialist in *Underworld*, "looked at all that soaring garbage":

> He imagined he was watching the construction of the Great Pyramid at Giza. ...All this ingenuity and labor, this delicate effort to fit maximum waste into diminishing space. The towers of the World Trade Center were visible in the distance and he sensed a poetic balance between that idea and this one. (184)

DeLillo's *Underworld* in its very title captures that vertical dig towards some inner discovery of new Urban quests. One of the quests in that novel is the search for a baseball. The ball in question is the "authentic ball" (96) with which a home run was hit in a big game in 1951. I cannot go into all of the intriguing lines of association that DeLillo ingeniously builds around this ritual of male competition, body power, historical period of witch hunts and reaction, of the yearning for originals in an age of copies and cyber-virtualities. What I do wish to comment upon is that this quest is left hanging, with loose ends, as befits an ironic and compromised holy grail, and secondly, it further problematises old quest myths by being linked not to any lost tribe or city or immense wealth, but to the random, the accidental arena of metonymy. As Nick explains, the ball is about the randomness of the bad luck of the loser in that game, Ralph Branca (97) or as Nick's friend explains, "[Nick] wonders what it is that brings bad luck to one person and the sweetest of good fortune to another" (99).

What is highly significant is that this baseball, paradoxical metaphor for the metonymic, finds its natural site underground, as opposed to across the seas. It finds its museum in the basement of the city, a basement belonging Marvin Lundy. This underground, underworld space is the new site of male escape from the domestic—the alternative to Mungo Park's expedition to Africa. As Lundy himself puts it:

> "People who save these bats and balls and preserve the old stories through the spoken word and know the nicknames of a thousand players, *we're here in our basements*. ...
> "Men come here to see my collection."..."They come and they don't want to leave. The phone rings, *it's the family—where is he? This is the fraternity of missing men*". (182, my emphases)

What are the links between the Quest, this vertical plane—these basements and high rise buildings—and the bodies of these domesticated late twentieth century men? We have watched Fred Pfeil chart the relationship between these bodies and architecture when he analyses films like *Rambo* and bodies like Sylvester Stallone's. In the conclusion to his paper, "From

Pillar to Postmodern: Race, Class, and Gender in the Male Rampage Film", subtitled "Bodies and Buildings, Open and Shut", he says:

> These buildings/bodies, moreover...these sites or spaces both ruined and saved: do they not rhyme in turn, or even coincide with the bodies of our oh-so-desirable heroes themselves, simultaneously displayed as beefcake and mortified as beef? (1998, 173)

The ridiculous, built torso of Rambo, playing in Roscoe's crumbling Moroccan *Cinema Le Paris* in North Africa underlines the anachronism of the white, male, Tarzan body on display and brings us to the next section.

The Hollowing-out of Phallic Authority #1: The Wounded Body

> Danny "wondered if there was some equally effective spell for making your dick go down". (*The Spell*, 224)

What did the irony of seeking such a spell conceal? If Hollinghurst had indeed found the formula for reducing the damage of Imperial Patriarchy, by way of the flaccid penis, what longings and frustrations accompanied such abstinence? His failed architect, Robin, of *The Spell* with the eye patch and the longing for contented celibacy, had staked his claim to rural England and the literary canon imprecated in it. But we saw him reduced as a creative, zestful man, by comparison with his youthful fervour in the desert of Arizona, questing after the genius of a Frank Lloyd Wright. Fred Pfeil looks for the roots of what he calls *"a hollowing-out of Phallic authority"* (1998, 169, my emphasis).

What is striking, in both popular and more serious film and fiction, and has been apparent in this book, is the recurrence of the wounded white male body. He is DeLillo's, Marvin Lundy, curator of the quest for baseball memorabilia, who is dying from prostate cancer—"an old recluse with half a stomach" (169). And again DeLillo hones in on reduced masculinity, linked by negative comparison with the heterotopia of ancient Egypt and embroiled with the new late twentieth century architecture. A character in *Underworld* imagines a cheap affair with "a secretary from Queens", and his sperm buried in the garbage, like Ramses's body preserved in the depths of the pyramid:

> And he gives her gifts and she gives him condoms, and it all ends up here, newsprint, emery boards, sexy underwear, coaxed into high relief by the rumbling dozers—think of his multitudinous spermlings with their history of high family foreheads, stranded in a Ramses body bag and rollered snug in the deep-down waste. (185)

Male sexuality amounts to nothing more than sordid, casual encounters, blighting future generations. These wounded men are all different and perplexingly the same as part of a cultural change in the image of masculinity. They are Brad Pitt as kick boxer or Stallone as Rocky or Rambo. Ivan Illich, in making "a plea for body history" suggests that "each historical moment is incarnated in a epoch-specific body" (344). The white male body, specific to our epoch is battered, bruised and bloodied.

We have seen versions of this body in the foregoing chapters. And again, this broken, white male flesh takes on a critical politics when bonded by these writers to an exposure of the master text of imperialism as a tall tale told by naked and ailing Empire builders. Hollinghurst's spell of eternal youth and perfect flesh was broken, or at least transferred to drug induced pleasures in the context of vulnerable, ageing. The weakened symbolic phallus manifested itself as the spectre of AIDS in Hollinghurst's *The Spell* and of aging in that novel—Robin with the eye patch. In *The Swimming-Pool Library*, Charles is first encountered collapsing in the loo and later Will's perfections are scarred as the result of being mugged by a bunch of thugs. There were the lepers stamped on Richard's soul in *the Lost Oasis*, lepers, who metamorphosed into the androgenous elephant creature in the desert. There was Abish's Zacherey in "Crossing the Great Void", who was deaf and Hugh in Thorpe's *Pieces of Light*, who was mentally unstable, old and visually impaired, as was Lemprière, protagonist of Norfolk's first novel. In his later, *The Pope's Rhinoceros*, Norfolk went to battle against the patriarchal Phallus with his depiction of the clay penis as part of the sacred metal working of the Benin master craftsman.

Recent popular culture abounds with images of the damaged white male body. What are the gender politics that flow from the mutilation of this body, the ripping apart of its perfections? Pfeil suggests, with nuance and caution, that we may be optimistic that what these bodies herald is, if not transformation, a growing climate of possibility that the old hard core masculinity is mutating:

> The wild, violent, mortified, desirable white male body at the centre of these films can hardly be taken as an icon of progressive movement, or even of its unambiguous possibility; yet the permeability that comes along with that body's persistence, the sensitivity that accompanies its violence...all at least suggest something is loose and shaking in the old centered, hard-shell masculinity they simultaneously defend and subvert. (1998, 174)

In this, Pfeil would be concurring with Kaja Silverman, whose *Male Subjectivity at the Margins* was dedicated to "some 'deviant' masculinities" (1) and concluded with the belief in the possibility of "some alternative ways of inhabiting a ... masculine body" (389).

There is a viewpoint that is less optimistic. David Savran, in his tellingly entitled paper "The Sadomasochist in the Closet: White Masculinity and the Culture of Victimisation", agrees with the fact that in our era, there is "a new, white masculine fantasmatic" (126). This he identifies as a newfound freedom to be both masculine and feminine (141). This feminine side then manifests itself as victim, as wounded, objectified flesh. It

> authorizes him to be both wild and domestic, to cultivate a "feminine" part of the self (or at least to endure his feminized flesh) and at the same time to subjugate it violently. ...It allows him to play the part of victim and yet be a man. (140–1)

Savran, in other words, resists the possibility that "the ascendancy of the white male as victim...offers radically subversive possibilities" (143). Instead, this "bifurcation" enables him to be more resiliant and responsive to our times, without "phallic divestiture" (144). He is what Rowena Chapman refers to in the title of her paper as "The Great Pretender"—"hybrid masculinity" being merely an adaptation that is "more suited to retain control" (235). She satirises this "new man" so viciously, however, that she must also fear him and we must suspect there is more to 'the pretender' than the mere sham she insists upon:

> Tough but tender, he knew his way around a Futon, and could do more than just spell clitoris. Not for him the wham-bam-thank-you-mam thrust of the quick fuck. He was all cuddles and protracted arousal, post-penis man incarnate, the doyen of non-penetrative sex. (227)

She does, I think, place this man in a rather no-win situation:

> He is everywhere. In the street, holding babies, pushing prams, collecting children, shopping with the progeny, panting in the ante-natal classes, shuffling sweaty-palmed in maternity rooms, grinning in the Mothercare catalogue, fighting with absentee mums and the vagaries of washing machines in the Persil ad. (226)

We should be so lucky that he is everywhere, because, in truth, he is not, although this man, who is trying hard to be different, is very visible in the fiction examined in this book in some detail. The dilemma for him is captured by Michael Flynn in his "Searching for Alternatives: Autobiography and Masculinity at the Bimillenium":

> Many young men are frightened by the ease with which they inhabit styles of masculinity antagonistic to the mutuality they desire, forms that operate on domination and indifference, forms that ensure alienation and nihilism. They want the liberty to express gentleness, sadness, and confusion outside the confines of the barroom or the postconjugal embrace. They want it without having to adopt the

affectations of either sensitivity or androgyny; there are certain aspects of a traditional masculine stance they don't seek to jettison. (247–8)

This is precisely what Boyle, in humourous mode, was saying in his "The Descent of Man" story, where he portrayed the sapped male, who lost his image of his body and his mind, because he could neither be a man in the old mould or happily domesticated in the new. Sadly, we saw that the new was impossible because of the threat posed by his professional female partner. If anything hollows out the authority of the man, it is seen to be the feminism that has transformed the woman.

The Hollowing-out of Phallic Authority #2: The Threat Posed by the Woman

> Then Adam Burden put down his rifle. Madelene and the ape retreated towards the door. Adam followed them, unarmed, awkward. (*The Woman and the Ape*, 226)

The ape found the spell that Danny ironically called for and had caused Adam's 'dick' to go down—a lot more about apes shortly. For now, let us remember all the Madelenes, Ailies, Hopes, Mothers and, most especially, the many Janes—all powerful and threatening women.

A strong, career oriented Jane appeared to be independent enough to return his rib to Tarzan in the Edenic Jungles of Africa, and then to stab him in the back with it. Late twentieth century white woman is finding her own language, quests and goals and in so doing, she is seen by white men as emaciating them. What is quite unexpected in the fiction under consideration is the degree of threat to their self-esteem that many of the writers perceive from white women. She was often his obstacle and his snare and, perplexingly, seldom, in all this genuine confrontation with patriarchy, his ally and companion.

By coincidence, or perhaps the archetypal unconscious, many of these women were called "Jane". This is so, at least in part, given the shared Western culture of Tarzan and Jane, who like Adam and Eve, are the parents of our explorers and travellers and also like them, have been expelled from the Edenic jungle of post-independence Africa. We saw that this archetype has been reinforced by the more recent icon of Jane Goodall and her link with Africa and primates.

There was Jane Good in Boyle's "Descent of Man," and various Jane Goodall clones, such as Boyle's Beatrice Umbo in another story and Ludmilla Rauhschutz in *Great Apes*. In *The Spell*, Robin's former wife was called Jane "a Distinguished Professor now, who wrote acclaimed books in an idiolect Robin couldn't understand" (1998, 60) and Robin describes her as "fierce and fit" in photograph of her with Danny (1998, 92). "Fit" means physically strong and buttresses fierce, as in hostile and threatening. This may have specific context for a gay man viewing his bisexual past, but the portrayal is familiar across many of the writers.

In *Riven Rock*, in a final reversal of the Tarzan tale, with yet another Jane, the hint was that Katherine and fellow suffragette, Jane Roessing, find lesbian comfort in each other, out of this distasteful world of bullish men, another stereotype about feminists being that they are 'dykes'. There were other powerful, independent white women and none of them were entirely trustworthy—Madelene (*The Woman and the Ape*), Katherine (*Riven Rock*), and to a somewhat lesser extent, Hope Clearwater, (*Brazzaville Beach*). And nowhere was this image of emasculation by professional women more ruefully and humorously, yet deadly seriously, captured, than in T. Coraghessan Boyle's "Descent of Man", where the poor narrator was totally undermined, whose wee "wouldn't come" (1987, 5) and whose instructions are to "vacuum rug and clean toilet" (1987, 12).

These are the women who are punished, in one way or another, in Pfeil's description of movies of rampaging, wounded men. They are women who are "business-suited, dress-for-success professionals pursuing careers that take them away from home" (1998, 162), women who, like men, have "their own salaried jobs in tall buildings" (1998, 163). Even here, in these popular films of only partially wounded and minimally reconstituted men, the message with regard to these career women is mixed:

> We are not invited to vote openly against this professional woman's pursuit of a career. For one thing, McClane [in the first *Die Hard*] does not seem to know or credit what we know: that she [his wife] is still a fully domesticated family woman underneath...in favor of her traditional Christmas vision of "families, stockings, chestnuts, Rudolf and Frosty," even as she strides down the corridor to look at some spreadsheets. (Pfeil, 1998, 163)

Different ways of conceptualising woman do at times glimmer beneath the surface. The mothers may be rejecting, cold or threatening (*Pieces of Light, The Lost Oasis, Water Music*) but they also sometimes imply alternatives, if not positively to enact them. For example, Ailie is simultaneously a woman of great potential and passion, who is snuffed by her exploring, ego-centred husband. While Roscoe's crazed mother offers but little, she does speak in a language that departs from that of the controlling metaphors of the father. Most intriguingly, I think, there was the Mary Kingsley styled alternative to the big white male ego, with the possibility of a female entry into a magnificent African crater lake, held out as a tantalising loose end in *Pieces of Light*.

Why this perceived threat from the emasculating Janes was so unexpected was that these writers, without exception, are clearly themselves unconventional men, who have exhibited great awareness and sensitivity to issues of history, race and gender in their writing. There seems to be a tendency in some late twentieth century men, however, of ambiguity about strong, powerful women, who potentially emasculate them and produce in them a poor body image. This is so notwithstanding their genuine rejection of dominant and conventional masculinity. Is there a lurking fantasised resolution of these tensions for these particular writers, who set their fictions in Africa, in terms of race, in terms, of the fantasy of becoming Black? And what might be the political consequences of this fantasy?

The Hollowing-out of Phallic Authority #3: The Longing to be Black

> The Water-man was black. (*The Pope's Rhinoceros*, 663)
> For Salvestro there is only the Water-man now, and the Water-man is himself (*The Pope's Rhinoceros*, 741)

> That night I experimented with cinders from the stove, rubbing them into my face. Then I tried my father's blacking, the stuff he brushed briskly but thoroughly into his mosquito boots twice a week. (*Pieces of Light*, 12)

In *The Pope's Rhinoceros*, Salvestro, during moments of identity introspection, saw himself reflected in the image of a black person; Hugh in *Pieces of Light* desperately tried to become Black; One of Boyle's personas in *Water Music* was the African guide, Johnson and Boyd in *Brazzaville Beach* constructed his Everyman, his Usman, as Egyptian, and played out his own desire to have an activist role in Africa through Amilcar, the Black revolutionary.

What is striking is that in the absence of the white woman as loving mother and nurturer, this role of support is played, but in quite a circuitous way, by blackness. It is circuitous in the sense that what we have, for the most part, are devices and imaginaries, rather than flesh and blood African characters.

Again, Pfeil points to this in the context of the rampage film. He describes what he calls "proto-sexual healing of the white man by the black" (1998, 158). Furthermore, in the *Lethal Weapon* films, for example, "only thanks to the presence and influence of the nurturant, supportive, domestic black buddy can the white hero at last let himself be straightforwardly soft and sensitive too" (1998, 159). This freedom emerges in part, I think, due to the cultural stereotype of the black body as unquestioningly virile and potent, about which more in a moment. If a black hunk of an action policeman can be soft and emotional on occasion, this clears the space for the white guy, with his male hang-ups, to follow suit with greater impunity.

This role played by blackness is crucial and needs to be unpacked rather a lot. What I think we have seen happening is that many of the writers under discussion identified with black skins and desired to enter black bodies in interesting ways. The splintered identities, fractured narratives and damaged bodies of postmodern writers more broadly, took a specific turn when that fiction was set in Africa. And it did so particularly in terms of race.

This returns us to Alice Jardine's concept of "gynesis" discussed at some length in chapter three. What we added to Jardine's propositions was that the writers, who populate this book, with its particular interest in how Africa and Africans are depicted, used race, perhaps more than gender, as that space of self-exploration, a space that is intriguingly less flesh and blood than metonymic jingle and alphabetic sign.

And as always, the ice is dangerously thin. Let us go deeper with Jardine into her gendered paradigm and see how much it reverberates with that of race and with many of the fictions examined in this book. She asks whether 'gynesis' invariably, in spite of its best intentions, is bound to "reintroduce very familiar representations of women" (26). She does appear to retain the possibility and the hope that "these texts offer new ways of connecting the most radical insights of feminism to the larger questions facing the West as it moves toward a new century" (26).

With this hope in mind, let me reinforce the nub of my argument here. Firstly, I think that the paucity of developed African characters is not in itself a problem. In fact, it could be part of the realization of the difficulties in constructing such portrayals, without Othering and making arrogant assumptions about cultures and people that could be naïve and damaging. This we identified in the introduction as the pitfall into which David Caute fell in his *Fatima's Scarf*. While I suggested there, and have not changed my mind here, that there are no prohibitions on who may depict whom, there are certainly hazards and injunctions on how to do so, depending on the space occupied by the particular writer. And I do think that much of the writing we have been celebrating is exquisitely tactful in this regard.

Secondly, I think that the ways in which most of the writers in this study have attempted to bring into the guts and mechanics of their narratives the space of blackness, as a necessity, is wise and complex. The necessity is that of re-thinking their own maleness and their own inadvertent participation in the imperial past, in the late twentieth century present, and is one of the most positive aspects of their endeavours.

Thirdly, (not as an 'however', but as an 'in addition') I think that they encounter obstacles to this fierce and committed cultural politics in two linked ways. The first we have seen occur when writers avoid dealing creatively with the transformations occurring in late twentieth century women. The second, which we will come to now, is that blackness sometimes, fatally, doubles up as body. When blackness rears its private part as stereotypically enormous penis, then, and only then, by definition, I think, writers fall back into the bad old ways of the discourse and of "double representation", discussed in chapter one (Mudimbe, 1988, 8 – 9). It is in fear and trembling of their emasculated bodies, in relation to white women, that some of these men set out in search of the mystical lost tribe of virile male origins, labelled Black and African, with our close relative, the ape, waiting in the wings to detonate the fiction.

A writer like Alan Hollinghurst was simultaneously aware of the dangers inherent in white male desire for black bodies, and also torn by a degree of self-aware collusion with this cultural stereotype. This explains the somewhat love/hate relationship with his protagonist, Will, which we saw in *The Swimming-Pool Library*. This simultaneous critique and collusion occurred in *The Spell* where Hollinghurst appears to be making the link between pornography, Empire and black bodies by recasting an image out of Conrad's *The Nigger of the Narcissus*. Hollinghurst's Dave, runs a porno outfit and is big and black:

> Dave sat among the shiny flesh-colours of shrink-wrapped pornography and rubber sex aids *like a big black deity in a garish little shrine*. He had the jaw and the firm weight of a boxer. ...(1998, 79, my emphasis)

Look at the echoes in Conrad's description of Jimmy, 'nigger' of Conrad's title:

> In the evening, in the dog-watches, and even far into the first night-watch, a knot of men could always be seen congregated before Jimmy's cabin. They leaned on each side of the door peacefully interested and with crossed legs;...*The little place, repainted white, had, in the night, the brilliance of a silver shrine where a black idol*, reclining stiffly under a blanket, blinked its weary eyes and received our homage. (1961, 105, my emphasis)

Conrad's Jimmy is fetishized and worshipped because he signifies mortality. Far from being body, he is skull, death, disease and Africa incarnate:

> He was unique, and as *fascinating as only something inhuman could be*. ...He was becoming immaterial like an apparition; his cheekbones rose, the forehead slanted more; the face was all hollows, patches of shade; and the fleshless head resembled a disinterred black skull, fitted with two restless globes of silver in the sockets of eyes. (1961, 139, my emphasis)

The Nigger of the Narcissus, first published in 1912, quintessentially embodies colonialist discourse. Hollinghurst gleefully reverses this image and turns Dave into material, fleshy reality, but he retains the false idol of the great black body, even as he attempts to de-fetishize it. He is playing with fire. Look at the gift he gives to dear Hugh, a sweet character, who has not had the best of luck up until this moment near the end of *The Spell* when Hugh tells his friend, Alex, about his new Nigerian boyfriend:

> [Alex] knew what question Hugh wanted him to ask next, and he brought it out with airy courtesy: What's his dick like, by the way?' Hugh's glow of tactfully suppressed pleasure deepened to a triumphant blush. (1998, 245)

The problem is that while Hollinghurst is bashing icons by taking off Conrad's colonialist discourse, he runs the risk of returning this discourse through the back door and another version—that of the Black man's well hung brawn.

Equally, look at Boyle's version of the black body stereotype in *Water Music* where a cameo incident occurs in London involving an African character called Jutta Jim. Jutta Jim, according to Ned Rise, right near the beginning of the novel, is "the black nigger of the Congo", who works for a decadent member of the aristocracy, tellingly called Lord Twit. Ned "leases" Jutta Jim from Twit, in order to mount an entertainment, a public orgy, in which Jutta Jim "performs" with a white, underclass woman, Sally. Jim is "bare-assed, buck black naked, his member slick and hard in the light from the oil lamps (1981, 20). And Sally, who describes Jim as a cannibal with the breath of "a fookin' chamberpot", concedes that "he's got a tool on 'im, though—I'll say that for the beast" (1981, 20). If English decadence and moral turpitude is demonstrated by all of this, then it is done so at the expense of Jutta Jim, who is the stereotypical black stud. And if, as we saw in chapter two, this is given ironically in the inimical Boyle style, the irony is not appropriate for the purposes of hammering the stereotype. This brings us to remember the chapters dealing with humans who mix genes with apes.

The Hollowing-out of Phallic Authority #4: Human Hybrids and Apes

Chapters four and five examined a range of short and longer fiction, in which men merged with chimps and the resulting mutant bodies were pumped with power and vigour. We saw Konrad, Boyle's chimp, who had the best of both worlds—human knowledge and great physical prowess. Then there was Howie, a man with chimp attributes. Boyd's ape, Conrad, was disconcertingly human and reverberations between chimp and local civil wars, put us in mind of boundary crossings. Then there was Erasmus, the hybrid human ape in *The Woman and the Ape* and Simon Dykes, the mutated human/ape fantasy. What I suggested at the end of chapter five is that given the history of Tarzan lording it in the jungle with apes, who merge with local inhabitants in many popular accounts, these particular boundaries are crossed with problematic consequences. White men may, out of a sense of insecurity, appear to be affirming their black brothers when they yearn for their supposed pecs, power and potent penises, but the type-casting and history ensures that this only ends badly.

The fiction we have been looking at also abounds with cyborgs of varying weird and wonderful constructions and we have to wonder what this means. There are wolf men, leopard men, rhino men, a boy bonded with a white horse, aeroplanes with insect bodies and human bodies turned insectoid. And in this preoccupation with species crossing in general, and cyborgs in particular, the novels discussed in this book participate in a seminal image that touches late twentieth century imaginaries as a whole. This is, in fact, a reason that Donna Heiland proposes for the renewed interest in the eighteenth century, the century in which both Boyle and Norfolk set one of their novels:

> In the late twentieth century we have become obsessed with the question of what it means to be human, cyberspace making us all wonder whether we are not pure mind as opposed to body, and cyborgs making us wonder just the opposite. With these questions in mind, it makes sense to look back to the origins of that dualism—to look back, in other words, to Decartes' articulation of the idea that human beings were defined by their minds in opposition to their animal/mechanical bodies, and to the reception of his ideas over the next century or so. (109)

We could remember here Fred Pfeil's suggestion in chapter four that "when certain bodies are mutating" and disturb the "social-symbolic imaginaries" then, given that "no psycho-social body is ever finally closed" and "no imaginary ever complete or fully resolved" then something new and radical may be "up for grabs" (1998, 32–3). Or there is Cynthia Fuchs's suggestion that "Robocop is always an inconsistent (if highly unlikely) underdog, the site of intersecting cultural anxieties and social disruptions"(116). In other words, when identities are splintered, when solutions are being sought, when race and gender are being interrogated, when cyborgs are being born, then what may be possible is not a foregone conclusion. This brings us to a paradoxically optimistic connection between mutating bodies and the recurrence of fractured minds.

Mutating Bodies and Fractured Minds: Late Twentieth Century Schizophrenia

If bodies were mutating at quite an alarming rate, then minds too were being lost and sometimes found in strange spaces. There were many versions of schizophrenia in Boyle's fiction, including Konrad as schizophrenic ape in "The Ape Lady in Retirement", to say nothing about the ape lady herself, who was split and peculiar. All of this culminated in Boyle's insane Stanley McCormick in *Riven Rock*; John Clearwater, lost his mind and took his own life in *Brazzaville Beach*, which brings to mind Salvestro, who, likewise killed himself; Richard's mother and sister were both schizophrenic in *The Lost Oasis* and his brother's body was so wracked by headaches as indicators of his unhappy mind, that he literally had to run away, never to be heard from again. In *Pieces of light*, Hugh, as well as the father who raised him and also his biological father, were all mentally unstable, with much of Hugh's narrative serving the function of therapy and written from within an asylum.

We need to interpret all of this insanity, in the light of the difficulties inherent in 'normal' subject constitution, discussed in chapter one of this book. We saw there how thinkers like Gilles Deleuze and Felix Guattari posed a model of a kind of schizophrenic escape from the tentacles of Oedipal 'normality', as endemic to the late twentieth century. We saw quite clearly, and have been confirming throughout, that the predetermined route from the Imaginary to the Symbolic zones, both enables the mature male to emerge, but simultaneously arms him with a language and an ideology that tends to be Patriarchal, Imperialistic and Phallic. We have also witnessed writers who are deviant, who resist patriarchy and imperialism and who seek alternatives in their often scarred, wounded, profound and wonderful fictions.

What Deleuze and Guattari pose as the alternative to Phallic subjectivity is a Body without Organs. What is this Body without Organs? It is linked to the wounded body we have already talked about, wounds that are therefore potentially regenerative in the way that the perfect, built body of Superman or Tarzan, was not. The "Bodies without organs" are the drugged, masochist, "sucked-dry, catatonicized, vitrified, sewn-up bodies", but, and here is the paradox, these damaged bodies, with their potential for metamorphosis and transformation are "full of gaiety, ecstasy, and dance" as described in *A Thousand Plateaus*, which is Deleuze and Guattari's second volume of *Capitalism and Schizophrenia* (1987, 150). It is only this strange, weird and deformed body that has the malleability and magical capacity to inaugurate "strange becomings" (1987, 151).

These "becomings" are played with in a chapter of *A Thousand Plateaus*, which is entitled " 1730: Becoming-Intense, Becoming-Animal, Becoming-

Imperceptible...". The dots are theirs and imply the infinite possible Becomings. 'Becoming', rather than being fully and finally constituted, is the nature of the schizoanalytic unconscious—"Becoming is always of a different order than filiation" (Deleuze & Guattari, 1987, 238). Becoming does not entail the consolidation of familial relations. Deleuze and Guattari ask the question: "How can we conceive of a peopling, a propagation, a becoming that is without filiation or hereditary production?" (1987, 241). They reply that this "is quite simple" and they list their demonic preferences, which obliterate family, sexuality and structure, predictability, design and meaning. Instead, "bands, human or animal, proliferate by contagion, epidemics, battlefields, and catastrophes (1987, 241). And so:

> The vampire does not filiate, it infects. The difference is that contagion, epidemic, involves terms that are entirely heterogeneous: for example, a human being, an animal, and a bacterium, a virus, a molecule, a microorganism. Or in the case of the truffle, a tree, a fly, and a pig. ...We know that many beings pass between a man and a woman; they come from different worlds, are borne on the wind, form rhizomes around roots; they cannot be understood in terms of production, only in terms of becoming. (Deleuze & Guattari, 1987, 241–2)

These "dark assemblages", paradoxically, appear to be sinister, but are also radical and fraught with the possibility of escaping the stranglehold of the phallus, of discourse, of patriarchy and of the Law of European domination. They are to be contrasted with "organizations such as the institution of the family and the State apparatus" (Deleuze & Guattari, 1987, 242). Instead of the son or the father, the families at the heart of Oedipal subjectivity, there is the sorcerer, and the sorcerer is none other than our writers, who are weary of being sons:

> If the writer is a sorcerer, it is because writing is a becoming, writing is traversed by strange becomings that are not becomings-writer, but becomings-rat, becomings-insect, becomings-wolf, etc. (Deleuze & Guattari, 1987, 240)

If the writer is sorcerer, he is also outsider, ostracised by the respectable citizens. He is Charles imprisoned for Sodomy, Salvador tied to the tree, Salvestro hounded to his self destruction and his mother, murdered as a witch:

> Sorcerers have always held the anomalous position, at the edge of the fields or woods. They haunt the fringes. There are at the borderline of the village, or *between* villages. (Deleuze & Guattari, 1987, 246)

They are the incarcerated madman of *Riven Rock* speaking the language babble of merged, mirrored non-subjectivity and the crazed rhino-man,

Hargreaves, or his 'son', leopard-man Hugh, of *Pieces of Light*. They are "feminized men", "anti heroes" with no way to speak "without lapsing into paranoia" (Sciolino, 158). They will not have sexual relations with women, relations, which could perpetuate families. There are also, and here I must sound a cautionary note, African desert winds and jungle storms, which perpetuate a strange species through the "bacteria sowing contagion", powerfully evoked in William Boyd's *The New Confessions*. Here Boyd ominously entwines the Uncertainty principle with the landscape of Africa. Boyd describes a certain kind of stink ant "that lives on the floor of the West African rain forest":

> In this forest there is a particular type of arboreal fungus that flourishes at the top of the great forest trees. At certain times this fungus releases its millions of spores into the air. ...This one minute fungus spore falls on the stink ant and is absorbed into its ant system.
> It drives the ant mad. Remember the stink ant's habitat is the ground, but the lethal poison of the fungus spore engenders in it the sudden desire to climb. So the stink ant, for the first and last time in its life, leaves the ground and begins to ascend. It climbs up and up, higher and higher, until it can climb no more. There, at the very top of the tree, it sinks its mandibles into the ultimate twig—fast, immovable—and abruptly dies. Inside the dead ant the fungus peacefully grows, nourished by ant meat, warmed by the sunlight at the top of the tree. The ant is consumed and a new fungus is born.
> Sometimes I look back on my life and I feel like a maddened stink ant driven on by my one random fungus spore. Today, I sense, the time has come to sink my mandibles into the bark at the top of the tree. (1989, 471)

The maddened human Becomings-animal-stink-ant reproduces itself like a vampire bat, merging with fungus and tree. The problem, however, which rears its bloodied fangs is that Africa, replete with its stink ants, leopard men and chimps, becomes the ideal explorative experimental space for imagining these strange Becomings, where a spider-like Boyd catches his horseflies, which he transforms into miniature aeroplanes to expose, only ambivalently, the male urge to swing from the dizzy heights of the branches with Tarzan once more. Likewise, it is the North African Desert that is the space chosen by Roscoe as appropriate for his brave quest to empty his mind and heart of the language of Africanist metaphor. Deleuze and Guattari themselves, are to some extent trapped in this Symbolic, Africanist metaphorical landscape at the very moment when they are attempting precisely to provide a manifesto for its annihilation:

> We knew the schizo was not oedipalizable, because he is beyond territoriality, because he has carried his laws right into the desert. (1984, 67, also 102)

And in their later work, as you struggle to reach your Body without Organs, you are "scurrying like a vermin, groping like a blind person, or running like a lunatic: desert traveller and nomad of the steppes" (1987, 150). What does this say to the flesh and blood nomads, whose way of life is thus troped and moulded? Why have Deleuze and Guattari not unravelled the implications of what we could surely call the dregs of the Oedipal Symbolic in their demonstration that "nothing is primal" in the schizo unconscious of Nijinsky, who wrote:

> "I am God I was not God I am a clown of God; I am Apis. *I am an Egyptian. I am a red Indian. I am a Negro.* I am a Chinaman. I am a Japanese, I am a foreigner, a stranger. I am a sea bird. I am a land bird. I am the tree of Tolstoy. I am the roots of Tolstoy. ...I am husband and wife in one. (1984, 77, my emphasis)

And in case we imagine that the inclusion in the list of blacks and foreigners is simply part of the fortuitous metonymic chain, which here includes birds and Tolstoy mutated into tree, they enlarge later, blandly, that "there is no signifying chain without a Chinaman, an Arab, and a black who drop in to trouble the night of a white paranoiac" (Deleuze & Guattari, 1984, 98).

In other words, and perplexingly, Hollinghurst's very choice of the pyramid as the sacred shape which requires de-fetishing, before the English countryside may be claimed, uses African monuments and history for the purposes of enhancing white, male identity. Roscoe, whose perception of the dire necessity of debunking quests in Africa before a new gay liberated man could emerge, simultaneously bonded that liberation to the cleansing effects of the desert and a shard of Orientalised African landscape slips in through the back door. Boyle travelled back in time and space to re-make Mungo Park in a new mould, only to recover his working class persona through the desire to laud it over the pygmies in some idealised African landscape; Norfolk, whose Salvestro is one of the most moving of protagonists in his sadness and his gentle sexuality, inadvertently mythologized Africa as he transplanted a Southern African tragedy into West Africa in different century. This is the labyrinth that continues to discombobulate writers, whose new quest was not for lands, power and jungle kingdoms, not for river sources and lost cities, but precisely for a way out of this labyrinth. They will not beat a path, without speaking a new language.

Speaking in Tongues: Alphabetical Africa

> Once my brother and sister and I had a private language built exclusively upon the names of places. For us, Paris and Rome acted as verbs, Rio de Janeiro as adjective, Singapore as improper noun. We learned long ago that this could be the only way to

> tell our story—through a language where Barcelona means love and Mombasa means sorrow and all gods are summoned by means of prayers that begin something like: Jakarta, Manila, Copenhagen, hallowed be thy name.
> And what did Mexico mean?
> And when did I forget this secret language? (*The Lost Oasis*, 319)

What has become clear is that without confronting language and its cultural metaphors themselves, the tenacity of the discourse surfaces and overwhelms attempts at writing a different version of history from that of the European patriarch. The writers, who stand the best chance of writing an alternative to the old Master text, are those who themselves have come to this insight, writers, in other words, who recognise the imperative of reversing the rhetorical narrative codes, linked to representation in a postcolonial context.

This recognition does not lead to simple alternatives and late twentieth century narrative has been described as being in something of a crisis. For example, we referred to Alice Jardine's discussion of Abish's story in chapter eight. This she did in the context of Jean-Francois Lyotard's postmodernist "incredulity with regard to the master narratives". The consequences of this incredulity are that "the narrative function loses its foundations, the great hero, the great perils; the great quests, and the great goal" (65). She emphasises that the ambivalence with regard to heroic questing is motivated by a "crisis in the status of *knowledge*" (65, her emphasis). And with the absence of God, with Fathers, who are missing, comes a new exploration that "of the figural", or metaphorical, an exploration seen as a necessity "by those philosophers attuned to the violence of technique and its technologies in the twentieth century" (76). Jardine emphasises that "the crises in figurability intrinsic to modernity are numerous and complex:

> For whatever the status of the Father throughout his history, he has served as the ultimate judge, the self-sufficient Idea that has given the Western world its contours. Recent analyses of the demise of the paternal function in the West have therefore not failed to link the presence or absence of his image to the crises in figurability at the roots of modernity. (80)

She then links crises in figurability to a distinction to which I have been returning in this book, namely the difference between metonymy and metaphor (80). And this characterises many of the twentieth century male novels that Jardine analyses. With the abandonment of the quest for the Father, for Meaning, metaphor gives way to metonymy as the preferred dominant mode of writing. For example, in a chapter entitled "The Fault of the Pronouns", Jardine describes how in Philippe Sollers's *Drame,* "the man searching for something…is not *a* man but a textual assemblage of pronouns spinning around an empty space which is to be filled with—no One" (240).

The assemblage of words, classified not according to meaning, but to characteristics such as their parts of speech, their letters of the alphabet, as in dictionaries or encyclopaedias, characterises the randomness of the metonymic. This is why Thomas Pynchon names his first novel after a letter, *V,* and, as we saw in chapter three, sends us on a goose chase of meaningless quests to find the ultimate significance of the letter, precisely in its chance insignificance. In a lovely tiny incident in the novel, Pynchon captures the connections between the body, the phallus, chance and the anti-quest. Profane, one of the protagonists in the novel, whose name already signals his refusal of higher planes, has been sexually fantasising:

> He'd thought himself into an erection. He covered it with the Times classified and waited for it to subside. …
>
> He happened to look down. His erection had produced in the newspaper a crosswise fold, which moved line by line down the page as the swelling gradually diminished. It was a list of employment agencies. OK, thought Profane, just for the heck of it I will close my eyes, count three and open them and whatever agency listing that fold is on I will go to them. It will be like flipping a coin: inanimate schmuck, inanimate paper, *pure chance*. (214–5, my emphasis)

Penis, not phallus, by any stretch, is the dice producing action on the basis of happenstance. What Pynchon is playing with, is the impossibility of language without polluted meaning. Likewise, Don DeLillo has Nick observe in *Underworld*:

> And I thought the problem is the language, I need to change languages, find a word that is pure word, without a lifetime of connotation and shading. (296)

Nick's brother in the novel, the ambivalent nuclear physicist called Matt, says the same thing differently, invoking the desert and the bible, brimming with their cultural meanings, but carrying the random, metonymic flow:

> and the biblical wind that carries sagebrush, sand, hats, cats, car parts, condoms and poisonous snakes, all blowing by the desert dawn (DeLillo, 413)

Or there is the cultural guru, Lenny Bruce in the same novel, comedian and prophet of his age, who shouts the cleansing gibberish into the faces of the property barons, the 'men in full', who have had their day:

> Lenny broke off unexpectedly and leaned into the face of one of the real-estate barons sitting ringside…
> "Mick spic hunky junkie boogie."

> There was no context for the line except the one that Lenny took with him everywhere. *The culture and its loaded words.* He looked around some more. He seemed to need a particular kind of face into which to deliver his scripture.
> One of the college profs smiled invitingly and Lenny obliged with, "Fuck suck fag hag gimme a nickel bag."
> In fact the words were thrilling. (DeLillo, 584–5, my emphasis)

Or as Martina Sciolino puts it, in relation to "the Postmodern 'Masters'" including Pynchon, but here with reference to Donald Barthelme's *The Dead Father*—"Barthelme's desublimation of the quest is carried out by a rhetorical striptease that deflates the metaphorical significance of the object" (161).

Perplexingly, metonymy has been linked both to Realist and Postmodern conventions, but this does make a degree of sense. While nothing is fixed in advance, what is true is that it is Modernism, with its predilection for metaphor and myth, quests and dark hearts concealing black horrors, that tends towards reinforcing colonialist discourse. This is the discourse that these weary sons have tried hard to explode. This is not to fall back on conventions of Classical Realism or to worship the sexy, experimental acrobatics of Postmodernism. It is to say, that an awareness of the evil ends to which figurative language has been put, as it manipulates Africa and Africans, means that sometimes a detailed and realistic and historical treatment of the subject may avoid such puppet-mastering. It means, paradoxically and at the opposite end of the language scale from Realism, that the Postmodern exposure of the mechanics of words for the assemblages they are, could alert the reader to the machinations of discourse.

Fred Pfeil's argument once again has resonance here when he indicates that the surprising fractures and dents to traditional manhood in some popular movies is brought about by the fact that these male rampage films are "surprisingly postmodernist" (1998, 147). Pfeil examines what these films' "*formal* postmodernity…might signify" (1998, 171). What precisely makes these films postmodern is explained best in the Coda to the paper of 1996, when Pfeil adds *Pulp Fiction* to his list of male rampage movies. This film "gives up all pretence of offering us…an authorized developed narrative" (1998, 181). In it we have

> the devolution of the white male protagonist himself into an only peripherally related assortment of white boys (Travolta's Vince, Willis's Butch, Tim Roth's Pumpkin) cruising around their landscapes of interchangeable parts splattered here and there with the messes they make, and laced with their hilariously obscene yet *insipid dialogue, itself the verbal equivalent of the gelatinous world* they drift across. (1998, 181, my emphasis)

That "insipid" dialogue, bereft of meaning, is the predominance of the metonymic, precisely reflecting the fact that these outlaws have not entirely entered the Symbolic and achieved subjectivity by way of the Phallus (although Pfeil possibly goes too far in his wishful optimism of transformed masculinity). Pfeil relates the anomy of these films quite precisely to a fracturing of the Oedipal story and a process whereby

> a once organic interrelationship between nationality, territoriality, and authorized Fordist-Oedipal man and the whole economy of pleasure based upon it, fall away in the face of a new postnational landscape of giddy de-rangements, zigzagged across by so many deauthorized, pre-Oedipal/post-Fordist, havoc-wreaking guys offering us a new set of kicks. (1998, 181)

Instead of wreaking havoc, what politically sophisticated writers, like Walter Abish, attempt to do is to explore creatively the politics of this metonymic, postmodern language of random proximities, of alphabets, lists, strangers and coincidences. In this way, they hope to free the deep language of our subjectivity, which has been forged in a polluted unconscious. But we have seen, over and again, how difficult this is in practice, and how the discourse tends to enter through the back door, no sooner have the writers bolted and sealed up the front entrance.

After the breakdown of old tropes, new meanings emerge, new metaphors are forged. But are they new? Does the empty space loom out of the page and become sand dune and pyramid, North Africa, populated by lepers and beggars, whose landscapes offer dangerous old metaphors in place of eagerly sought new languages?

Language in *The Lost Oasis* was twisted into the distorted metaphors of the crazy father, whose wounded children landed up in asylums, missing or secreted in gay closets. All three of those children inhabited a world in which

> around us jangle words and music we do not understand; to be surrounded by strangeness is for us the most natural condition. Arabic, Swahili, Hindi: take your pick. (320)

These languages of the world, which produce meaning and subjectivity for their native speakers, are for these children the meaningless sing-song of the jangle. And as Richard battles against the distorted subjectivity bonded to acquiring that strange language of their own, he first has to empty words of meaning and the Law of its Religious significance. Ultimately, however, the light of this lost oasis is a new religion, new Law that cuts across the established Orders and is given in the nursery rhyme rhythm of metonymy:

> The blanket floats around my shoulders like the robes of a new religion whose God is summoned by a prayer that begins: Tan-Tan, Tarfaya, Layounne, hallowed be thy name. And Smara is heaven and Dakhla is hell, and from the sand rises a transparent cathedral or synagogue or mosque, reaching among the stars, curving through heaven's vast vault. (322)

Muslim, Catholic, or Jew, whatever. Nonetheless, from the desert sand arises new Laws, a holy place, whose liberated transparency signifies the obliteration of the cramped, colonial, gay hotel rooms, pyramids and closets. And here is the conundrum. This opening out into the light, induced by the metonymic emptying of prior meaning, takes place through the mechanism of the metaphor, the old Africanist trope, of emptiness, embodied in Africa in general and the North African Desert in particular. At the same time, Roscoe opposed this old troping with his lovely, concrete building, that of the commonplace Café Oasis, a tearoom offering sustenance in place of Mitch's dangerous metaphorical lost desert utopia.

When Deleuze and Guattari proposed their "fundamental difference between psychoanalysis and schizoanalysis", they emphasised that the latter "attains a nonfigurative and nonsymbolic unconscious" (1984, 351). This brings us back to the distinction between the metaphoric and the embedded tropes of colonial discourse, as contrasting with the more literal and potentially more liberated use of literal language.

The alternative to creating new meaning is to butcher narrative to the point that what we have is unreadable. And indeed there are many such "novels" where scholars may grit their teeth and sweat through texts without characters or events, but such works betray one of fiction's sacred briefs, which is to engage and compel the reader. One such miserable book is the novel that Abish published the year before the short story collection came out, a novel, which expresses his determination to delay metaphor indefinitely, his uncompromisingly metonymic *Alphabetical Africa*. Abish says on the back cover that he wrote it "feeling a distrust of the understanding that is intrinsic to any communication" (1974). That is all very well, but communicate writers must, and a book which starts "only with words beginning with the letter A, then incorporates words beginning with B, so adding until the repertoire fills, and then empties again, as he takes away letters one by one" (Bradbury, xi), is very unpleasant to read, even if it makes its point about the dangers of narrative and of meaning. *Alphabetical Africa* ends with lists of 'anothers' and only words beginning with the letter 'A':

> Another avid avowal another awareness another awakening another awesome age another axis another Alva another Alex another Allen another Alfred another Africa another alphabet. (1974, 152)

The conundrum persists. To abandon quests, meaning, language, plot and narrative, may empty life of its colour, spirituality and purpose. To embrace all of these is to risk conscription into dubious ventures and voyages, unjust wars and lost causes.

Finally, therefore, having cast aspersion on Abish's alphabet of Africa, I would like to remember how fine is the project, and how hard the task, of abolishing the old meanings. I will pay homage to Abish's, Roscoe's and Norfolk's alphabetic acrobatics by hazarding a concluding one of my own.

A Weary Son of the Century: an Imaginary Biography

A challenge that is irresistible for a book researched over two different centuries and written within the midst of millennial fever, is to construct an imaginary figure of the aware and reconstituted late twentieth century white male writer, with a special interest in Africa. Mary Louise Pratt in her book, *Imperial Eyes*, undertook this task and constructs a wonderful image of the eighteenth century Enlightenment man, the ambivalent and contradictory "Anti Conquest" man, who is as much gentle naturalist as imperial pawn. Pratt's archetype of this man is none other than Mungo Park, the inspiration behind T. Coraghessan Boyle's first full-length novel, *Water Music*. This figure is more the ancestor of our writers than his late nineteenth century counterpart, "the all seeing man", whose hunting, conquering and acquisitive impulses were more suited to the age of the official "scramble" for African possessions (Pratt, 1992).

But how to approach such a daunting task? The device of the alphabet, the figure of Nat Tate and the genre of the fictional biography, presented a possibility. Lawrence Norfolk used the device of the dictionary in his first novel in ways that enabled him to demonstrate in language, what he was grappling with in history and politics. He uses the device again in the much smaller, journalistic piece entitled "A Bosnian Alphabet" (1993). He describes the Bosnian conflict by the staccato and disjointed mechanism of taking us through his apparently random, disconnected thoughts, triggered only by the next letter, yet paradoxically he felt that this mechanism provided an appropriate structure—"A should be for Alphabet: the device I am resorting to in some desperation *to structure my thoughts* on this subject" (1993, 213, my emphasis). What he likes about this structure "is its transparency" (1993, 213). It is transparent, as we have seen in foregoing chapters where we have touched on the use of metonymy rather than metaphor, in the sense of restoring the visible tools of the language and refusing the dominant fictions of the age.

Coincidences continue to intrigue me. I was reading the *Times Literary Supplement* and on the same page as a review of Norfolk's *Lemprière's Dictionary*, my wondering eye happened to catch a review of a book by

Julian Symons called *Portraits of the Missing: Imaginary Biographies*, in which the reviewer, J.K.L. Walker, tells us that Symons warns the reader "not to seek to identify any single individual":

> The characters, he tells us, are composite figures in which "the characteristics of two or three people have gone to the making of each biography, along with fragments of their lives". (21)

This brought Nat Tate to mind. Who is he? In 1998, William Boyd, whose *Brazzaville Beach* was the focus of chapter five, published his *Nat Tate: An American Artist: 1928–1960*. Apparently the biography of this minor artist, replete with photographs and acknowledgements, was a great hoax, a take off of the art world. Or was it? Nat Tate may have been a fiction of Boyd's mind, but we learn a great deal about Boyd himself, his fears about his writing, his aspirations as a minor artist himself, and his dislocated roots, in terms of his own sense of belonging. William Boyd uses the fictional biography of Nat Tate to write a fragment of the autobiography of William Boyd.

I now beg the indulgence of my reader to allow me to play a little as my study draws to its close.

A stands for **Adam**, not the biblical, Oedipal first man, originator of humanity, but late twentieth century man, wizard, schizo-writer, like Adam Thorpe, whose fiction demonstrated how white men can write, and have written, interestingly and wisely about Africa. Adam is also, coincidentally, the name of my son, one of the people acknowledged in this book.

B is for **Books**. Adam is an intellectual. He is enormously well read. He attended Cambridge University, about which he is quite dismissive. He is ambivalent about all of his book learning and will, on occasion, indulge in a degree of self-hatred in this regard. He has strong moral principles, but balks before notions of Truth or Absolutes.

C is for **Cyborgs**. Adam is bonded to his computer and is a late twentieth century cyber-traveller. As an insider/outsider to his own society, he metamorphoses in his mind travels. Not the creator of Frankenstein monsters, that modernist project of the search for boundaries and ethics, but as a postmodern man, flying free and changing form, he experiences his identity as unstable. He is a wolf, a rat, an insect, a Robocop. He is beefcake Schwarzenegger only in his most shameful and secret fantasies. Sometimes he is weird and mutters obscenities, or some kind of strange gibberish.

D is for **Damaged**. It is not for **Darkness**, as in **Heart of** as he is aware of those pitfalls and studiedly avoids the most obvious one of all. His Africa is not dark, although it sometimes is the other bad things he is also trying very hard to avoid. Adam experiences his body as imperfect. When he becomes a rat or an insectoid, it is his body that he perceives as remaining true to its puny self. He would rather die than admit it, but he wonders about the legends relating to black bodies.

E is for **Emotional**. Although he finds this hard, and his upbringing and education discouraged it, Adam tries to be close to his feelings and to express them. His writing helps, and the fact that, also not true to form, he has learnt to bond with other men and to talk about his fears and inadequacies with them.

F is for **Feminist**. Adam believes passionately in the equality of women and is a reconstituted husband and father. He shares the burden of domestic chores and childcare, although he sometimes secretly envies colleagues, who have more 'traditional' arrangements. He is however, quite afraid of powerful career women, especially when he feels criticised by them. He resents being criticised simply because he is a white man—how can he help that?

G is for **Green Movement**. Adam, like Adam Thorpe, his namesake, is an environmentalist and although he is a city man, who lives in London and loves the architecture of American high-rise, he is firmly rooted in his devotion to the English countryside. Funnily enough, having rejected much of the values and ethics of his family and Cambridge cohorts, he shares this love with them. He also has read and is well informed about rain forests and conservation debates in the Third World. When he thinks about the earth, he has a global perspective, which he tries to make as concrete as possible, understanding as he does that myths of darkness or light have played an unsavoury and imperialistic role. However, when he plays with the fantasy of roaming free, of finding himself on the edge of the planet, he involuntarily pictures the desert.

H is for **Horror,** which both is, and is not "The horror! The horror!" (See **darkness**, above). The horror is of the lepers and the leopard men, the archetypal terrors and ghosts returning as the repressed fears of white society, fears that Adam has not entirely exorcised.

I is for **Identity**. There is a genuine problem with regard to his male identity, as Adam lives through an era of gender transformation. He questions what it means to be male when many of the defining body and economic functions have come under scrutiny and yet he needs an outlet to define his manhood. He does not wish to be a soft man and is too old to be a hippie, but neither is he a patriarch in the mould of his father. He does not feel that women are able to assist in this identity crisis as, by definition, this reinforces his sense of loss of empowerment in relation to his partner. Black men, who do not form part of the cabal of white male power, are the friends with whom he feels most comfortable in his search for an alternative role, one which has him neither pecked by hens nor whooping from the tops of faraway trees.

J is for **Juju**, the West African concept of the fetish. Adam is a very secular man, believing neither in god, nor in magic. He eschews superstition, but has tremendous respect for the beliefs and customs, particularly of people coming from very different backgrounds from his own. He is less tolerant of people's religious convictions, which were once his own and from which he has departed. This presents a bit of a perplexing situation where juju is concerned. He will be careful about dismissing such belief as primitive (the 'p' word does not cross his lips) but he will work hard to de-mystify and de-fetishize myths, icons, metaphors and Master texts for the props and evil weapons that they are.

K is for **Kind**, which Adam is very. He is a gentle person, who wishes to do right in the world. I like and trust him a lot, more, I suspect, than he likes and trusts me.

L is for **Language**, which is his passion and his prison, and this he knows. He tries to find a tongue for speaking that does not tie him to the voice of his father. Like me, he has become interested in alphabets. He knows that if his writing is to be truly transformational, liberating it and himself from Empire, it has to find new ways of speaking and not simply new things to speak about.

M is for **Machine**, which, cyborg that he is, takes on an organic characteristic in his existence. He writes on a machine; his home is wired up with labour saving devices, whose rhythm and cycle merge with his sense self of body and of self. He may write about Africa, and visit it fictionally, but he is the product of the most technologically advanced sites of the information age.

N is for **Nervous**. Adam has bouts of depression and fear and these emanate from his sense of dislocation from the culture and language of his Fathers. He worries about being a rat and about fantasising about mating with a wolf and about the gibberish that sometimes overtakes his stream of consciousness.

O is for **Opaque**, which colours his world. He is not filled with certainties, yet, unlike some of his postmodern fellow writers, Adam believes in discovering purpose and defending a moral code. Purpose and morality, however, are not light as opposed to darkness, but the shade of opaque.

P is for **Penis** and not for Phallus. Adam hates the fetish of the phallus and would like to be liberated from it. However, he does not know what to substitute and still labours under the worry that his concrete, flesh and blood penis may not be adequate in his world, which is no longer bolstered by traditional male power.

Adam's **Q** for **Quest**, is, partly, to re-think his body. Questing is for Hunters, Adventurers on the High Seas, Tarzan and Cecil John Rhodes. Not entirely recognising the nature of his own quests, and yet needing big goals and worthy purpose, within his crisis of male identity, makes him ambivalent about the dreams of his rejected forefathers.

R is for **Race** and one of the most interesting things about Adam is that he fully appreciates the fact he is a man of a colour, which is called white. In other words, he does not regard himself as the neutral norm and is aware that he is gendered male and has enjoyed the privileges of his European background. This gives him a very attractive humility.

S is for **Son**, which he is ambivalently. Adam thinks he may have been adopted. He has nothing in common with his father and dreads Christmas and family gatherings. He is a son in name only and is sure that he is a different kind of father to his own children.

T is for **Tactful** in the sense outlined in the introduction to this book. He writes about faraway people and places, but does so with the awareness of his own race and gender, history and background and attempts to capture this humility in his fiction. He also achieves this grace through his unflinching acknowledgement of the inadvertent benefits that have accrued to him, as part of the white, male, Western world. This is the basis of his acceptance of collusion and also underlies his tactfulness, which is politically profound.

U is for **Underworld**, a space that draws Adam as the flip side of the deserts of Africa. If Africa is vast space, then London, the city he lives in, is vertical, high and low and it is in digging beneath the foundations of the city that his buried and archetypal fears are to be found, full of scurrying rats and unconscious fears.

V is for the **Vermin** that populate Adam's underworld, which occupy his nightmares and signify his identity dilemmas.

W is for **Weary**, the exhaustion that overtakes him in the face of all the work of re-making, re-thinking and re-talking.

X is for **Xantippe**, querulous and nagging wife of Socrates, who stands for all quarrelsome women and is the fear and horror of men like Adam, who cannot deal with this conflict in the Patriarchal ways of their fathers, but have not discovered other defences at hand.

Y is for **Yamasaki**, the architect, who designed the World Trade Center in New York. Adam has written a journalistic piece about him, which was published in *Granta*. Adam found the vision of this extraordinary architect intriguing and inspiring. Yamasaki is one of the new brand of urban explorers—he is an astronaut, who has scaled vertical frontiers and risen above the depths of the underworld.

Z is for **Zaire**, the post-independence name for the Congo, site of the *Heart of Darkness*. It is a concrete place, which Adam wishes to portray realistically in his writing. He attempts to purge it of the image of the dark heart, against whose grain he tries to write. He has confronted his past with a full frontal gaze at his scarred nakedness; he has identified these scars as the marks of his white man's burden. Son of Conrad, he is weary of shouldering this load.

BIBLIOGRAPHY

Abish, Walter, 1974, *Alphabetical Africa*, New Directions Books, New York.
——, 1977, "Crossing the Great Void", *In the Future Perfect*, New Directions Books, New York, 98–113.
Achebe, Chinua, 1991, "African Literature as Restoration of Celebration", in Petersen, Kirsten Holst & Rutherford, Anna (eds.) *Chinua Achebe: A Celebration*, Heinemann & Dangeroo Press, London & Sydney, 1–10.
Adams, Elizabeth, 1991, "An Interview with T. Coraghessan Boyle", *Chicago Review*, 37.2–3, 51–63.
Aijaz, Ahmad, 1992, *In Theory*, Verso, London.
Althusser, Louis, 1971, *Lenin and Philosophy*, New Left Books, London.
Animal People, 1997, Editorial, "Them Bones, Them Bones," Jan./Feb. http://www.*animalpepl.org/97/1/editorial.html*
Appadurai, Arjun, 1993, "The Heart of Whiteness", *Callaloo*, 16.4, 796–807.
Appignanesi, Lisa & Maitland, Sara (eds.) 1989, *The Rushdie File*, ICA, London.
Ashcroft, W.D., 1989, "Is That the Congo? Language as Metonymy in the Post-Colonial Text", *World Literature Written in English*, Vol. 29, No. 2, 3–10.
http://www.*awerty.com/divine.html*
Bann, Stephen, 1990, "From Captain Cook to Neil Armstrong: Colonial Exploration and the Structure of Landscape", in Pugh, Simon, (ed.) *Reading Landscape: Country-City-Capital*, Manchester University Press, 214–230.
Barrell, John, 1980, *The Dark Side of Landscape: The Rural Poor in English Painting 1730—1840*, Cambridge University Press.
Barthes, Roland, 1979, *The Eiffel Tower and other Mythologies*, Hill & Wang, New York.
Bedini, Silvio A., 1997, *The Pope's Elephant*, Carcanet Press, Manchester.
Beer, Gillian, 1983, *Darwin's Plots: Evolutionary Narrative in Darwin, George Eliot and Nineteenth-Century Fiction*, Routledge and Kegan Paul, London.

Bermingham, Ann, 1986, *Landscape and Ideology: The English Rustic Tradition, 1740—1860*, University of California Press, Los Angeles.
Bhabha, Homi K., 1994a, "Signs Taken for Wonders: Questions of ambivalence and authority under a tree outside Delhi, May 1817", *The Location of Culture*, Routledge, London, 102–122.
——, 1994b, "How newness enters the world: Postmodern space, postcolonial times and the trials of cultural translation", *The Location of Culture*, Routledge, London, 212–235.
Bilston, John, 1992, "Chronicles of Albion, Adam Thorpe, *Ulverton*", *Times Literary Supplement*, May 8, 20.
Boehmer, Elleke, 1995, *Colonial and Postcolonial Literature*, Oxford University Press, Oxford.
Boone, Joseph A., 1995, "Vacation Cruises; or, The Homoerotics of Orientalism", *PMLA* 110.1, 89–107.
Boyd, William, 1981, *A Good Man in Africa*, Penguin Books, London.
——, 1989, *The New Confessions*, Penguin Books, London.
——, 1990, *Brazzaville Beach*, Penguin Books, London.
——, 1992, "A Pole Apart," *Transition*, no.55, 74–178.
——, 1993, *The Blue Afternoon*, Penguin Books, London.
——, 1995, "A Man of Peace Condemned by a Cynical Tyranny," *Sunday Times*, November 12, 22.
——,1998a, *Armadillo*, Hamish Hamilton, London.
——, 1998b, *Nat Tate: An American Artist: 1928–1960*, 21 Publishing Ltd, Cambridge.
Boyle, T. Coraghessan, 1981, *Water Music*, Granta Books, London.
——, 1986, *Greasy Lake & other Stories*, Penguin, London.
——, 1987, "Descent of Man," in *Descent of Man*, Penguin, London, 3–16.
——, 1989, "The Ape Lady in Retirement," in *If the River wasWhiskey*, Penguin, London, 193–213.
——, 1994, *Without a Hero & other Stories*, Viking.
——, 1998, *Riven Rock*, Bloomsbury, London.
Bradbury, Malcolm, 1977, "Introduction" in Abish, Walter, *In the Future Perfect*, New Directions Books, New York, ix–xiii.
Britannica Micropaedia, 1993 edition, No. 4, 548.
——, No. 9, 1993 edition, 445.
——, No. 1, 1993 edition, 559.
——, No. 18, 1993 edition, 490.
Brookner, Anita, 1990, "Catastrophe but not the Death of Hope", *The Spectator*, September 15, 38.
Bryld, Mette & Lykke, Nina, 1999, *Cosmodolphins: Feminist Cultural Studies of Technology, Animals and the Sacred*, Zed Books, London.

Bunn, David, 1994, "'Our Wattled Cot': Mercantile and Domestic Space in Thomas Pringle's African Landscapes", in Mitchell, W.J.T., (ed.), *Landscape and Power*, University of Chicago Press, Chicago, 127–173.

Burroughs, Edgar Rice, 1920 [1917], *Tarzan of the Apes*, Methuen, New York.

Casarino, Cesare, 1994, *The Voyages of Heterotopia: Meditations on Modernity, Crisis and the Sea*, Doctor of Philosophy Dissertation, The Literature Program in the Graduate School, Duke University.

——, 1997, "The Sublime of the Closet; or, Joseph Conrad's Secret Sharing", *Boundary* 2, 24.2 (Summer), 199–243.

Caute, David, 1998, *Fatima's Scarf*, Totterdown Books, London.

Chambers, Iain, 1996, "Signs of Silence, Lines of Listening", in Chambers, Iain & Curti, Lidia, (eds.) *The Post-Colonial Question: Common Skies, Divided Horizons*, Routledge, London, 47–62.

Chambers, Ross, 1993, "Messing Around: Gayness and Loiterature in Alan Hollinghurst's *The Swimming-Pool Library*", in Still, Judith & Wonton, Michael, (eds.) *Textuality and Sexuality: Reading Theories and Practices*, Manchester University Press, Manchester, 207–217.

Chapman, Rowena, 1988, "The Great Pretender: Variations on the New Man Theme", in Chapman, Rowena & Rutherford, Jonathan (eds.) *Male Order: Unwrapping Masculinity*, Lawrence & Wishart, London, 225–248.

Cheyfitz, Eric, 1997, *The Poetics of Imperialism: Translation and Colonization from The Tempest to Tarzan*, University of Pennsylvania Press, Philadelphia.

Clement, Catherine, 1987 [1978], *The Weary Sons of Freud*, Verso, London.

Connell, R.W., 1995, *Masculinities*, Polity Press, Oxford.

Conrad, Joseph, 1961 [1912], *The Secret Sharer, An Episode from the Coast*, in *The Nigger of the Narcissus and other tales*, Oxford University Press, Oxford.

——, 1987 [1988], *Heart of Darkness*, Ad Donker, Cape Town.

Cooper, Brenda, 1992, *To Lay These Secrets Open*, David Philip, Cape Town.

——, 1998, *Magical Realism in West African Fiction: Seeing with a Third Eye*, Routledge, London.

Core, Philip, 1984, *Camp. The Lie that Tells the Truth*, Delilah Books, New York.

Cosgrove, Denis, 1998 [1984], *Social Formation and Symbolic Landscape*, The University of Wisconsin Press, Wisconsin.

Cover, Rob, 1999, "Queer with Class: Absence of Third World Sweatshop in Lesbian/Gay Discourse and a Rearticulation of Materialist Queer Theory", *Ariel*, 30.2 (April), 29–48.

Daniels, Stephen, 1988, "The Political Iconography of Woodland in later Georgian England", in Cosgrove, Denis & Daniels, Stephen, (eds.) *The Iconography of Landscape: Essays on the Symbolic Representation, Design and Use of Past Environments*, Cambridge University Press, Cambridge.
——, 1993, *Fields of Vision: Landscape Imagery and National Identity in England and the United States*, Polity Press, Oxford.
Deleuze, Gilles, & Guattari, Felix,1984 [1972], *Anti-Oedipus: Capitalism and Schizophrenia*, The Athlone Press, London.
——, 1987 [1980], *A Thousand Plateaus*, The University of Minnesota Press, Minneapolis.
Dellamora, Richard, 1993, "Textual Politics/Sexual Politics", *Modern Language Quarterly*, 54.1 (March), 155–164.
——, 1994, *Apocalyptic Overtures: Sexual Politics and the Sense of an Ending*, Rutgers University Press, New Brunswick, New Jersey.
DeLillo, Don, 1999 [1997], *Underworld*, Picador, London.
deMan, Paul, 1979, *Allegories of Reading: Figural Language in Rousseau, Nietzsche, Rilke, and Proust*, Yale University Press, New Haven.
Denina, Chris, 1997, "Will the real Boyle please stand up?" *Daily Trojan Diversions*, Tuesday, October 7th, Vol.132, No.27, 1–8.
Dreifus, Claudia, 1999, "Jane of the Jungle", *Modern Maturity*, Nov. — Dec., 1–8.
Dukes, Thomas, 1996, "'Mappings of Secrecy and Disclosure': *The Swimming-Pool Library*, the Closet, and the Empire", *Journal of Homosexuality*, 31.3, 95–107.
Dunn, Douglas, 1993, "Divergent Scottishness: William Boyd, Alan Massie, Ronald Frame," in Wallace, Gavin & Stevenson, Randall, (eds.) *The Scottish Novel Since the Seventies: New Visions, Old Dreams*, Edinburgh University Press, Edinburgh, 149–169.
Durham, Deborah & Fernandez, James W., 1991, "Tropical Dominions: The Figurative Struggle over Domains of Belonging and Apartness in Africa", in Fernandez, James W., *Beyond Metaphor: The Theory of Tropes in Anthropology*, Stanford University Press, Stanford, 190–210.
Dyer, Richard, 1997, *White*, Routledge, London.
Edwards, Thomas R, 1991, "Good Intentions", *The New York Review of Books*, October 10, 33–4.
Fabian, Johannes, 1983, *Time and the Other: How Anthropology Makes Its Object*, Columbia University Press, New York.
Farki, Neville, 1985, *The Death of Tarzana Clayton*, Karnak House, London.
Fleck, Linda L., 1998, "From Metonymy to Metaphor: Paul Auster's *Leviathan*", *Critique*, Spring, vol.39, no.3, 258–270.

Flynn, Michael, 1997, "Searching for Alternatives: Autobiography and Masculinity at the Bimillennium", in Strozier, Charles, B., & Flynn, Michael, (eds.) *The Year 2000: Essays on the End*, New York University Press, New York, 239–249.

Forster, E. M., 1972, *The Life To Come and Other Stories*, Edward Arnold, London.

Foucault, Michel, 1986 [1967], "Of Other Spaces", *diacritics*/spring, Vol.16, 22–27.

French, Sean, 1990, "Divergence Syndromes", *New Statesman*, September 14, 38–9.

Friend, Tad, 1990, "Rolling Boyle", *New York Times Magazine*, Dec. 9, 50, 64–68.

Fuchs, Cynthia, J., 1993, "'Death Is Irrelevant': Cyborgs, Reproduction, and the Future of Male Hysteria", *Genders*, No. 18, Winter, 113–133.

Galligan, David, 1997, "Beneath the Surface of *The Swimming-Pool Library*: An Interview with Alan Hollinghurst", *The James White Review*, 14.3, 1, 3–7.

——, 1998, "On Hampstead Heath: An Interview with Alan Hollinghurst", *The James White Review*, 15.1, 10–13.

Gifford, Terry, 1999, *Pastoral*, Routledge, London.

Gikandi, Simon, 1996, *Maps of Englishness: Writing Identity in the Culture of Colonialism*, Columbia University Press, New York.

Gilman, Sander, 1992, *Difference and Pathology: Stereotypes of Sexuality, Race and Madness*, Cornell University Press, Ithaca.

Goodchild, Philip, 1996, *Deleuze & Guattari: An Introduction to the Politics of Desire*, Sage Publications, London.

Gorra, Michael, 1991, "Tact and Tarzan", *Transition*, no.52, 80–91.

——, 1997, *After Empire: Scott, Naipaul, Rushdie*, The University of Chicago Press, Chicago.

Graeber, Laurel,1994, "Truth, Fiction and Achondroplasia", *New York Times Book Review*, Sept. 4, 1994, 1, 22.

Greenblatt, Stephen, 1980, *Renaissance Self-Fashioning: From Moore to Shakespeare*, University of Chicago Press, Chicago.

Gruesser, John Cullen, 1992, *White on Black: Contemporary Literature about Africa*, University of Illinois Press, Urbana, Illinois.

Hagenauer, Sabine, 1996, "An Interview with Adam Thorpe", http://webdoc.sub.gwdg.de/edoc/ia/eese/artic96/hagenau/396.html, 1–9.

Hall, Kim F., 1995, *Things of Darkness: Economies of Race and Gender in Early Modern England*, Cornell University Press, Ithaca.

Hall, Stuart, 1996, "When was 'The Post-Colonial'? Thinking at the Limit", in Chambers, Iain & Curti, Lidia, (eds.) *The Post-Colonial Question: Common Skies, Divided Horizons*, Routledge, London, 242–260.

Haraway, Donna, 1989, *Primate Visions: Gender, Race and Nature in the World of Modern Science*, Routledge, London.
——, 1991, *Simians, Cyborgs and Women: The Reinvention of Nature*, Free Association Books, London.
——, 1992, "The Promises of Monsters: A Regenerative Politics for Inappropriate/d Others," in Grossberg, Lawrence, Nelson, Cary, & Treichler, Paula A., (eds.) *Cultural Studies*, Routledge, London, 295–337.
——, 1997a, *Modest-Witness @ Second-Millennium. FemaleMan_Meets—OncoMouseTM: Feminism and Technoscience*, Routledge, London.
——, 1997b, "Mice into Wormholes/A Comment on the Nature of No Nature", in LeeDowney, Gary, & Dumit, Joseph, (eds.) *Cyborgs & Citadels*, School of American Research Press, J. Santa Fe, 209–243.
Hayles, Katherine, 1990, *Chaos Bound: Orderly Disorder in Contemporary Literature and Science*, Cornell University Press, Ithaca.
Heiland, Donna, 1997, "Historical Subjects: Recent Fiction about the Eighteenth Century", *Eighteenth-Century Life*, 21, February, 108 – 122.
Hickey, Dennis & Wylie, Kenneth C., 1993, *An Enchanting Darkness: The American Vision of Africa in the Twentieth Century*, Michigan State University Press, Ann Arbor.
Høeg, Peter, 1994, *Miss Smilla's Feeling for Snow*, Flamingo, London.
   1996, *The Woman and the Ape*, Harvill Press, London.
Hollinghurst, Alan, 1980, "The Creative Uses of Homosexuality in the Novels of E.M. Forster, Ronald Firbank and L.P. Hartley", M.Litt. thesis, Bodleian Library, Oxford University.
——, 1983, "A Thieving Boy", *Firebird 2: Writing Today*, Penguin Books, London, 95 – 109.
——, 1989a, *The Swimming-Pool Library*, Vintage, London.
——, 1989b, "Dry Season Nights" in Christopher Reid, (ed.) *The Poetry Book Society Anthology, 1989–1990*, Hutchinson, London, 54.
——, 1998, *The Spell*, Chatto and Windus, London.
Ignatiev, Noel, 1995, *How the Irish Became White*, Routledge, London.
Illich, Ivan, 1987, "A Plea for Body History", *Michigan Quarterly Review*, 26.2 (Spring), 342–348.
Irving, John, 1994, *A Son of the Circus*, Bloomsbury, London.
Jakobson, Roman & Halle, Morris, 1956, *The Fundamentals of Language*, Mouton, The Hague.
Jameson, Fredric, 1988, "Periodizing the 60s", *The Ideology of Theory Essays 1971–1986, Volume 2: Syntax of History*, Routledge, London, 178–208.
——, 1991, *Postmodernism or the Cultural Logic of Late Capitalism*, Duke University Press, Durham.

Jardine, Alice, 1985, *Gynesis: Configurations of Woman and Modernity*, Cornell University Press, Ithaca.
Jensen, Hal, 1998, "Pastoral in Passing: Alan Hollinghurst *The Spell*", *Times Literary Supplement*, June 28th, 25.
Jordan, Justine, 1998, "*Pieces of Light* by Adam Thorpe", *London Review of Books*, 29 October, 25.
Kayo, Patrice, 1984, "Song of the Initiate", in Moore, Gerald & Beier, Ulli, (eds.) *The Penguin Book of Modern African Poetry*, Penguin, London, 55.
Keates, Jonathan, 1996, "A Monster for the Medici", *Times Literary Supplement*, April 26, 21.
Keller, Evelyn Fox, 1992, *Secrets of Life, Secrets of Death: Essays on Language, Gender and Science*, Routledge, London.
Keough, Peter, 1996, "Oeuvrestuffed", Boston Phoenix Online, Oct., 1–2. http://www.*bostonphoenix.com/alt1.archive/books/reviews/10–96/ POPE.html*
Kingsley, Mary H., 1900 [1897], *Travels in West Africa*, Macmillan, London.
Koven, Seth, 1992, "From Rough Lads to Hooligans: Boy Life, National Culture and Social Reform", in Parker, Andrew, Russo, Mary, Sommer, Doris & Yaeger, Patricia, (eds.) *Nationalisms and Sexualities*, Routledge, London, 365–391.
Kurth, Peter, 1998, "*Riven Rock* by T. Coraghessan Boyle," Salon Magazine, Jan. 28, 1–3. http://www.*salonmagazine.com/books/sneaks/1998/ 01/28review.html*
Lacan, Jacques, 1977, "Preface" in Lemaire, Anika, *Jacques Lacan*, Routlege & Kegan Paul, London, vii–xv.
Lanchester, John, 1988, "Catch 28", *London Review of Books*, 3 March, 11–12.
Lane, Christopher, 1995, *The Ruling Passion: British Allegory and the Paradox of Homosexual Desire*, Duke University Press, Durham.
LeBihan, Jill, 1992, "Gorilla Girls and Chimpanzee Mothers: Sexual and Cultural Identity in the Primatologist's Field", *Journal of Commonwealth Literature*, 27, no. 1, 139–148.
Lemaire, Anika, 1977, *Jacques Lacan*, Routlege & Kegan Paul, London.
Levine, June Perry, 1984, "The Tame in Pursuit of the Savage: The Posthumous Fiction of E.M. Forster", *PMLA*, 99.1, (January), 72–88.
Lock, Charles, 1999, "Sentenced to the Century: The Novels of Adam Thorpe", *Anglofiles,* No. 110, February, 25–27.
Lodge, David, 1977, *The Modes of Modern Writing*, Edward Arnold, London.
Lorenz, Konrad, 1966, *On Aggression*, Methuen, New York.

Low, Gail Ching-Liang, 1996, *White Skins, Black Masks: Representation and Colonialism*, Routledge, London.
McCaffery, Larry, 1982, "An Interview with John Irving", *Contemporary Literature*, 23(1), Winter, 1–18.
McClintock, Anne, 1995, *Imperial Leather*, Routledge, London.
Mercer, Kobena, 1991, "Looking for Trouble", *Transition*, No. 51, 184–197.
——, 1992, "'1968': Periodizing Postmodern Politics and Identity", in Grossberg, Lawrence, Nelson, Cary & Treichler, Paula A., (eds.) *Cultural Studies*, Routledge, London, 424–438.
——, 1994, *Welcome to the Jungle: New Positions in Black Cultural Studies*, Routledge, London.
Miller, Christopher L., 1985, *Blank Darkness: Africanist Discourse in French*, University of Chicago Press, Chicago.
Mitchell, W.J.T., 1994, "Imperial Landscape", in Mitchell, W.J.T., (ed.) *Landscape and Power*, University of Chicago Press, 5–34.
Moore, Steven, 1996, "The Beast in the Vatican", *Washington Post Online*, Sept. 15, 1–3. http://washingtonpost.com/wp-srv/style/longterm/books/review /popes rhinoceros.html
Mudimbe, V.Y., 1988, *The Invention of Africa*, Indiana University Press, Bloomington.
——, 1994, *The Idea of Africa*, Indiana University Press, Bloomington.
Ngugi, wa Thiong'o, 1981, *Writers in Politics*, Heinemann, London.
Norfolk, Lawrence, 1991, *Lempriere's Dictionary*, Harmony Books, New York.
——, 1993, "A Bosnian Alphabet", in Buford, Bill, (ed.) <u>Granta</u>, London, 43, 213–222.
——, 1994, "The Honesty of Pagemonsters", *Times Literary Supplement*, September 2, 6.
——, 1997, *The Pope's Rhinoceros*, Minerva, London.
Parini, Jay, 1996, "Political Animal", *New York Times Book Review*, Nov. 10, 60.
Park, Mungo, 1954, [1799, first journey, 1815 from notes of second journey], *Travels in Africa*, J.M. Dent & Sons, London.
Peires, J. B., 1989, *The Dead Will Arise: Nongqawuse and the Great Xhosa Cattle-Killing Movement of 185-7*, Ravan, Johannesburg.
Pfeil, Fred, 1995, *White Guys: Studies in Postmodern Domination and Difference*, Verso, London.
——, 1998, "From Pillar to Postmodern: Race, Class, and Gender in the Male Rampage Film", in Lewis, Jon, (ed.) *The New American Cinema*, Duke University Press, Durham, 146–186.
Porges, Irwin, 1975, *Edgar Rice Burroughs: The Man Who Created Tarzan*, Brigham Young University Press, Provo, Utah.

Porter, Dennis, 1991, *Haunted Journeys: Desire and Transgression in European Travel Writing*, Princeton University Press, Princeton.
Pratt, Mary Louise, 1992, *Imperial Eyes. Travel Writing and Transculturation*, Routledge, London.
——, 1994, "Edward Said's *Culture and Imperialism*: A Symposium", with Robbins, Bruce, Pratt, Mary Louise, Arac, Jonathan R. Radhakrishnan & Said, Edward, *Social Text 40* (Fall), 9–15.
Pynchon, Thomas, 1995 [1961], *V*, Vintage, London.
Radhakrishnan, R, 1994, "Edward Said's *Culture and Imperialism*: A Symposium", with Robbins, Bruce, Pratt, Mary Louise, Arac, Jonathan R. Radhakrishnan & Said, Edward, *Social Text 40* (Fall), 9–15.
Roscoe, Patrick, 1994, "The Beginning of the World", in *Love Is Starving for Itself*, The Mercury Press, Stratford, Ontario, 9–24.
——, 1995, *The Lost Oasis*, McClelland & Stewart, Toronto.
Ruegg, Maria, 1979, "Metaphor and Metonymy: The Logic of Structuralist Rhetoric", *Glyph*, 6, 141–157.
Rushdie, Salman, 1988, *The Satanic Verses*, Viking, London.
——, 1995, *The Moor's Last Sigh*, Vintage, London.
——, 1999, *The Ground Beneath Her Feet*, Henry Holt &Co., New York.
Rutherford, Jonathan, 1997, *Forever England*, Lawrence and Wishart, London.
Said, Edward, 1985, *Orientalism*, Penguin, London.
——, 1989, "Representing the Colonized: Anthropology's Interlocutors", *Critical Inquiry*, 15, winter, 205–225.
——, 1993, *Culture and Imperialism*, Chatto & Windus, London.
——, 1998, "Between Worlds, *London Review of Books*, 7 May, 3–7.
Savran, David, 1996, "The Sadomasochist in the Closet: White Masculinity and the Culture of Victimization", *differences*, 8.2, 125–152.
Schama, Simon, 1995, *Landscape and Memory*, HarperCollins, London.
Sciolino, Martina, 1994, "Objects of the Postmodern 'Masters': Subject-in-Simulation/Woman-in-Effect", in Morgan, Thais, E., (ed.) *Men Writing the Feminine: Literature, Theory and the Question of Genders*, State University of New York Press, New York, 157–171.
Scott, A. O., 1998, "As Luck Would have It," *The New York Times Book Review*, November 22, 10.
Sedgwick, Eve Kosofsky, 1990, *Epistemology of the Closet*, University of California Press, Los Angeles.
——, 1992, "Nationalisms and Sexualities in the Age of Wilde", in Parker, Andrew, Russo, Mary, Sommer, Doris & Yaeger, Patricia, (eds.) *Nationalisms and Sexualities*, Routledge, London, 235–245.
Segal, Lynne, 1990, *Slow Motion: Changing Masculinities, Changing Men*, Virago, London.

Self, Will, 1998, *Great Apes*, Penguin, London.
Shostak, Debra, 1994, "The Family Romances of John Irving", *Essays in Literature*, vol. 21, part 1, 129–145.
Silverman, Kaja, 1992, *Male Subjectivity at the Margins*, Routledge, London.
Sontag, Susan, 1964, "Notes on Camp", in *Partisan Review*, 31.4, (Fall), 515–530.
Spurr, David, 1993, *The Rhetoric of Empire: Colonial Discourse in Journalism, Travel Writing and Imperial Administration*, Duke University Press, Durham.
Stallybrass, Oliver, 1972, Introduction to Forster, E. M., *The Life To Come and Other Stories*, Edward Arnold, London, vii–xxi.
Suleri Sara, 1992, *The Rhetoric of English India*, University of Chicago Press, Chicago.
Theroux, Paul, 1985, *Sunrise with Seamonsters*, Penguin, London.
Thomas, D. M., 1998, "Men Who Love Too Much", *The New York Times Book Review*, Feb. 8, 8.
Thorpe, Adam, 1988, *Mornings in the Baltic*, Secker & Warburg, London.
——, 1998a [1992], *Ulverton* Vintage, London.
——, 1996 [1995], *Still*, Minerva, London.
——, 1998b, *Pieces of Light*, Jonathan Cape, London.
Thorell, Tsomondo, 1989, "Metaphor, Metonymy and Houses: Figures of Construction in *A House for Mr. Biswas*", *World Literature Written in English*, Vol. 29, No. 2, 83–94.
Torgovnick, Marianna, 1990, *Gone Primitive: Savage Intellects, Modern Lives*, Chicago University Press, Chicago.
——, 1997, *Primitive Passions: Men, Women and the Quest for Ecstasy*, Alfred A. Knopf, New York.
Vaid, Krishna Baldev, 1996, "Franz Kafka Writes to T. Coraghessan Boyle", *Michigan Quarterly Review*, 35.3, 532–47.
Walker, J.K.L., 1991, "A Period in Progress: Julian Symons, *Portraits of the Missing: Imaginary Biographies*", *Times Literary Supplement*, August 23, 21.
Walker, Michael, 1994, "Boyle's 'Greasy Lake' and the Moral Failure of Postmodernism", *Studies in Short Fiction*, 31, 247–55.
Wall, Stephen, 1990, "Mockmen", *London Review of Books*, September 27, 19–20.
White, Hayden, 1972, "The Forms of Wildness: Archaeology of an Idea", in Dudley, Edward, & Novak, Maximillian, E., (eds.) *The Wild Man Within: An Image in Western Thought from the Renaissance to Romanticism*, University of Pittsburgh Press, Pittsburgh, 3–38.

Wilde, Oscar, 1910, [1890], *The Picture of Dorian Gray*, Simpkin, Marshall & Co, London.

Wilden, Anthony, 1972, *System & Structure: Essays in Communication and Exchange*, Tavistock, London.

Williams, Raymond, 1973, *The Country and the City*, Chatto & Windus, London.

Woods, Richard, 1999, "Eye Surgery lifts Salman Rushdie's brooding looks", //content.40/http:www.*Sunday-times/99/03/21*, 1–3.

Zweig, Paul, 1974, *The Adventurer*, Basic Books, London.

INDEX

A

Abish, Walter 229, 232, 300, 313, 316, 317–318
Achebe, Chinua 2, 12, 180, 293
Ackerley, J.R. 186
adventurers *see* explorers
Africa, representation of 31–2, 97, 124, 132–4, 211, 263–5
Africanist discourse 10–21, 28, 231, 247, 293–4
  and Tarzan 105–106
  in *Brazzaville Beach* 133
  in *Great Apes* 152
  in *Pieces of Light* 254, 261–2
  in *The Pope's Rhinoceros* 98
  in *Water Music* 36, 49–50, 61, 63
Agassiz (character in *The Ape Lady in Retirement*) 120, 124
Agassiz, Louis 124
AIDS 7, 203, 204, 236–7, 300
alphabet 317–23
Althusser, Louis 15
Amilcar (character in *Brazzaville Beach*) 136–8, 140, 142, 149, 296, 304
anti–imperialism 297; *see also* imperialism
anti–pastoral tradition 244, 251–2; *see also* pastoralism
apes 4, 103–106, 125, 307–308
  and black people 104, 106–108, 112–14, 133, 138
  as fictional characters *see* Agassiz; Conrad; Erasmus; Julius; Konrad; Kong
  human attitudes to 112–13
Appadurai, Arjun 2, 5, 28
archaeology, imagery of 260, 296, 297
architecture, imagery of 194–5, 203, 232–7, 296–8, 299

Arkwright, Hugh (character in *Pieces of Light*) 241, 246, 255, 257–90, 304, 309, 311
Ashcroft, W.D. 211

B

Bann, Stephen 69–70
Barrenboyne, Prentiss (character in *Water Music*) 58–9
Barrell, John 247, 249
Barthelme, Donald 23, 315
Barthes, Roland 16
Beckwith, Will (character in *The Swimming–Pool Library*) 162, 191–6, 198–9, 201–204, 206–208
Bedini, Silvio A. 71, 95–6
Benin, Kingdom of 73, 76–7, 80, 82, 86–8
Bermingham, Ann 248
Bhabha, Homi 53–4, 56, 96–7
Biafran war 136, 137
Bilston, John 251
biography, fictional 318, 319
black bodies
  exploitation of 204–205
  stereotype of 304–307
blacks, representation of 12–13, 95, 106, 111–12, 304–307
Blixen, Karen 146
Boehmer, Elleke 296
books 53–4, 67–8; *see also* stories
Boone, Joseph 169
Bosnia 79, 318
Bowles, Paul 168
Boyd, William 2, 104, 110, 144–5, 153, 294
  A Good Man in Africa 139
  Armadillo 145
  The Blue Afternoon 146
  Brazzaville Beach 103, 112, 129, 131–50, 169, 219, 296, 304,

Nat Tate: An American Artist 318, 319
The New Confessions 311
Boyle, T. Coraghessan 2, 35–6, 37–8,
    104, 110, 153, 294
    The Ape Lady in Retirement 103, 120–4
    characterization in 76, 120–1; *see also* under names of specific characters
    Descent of Man 103, 116–20, 239, 301–302, 303
    Greasy Lake 37–8
    If the River was Whiskey 103
    Rara Avis 42–3
    Riven Rock 103, 124–8, 303, 310
    schizophrenia in 309
    Water Music 6–7, 35–68, 69, 216, 296, 312, 318
Boyles, Billy (character in *Water Music*) 36, 60–2
Bradbury, Malcolm 229
bronze–casting 77, 80–2
Brookner, Anita 132, 142
Bryld, Mette 70
Bunn, David 279
Burden, Adam (character in *The Woman and the Ape*) 155–6
Burgkmair, Hans 12, 95–6
Burroughs, Edgar Rice 105, 106, 119, 125, 157; *see also* Tarzan

C

Cabral, Amilcar 138
Cain, mark of 215, 216, 219, 225
Caliban, 3, 179–80
Camp, language of 177–8, 180–1, 188, 189
    in *The Spell* 234, 239–40
    in *The Swimming Pool Library* 194, 207
capitalism, patriarchal 17–18
Casarino, Cesare 162, 164, 166–8
Castro, Fidel 38
cattle killing, South African 85–6, 97, 312
Caute, David 24–7, 29–31, 144, 169, 305
Chambers, Iain 5, 78, 85, 96
Chapman, Rowena 301
Cheyfitz, Eric 106
chimpanzees 120, 132, 133–7, 141–2, 219
Christianity 182–5, 282

civil wars 133–8, 142, 131, 140, 144, 210, 219–21
Clearwater, Hope (character in *Brazzaville Beach*) 129, 131, 132–50, 296, 303
Clearwater, John (character in *Brazzaville Beach*) 131, 142–3, 309
Clement, Catherine 2
closet 161–3, 168–70, 172, 175, 203
    glass 165, 173, 178–9, 181–2, 188, 215–16
colonialist discourse 3, 6, 18, 104, 119, 163, 315, 317; *see also* Conrad, Joseph
colonisation 5, 13, 192, 197
coming out 169, 192–3, 202–203, 210, 212, 214, 225
concealment, tradition of 161–3, 165, 177–8, 187
Conrad (character in *Brazzaville Beach*) 129, 138, 141–2, 149, 155, 307
Conrad, Joseph 10, 12, 109
    Heart of Darkness 11, 12, 149–50, 167, 180, 197, 198, 218
    influence of 2, 4, 38, 63, 118–19, 271, 280
    The Nigger of the Narcissus 306–307
    The Secret Sharer 163–8, 178, 208
Constable, John 248, 250, 253–4, 280, 287, 289
Core, Philip 177, 181
Cosgrove, Denis 255
cyborgs 99, 113–16, 145–50, 153–4, 157–8, 296, 308

D

Daniels, Stephen 250, 253–4, 267
Dante 282, 283
Daruwalla, Farrokh (character in *A Son of the Circus*) 7–10, 27–8
Darwin, Charles 114, 116
de–fetishisation 91, 234, 307, 312
Deleuze, Gilles 22–3, 128, 277–8, 309–12, 317
DeLillo, Don 297–8, 299, 314
Dellamora, Richard 163, 197
DeMan, Paul 211, 226
Denina, Chris 37

Index

desert
  North African 229–32
  in *The Lost Oasis* 209–11, 217, 295, 311, 312, 317
  North American
  in *The Spell* 232–3, 236–7, 240, 299
Dickens, Charles 8, 26–7, 31, 36, 54
Dikes, Simon (character in *Great Apes*) 151–4, 156, 158, 308
discourse 14, 18; *see also* Africanist discourse; colonialist discourse
Doolittle, Eliza: myth 58–9
Dorian Gray parable 175–6, 178–80, 188, 216
Dunn, Douglas 145
Durham, Deborah 20
Dyer, Richard 5, 152

E

Eboe (character in *Water Music*) 55–7
Edwards, Thomas 132
Egypt 144, 163, 168–74, 177, 203, 232, 233, 249, 297
Erasmus (character in *The Woman and the Ape*) 155–7, 308
Erasmus, Desiderius 155, 156
ethnic cleansing 79, 114
Eusebia *see* Usse
evolution 107, 114, 116, 158
explorers
  female 284, 285–6, 287, 303
  male 4, 70, 211
    in *Brazzaville Beach* 146–7
    in Hollinghurst 197, 233
    in *The Pope's Rhinoceros* 74, 75–6
    in *Water Music* 39–40, 43–4, 46, 49–50, 295–6
Eze Nri (character in *The Pope's Rhinoceros*) 80–2, 88
exploitation 253–4

F

Fabian, Johannes 86
Fanon, Frantz 24, 36, 38, 205
Farki, Neville 106
fathers 15–16, 26–7, 78–80, 198, 258–9
  false 2–3, 38–9, 71, 201, 266, 274, 288
gay 178; *see also* E.M.Forster; O.Wilde
  new 28–9, 35–6, 38–9, 65–6
  quest for 229–31, 313
    in *The Lost Oasis* 209–10, 211–12, 214–15, 220, 222–5, 295
Fatima (character in *Water Music*) 48–9
Fernandez, James W. 20
fetishes 204–205
  in *Pieces of Light* 259, 260, 267–8
  in *The Pope's Rhinoceros* 80–1
  in *The Spell* 236
  in *The Swimming–Pool Library* 197, 199, 208
  in *Water Music* 36–7, 47–8, 55–6, 58, 65–7
fiction, eighteenth century 69, 295–6, 308;
  see also Boyd, W. *The Pope's Rhinoceros;* Boyle, T.C. *Water Music*
  films 146, 250–1
  male rampage 298–9, 303, 304, 315–16
  pornographic 201–203, 206
  Tarzan 112–13, 115
Firbank, Ronald 177
Fleck, Linda 19–20
flying, symbol 123–4, 145–8, 150, 297
Flynn, Michael 301
forest, African 11, 182, 261–2, 269–70
Forster, E.M. 11, 163, 168, 177, 194, 208
  The Life to Come 181–8
Fossey, Dian 110–11, 118, 142, 153
Foucault, Michel 164–5, 169
French, Sean 132, 142
Freud, Sigmund 2
Fuchs, Cynthia 308

G

Gabriel (character in *The Swimming–Pool Library*) 206–207
Galdikas, Berute 110, 118, 120
Galligan, David 171, 173, 202, 205
gay liberation 162, 163, 191
gender 1, 11, 111, 116, 133; *see also* masculinity; patriarchy; women
Gide, Andre 168
Gifford, Terry 244, 252, 253
Gikandi, Simon 5, 11–12, 29, 231
globalisation 3–4, 5

Gombe National Park, Tanzania 110, 112, 132
Good, Jane (character in *Descent of Man*) 116–18, 120, 126, 156, 302
Goodall, Jane 104, 110–12, 135, 138
  in fiction 116, 118, 153, 302
    Brazzaville Beach 129, 131–2, 140, 142–3
Goodchild, Philip 22–3
Gorra, Michael 6, 30, 105, 109, 145
Graeber, Laurel 28
Greenblatt, Steven 94
Greystoke: The Story of Tarzan 112–13
Gruesser, John Cullen 294
Guattari, Felix 22–3, 128, 277–8, 309–12, 317
Guevara, Che 35
gynesis 98, 305

H

Haklle, Morris 19
Hall, Stuart 79
Harraway, Donna 107, 110–15, 132, 135, 149, 150, 157–8
Hardy, Thomas 238–9, 240
Hayles, Katherine 115
Heiland, Donna 69, 308
heterotopia 164–5, 182, 193, 194
  North Africa 169, 172, 174, 203, 295, 299
Hickey, Dennis 11
Høeg, Peter 110, 150
  The Woman and the Ape 103, 154–7, 303
Hollinghurst, Alan 2, 166, 177, 215, 294
  A Thieving Boy 168–72, 177–8, 198, 202
  and de-fetishisation 91, 306, 312
  Dry Season Nights 189
  The Spell 163, 232–40, 295, 296–7, 299, 300, 302, 306–307
  The Swimming–Pool Library 163, 171, 175, 189, 191–209, 216, 232, 236
    structure of 173, 192, 194–5
homosexual fiction 161–89, 208
Howie (character in *The Ape Lady in Retirement*) 120, 123, 125, 146, 307
hybrid man 154, 156, 257, 301; *see also* cyborgs; mutants
hybrid zones 144; *see also* North Africa; Mexico

hybridity 3, 5, 144, 169, 195

I

icons 195–7, 199, 236–8
identity, male: quest for 150, 151, 158
  by Tarzan 108–109
  by T.C. Boyle 35–6, 60, 62, 63, 116, 295
  in *Pieces of Light* 259, 266
  in *The Pope's Rhinoceros* 75–7, 93–4, 97
ideology 14–15
Ignatiev, Noel 59–60
Iguedo (character in *The Pope's Rhinoceros*) 81
Illich, Ivan 300
imagery 1
  homosexual 199, 295
  light & dark 149–50, 182, 247–9, 261–2, 267, 271–2, 276
  in *Pieces of Light* 246–7, 260, 280–1
  in *The Pope's Rhinoceros* 76–7, 83, 87, 89
  in *The Spell* 236
  in *The Swimming–Pool Library* 236
  water 38, 39, 146
imperialism 1, 3–4, 27, 232, 248, 253–4
  and Tarzan 152
  in Boyd 153
  in Boyle 153
  in Forster 183, 187
  in Hollinghhurst 197, 199, 206
  in Norfolk 69, 72, 295
  in Thorpe 250, 279–80, 295
India 5, 11, 18, 28, 188, 194
insanity *see* schizophrenia
irony 184–5
  in *The Pope's Rhinoceros* 72, 88–9
  in Thorpe 251, 254, 282
  in *Water Music* 39–40, 48–50, 54–6, 307
Irving, John 5, 18, 31
  A Son of the Circus 7–10, 26–8
Isaaco (character in *Water Music*) 41, 52–3, 57, 58
Ishiguro, Kazua 145

J

Jakobsen, Roman 19, 21
James, Henry 23, 92

Index

Jameson, Frederic 38–9, 296
Jane 103, 106, 110, 112, 135, 139; *see also* Jane Good; Jane Goodall; Jane Roessing; Tarzan
Jardine, Alice A. 98, 231, 305, 313
Johnson, Amy 273, 284
Johnson (character in *Water Music*) 36, 40–1, 44, 47, 50–7, 59, 67–8, 196, 304
Jordan, Justine 241, 243, 287
Julius (character in *Riven Rock*) 125, 127–8

K

Kabila, Laurent 138
Kapuscinski 132, 134
Kayo, Patrice 289
Keates, Jonathan 73
Keller, Evelyn Fox 111
Kelman, James 145
Keough, Peter 72, 73
kidnapping 112, 132, 136, 138, 158
Kingsley, Mary 284, 285–6, 303
Kipling, Rudyard 3, 11, 289
Klu Klux Klan 96
Kong (character in *Great Apes*) 151–2
Konrad (character in *The Ape Lady in Retirement*) 120–4, 125, 128, 146, 150, 156, 307, 309
Konrad (character in *Descent of Man*) 117–19, 307
Kureishi, Hanif 145
Kurtz (character in *Heart of Darkness*) 4, 46, 64, 95, 107, 150, 167,198, 282

L

Lacan, Jacques 15, 17, 18, 19–22, 31
landscape 242
    African 11, 86–7, 199–200, 213, 229, 231–2, 310–11, 312
    British 163, 236, 238–40, 241, 267
    hybrid 255, 259, 267, 276, 279–81, 290
    see also desert; forest
landscape painting 247–8, 250, 279, 280
Lane, Christopher 181–2, 186, 188
language 14–15, 312–14
    alternative 165–6, 213
    loss of 175–6, 178, 188
    see also Camp; metaphor; metonymy
law 14–18, 208–210, 231

challenges to 44–5, 164, 172, 182, 188–9, 237
new 38–9, 128, 316–17
The Pope's Rhinoceros 80–2, 88, 89, 94
Leakey, Louis 131–2
LeBihan, Jill 111–12
Lemaire, Anika 16–17, 18
Lemumba, Patrice 289
Leo X 71, 83, 88–9, 90, 93
Levine, June Perry 186–8
livestock, sacrifice of 83–4, 85–6, 97, 312
Lock, Charles 242
Lodge, David 13, 21
Lorenz, Konrad 118–19, 156
Low, Gail Ching–Liang 280
lycanthropy 267–8
Lykke, Nina 70
Lyotard, Jean–Francois 313

M

McCaffery, Larry 8
McClintock, Anne 11, 17, 67, 197
McCormick, Katherine Dexter 125, 126–7
McCormick, Katherine Dexter (character in *Riven Rock*) 125, 126–8, 303
McCormick, Stanley 124
McCormick, Stanley (character in *Riven Rock*) 124–7, 128, 142, 309
McKillip, Kenneth 126
magical realism 36, 53, 54–5
Mallabar, Eugene (character in *Brazzaville Beach*) 131–2, 133–4, 143–4
Mandel, Ernst 39
Mapplethorpe, Robert 204–205
mark 140–1, 264; *see also* Cain
Marquez, Gabriel Garcia 36, 53, 54–5
masculinity 32, 299–301
    alternative 13–14, 151, 294
    in Boyd 148, 150
    in Boyle 116, 121, 125, 128, 295
Mercer, Kobena 2, 204–205
metaphor 10, 19–22, 30–1, 82, 92, 119,167, 313
    and Africa 11–13, 16, 18, 43, 63, 311
    and apes 106, 107, 113, 121
    and concealment 161, 179
    in Hollinghurst 232
    in *The Lost Oasis* 211–14, 218, 222–6, 229, 316–17

in *Pieces of Light* 259, 278
in *Riven Rock* 124–5
metonymy 19–22, 24, 91, 120, 211, 313–18
  in Hollinghurst 235, 237
  in *The Lost Oasis* 217, 220–1, 224, 226
  in *Pieces of Light* 258, 260, 263, 275, 288
Mexico 175, 177
  in *The Lost Oasis* 212–13, 216, 221–4
  in *Pieces of Light* 242, 259, 263, 267, 270, 273–4, 281–8
  in *The Pope's Rhinoceros* 73–5, 93, 310
  in *Water Music* 303
Mudimbe, V.Y. 2, 12–13, 95–6, 288, 306
Muslim fundamentalism 29–30
Mustafa (character in *A Thieving Boy*) 169–74, 177, 179, 202
mutants 98–9, 113, 145, 151–7, 307–11

N

Naipaul, V.S. 109
Nantwich, Charles (character in *The Swimming Pool Library*) 191–2, 194–203, 207, 310
narcissism 165, 179–80, 182, 184–5, 215
narrative structure 312–13
  in *Brazzaville Beach* 139
  in homosexual writing 163, 174, 178, 187–8
  in *Pieces of Light* 258, 263, 265–6, 272
  in *The Pope's Rhinoceros* 85, 97–8
  in *The Swimming-Pool Library* 194–5, 199
  in *Ulverton* 243–6, 249, 252
Nature 39, 42
neo–colonialism 39
Ngugi wa Thiong'o 2, 12
Niger River 35, 40–1, 46, 116, 216, 235, 295
  imagery 38, 39, 146
Niklot (character in *The Pope's Rhinoceros*) 76–7, 79, 93
Nongqawuse 86
Norfolk, Lawrence 2, 68, 148, 318
  Lempriere's Dictionary 69–70, 88, 90–3, 98–9, 297, 300
  The Pope's Rhinoceros 35, 70–99, 268–9, 288, 295, 297, 300, 304, 312

North Africa 168–72, 175, 203, 209–10, 295; *see also* Egypt
nullity 11

O

Odysseus myth 44–5
Oedipus myth 22–3, 84, 272–7, 309, 310, 312, 316
O'Kane, Eddie (character in *Riven Rock*) 125–6
Okri, Ben 2
Orientalism 6, 10–11, 14, 21, 28–9, 231, 253
  African 218, 253
  in Caute 24–5, 27, 31
  in Boyle 48–50
  influence of 7–10
  simian 107–108
Out of Africa 146

P

paintings 195–6, 242, 257–60; *see also* J. Constable; landscape painting
Park, Ailie (character in *Water Music*) 45–8, 49, 67, 126, 140, 148
Park, Mungo 35, 43, 318
Park, Mungo (character in *Water Music*) 36, 39–42, 44–6, 49, 116, 125, 128
  comparison with Ned Rise 57–8, 61–3
pastoralism 241, 244, 247, 249, 251–3, 254, 280
patriarchy 1, 17–18, 44, 48–9, 75, 88, 293, 294
Peires, J.B. 85–6
Pfeil, Fred 32, 298–9, 300, 303, 304, 315–16
  mutants 115, 158, 308
phallus 17, 22, 31–2, 66, 80–1, 310, 315
Phillips, Caryl 145
photogrpahs 198–9, 204–205, 249, 263–6
Pinmay, Paul (character in *The Life to Come*) 182–6
Pitt, Brad 300
poetry 189, 244–5, 271
Porges, Irwin 105
pornography 201–203, 306
Porter, Denis 13
postcolonialism 23–4
postmodernism 21, 23–7, 31, 315
  in Boyle 119

Index

in Hollinghurst 233–5
in Norfolk 78, 85
in Thorpe 245, 296–7
Pratt, Mary Louise 3–4, 41, 43–4, 105, 318
Pringle, Thomas 279
Proust, Marcel 192, 208, 215–16, 226
Pulp Fiction 315
pygmies 65–7
Pynchon, Thomas 75, 91–2, 94–5, 98, 231, 295, 297, 314
Pyramids 169, 172–4, 233, 235–7, 295, 312

Q

quests 294–6, 312
  for meaning of life 12
  see also under fathers; identity, male

R

racism 1, 5–6, 30, 180, 186–7, 247, 305
  and Tarzan 106, 109
  in *Brazzaville Beach* 133
  in *The Swimming-Pool Library* 203, 206
  in *Water Music* 41–2, 59
Radhakrishnan, R. 29
Rambo 110, 222, 237, 298–300; *see also* Tarzan
rape
  in *The Pope's Rhinoceros* 74–5, 76, 294
  in *Riven Rock* 126
Rauhschutz, Ludmilla (character in *Great Apes*) 153, 302
realism 31, 36, 315
  magical 36, 53, 54–5
Redford, Robert 146
Richard (character in *The Lost Oasis*) 209–26
Rise, Ned (character in *Water Music*) 35, 36–7, 41, 57–63, 65–6, 116, 124, 125–6, 296
Robin (character in *The Spell*) 232–40
Rocky 300
Roessing, Jane (character in *Riven Rock*) 127, 303
Roscoe, Patrick 2, 166, 177, 189, 232
  The Beginning of the World 175, 188, 216

The Lost Oasis 163, 175, 209–26, 230, 285, 295, 309
  imagery in 203, 229, 237, 297, 299, 300
Ruegg, Maria 21–2
Rushdie, Salman 5, 27, 109
  influence of 2, 8, 24–6, 53, 144, 145, 169
  The Ground Beneath her Feet 45
  The Moor's Last Sigh 8
  The Satanic Verses 6, 25, 29, 96–7
  Shame 3

S

Said, Edward 3–4, 6, 7, 10, 28–9, 107, 231–2
Salvador (character in *The Beginning of the World*) 175–6, 178, 188, 211, 310
Salvestro (character in *The Pope's Rhinoceros*) 72–80, 87–9, 93–4, 97, 98, 288, 295, 304, 309, 310
Saro–Wiwa, Ken 138, 140
Sartre, J–P 38
Savran, David 297, 301
Schama, Simon 246
schizophrenia 22–3, 123–5, 128, 277, 296, 309–10
Schwarzenegger, Arnold 110, 115, 154
Sciolino, Martina 97–8, 315
Scott, A.O. 145
Sedgwick, Eve Kosofsky 161–2, 165, 178, 180, 208–209, 215, 221
Segal, Lynne 293
Self, Will 110, 150
  Great Apes 103, 151, 158
Shostak, Debra 26–7
Shoukry, Usman (character in *Brazzaville Beach*) 144–50, 151, 169, 296, 304
Silverman, Kaja 13–15, 300
social realism 36
Soller, Philippe 313
Sontag, Susan 178, 240
sorcerers 310–11
Soyinka, Wole 2, 109
spaces *see* heterotopia
Spurr, David 18, 87
Stallone, Sylvester 298, 299
stereotypes 1, 86, 133, 211, 206, 231, 258; *see also* women
Stonewall Inn, New York 161–2

stories
    in *Pieces of Light* 98, 260–1, 268–9
    in *The Pope's Rhinoceros* 73–5, 77–8, 80, 82–5, 93, 96, 268–9
Streep, Meryl 146
Suleri, Sara 3, 10
Superman 31
symbols 123–4, 145–8, 150, 270–1, 297

T

talisman 184, 185; *see also* fetishes
Tarzan 4, 30, 31, 66
    and women 110–12, 143–4
    discourse 99, 103–106, 145, 151–3, 158, 308, 309
    films 112–13, 115
    re–evaluation 108–110, 139, 278, 289
    see also Jane
taxidermy 277–8
The Terminator 115
Theroux, Paul 104–105
Third World 38, 39
    abuse of 113
    writers of 3–7, 36
Thorpe, Adam 2, 295, 297
    Pieces of Light 141, 240–3, 246–7, 250, 254, 255, 257–90, 300, 303, 304, 310
    Still 242, 247, 250, 252, 254, 255
    Ulverton 241, 243–6, 247–9, 250–2, 255, 272–3, 276, 281
Torgovnick, Marianna 108–109, 111, 112–13
travel 11, 13, 104–105; *see also* explorers

U

Umbehr, Otto 122
Umbo, Beatrice (character in *The Ape Lady in Retirement*) 120–4, 126, 146, 150, 153, 302
Usse/Eusebia (character in *The Pope's Rhinoceros*) 77–81, 83–4, 85, 90, 93, 97, 98, 269

V

Vail, Ian (character in *Brazzaville Beach*) 135, 136, 137
Vietnam War 36, 38, 50, 66
Virgil 244

Vithobai (character in *The Life to Come*) 182–6, 187–8
violence 42–3, 95, 119, 171; *see also* rape; wars

W

Wall, Stephen 132
wars 136, 137; *see also* civil wars; Vietnam War; World War I
water imagery 38, 39, 146
Water–man 76–7, 89, 93
Weismuller, Johnny 115
White, Hayden 44, 62
Wilde, Oscar 163, 165, 168, 184, 189, 200, 208
    The Picture of Dorian Gray 178–80, 181, 188
Williams, Raymond 252, 253
women
    primatologists 103–104, 110–112
    in fiction 116–24, 129, 131, 149, 153, 302–304;
        see also Beatrice Umbo; Hope Clearwater; Jane Good
    relationships with 46–9, 120, 128, 139–40, 151, 302–304
    representation of 97–8, 104, 126–7, 142, 305
    stereotypes 104, 127, 153, 302–304
    see also mothers; names of specific characters e.g. Jane; Usse etc.
Wordsworth, William 289
World War I 250, 253, 282–5, 287, 288
Wright, Frank Lloyd 232–3, 234, 296–7, 299
Wylden, Anthony 19
Wylie, Kenneth 11

Z

Zachary (character in *Crossing the Great Void*) 229–31
Zaire 112, 132
Zedong, Mao 35–6, 38
Zweig, Paul 45, 46

TRAVEL WRITING ACROSS THE DISCIPLINES

THEORY AND PEDAGOGY
Kristi Siegel, General Editor

The recent critical attention devoted to travel writing enacts a logical transition from the ongoing focus on autobiography, subjectivity, and multiculturalism. Travel extends the inward direction of autobiography to consider the journey outward and intersects provocatively with studies of multiculturalism, gender, and subjectivity. Whatever the journey's motive—tourism, study, flight, emigration, or domination—journey changes both the country visited and the self that travels. *Travel Writing Across the Disciplines* welcomes studies from all periods of literature on the theory and/or pedagogy of travel writing from various disciplines, such as social history, cultural theory, multicultural studies, anthropology, sociology, religious studies, literary analysis, and feminist criticism. The volumes in this series explore journey literature from critical and pedagogical perspectives and focus on travel as metaphor in cultural practice.

For additional information about this series or for the submission of manuscripts, please contact:

        Peter Lang Publishing. Inc.
        Acquisitions Department
        P.O. Box 1246
        Bel Air, MD 21014-1246

To order other books in this series, please contact our Customer Service Department:

        (800) 770-LANG (within the U.S.)
        (212) 647-7706 (outside the U.S.)
        (212) 647-7707 FAX

Or browse online by series:
        www.peterlangusa.com

OHIO UNIVERSITY LIBRARY

Please return this book as soon as you have finished with it. In order to avoid a fine it must be returned by the latest date stamped below. All books are subject to recall after two weeks or immediately if needed for reserve.

MAY 0 9 2005

MAY 1 9 2005

CF